THE HEART MUST BREAK

James Mawdsley was brought up in Lancashire with his sister and two brothers. He went to Bristol University to study physics and philosophy, but left to live in Australia. He was working in New Zealand when he first met exiles from Burma.

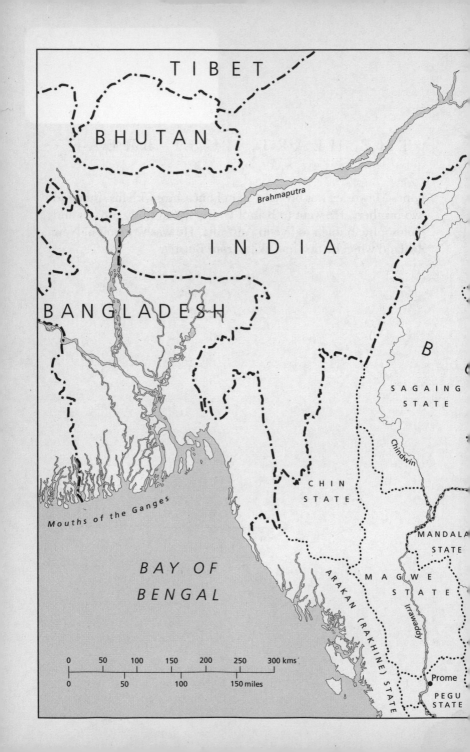

THE HEART
MUST BREAK

The Fight for Democracy
and Truth in Burma

JAMES MAWDSLEY

ARROW

Published by Arrow Books in 2002

1 3 5 7 9 10 8 6 4 2

Copyright © James Mawdsley 2001

James Mawdsley has asserted his right under the Copyright, Designs and Patents Act, 1988 to be identified as the author of this work

First published in the United Kingdom in 2001 by Century

Arrow Books Limited
The Random House Group Limited
20 Vauxhall Bridge Road, London SW1V 2SA

Random House Australia (Pty) Limited
20 Alfred Street, Milsons Point, Sydney,
New South Wales 2061, Australia

Random House New Zealand Limited
18 Poland Road, Glenfield
Auckland 10, New Zealand

Random House South Africa (Pty) Limited
Endulini, 5A Jubilee Road, Parktown 2193, South Africa

The Random House Group Limited Reg. No. 954009

www.randomhouse.co.uk

A CIP catalogue record for this book is available from the British Library

Papers used by Random House are natural, recyclable products made from wood grown in sustainable forests. The manufacturing processes conform to the environmental regulations of the country of origin

ISBN 0 09 9426943

Typeset by SX Composing DTP, Rayleigh, Essex
Printed and bound in Denamrk by
Nørhaven Paperback A/S, Viborg

To my mother

FOREWORD

JAMES MAWDSLEY is one of the most outstanding young people Britain has produced since World War Two. I first met James when he came to see me at Westminster. I had recently compiled a Jubilee Campaign report on human rights abuses in Burma, in particular on the plight of the Karen people. James wasted no time in sharing his anger about the situation in Burma – one vast concentration camp – and in enlisting my support for his proposed return.

He had already spent time in Burmese prisons and had suffered various privations and cruelty. None of this crushed his resolve to continue challenging the military regime. He was driven by a mixture of hardheaded idealism, gallantry and religious faith, and James's motives and outlook reminded me of the soldiers who, in 1945, returned from the hostilities determined to learn the lessons of totalitarianism and to build a more socially just society.

James was brought up to believe in the straightforward principle of duty. He is deeply aware that the liberties which we enjoy were won at a great price and that we must continue to defend those liberties – and still at great price. This awareness expresses itself in a passionate outpouring of concern for others.

When I returned from my own visit to Burma and the Karen refugee camps, Lady Mountbatten told me that her father regarded the Karen as our bravest and most loyal allies: 'Today they are our forgotten allies.' For James, Britain's abandonment of its allies remains unfinished business. During our first encounter and through his subsequent actions, James has made it abundantly clear that Burma is not 'a far away country about which we know very little', but a country and a people about whom we know a great deal and to whom we owe a debt of honour.

I warned James that if he returned to Burma there could be no certainty about the outcome; no certainty of his safety; and no certainty that his actions would not be caricatured as those of an adventurer. However, there was always the chance that his personal stand would stir consciences and remind the world of the continuing heartbreak of the Burmese people. He weighed those odds realistically and put himself on the line.

James's passion is matched by a powerful intellect: appreciation of strategic geo-political questions and a forensic grasp of the psychology of how a brutal dictatorship works. Without this combination of strengths, reinforced by his dogged Lancashire faith, it is difficult to see how James's mission could have so successfully achieved its objective. He comes from the recusant village of Mawdesley where, four hundred years ago, people died rather than give up their faith. It produced a young man called John Rigby, who was executed at Lancaster. His executioner said he had never encountered anyone of such singular virtue. James Mawdsley's Burmese captors might have had similar thoughts.

During the campaign to free James, small stones were distributed to those who attended demonstrations and meetings. Why? Because when small stones move, landslides happen. James Mawdsley put his life on the line because he cares about human rights; because he knows that when totalitarian regimes remain unchallenged it threatens the security of us all; and because he believes that when right and justice are pitted against an obnoxious regime, its days will be numbered.

In achieving his objective of forcing the world to take note of the plight of the indigenous Burmese, James became too much trouble for the Burmese regime. They beat him; they left him in isolation for over a year; they had hoped to break his remarkable spirit. Having failed to do that, they simply calculated that he would be less trouble outside the country than in.

In the long term this may prove to be yet another

miscalculation by a regime notorious for its use of brute force rather than finesse. One day James Mawdsley will bring his gifts into the political arena – where he will make an outstanding contribution. From childhood James has been reared in the principles of civic duty and personal responsibility. His upbringing has been a preparation for political service. Politics today has become a world of soundbites and careers predicted by a slavish adherence to the party line. It is a refreshing change to encounter someone who is not intoxicated by careerism and who has principles for which he is prepared to fight – and, if necessary, for which he will give up everything.

As this book reveals, this extraordinarily articulate young man has become an authoritative moral voice with access to milllions of hearts and minds. What is he using his voice to say? In telling us his story he does not focus on his own privations and mistreatment, but instead reminds us of the denial of basic democratic rights to the elected government of Aung San Suu Kyi and turns searchlights on to the genocide inflicted on the Karen, the Karenni and the Shan.

Over 30,000 Karen civilians have died as a result of Burmese military action since 1992; over 300,000 Karen and a similar number of Shan are internally displaced. Many are killed on sight when discovered. About 120,000 Karen and 100,000 Shan have been forced to flee to Thailand to escape the atrocities of the Burmese Army.

A report by the International Labour Organisation, in 1998, was a 254-page horror story. Since then, the United Nations Special Rapporteur on Burma, Mr Rajsoomer Lallah QC, has detailed horrific evidence of terrible atrocities in Burma. Mr Lallah says: '. . . violations include extrajudicial and arbitrary executions (not sparing women and children), rape, torture, inhuman treatment, forced labour and denial of freedom of movement. These violations have been so numerous and consistent over the past years as to suggest that they are not simply isolated acts of individual misbehaviour of middle and lower rank officers but are rather the result of policy at the highest level entailing political and legal reponsibility.'

The ILO has stated that: 'There is abundant evidence before the Commission showing the pervasive use of forced labour imposed on the civilian population of Burma by the authorities and the military,' and that this is 'a crime against humanity'.

What is happening in Burma today should certainly make the heart break, but it should stir our consciences too. History teaches us that tyrants are emboldened when free nations and free people fail to act. It is worth remembering the thoughts of Rev. Martin Niemoller:

First they came for the Communists, and I didn't speak up, because I wasn't a Communist.

Then they came for the Jews, and I didn't speak up, because I wasn't a Jew.

Then they came for the Catholics, and I didn't speak up, because I was a Protestant.

Then they came for me, and by that time there was no one left to speak up for me.

James's story is an account of courage and integrity. It will have meaning if those who read it then act for the 1500 political prisoners who remain in Burmese jails and the hundreds of thousands of ethnic minorities whose suffering continues unabated.

David Alton

David Alton is an independent crossbench peer, professor of citizenship at Liverpool John Moores University and a founder of the Jubilee Campaign.

GLOSSARY

ABSDF	All Burma Students Democratic Front
BBC	British Broadcasting Corporation
BSPP	Burma Socialist Programme Party
CRPP	Committee Representing the People's Parliament
DAB	Democratic Alliance of Burma
DVB	Democratic Voice of Burma
FCO	Foreign and Commonwealth Office
KNPP	Karenni National Progressive Party
KNU	Karen National Union
MFA	Ministry of Foreign Affairs
MI	Military Intelligence
NGO	Non Government Organisation
NLD	National League for Democracy
RFA	Radio Free Asia
SLORC	State Law and Order Restoration Council
SPDC	State Peace and Development Council
SRC	Student Relief Committee
Tatmadaw	Burmese Army
UDHR	Universal Declaration of Human Rights
UNHCR	United Nations High Commission for Refugees
VOA	Voice of America

I'm leaving this world where either the heart must break or turn as hard as iron.

Sebastian-Roch Nicholas Chamfort

CHAPTER 1

Stand for truth; it is enough.   Ben Jonson

I SQUATTED DOWN in the market place and reached into my small bag. Sick with apprehension I pulled the letters and cassettes out, expecting to be arrested at any moment. My heart felt utterly lame. Was there to be nothing that would stop me, no final realisation or excuse, no earthquake or Armageddon? No, there was just the misery of poverty and oppression all around. The drizzle falling made everything look even more rotten. I was in Tachilek, a small town on the Burma–Thai border, gateway to the Golden Triangle.

The military junta in Burma are destroying the country. They imprison those who dare to speak the truth, and are committing genocide against minority nations on the borders. They had killed eight of my friends. I was there to protest.

'*Kyaungtar khaung zaung Min Ko Naing hnit naing ngan yey a kyintha, lut myowt yey!*' I shouted, hurling the first fistful of letters into the air. I began walking through the market stalls, dropping audiocassettes of democratic songs at short intervals, and throwing letters and stickers to left and right. Tired-looking men stood behind stalls of fish paste or clothing but few were buying. There were plenty of vendors but otherwise the market seemed empty, subdued. Exhausted-looking women laid vegetables out on sacks or on the ground and waited for rare customers. Yet I could not really see anything around me; I was too nervous to take in much detail.

'Release the student leader Min Ko Naing and all political prisoners!' A few of the locals stared at me with astonished eyes but none made any move.

'Reopen the universities!' I shouted. Nobody would understand my appalling Burmese pronunciation, but the message was down there on the letters. I wanted to cover as much ground as possible so it didn't look like I had selected a special area.

'*Demokrasi! Khinmya doh ayey-ha, janore ayey bar beh*!' The local people had to hide their surprise. It was not safe for them to show an interest. Many tried to pretend I was not even present, they looked right through me. But that was perfect; it would be a disaster if anyone joined in.

'Your cause is my cause!' I called out, feeling a touch self-conscious. Protesting like this is not at all dignified. Fumbling, I dropped the last dozen cassettes in a clattering heap, not even looking behind me to see if anyone moved forward to swipe one. Suddenly I was out of the market, heading down a muddy lane that was becoming quieter and quieter. I felt scared and doubled back. Whatever was about to happen to me, I wanted there to be witnesses.

'*Shi lay lone sait dat, shin tan yey*!' Then a girl, perhaps twenty years old, ran up from nowhere, stopping abruptly in front of me and teetering off balance. Her dark cheeks were decorated with *thanaka,* a yellow powder used to keep the skin young, and her wide brown eyes were fixed on the letters in my hands. What a thirst there was in her eyes – for something to read! And something that was pretty obviously to do with freedom, to do with a fight against the brutal military junta. I gave her a couple of the letters and she bounded off. For a few moments my soul sang. Yes, what I was doing was right; it *did* mean something to the Burmese.

But it still looked ridiculous. 'Hey, you!' screamed out a uniformed man in front of me. He was thin and seemed afraid, uncertain. 'Hey, you! What are you do!' He and another barred my path. 'Stop!'

'Are you a policeman?' I asked him aggressively and barged past. 'DEMOCRACY!' I shouted at the top of my voice. I managed one more lap of the market, now shedding the letters very quickly. One fluttered down on to a table where three old men were drinking tea. They looked at it as if it were a bomb, not daring even to brush it off the table in case it appeared that they were reaching out to read it. The nearest man had prickly white stubble on his drooping chin and his face was a sketch of sorrow, alarm and fear.

Around the next corner there were five men glaring at me, two of them in brown uniform. 'What you do?' they demanded in fury. 'Stop now.'

As I passed they grabbed my arms and shirt but I shook their hands off and continued. They were uncertain. How rough could they be with a foreigner?

'*Khut daung sait dat, shin tan ja!*' By now there were a lot more people around. They snatched glances at me but I did not want to make eye contact with anyone in case an informer noticed it and chose to make something of it. I had been going for about ten minutes and really that was enough. It was clear by now that I was hollering something about democracy and that I was not well pleased with the authorities. And today, the last day of August 1999, they moved quite fast.

Suddenly a dozen angry men surrounded me. I would not be able to get much further.

'*Lut lat yey*!! Freedom!' said I, loud like, and happy to have got rid of the last letters. Then I remembered two handfuls of stickers stuffed down my socks. That was in case my bag had been confiscated before I could begin. I reached down to my foot and the eyes of one uniformed man opened wide with shock. Did he think I was going to pull out a knife?

'*Koe lay lone*,' as I threw it over their heads. They shot their arms up to stop me just a second too late. With a strange slowness I remembered again the other sockful and reached for that. Again, 'DEMOCRACY!' as I threw this over the other side. And again they were just a second too slow to stop me, but by then they had had enough. Hands came from everywhere and took a very tight grip. One big bearded bear of a man began twisting my shirt round in his fist. It hurt. The intensity of hatred burning his face fell on me like a blow. Then my arms were behind my back and handcuffs were squeezed on. In the background a considerable crowd had gathered. They watched silently, looking shocked, worried.

'*Keitsa ma shi bar bu!*' [No problem!] was my final cry and I was frogmarched away from the market, trying to smile bravely, but gulping in apprehension.

The police station was only a few minutes away. They sat me down in a large room: a few desks, a few guns, lots of people, uniformed and un-uniformed, milling about. The desks were cluttered with paperwork. Hats, shirts, belts adorned many chairs. I was left alone as they searched my bag. There was very little in it. The police had recovered a handful of the cassettes I had dropped and a bunch of them went into a side room with a tape deck to listen to them. I hoped they enjoyed the songs, sung by Burmese exile, Mun Awng, about freedom.

Two began searching me and as a hand went into my back pocket I was overcome by a sudden dread. I had done the stupidest thing in my life. In the pocket was a list of four telephone numbers of my friends in Thailand. I had needed to hang on to the list until the last minute, but was supposed to destroy it before entering Burma. I watched with sinking spirits as the small scrap of paper was put with the rest of my belongings in a corner of the room. Now I felt really sick. My heart and mind began racing. I wondered how on earth I could retrieve it before they read it and just then a policeman decided to handcuff me to the chair. O Lord!

I started to sniffle and twitch my nose. In my bag was a roll of tissues. Maybe – just maybe – they would pass me the bag to get a tissue and then I could snatch the list. I asked for my bag, said there was a tissue in it. They looked amused and got me one from elsewhere. Did I think they were born yesterday?

O Lord, I was dying with shame. This was the third time I had been arrested in Burma for supporting democracy. Until now I had not let anybody down. The second time, in Moulmein, I had refused to give the names of my comrades despite being tortured. But this time I was giving telephone numbers away for free.

There were no names on the paper and the regime might already know the numbers, but it was a galling mistake.

After inspecting my passport, a senior officer with big jowls, a big body and an unhappy expression telephoned his bosses in the capital, Rangoon. I listened in to the conversation and eventually heard the word 'Moulmein'. That meant they now knew my history in Burma, which would at least make the interrogation easier. Then a miracle happened.

Another officer decided he wanted to search my belongings again and he called for his subordinates to put them on the table in front of me. Now the list was only about six feet away. There was a gaggle of men pawing through the kit and I was handcuffed to a chair, but it was pretty clear I would never get another opportunity to retrieve the list. But if I failed in my attempt, then I would only be drawing attention to its significance. Full of dread, I sprang forward, dragging the chair with me, barging my arm and shoulder between two men and seized the note. Before they could react I stuffed it into my mouth and swallowed as quick as I could. Once again hands from everywhere grabbed me, they held my head and squeezed my mouth open – but I had felt the paper go down. In blessed relief I did not resist as they opened my jaws and, more astonished than angry, peered into and poked around my empty mouth. I felt then that they could do what they liked, there was no way I was going to betray anybody.

The senior officer was not impressed. His unhappy expression turned even sourer. My belongings were removed and I was told to take off my shoes and socks, my belt and watch. I did not care; they had not got the list. The wooden floor felt cold to my feet.

'What is your name?' asked one of the chiefs.

'You have my passport. You can see for yourself.'

'Are you Mr James Mawdsley?'

'Yes.'

'What is your nationality?'

'You have my passport.'

'You are British.'

'Yes.'

'What is your year of birth?'

'You have my passport.'

'14 February 1973?'

'Yes.'

'Why do you come to Burma?'

'To talk about freedom, justice, democracy, human rights . . .'

'How many people are with you? Who helped you?'

I smiled at him and said, 'I am under no obligation to answer your questions. You are not the government. You are part of a terrorist regime.'

They soon moved me from the police station to the immigration office. Sometimes they left me alone, sometimes they tried to question me, but they got nowhere.

A colonel from the Military Intelligence (MI) came to try his luck. The Military Intelligence are Burma's not so secret 'secret police'. They are ruthless, cruel and without morality. They have informers everywhere and even the generals at the top of the junta are afraid of them.

'Why have you come to Burma?' asked the MI colonel.

'Because I love Burma, I love the people here and I hate what your regime is doing to them.'

'It is not your country. Why do you interfere?'

'It is one world. It is my sisters and brothers that you are torturing, raping and murdering. It is absolutely my business to protest against that.'

'Tell us who helped you. Do you know anybody in Tachilek?'

'I am under no obligation to answer that question.'

He looked at me for a few moments. The conversation changed tack. Whenever I was being questioned in Burma I wanted to make sure that the interrogator knew that I respected the country, that I was not out to destroy anything or shouting for the West to take over (as their crazy propaganda claimed). We got on to the subject of Burma's natural beauty – common ground on which everyone can agree no matter which side they think they are on. There was an interpreter present and he began rambling on about the loveliness of Shan State, and I agreed with everything he said. I felt sorry for him. He did not belong with this regime. His father, who had been a military attaché in London, was flying from Ireland one day and the plane had crashed. His father was killed. That was in the 1950s. The interpreter was lost in sorrowful reminiscence as he told me. Even now, forty years on, he was pining for Burma's glory days when the Japanese were gone, the British were gone and the Burmese had won their independence. They were Asia's brightest star, a parliamentary democracy, the world's foremost exporter of rice, unheard-of literacy rates and a country heaving with wealth: oil, teak, jade, gems, pearls, metals and magic. But the promise had miscarried.

'Oh, Shan State,' he enthused, 'the mountains so beautiful, the trees and rivers, the birds and the flowers by the roadside . . .'

'And the poppies!' I added, unable to resist. The poppies are for opium, the opium is for heroin. More heroin is produced in the Golden Triangle than anywhere else in the world (except perhaps Afghanistan). Laos forms one corner of the triangle. Yunnan Province in south-west China has replaced Thailand as a second corner. But the heart of it has always been Burma, Shan State. The Burmese junta work with local drug barons to produce and traffic heroin and methamphetamines. It is a vast source of revenue for them.

'What?' mumbled the interpreter, waking from his reverie.

'The millions of poppies on the roadside, very pretty too, hey?'

'No no!' he snapped, and I thought my ambitious joke had met its inevitable end. But then he delighted me. 'They don't grow the poppies by the roadside, they grow them further back so they cannot be seen.'

I clapped in delight. Brilliant! If it were in a script it would be corny. The MI colonel was livid.

'And there are no poppies there,' he insisted through clenched teeth, 'because our drug eradication programme is cutting all that out!' He fumed at the interpreter who suddenly realised his faux pas and looked like he had swallowed a ball. The colonel stood up and walked to the door, then he delivered his final warning. 'You know they will take you to Kengtung. They can torture you there.'

'They can do what they like, pal, I'm not saying anything.'

He scowled and left. My wrists were cut from the handcuffs being too tight. When I asked for them to be loosened the police had great sport pretending that the keys were lost. I had been through this before. Then I was taken to a small cell with a reeking bottle of urine in the corner. One of the guards looked about fifteen. He had an automatic rifle on his knee, carelessly playing with it, unaware that he was pointing it right at me. That was more unnerving than threats of torture from the regime. I was prepared to face anything the regime might do to me; I was not afraid of them. But I was frightened by this boy with his gun, frightened of a senseless accident. Fortunately, I was not there long. Half an hour later a long thick chain was attached to my handcuffs and I was led out into a nearby building. I sat on a bench against the back wall, police on either side and a knot of men outside the door. I was told to stand as three men filed in from another room. It was only as witnesses were summoned to testify that I realised with astonishment that this was my trial.

There were four witnesses. The first, a policeman, said he had seen me that morning, causing a disturbance in the market and he had arrested me. I was given the chance to question him.

'From where do you get your authority?' I asked. 'Who made you a policeman?'

He did not respond. The second witness said I had been caught distributing anti-government literature.

'What did I do that was anti-government?' I asked. 'Is it anti-government to call for freedom and justice? What have I written in my letters that is anti-government?'

The judge intervened. He said it did not matter what I had written in the letters. It was an offence to give out any literature that had not passed the censors. But still they persisted with mentioning anti-government literature.

'Tell me exactly what words I have spoken or written which are anti-government. What I have written is pro-democracy. It is pro-truth. It is not anti anything.'

Of course they could not show evidence of anything anti-government. I had been extremely careful in what I had written (for a copy of the letter see appendix, B). It was forthright, but from any legal point of view utterly unobjectionable.

'The letters ask for three things,' I said. 'That the universities be reopened. That all political prisoners be released. And that the SPDC [military regime] holds dialogue with the National League for Democracy. What is anti-government in that? These things are in Burma's best interests.' I was insistent. Eventually the judge agreed to drop all reference to anti-government activities or literature.

'I have a complaint. Your man' – I pointed towards a clerk – 'is not writing down in the court record what I say. After each translation he just sits there. It is not right that you do not record what I say.'

The judge and prosecutor conferred and the clerk pretended to write.

'And I want to speak with a lawyer. I have the right to a defence lawyer.'

The judge tilted his head towards the prosecutor. 'He is a lawyer.' Then they carried on. My request was ignored. The translator was patently disregarding things I said and, worse, he was failing to tell me what the witnesses were saying.

The third witness was the big bearded bear who had grabbed me that morning, apparently the market headman. He had really spruced himself up for court: a bright Hawaiian shirt, his smartest *longyi* (a Burmese sarong) and perhaps the best wash of his life. Again he said I was caught distributing anti-government literature. When I could speak I asked once more what, specifically, I had written that was anti-government. The judge was flustered. He looked about, agitated, and summoned colleagues forward for whispered consultations. Then, through the translator, he told me all anti-government references would be dropped. They were irrelevant to the charge.

I asked the market headman if he had seen the red and white stickers I had given out.

'Yes,' he replied.

'Did you read them? Did you understand them?'

'Yes,' he answered again.

The stickers read in Burmese, 'Treat people as human beings'.

'Then why don't you?' I demanded, remembering how rough he had been in dragging me to the police station.

He regarded me with his eyes blazing and then, striking his chest, he boomed in English, 'I am Myanmar!' He meant he was Burmese, and therefore he and his colleagues could do whatever they liked and foreigners had no right to interfere. That is fine if he is talking about cuisine, fashion or political systems. It is untenable on issues of systematic rape and genocide.

The last witness was an immigration officer. I had entered Burma that morning on a one-day visa, paid my five dollars for it and had my passport duly stamped. This officer confirmed that. The judge said that a condition of the visa was that one did not break any laws in Burma. As I had broken the law in giving out literature I had broken my immigration bond too, and this was the second charge. I could not believe it. If the first charge was Orwellian repression, this one was straight from *Alice in Wonderland*.

'Are you saying that it is illegal to break the law?' I asked in astonishment. I was not at all surprised by injustice, but I thought they would at least try to be a bit more intelligent about it. How on earth would this lunacy bear up to international scrutiny in the following months?

The court was a bit confused.

I asked the immigration officer, 'Are you saying that anyone who breaks the law can be charged for that offence, and then charged again because breaking the law is deemed illegal? That is idiocy.' I was quite enjoying the proceedings. It is very rare to get the chance to stand up in front of the authorities of various departments and speak one's mind. I wanted to make the most of it.

They did not have an answer for me. Instead, the judge chose this moment to wrap it all up: 'You are charged with breaking the Printers and Publishers Act of 1962. Do you plead guilty or not guilty?'

I paused for a while, wondering how to word my opening phrase. 'With a *little* bit of respect,' I began, 'you are not a judge, this is not a court, and I do not recognise the authority of the State Peace and Development Council [the military regime]. They have no constitutional, legal, moral or popular mandate to govern. Instead, I recognise the National League for Democracy as government, as they won eighty-two per cent of the seats in the 1990 election. The National League for Democracy is sovereign in Burma, and I will only answer to judges, policemen and officials who are appointed by them. I do not plead; neither "guilty" nor "not guilty".'

The court was not happy: 'You are charged with breaking the Immigration Act of 1947. Do you plead guilty or not guilty?'

'I have told you many times. I do not recognise your authority. You work for terrorists. The National League for Democracy is sovereign in Burma. They can try me. I have broken no law. I do not plead.'

This upset the court. They were nervous because I was the only Westerner they had had to deal with. There was some discussion and soon the judge, prosecutor and clerk left (I am sure to telephone the Military Intelligence in Rangoon). That left just the police and me. We grinned at each other, theatregoers sharing the novelty of it all, and enjoyed two cigarettes during the recess. This must have been quite an entertainment for them. My main concern was to try to look untroubled, which was not impossible. I believe with all my heart that the forces for freedom are stronger than the forces for oppression. I know justice will prevail. Very well, then, let me demonstrate that belief. With words I could reject the corrupt judiciary. With actions, by a calm, unruffled, even irreverent demeanour, I could dismiss the might of the regime. Let me laugh at this charade, because I know that tyrants are weak. Fearlessness, and public displays of fearlessness, are the greatest threat to a regime that rules by fear.

It was dark outside when the judge returned. I had no idea of what would happen next but was determined to stick to my guns. The judge started a long preamble. Then it all came so quickly. On the first charge they found me guilty. For that I was sentenced to seven years' imprisonment. On the second charge they found me guilty. Five more years. I was surprised that they had not mentioned my previous suspended sentence of five years, but they added that on later (without telling me).

So no lawyer, no consular access, no evidence shown in court.

Within just ten hours of entering the country I was in prison beginning a seventeen-year sentence. My feelings were of utter relief. For a start the fact they had gone through the charade of court meant that the interrogation was probably over. I was not going to be tortured. And I did not now have that great anxiety of waiting to see what would happen. Most important the junta had just ruined their chances of keeping me. My hope had been to make sure that my imprisonment would not only be utterly unjust, but also manifestly so. Had they given me three or four years it would have attracted little outside attention. But by giving me the ridiculous sentence of seventeen years they had given the media the kind of headlines they loved and thus the regime would draw flak from all sides.

Six months earlier I had warned family and friends that I would be arrested in Burma around August or September and that I would serve perhaps six to eighteen months of a long sentence, maybe fifteen years or so. Everything had gone so smoothly. As I began pacing around my filthy cell I could not stop a smile sliding on to my face. I felt a relief that almost bordered on exhilaration and, being back in a Burmese prison, I had the strangest feeling I was home. I had wanted to fight this military regime for years and my chance to do that had just begun.

CHAPTER 2

Our youth today love luxury. They have bad manners, contempt for authority, disrespect for older people. Children nowadays are tyrants. They contradict their parents, gobble their food and tyrannise their teachers.   Socrates (400 BC)

CHILDHOOD FOR ME was pretty idyllic. I grew up in Mawdesley village, Lancashire, with my sister and two brothers. We were very close in age and very close in everything we did. Emma was the eldest, then Jonathan, then Jeremy and I came together. We were absolutely spoilt with love but not in material things. Instead of toys we would be told to go outside and play together in the rich countryside that surrounded us. And there is nothing built by man, no toy or computer, which is as interesting or as much fun as building dams in streams, or collecting frogspawn, or climbing trees and sword fighting in forests. And when inevitably we returned home cut and bruised, Mum would not fuss over us with plasters and iodine; she would kiss the wound and tell us it would get better with God's fresh air.

Mum was Australian. She had arrived in England in her early twenties and was commissioned in the Queen Alexandra's Royal Army Nursing Corps. After a two-year posting to Malaysia, she returned to England and found herself nursing another officer. The patient, who was to become my father, had been an army fitness instructor and played much sport. He was now in hospital after injuring his leg in a rugby match. The two of them got on and, later, married. Soon afterwards Dad was piloting helicopters in the Middle East, fighting for the Sultan of Oman against South Yemenis. His courage was noted when he flew behind enemy lines to rescue a fighter pilot (who had been shot down) and, despite coming under heavy enemy fire, they got their man out. We kids did not hear these stories until many years later. Dad was Church of England but as his job meant that he spent many months a year abroad, my parents agreed that we would be brought up, as Mum was, Roman Catholic.

School was a very happy time. My best friend at the village primary school was John. He was dark-haired, strong and dauntless. We went through all sorts of trouble together. We both died at El Alamein, at the Bulge, in Colditz. Yet, unperturbed by details like death, we went on to overthrow the Chinese communists. Side by side, we were a tough team. School bullies learnt to avoid us. Like everyone else we were frequently in trouble with teachers too, but we respected them. In our schoolboy morality it did not matter so much if you did 'right' or 'wrong'. But what mattered was, when you were caught would you confess? To own up and accept punishment was to be a man. To try and deny it was spineless.

Despite our great friendship, John had two problems. The first was that he would sometimes pick on his younger brother. Whenever this happened it fell to me to protect Thomas, the younger one. John would be furious with me, telling me I had no right to interfere in his family affairs, that as Thomas was *his* brother I had no business in stopping John giving him a pounding. The only other shortfall John had was that he sometimes got involved in scenes that had nothing to do with him. This happened when my own younger brother, Jeremy, albeit only fifteen minutes younger, would step right out of line. When he annoyed me like that, and I would give chase in order to administer a beating, John would catch hold of me and stop me. I would be absolutely livid, demanding to know how he could justify his interference in my family affairs. Surely he could see that as Jeremy was my own twin brother I had every right to do what I liked to him, and that it was quite wrong for an outsider to stick his oar into family justice. Childish fights – John and I remain good friends.

School went on. My twin, Jeremy, would clean up on the sports field, winning the *Victor Ludorum* each year at sports day (while I sat in uniform with the other bozos too slow and malcoordinated to find an event), and I would do the equivalent academically, coming top each year. I was no swot, but as I enjoyed learning the results came easily.

Church, every Sunday, I found as difficult to follow as all other kids who would rather be outside getting muddy. Yet I remember that even as an eight-year-old I was intensely jealous of the apostles. They had seen Christ, seen the Messiah raising people from the dead, and therefore, or so I thought, they need have no doubt at all. If they were required to die they could do so easily, firm in the knowledge that they would soon be in paradise. The rest of us, though, have to discover proof for ourselves. It always seemed to me that the most important thing was to find out what we have been born for, what is our purpose, what is the meaning of life. What were the apostles so ready to die for? This, sometimes an insomniac obsession, probably marked me out – nose in a book, head in the clouds.

When I was twelve Mum and Dad told us they wanted a divorce. We four children were devastated. It was shattering news. Until then I do not think I knew what a problem was. This woke me up to pain. Innocence was over. Beforehand we kids lived in the perfect world. Now we shared the real world with everyone else. It taught me to be more self-reliant. As it went, Mum wanted to protect us and decided to delay the divorce until six years later when we had all flown the nest.

At thirteen a new boy came to our school. He was Burmese, named Aung Lin, and for no obvious reason at all his desk was placed next to mine. He was the deepest thinker I had ever met. We spent our lunch breaks discussing life, the universe and everything: free will, space–time, objective truth. We never got anywhere but we became excellent friends. He told me about his country. It seemed a far-off land, a magical one – so ancient, so different, so interesting. Were all Burmese people as philosophical as Aung Lin? But I also learnt from him that the people in his homeland were suffering, suffering in ways beyond his description and beyond my comprehension. The military used to 'steal' the electricity. That is there would be power cuts every day as the army diverted the electricity supply to their own camps and projects. I tried to imagine the British army doing that.

Although Mum was Australian, she often seemed more British than most British. That meant honour, reserve and a sense of humour in adversity. She knew Britain's history inside out and her literature back to front. Personally, I was more inclined to science, but was blessed to have a mum and a sister, Emma, who showed me the value of the humanities.

Adolescent philosophy is mostly quite embarrassing, but there were two gems I discovered lying awake at night. The first was that nobody can do wrong to me. When we hurt somebody, in fact we hurt the whole, including ourselves. Such self-destruction can only be done from ignorance. Therefore, if I think somebody has done wrong by me, I should not take offence, or feel hatred towards them. I should recognise that it comes from their ignorance and it is best for me to reflect on how I make the same mistakes.

The second was that it is always to one's benefit to do what is right and to one's detriment to do what is wrong. Moral considerations are not something we can weigh against other arguments – what is easiest, or safest, or most fun, or most lucrative. Morality is supreme. If I think deceit is going to help me I am mistaken. If I think I can afford to be a coward I am in error. We reap what we sow.

School went on. At sixteen I had an operation that required a general anaesthetic. As the anaesthetic wore off, my body reacted badly. My breathing stopped and twice my heart stopped. The doctors discovered a *phaeochromacytoma* in my adrenal gland. It was as big as an orange and they left a two-foot scar across my torso in removing it. I was proud of the scar and quite oblivious to the danger.

Choosing a course for university had nothing to do with career but only with the continued search for the meaning of life. I went to Bristol to read physics and philosophy, believing that these two subjects both sought to understand the fundamental nature of everything. What is the universe made of and what is it for? What are its laws? What is our role in it?

But studying life is never as rewarding as living it. I made the best of friends at Bristol – friends I still have – and we had a wonderfully exhausting time. Work began to take a back seat to more pressing distractions: beer, cigarettes, women. Discovering these was a great deal of fun and, due to excess, a greater deal of shame. Spiritual hangovers were far more painful than chemical ones. If the physical and emotional sides of a relationship develop together, in balance, then there is no great problem. But it seems that when the physical side races way ahead then there is shame. Regardless of liberal theory, the heart knows that sex outside of love is destructive. It is profane. It was not sin itself which made me so ashamed, but the weakness which gives rise to it. I know what is right, I want to do what is right, yet time after time after time I do wrong, because I am weak.

I was never involved in any kind of student politics. I was as apathetic as everyone else; what was there to fight about? Many students in Britain have everything served to them on a plate. In the sixties they might have rallied to get better accommodation. In Bristol the newest student halls had en suite bathrooms! The whole money issue passed me by as well. The government paid for students' tuition fees and for some it contributed towards maintenance. I thought this was something we should be grateful for, rather than demanding more. During holidays I worked like a horse in the local supermarket. In term-time I worked at a student bar, being paid in beer tokens. In my second year I joined the Officer Training Corps, which meant being paid to dress in green and run around forests having fun. So in all my time at Bristol I never had to go into debt. Sure, I had no CDs, very few clothes and none of the trinkets students usually embellish their rooms with. But I was never short of money for beer.

At the end of the first year we sat our exams. In the seven papers for physics and maths I got straight A grades. I was not very encouraged by that. University seemed less serious. I had got straight As pretty much all my life but beforehand I had always concentrated enough to earn them. This year, however, had been spent in increasingly drunken folly and neglect of the course. Perhaps in any other subject I would have felt pleased to get away with a year of fun and then knuckled down to work. But the fact that I had even been given an A in quantum and relativistic physics, which is hard yards by anyone's reckoning, jolted me. I felt I understood next to nothing of them and here was the university awarding A grades. What was it for? Society put so much stock by getting a degree: 'Get a degree, then all will be fine. Get a degree, it is most important.' But here I could see that a degree was not important. It did not equate to knowledge or understanding. It only meant that one knew how to play the system, in this case, what kind of answers examiners liked.

As a child I had never doubted 'the system'. I had had absolute trust in parents, teachers, police, government. With alarming naivety I had believed that everyone in power knew what they were doing and furthermore they were all honourably devoted to the welfare of society. But over the past couple of years it had been slowly dawning on me that humanity does not know what it should be doing. And now my own experience with the exam results proved unequivocally that the system was flawed, that it gave honour where none was due.

Besides that, I was also beginning to realise that the Meaning of Life was not going to come to me in lecture halls or laboratories. Other than socially, I felt I was wasting my time at university. I could lose my degree without losing my friends. Much of life was good, but it did not seem to make up for the bad: homelessness; wife-beating; drugs destroying families. My trouble was that I did not use my own ears and eyes to assess the reality around, but instead I let myself be increasingly overwhelmed by disturbing reports from the media and elsewhere. Could it possibly make sense for me to pursue a degree, a career, a mortgage, a happy family life while all around the world people were starving to death and living in unspeakable fear? The crucifying injustices that paralyse my brother are, can I see it, crucifying me too. They must be my priority. There were more important things than gaining qualifications. I did not know what was the right thing for me to do. I did know that it was not a degree. Halfway through my second year I left the university.

I was thinking: 'If I want a rational, logical excuse for not going to my brother's aid, one rooted in eternal truth, it has to be a reason that satisfies me as the privileged and simultaneously satisfies the oppressed. But there is no such reason. Whatever excuse I contrive for accepting the imbalance of injustice, I know that I would immediately reject that excuse were I one of the oppressed.'

Why, then, did I not start doing something about it, something practical? Because I did not at that time believe in the power of the powerless. I did not know that it is enough to do all you can. I wanted immediate change and, while I was not so foolish as to believe I could get it, I was so foolish as to believe that therefore life held nothing. I did not want to share a world with evil. So for that, I tried to kill myself. It was not that I had lost my faith in God. On the contrary, it was the very fact that I knew there was a god and knew there was meaning that caused the problem. Because as much as I knew these existed I also knew that I had missed them, that the life I was looking at was not one worth living. I realised, of course, that Christianity prohibits suicide, but I had not yet learnt obedience – I was still at the stage where I thought mere mortals could bargain life's contract with God. But it is a mistake to think we have some say in our lives, opining what is reasonable and fair to endure and what is simply too much.

Death had never been a scary prospect. Rather, it seemed like the most exciting event in anybody's life; after death came all the answers, the final truth. In May 1993 I slit my wrists in a warm bath. I made a great mess of one arm and there was plenty of blood. But as the bath water began reddening I began to feel sorrowful. Each cut on my arm would bleed briefly, then slow down. I had to cut again and again, deeper each time, but each time I felt more frightened by what I was doing. It was as if I was cutting someone else's body. It seemed cruel. My own life began to seem achingly precious. It was not something to throw away wilfully. The feeling that I was killing somebody else, a young child, became stronger and stronger. Part of me was whimpering to another part, saying please do not do this, please do not carry on, please let me live. The cuts kept closing up. I had not been ruthless enough. As I lost my resolve to continue I felt an embarrassed relief. Had I really been driven to this by despair at the world's suffering? Or was it a more personal weakness: fear of failure, disillusionment or the feeling of being intensely alone? I am still not sure.

But certain things became clear after that. First I would never ever try to kill myself again. Life is too precious. Suicide felt like murder. And also my life was no longer my own. I had been all set to throw it away. In fact, I had thrown it away and it had been saved by some small voice which said, 'Don't.' *Well, God,* I thought, *if you want me alive for something, then you can have me. If I am called to it, I will do it. Anything.*

Meanwhile, I loved the city of Bristol and remained there to be near friends while working in warehouses to earn a fare to Australia. Over there I would see my mum's side of the family and a bit of the world.

Oddly enough I discovered the true value of university in the months after I had quit: it is for learning, for discovering, not for being taught. Increasingly, I was using the university library to read up on history, military history, revolution, economics. Here I read only what I wanted to read, chasing up themes through other books. And also fishing from the great pool of brains (which a university hopefully is) to catch new ideas, to share thoughts, to expand one's limits. And I would not have wanted to be anywhere else for it but Bristol.

CHAPTER 3

Politics is about people and you cannot separate people from their spiritual values. Daw Aung San Suu Kyi

IN 1988 BURMA hit the world's headlines. Millions of Burmese had taken to the streets, making non-violent marches calling for change and democracy. For twenty-six years they had endured oppressive military rule. This once-rich nation, abundantly fertile land, now knew poverty and starvation. The economy was a disaster. The people had no rights, no freedom. Liberty had been eroded and extinguished. In its place grew fear and the fear was well founded. The military junta responded to the protest marches by gunning down thousands. The shooting was indiscriminate. Housewives and schoolchildren were shot. Buddhist monks were bayoneted to death. Nurses, covered in the blood of their patients, pleaded with the soldiers to stop shooting. They were killed too.

In 1989 the leader of the democracy movement, Daw Aung San Suu Kyi, was put under house arrest. The following year she led the National League for Democracy (NLD) to a landslide election victory, winning eighty-two per cent of the seats. The military junta had never had any intention of handing over power. They had agreed to hold the election (the only one in decades) because they were so out of touch with reality that they actually thought they would win. So when they realised they had lost so overwhelmingly, they began imprisoning, torturing and murdering elected MPs, trying to force mass resignations from the NLD. Daw Aung San Suu Kyi remained under house arrest and in 1991 won the Nobel Peace Prize.

I was too young to understand what was happening, quite preoccupied with school, with exams. But these events caught my attention and, like the rest of the world, I marvelled at the dauntless courage and leadership of Daw Suu Kyi. And, like the male half of the world, I marvelled at her beauty. Burma seemed to me to be such a far-off land, even a different planet, but I had my Burmese friend Aung Lin, so I knew it was real. Many of those who were imprisoned and killed were the same age as Aung Lin and I. Many were younger. Did that mean that if Aung Lin had not come to England he might be dead now?

In 1995 Burma hit the headlines again. Daw Suu Kyi had supposedly been released from house arrest (but in reality most of the restrictions have remained in place). By this time I had travelled a fair bit in Europe, America and Australia, but my heart yearned for Asia. I was in love with jungle, so full of the unknown, so full of God's secrets, beautiful, wild. And I wanted to understand this magic land, a place so completely different from our world in the West. In 1996 my mind was made up by an article in the *Daily Telegraph*. The article was about forced labour in Burma. Even children were made to work. A photograph showed a young boy wielding a mattock, working to build a road for tourists. This seemed to me to be absolutely abominable. The child should have been at school. But who was allowing the current situation? Was it the child's parents who wanted him to work? Was it the military junta who forced them? Or was it we in the West, by demanding trade and tourism but neglecting justice? I had no idea whatsoever as to the answer and was quite sure I would not be able to find out unless I visited Burma. But how on earth could I do that? Two months later a door opened.

After Australia, I was working in New Zealand, assembling farm equipment at a plastics and metal factory. Quite by chance I met a student in a pub who had been to the Thai–Burma border. He showed me photographs of the guerrillas and their camps, and gave me human rights reports to read. They were horrifying. Not only slave labour of children, but arbitrary detentions, summary executions, gang rapes of ethnic women and slaughter of entire villages. How could any people deserve such suffering? How could any people perpetrate such cruelty? The camps he had stayed at were run by ex-students, those who had escaped from the slaughter of 1988 and had made their way to the border areas to join the ethnic groups who had been fighting for their land for decades. The largest group of students was called the All Burma Students Democratic Front (ABSDF).

I asked him if he thought they would welcome me there. He suggested that if I offered to teach English then certainly they might find a place for me. He gave me a contact name and telephone number in Bangkok, and wished me luck. That was it.

My family may have been geographically dispersed but we were always in close touch and I kept them well informed on the developing plans. I had resolved to fly to Bangkok before the New Year and so spent the next three months working all the hours I could get. In time off I hunted out every single book I could find on Burma and think I got about three. Not very impressive. But one of them was *Freedom from Fear* by Daw Aung San Suu Kyi. What a perfect introduction to Burma and the short essay, which gave the book its title, was one of the most inspirational reads, showing with perfect clarity that to allow oneself to be trapped by fear is a fatal mistake.

I was also able to meet with a couple of Burmese exiles, two sisters. They had been involved in student demonstrations in the 1970s when dozens were shot and thousands arrested. I almost cried to hear it. I told them I wanted to go to Burma and confront the military regime, I wanted to make an appeal to them to put down their guns. Not that I expected they would put down their guns. I did not really know what to expect. I did not really care. I just wanted to confront them with the question and find out what the response would be. The elder sister told me I would be shot. I asked her the Burmese word for 'friend'. It was '*mae-sway*'. I wrote that down, a word I wanted to remember. When we said goodbye the elder sister had tears in her eyes.

Oh, New Zealand, dream land! What a gorgeous country. What

welcoming people. And what fantastic libraries in Palmerston North! If I had not been so thrilled to be heading to south-east Asia it would have been much harder to leave New Zealand. I was acting on an impulse which many of us feel. We see devastating suffering and we want desperately to do something about it, to stand against it. And too often this feeling is immediately overcome by one of helplessness – 'but what can I do? – I am only one'. For me though this refrain no longer had any power because I had no ties, no responsibilities, nothing better to do.

How do you introduce yourself to a guerrilla army? How do you make contact with the Foreign Affairs wing of an insurgent group? Almost certainly you want to keep a low profile, not let anybody else know what you are up to, and have your first meeting in some dark, unfriendly corner of town. I had been in Bangkok just one night and it was time to make my move.

Unfortunately, I didn't know how to use a Thai telephone. The guest house owner made the call for me and arranged the rendezvous. Very professional, James. Very low-profile. We were to meet outside McDonald's in front of a huge new shopping mall. Very Secret Service. Very cloak and dagger.

So there I was, twiddling my thumbs, scanning the heaving crowds of middle-class Thai schoolkids, looking for some hardened Burmese brute who would whisk me away to their hideaway. He was a little bit late. I began to worry that he had taken one look at me and decided to disappear. Grinning foreign idiot. The Thai schoolkids were immaculately turned out but perhaps only one in ten had any money to spend in the mall. It was just a place for them to hang out. Not quite the Bangkok I had imagined . . . one of them was smiling at me. But he was not a kid. He was certainly older, maybe twenty-five: very slight build, pressed white shirt, nicely combed hair, smart trousers, poncy leather satchel. He came right up to me.

'Zaw Min?' I asked, startled.

'No, Ko Chit. Zaw Min could not make it.' We stuck our arms out and shook hands. 'So . . . ?'

'Thank you for coming,' I said eagerly, 'thank you for agreeing to see me. Erm . . . can we talk? Shall we go somewhere?'

Ko Chit smiled. 'We can talk here,' he suggested. So we did. I told him what I knew about Burma, which did not take long. I told him how much I wanted to get involved, wanted to learn, so that one day I could help. I asked him about the massacres in 1988. He had been there, one of the students demonstrating, asking for change, asking for a chance at democracy. Well, he must be older than twenty-five then. I asked him if there was anything I could do which would mean that I could live inside Burma. Could I teach English in one of their jungle camps? After about twenty minutes' conversation he said we could go back to his office.

A couple of cramped bus rides later we arrived at a two-storey terraced house. Inside there were half a dozen Burmese men sitting around, some eating, some reading, some smoking. They were very hospitable. Did I want a drink? Tea? Something to eat? I was too nervous for anything. I found a spot on the floor and grinned foolishly.

There were people coming and going but any activity took place upstairs. Down here was for lounging about. I introduced myself. Shared some cigarettes. Explained again what I knew about Burma and I am sure they could see the passion behind my ignorance. One by one they told me their stories and the same pattern emerged. Students in 1988, they joined the pro-democracy marches and then dodged the bullets, saw their friends fall dead. Some were arrested and spent time in prison, some went into hiding, many did both before heading to Karen State along the Thai border, there to join the guerrilla armies at war with the regime. They fought in the jungle for years. Thousands of their comrades died in the fighting and thousands more died from malaria. Now they were here in Bangkok. There were two main offices. This one, the Foreign Affairs office, gave information to interested bodies/governments about their situation. The other office, Student Relief Committee, organised supplies for those still on the border and inside Burma.

There was also plenty of literature lying around explaining the history of Burma and the situation today. I spent my time listening, reading and trying to learn Burmese. Burma is an ancient civilisation, predominantly Buddhist. The 45 million population is made up of over a hundred ethnic groups, many of which have been fighting for centuries. The largest group, the Burmans, dominate the central lowlands while the remaining thirty per cent of the population live mostly in the mountainous border areas.

In the 1800s Burma became a British colony. The Burmese had revered their king but the British showed that guns were more powerful. And so certain Burmese came to revere the gun and to make the army more glorious than ever an army should be. After World War Two Burma won her independence but fighting between the ethnic groups and the Burman majority continued. There were fourteen brief years of parliamentary democracy, but then in 1962 a terrible thing happened. Ne Win, a man without brain or heart, took power in a military coup. There were protests but not enough; many Burmese trusted the army because, after all, it had been founded by their national hero, *Bogyoke* Aung San (father of Daw Aung San Suu Kyi). And ever since that coup Burma's fortunes have deteriorated, her suffering has increased. The only way the junta can remain sitting on top of the country is by murdering it, strangling it, by destroying the life in it. They have done this for forty years but it is becoming harder and harder for them to survive. They are tyrannical parasites whose greed is so extreme that they blindly suck the life from their host without realising such a process will be their own end.

As I tried to take in all the new information I was terribly nervous. What if the ABSDF decided I could be of no use to them and politely showed me the door? But the next day, New Year's Eve, great news came. I could teach English in Minthamee camp, Tenasserim Division, south-east Burma. Ordinarily to get there would require a lot of awkward travel – buses, motorbikes, long long treks. But as the gods were smiling, there were a couple of NGO (Non Government Organisation) workers driving there in two days' time. I could get a lift with them. Fantastic.

'We cannot afford to pay you, you know?' Ko Chit put in.

'Are you joking, man?' I replied. 'I should be paying you. For somewhere to stay, for whatever food I need . . .'

'Never mind. Thank you for your interest in our revolution.'

New Year's Eve in Bangkok. Midnight. Exciting? I slept through it.

The next day I went to a hospital to enquire about anti-malaria drugs and immunisation from hepatitis. In New Zealand the hep shot was too expensive and nobody knew which strain of malaria was prevalent on the Burma border (and I did not know then which part I would be going to). It would be useless to take the wrong drug. The Thai hospital was just as expensive. Well, I did not like drugs anyway. Better to use common sense. That was the excuse my wallet came up with.

I felt like a fish out of water but was determined that nothing would be a problem. My hosts had enough to worry about. They advised me to get a warm jacket.

'But it's boiling!' I said.

'Not at night, not on the border.'

Can't be colder than the north of England, I thought to myself.

'Get a jacket.' I got a jacket.

We arrived at the NGO office early. They were a Christian group, concentrating on supplying the refugees with rice. Officially they were only supposed to provide for those who were in camps inside Thailand, but with their heads screwed on they took the risk of supplying who they could in Burma too. Sarah, from the UK, was the boss, and Will her boyfriend. They wanted to spend three days at the camp to check on conditions and were happy to drop me off there. Ko Chit would come for the three days too.

I had expected an arduous journey. Instead, we went by air-conditioned four-wheel drive. Almost as soon as we had set off a policeman flagged us down. Sarah ignored him and drove on.

'What was that for?' I asked.

'Nothing. Speeding. He just wants our money.'

'Were you speeding?'

'Course not.'

I watched the tourist sites of Bangkok go by – pagodas, palaces, parks. Not interested. Goodbye to the concrete jungle.

Many hours later we reached the first of several border checkpoints. The road by now was just an unsurfaced track. Burma and Thailand share a 2000-kilometre border. On this there are just three towns where one can apply to cross on a one-day visa. Certainly tourists cannot cross anywhere else. But as any Burmese will tell you, there are ways and means. And in reality, any 2000-kilometre border, which runs mostly through mountains, forest or jungle, is as porous as a broken net. At each checkpoint I expected the Thai soldiers would ask me where the devil I thought I was going and had I never heard of a visa. But nothing happened. Ko Chit and Sarah would get out and have a few words. Then we would proceed. The Thais would radio ahead to the next checkpoint and we would just be waved through. Nevertheless, I tried my best to look either Burmese or invisible.

And then, beside the road there was a shoddy wooden sign: 'Entry absolutely forbidden. This is Karen State.' We had reached Burma. It had all been rather too easy. Four months earlier I had been on a drunken road trip in New Zealand with only the vaguest dreams of travel. Now I was inside Burma going to a jungle camp of soldiers to teach English. Surely there was something I should be worried about. I decided to worry about malaria.

We drove deeper and deeper into the jungle. At times it would grow greener, darker, denser – reaching over the track. Then it would thin out again, allowing light to play with the shadows. The four-wheel drive struggled sometimes in the sand or on the dry but steep river banks. We passed through more checkpoints but there were no delays here. These were manned by soldiers of the Karen National Union, 4th Brigade. The Karen, at 6 million, were the largest of Burma's ethnic minorities. They had been fighting against the Burmese regime for fifty years. I would find out more and more about the British debt to them.

We stopped briefly at a village where Ko Chit and Sarah knew some of the locals. It was poor. The air smelt unclean and the whole place looked diseased. Even the chickens looked unhealthy. A few dozen wood houses lined the dusty road. In one house was an ABSDF HQ, home to about ten members. We introduced ourselves. So much was new, the surroundings, the people, the situation, that it felt difficult to take in all the details. Some were friendly, some a little shy.

Then one more came forward. He dragged himself across the

floor and raised his left arm to shake hands. 'My name is', he said with some difficulty, 'Yan Kyaw Aung.' He was severely crippled, paralysed from the waist down. What a horror to live out here in that condition. But he was smiling. A big smile. Over the next few years he would work a miracle.

We set off again as the sky reddened and darkened. The jungle became exquisite: thicker, deeper, more mysterious. The last light was pink and then we were surrendered to the black night. It was comforting. Whenever we passed someone on the roadside Sarah would slow right down so they could jump into the back, picking up about a dozen people this way. At last the headlights picked out a large red sign: Minthamee Camp, All Burma Students Democratic Front, Battalion 201. We had arrived. The camp, like scores of others around Burma's borders, had been established in 1988–9 by students who had escaped from the massacres in central Burma.

There were people to greet us as soon as we stepped out of the vehicle. Ko Min Aung was the political leader of the camp. He had very short-cropped hair and a severe look. He made me think of communists, the dedicated and noble ones surviving in China's Yan'an caves in the 1930s. His English was excellent.

'Ah. We have been expecting you. Please, come this way.'

Someone offered to carry my bag. I said I was OK and followed into a fairly large hut. I could already feel the mosquitoes biting. Malaria hits at dawn and dusk. I was worried, keen to get the mossie repellent out of my bag and on to my skin. Nobody else seemed to think it was important.

In the hut a candlelit table was laid out with bowls. More were arriving. They had put on quite a feast for us: rice, soup, vegetables, bean sauce, fish paste, fried eggs, noodles, even a bit of pork. Burmese believe strongly in hospitality. There were about eight of us around the table. Sarah and Will seemed very comfortable. They had lots to talk about and only three days to do it. I was more than happy to sit back and listen. It did not take the brains of an archbishop to work out that this was a pretty special spread of food. Nobody else in the camp would eat as well as this. I was reluctant to tuck in.

Ko Min Aung told me to eat up. 'Don't be shy. Make yourself at home. *Ahmanabarne.*'

'*Aban mar nah nay*?' I repeated.

The eight or so people around the table laughed.

'*Ahmanabarne*,' said Ko Min Aung kindly. 'It means, "don't be shy".'

Still I was reluctant to eat too much. I tried to eat just rice and only take small amounts of the delicacies – eggs, pork, vegetables.

'You have to eat good,' said Will with a huge mouthful. 'You'll be no good out here if you get sick. You must eat a lot to stay healthy.'

I nodded but did not agree. Surely the locals would need the food more than me. The conversation turned to English teaching.

'I've never taught English before,' I explained. 'I haven't got any qualifications or anything.' Ko Chit had already told me in Bangkok that this would not be a problem.

'Never mind. That is not important,' said Ko Min Aung. He might have looked severe but he was kindness itself. 'When do you want to begin?'

I considered it for a few moments. I had just arrived so it would be nice to take two or three days to get to know the area and my hosts before launching into the formalities.

'He could start tomorrow,' volunteered Sarah. She looked at me. 'Is tomorrow morning OK.'

I was startled.

'Excellent,' agreed Ko Min Aung. 'How about ten o'clock?'

I opened and shut my mouth a few times.

'Ten o'clock, then?'

Oops.

By now it was past midnight. Time to find our quarters. Sarah went off to sleep in a hut with two women. Will and I were to sleep in the library. A dark-skinned student, Ye Min Aung, offered to show us the way. The library turned out to be a bamboo room with three shelves of extremely mouldy papers. Among all that one could probably have salvaged about a score of what we in the West would call 'books'. But anyway, it was somewhere to sleep. Will had a huge mosquito net and set that up for both of us. Ye

Min Aung found us a few blankets and warned us that it would get very cold by morning.

Lying there trying to nod off, I think I had forgotten about malaria. Neither was I worried about being in a war zone. 'English class at ten!' I thought, absolutely stricken. 'They'll throw me out of here within the week.'

CHAPTER 4

The exercise of power is governed by thousands of interactions between the world of the powerful and that of the powerless, all the more so because these worlds are never divided by a sharp line: everyone has a small part of himself in both.   Václav Havel

THE FIRST MORNING was a bit of a mêlée. There were about two hundred people in the camp: eighty children, forty women and eighty men. Of the men most were soldiers on R&R (Rest and Recuperation). Depending on whom you asked, the fighting was five days away or five hours. In any case, everybody agreed we were quite safe here. The camp had been established shortly after the 1988 uprisings and although many had been living in the jungle since then, they still classed themselves as students. They might spend six months to two years in the front line and then retire here to Minthamee for a few months' rest. And the front line, of course, was not a line at all but part of vast tracts in Burma where territory is disputed, where resistance fighters follow guerrilla tactics and the *Tatmadaw* (Burmese army) terrorises locals. Many of the students were Burmans, the ethnic majority forming seventy per cent of Burma's population. But there were also members of other ethnic groups: Karen, Mon, Arakanese, Chin, Kachin and more. Over the past decade this had had the important effect of unifying various groups against their common enemy. The conflict became drawn less along ethnic lines and increasingly on political lines: pro-freedom v. totalitarianism.

Another great effect the students have had is to have articulated their country's pain to the outside world. We are now better informed than ever about what is happening in Burma and that is in large part due to the students who still carry the message and who still risk their lives returning to central Burma to gather information.

About thirty students wanted to sign up for English lessons. Ye Min Aung, tall and the same age as me, helped organise everything. Over the following days a timetable emerged. The 'advanced' class for two hours in the morning. An 'intermediate' class for two hours in the afternoon. And a beginners' class for an hour and a half. This was Monday to Friday. Saturday morning was a voluntary lesson for anybody keen enough and the rest of the weekend was free. I had managed to dig a 1950s American textbook out of the 'library' and tried to base lessons on that.

The students were, to put it mildly, keen. The natural thirst for education had been sharpened by years of denial. And learning English was particularly useful. It meant students could communicate directly with international agencies about their situation. They could tell their story to the media, give facts to NGOs, appeal to foreign governments. A second-hand translation is feeble in comparison with a face-to-face talk. And those who excelled could produce their own pieces for the international media, they could set up their own NGOs and they could better understand the position of foreign governments which might influence their country. Learning English also opens up tremendous new horizons, for example, by enabling a student to read widely. The Orwellian regime censors all printed matter to a Draconian extent. There is precious little of worth printed in Burmese (other than poetic and religious material). And anyway, even if my lessons were not going to be especially educational, they would at least be a diverting distraction.

The very first part of each lesson would be pronunciation practice. I would write out a passage on the board (we had chalk and a blackboard!) and the students would stand up in pairs to read it out, alternating sentences. Initially, in a mood of inspirational folly, I took the passages from *Crime and Punishment* by

Dostoevsky. It was one of the very few books I had salvaged from the library. The students' English was good, but this was a bit much. After a few days Ye Min Aung took me to one side and politely suggested a change. So we went on to magazines of the democracy movement – far more appropriate.

Following this would be prepared sessions on grammar and vocabulary, but we would finish off with a general discussion that went anywhere. Through the lessons I began to learn about Burma and about them, their histories. Ye Min Aung was one of the best English speakers. He and others were always keen to talk about politics and wanted me to teach them about it. Very quickly we found out that they knew far more of the American Constitution and the British political system than I did. So I would listen in, occasionally correcting points of grammar in order to earn my rice.

The American textbook was of limited use. It was full of sentences like, 'John works as an accountant', 'Bill watches TV all evening', 'Susan drives from the airport to the hotel'. It was not just that much of this vocab seemed irrelevant, but I became acutely embarrassed by the triviality of Western life. Could Westerners really lounge around watching TV all night, and have money for hotels and flights, and still share a planet with civil wars where people were starving to death? I made the necessary changes. Accountants and lawyers became farmers and soldiers. TV and newspapers became watering the plantation and standing guard duty.

We had a lot of fun in the lessons, but other than a marked improvement in pronunciation, I do not think there were any scholastic benefits. In Burma all teachers are shown great respect. I was included in this but it felt odd. Time and again I told them that it was the other way around, I was the student and they, all 200, were my teachers.

After the first night I slept with three room-mates in a hut joined to the library. The view was beautiful, overlooking the Tenasserim river and the jungle-clad hills behind. We would walk down the steep hundred-foot bank to the river to have a wash. Burmese prefer to wash in the cool of the day, late afternoon or dusk. I was typically English and keen on getting a tan, so went at midday. Sometimes I would go down at dawn when the river was covered in mist. I cannot fairly describe that heavenly beauty: pink mist and palm trees, gorgeous sand by gently flowing river.

Sarah and Will wished me luck and returned to Thailand. I began to fall in love more and more with my hosts and their country.

Ye Min Aung, although one of the best English speakers, was one of the few who had never been to university. He had joined the Burmese army after school and was soon sent to the borders to fight against the ethnic minorities. He told me how as soldiers they would round up local villagers to make them carry rations or ammunition to the front line. These 'porters' would receive no pay, no food, no shelter, no medicine. They would be taken, one or two from every household in a village, and made to work for a week, a month or longer. If a household could not provide a person they had to pay a fine. If they could not pay the fine a person would be taken by force: children, pregnant women, the sick. The Burmese junta try to explain to the world that this is not forced labour. They say it is a tradition in Burma for locals to volunteer for work on local projects. It is an alternative to taxation. That was fine in the past when people really would work on local amenities, but it is different from being dragged to the front line to be used as a human minesweeper.

One day Ye Min Aung saw one of the porters fall. He was over sixty years old and utterly exhausted. He could not go on. A sergeant came to the spot and made a decision. He ordered Ye Min Aung to shoot the old man. Ye Min Aung refused. The sergeant was furious and shot the man himself. I could hardly believe what I was hearing.

'How did you desert?' I asked.

'We were fighting. It was very bad. I was sick.' He was speaking animatedly. 'Usually I would go right to the front and fight, but this time I was sick. I could not move. A corporal came and started to hit me in the face with his *boots . . .*' He made a pounding motion.

'His *boots*?' I interrupted.

'Yes. He hit me again and again in the face with his *boots* so I . . .'

I did not want to interrupt again but the pounding motion did not seem to fit. 'His *boots?*'

'Yes,' answered Ye Min Aung, 'with the *boots* of his rifle . . .'

'Oh, the butt! He hit you with the butt of his rifle.' Now I understood.

Ye Min Aung looked at me as if to say, 'That is what I said' and carried on: 'He was hitting me and I was sick, and I had had enough. So I put down my gun . . .' He mimed levelling his rifle. 'And dah! dah! dah! dah! I shot to one side of him.'

Blimey, I thought with my eyebrows high. 'What happened?'

'The company sergeant major ran over to us to stop me.' He paused briefly. 'So I pointed my rifle to the side of him and dah! dah! dah! dah! After that they left me. When I was better I deserted. I joined the ABSDF.' He showed me photographs of his early days in the ABSDF. Of course, none of the students had had military experience. They were trained by the Karen or on the Chinese border by Shan and Kachin, and on the Bangladeshi and Indian borders by Arakanese and Chin rebels. But Ye Min Aung was already experienced so he was soon made an RSM (Regimental Sergeant Major). I saw photographs of him leading parades. Very smart. And very hard, too. Since then he had used every opportunity he could get to educate himself. If he could find a book, he would work through it, even if it were just a dictionary. He was a tough soldier, but his passion was for education. He always had his eye on the long term, and knew what his country would need when democracy came.

Ye Min Aung lived in barracks a couple of hundred yards from my hut, but he would visit most evenings. We would play 'Spendygame' (Scrabble) with my room-mates. Almost inevitably these games would be won by Kawn Sheim. He was Mon, an ethnic group from south-east Burma, but to me he looked just like he had swept down from the Mongol Steppe. He had a spiky moustache, sharp eyes and in the cold evenings he wore a blue bobble hat. I thought it very rude of him consistently to beat his English teacher at Scrabble, but he was not the only one. I would trail in third or fourth, convinced they thought I was making up words when occasionally I won. We had a children's picture dictionary to hand and that rarely helped in adjudicating. Kawn Sheim had a wicked laugh. He was full of humour and did not seem to notice the hardship of the jungle.

I had been so paranoid about trying to be useful that I had not even found time out of teaching to look around the camp. After a fortnight Kawn Sheim and Ye Min Aung offered to take me on a tour. The main office I knew. That was where we had dined royally on the first evening and it was where the English lessons were held. Attached were the political leader Ko Min Aung's quarters, which he shared with the cook, Ko Ko Oo. And I had already seen Ye Min Aung's barracks where he lived with a couple of dozen other soldiers. Minthamee also had its own hospital, primary school, monastery, family village area, more barracks, a generator room and even a gaol.

The gaol held one student. He was there for taking drugs in the front line. There were no guards, the door was not locked, and he was allowed out all day to do whatever he liked. He slept there but that was it. Sensible system.

The monastery was by far the grandest building in the camp. All the others were mostly small and made of bamboo. The monastery, with four *pongyis* (monks), was huge and made with beautiful polished teak. I spent one afternoon there discussing Buddhism with the youngest monk. Throughout the talk I was being assailed by spiders and ants, but being in a monastery I thought it would be rude even to brush them aside. Unfortunately, I was not well-mannered enough to refrain from occasionally correcting the monk's pronunciation. I blame the fact that I had been so heavily in 'teacher mode'. When we left Ye Min Aung told me the *pongyi* had a speech impediment. I nearly died.

I had a camera with me and Kawn Sheim snapped a shot of me speaking with the *pongyi*. Months later I saw the photograph. I was sitting cross-legged, vainly trying to keep my head slightly lower than his, as he sat on a low platform. I thought I was doing OK. In Burma, though, one should always tuck one's legs away, underneath or to one side, when facing a *pongyi*. My crossed legs were an insult or at best a sign of great uncouthness. I have found this throughout my visits to Burma. You cannot stop making faux pas, and mostly in utter ignorance. I must have seemed like a child. I could not cook for myself, I could not speak the language and I even needed lessons in how to wash my clothes in the river. What a baby.

We looked in at the hospital. It was run by Moe Zaw Aung. Previously he was a mathematics student. Now he was one of the stars of the 'advanced' English class. Inside were about eight beds, two occupied by young boys with dysentery, two for malaria patients (out for the day) and one by a baby. The baby was sitting in her father's arms. She had had twenty-six loose bowel motions that day. There was virtually no equipment, scarcely any medicine. The medic told me they had no drips to give her and in any case it was difficult to put a baby on drips. Instead, her father was gently ladling spoonfuls of orange juice to her mouth, trying to give her sugar. He looked frightened. Moe Zaw Aung was helped out by two students from the 'beginners' English class, Tin Yu Shwe and Sein Sein Aye, very gorgeous, very unmarried, very shy, very very distracting.

Moe Zaw Aung and his wife invited me to their hut for *mohinga*. It is a favourite Burmese dish, basically noodles with many accompanying vegetables, chillies and nuts. Delicious.

We dropped by the primary school and our last call was to Martyr Hill, the graveyard. It was about fifteen minutes' walk from the camp. Sixteen wooden markers giving the names and dates of those who had died. There was a captain, a lieutenant, a CSM, a sergeant and privates. Most had died in combat – their bodies were still at the front line. Some had died of malaria. One of the graves was dated 8.8.93. It was the anniversary of the massacres, which were at their worst on 8.8.88. I asked Ye Min Aung about it. He told me it belonged to a soldier. He had been twenty-four years old and had committed suicide on the anniversary of Burma's sorrow (see photograph).

And there was another suicide, beside the grave of the lieutenant, his wife. About six months after he died in the front line she killed herself. She had been twenty years old, a medic.

That evening we heard that a baby had died. She had been suffering from malaria for about a week and chronic diarrhoea had finished her off. She was an only child. That same night she was buried on Martyr Hill, and for the next three days the camp held a kind of vigil at her parents' house. They set up a TV and video there (powered by the generator), much food was brought, also as much alcohol as could be found and the camp tried to comfort the parents. But there was no one there who had not already known similar loss.

After three weeks I became very sick. I could hardly get out of bed and when I did I nearly fell over. The incubation period for malaria was three weeks. Damn. I had got it on my very first night! I had been very careful to wear long-sleeved clothes at night, pale colours to deter the mossies and plenty of repellent. I had a mosquito net, too, and had been scrupulous about using it. I was pretty annoyed. But I did not see it as a reason to stop the English lessons.

That morning I skipped the usual breakfast of rice, lettuce and bean paste. I turned up at the main office, where the English lessons were held, looking whiter than usual. Ko Min Aung had already heard that I was off colour and said they would take me to a nearby clinic. I declined, and said I should carry on teaching. Maybe it was not malaria, maybe it would pass. Ko Min Aung was not convinced. He had a word with Kawn Sheim.

Until then I had been teaching pretty solidly and the students were always very keen and very punctual. This morning, however, only three students turned up: Kawn Sheim, Ye Min Aung and Cho Too. I smiled weakly at them. We waited a few minutes.

'Where is everyone,' I eventually asked.

'They busy,' answered Cho Too.

'They are busy,' I corrected him.

'Yes,' he answered, 'they busy.'

'Today', announced Kawn Sheim, 'the students have duty.'

'Duty,' added Ye Min Aung with authority. That seemed to be that, they thought.

'Well, we can carry on then,' I said, leaning against a table so I would not fall. 'Shall we . . .'

The lesson began but the three were not paying much attention. They seemed quite uncomfortable, in fact, even disruptive.

'I think you are sick,' said Ye Min Aung.

'I'm OK. You have all had malaria, haven't you.' It was true. Every single person in the camp had had malaria and suffered the recurrent bouts a few times each year. Malaria does not go away. I tried to get on with the lesson but they would have none of it.

'Come with us to Htee Htar. It is a nearby village,' said Ye Min Aung.

I was tempted. For three weeks I had not left the camp. It would be good to have a day out. But I had heard enough of their histories to know that sickness was no excuse for a day off.

'We can go by boat,' put in Kawn Sheim. That clinched it. I love water. To go on a boat up the river, through the jungle, fabulous.

'Right. Good idea,' I agreed, 'lesson over.' The boys were delighted and ran off to make preparations. Soon we were loaded into the long, narrow boat and were ready to set off. But we did not. We waited. And waited.

'Sorry,' said Ye Min Aung, 'got to find boat driver.' He had been there a few minutes before but had slunk off. At length he returned, being herded in by a laughing Kawn Sheim.

'Ah, Mr J!' shouted the boat driver excitedly, 'I am Here. My name is Here.' He was perhaps a touch hung-over, but braving it very well. 'Let us go now, let us go to Htee Htar.'

He pushed the boat out and started up the motor. It was very kind of them to use the boat; diesel did not come cheaply.

'Why did no one come to the lesson this morning?' I asked Kawn Sheim.

He grinned. 'Students boycott your lesson!' The rest was left unsaid. They knew I was sick, they were going to take me to the clinic in Htee Htar.

By the time we got there I had almost recovered. It was just under two hours upstream and the views had been glorious. Lazy sandbanks baked under the hot sun but we enjoyed a cool breeze as we motored through the rushing water. Occasionally the long boat struggled against rapids and sometimes its belly or propeller would strike a rock. But then the river would widen again, deepen again and we roared ahead, unable to hear any of the birds we saw. Islands to the left of us, islands to the right of us, and although it was the hottest time of year the magnificent jungle did not appear to be suffering from thirst.

Refreshed, we disembarked and started making our way through the Karen village. It seemed more like a town to me. There must have been at least 2000 inhabitants and, unlike Minthamee's tiny bamboo huts, here some of the houses were great big structures made from teak or other hardwoods. There was a beautiful great church. We wandered along a road to the edge of the village, past a sawmill and arrived at the breeze-block clinic. A young Karen medic pricked the end of my thumb, then went off to put the blood under a microscope. This kind of service was courtesy of efficient Karen organisation and generous donations from abroad. Even so, the clinic was very basic and had scarcely any equipment or supplies. It also served a vast area. We waited. I wanted to know about the sawmill. There were over a hundred workers being paid 80 Baht per day for a ten-hour day and a six-day week. There was a break for lunch. Fifteen pence per hour. The work was very dirty, quite dangerous and incredibly noisy. No chance of ear defenders, I am sure all the workers were going deaf.

Burma holds eighty per cent of the world's teak. One notices the dramatic change in the forest from the Thai side of the border to the Burma side. The former is made of thin young trees, not very impressive at all. In Burma however the forest is thick. You can call it jungle. And as much of the hardwood has already been ripped out of Thailand, entrepreneurs have now turned to Burma.

Burma also grows much of the world's opium, later refined to heroin. This is in addition to the boom industry of amphetamines. The Burmese military regime and certain ethnic groups use the drug money to fund their wars but the Karen refuse to do this.

Previously they made sufficient money by placing a ten per cent tax on the vast quantities of goods smuggled across the border (mostly into Burma). More recently they sell logging rights to Thais. Back in the West we cry out that we must save the rainforests. Perhaps we should concentrate on saving the Karen, then they would not have to sell off their forests. They are fighting to defend their land, their villagers, their lives. It is peculiar to ask them to put the trees first.

The medic came over with the results. No malaria. Probably just a mouthful of dicey river water. Phew.

In any event I was sure the sickness did not come from Ko Ko Oo's cooking. Although he cooked in just a tiny dirt-floor kitchen, everything was scrupulously hygienic. Ko Ko Oo was perhaps the best-natured man in the world and certainly he has the best smile. The food he turned out was also delicious. Rice came from Thailand. Vegetables were grown in plantations beside the river. They grew lettuces, cabbages, cucumbers, rosily, spinach, long beans and even tomatoes. To be sure there were very few of these. Mostly soldiers ate just rice and a few boiled leaves. I was astonished to hear they grew carrots; I had not seen one for weeks and was suddenly very keen to try. But the carrots turned out to be parsnips . . . well, delicious too.

One day down in the plantation I saw a chap working away, mud up to his knees and elbows. I went over to talk. He was cheerful and friendly. Our conversation went on and I discovered he was Ko Htay Aung, the military leader of the camp. I had kept my distance from the military side of things, not because I was not interested, but because I wanted to respect their security and not come across as a teenager on an adventure; it was important to earn trust before probing to the heart of things. But the equality of it struck me. Ko Min Aung was the political leader of the camp, but Ko Htay Aung was even more senior. And here he was muddied up, irrigating the plantation. No conceit at all.

Meat was rare, though animal life was prolific. There were cats and dogs everywhere. They were not territorial but wandered wherever they liked in the camp, spawning litters with abandon. Every time you turned you would see ducks, or chickens, or bantams, or peacock-type things (fat, with no tail and collared-dove-coloured), all pursued by their stumbling broods. There were cows and oxen distinct, pigs, goats, catfish and to top it off, one day near Htee Htar, I saw a real-life huge dirty elephant with droppings to match. In the wild there were monkeys, Burmese pythons, vipers, geckos, tadpoles/toads, mosquitoes – all these I saw, and it was wonderful. The beneficent variety of Allah!

But it was not all variety. 'Ah Minthamee!' I thought to myself, sitting on a bamboo mat in a bamboo hut before a bamboo table eating bamboo soup with a bamboo spoon from a bamboo bowl. 'Ah, Minthamee!' The word means 'actress'. The other side of the river was 'Mintha' – 'actor'.

One day a group of six men arrived in the camp. They had come by boat upriver and then climbed the bank behind my hut. There was some excitement in welcoming them back. They were dressed in fighting kit and seemed well armed and well tired. Among them was Phoe Ni, which means axe. He appeared every bit the guerrilla soldier: fit, tough, watchful. When he passed me he looked away – bloody foreigner. His group had just spent ten months at the front line. He knew the reality of suffering and fighting in Burma. Like many others, Phoe Ni was a bit sick of foreigners who seem to regard themselves as all-important angels of deliverance come to save the blighted poor folk. Foreigners are full of grand words and deepest sympathy, then retire to their air-conditioned hotel for huge meaty meals before catching the flight home.

I was standing in dumb, awed respect as the soldiers filed by. Bursting with a million questions, I did not dare to impose on their time. I just smiled and nodded as they disappeared, hoping to get to know them later.

Another time a student returned from a hunting trip. The prize of it was an eleven-foot Burmese python, gold with the dark diamond outlines. It was odd to see it there. Pythons belonged in zoos I thought. And this was your quintessential cartoon Python: the huge length and classic markings. I remembered vaguely that zoos called them Burmese pythons. It was strange to think that this was their real home, this was where they came from first. The hunter had also bagged a couple of monkeys. The meat was incredibly tough and tasted pleasantly of charcoal. But there was more than just the meat.

'Have some monkey shit stew,' offered Ye Min Aung kindly.

My eyes popped. 'You what?'

'Monkey shit stew. Very delicious.'

'I don't believe it,' I replied. 'Are you sure it is monkey shit.'

'Yes. We take from inside the monkey,' he assured me evenly. 'Very delicious. Very healthy. You know, monkey, he never get malaria. He eat the right herb.' Ye Min Aung pointed to some leaves. 'He never get malaria. Very clever. You eat monkey shit stew. Good health.'

I was more than dubious. But a couple of hours later there were a few steaming bowls of it and the boys were tucking in. I did not want to eat monkey shit, no matter how many herbal wonder cures it contained. But I did not want to be churlish either and throughout my stay I had made a point of trying to live as they lived, to share what I had by way of advantage (mostly cigarettes) and to decline most privileges where offered. The boys were happily spooning mouthfuls of the brownish-green soup and licking their lips. Well, I thought, a little taste cannot hurt.

'Bitter, bitter,' said Ye Min Aung.

'Yes,' I agreed, with my face screwed up. It was bitter but not inedible. Actually, quite nice. Maybe. For the sake of revolutionary solidarity, I would eat monkey shit.

The next day in our English class I decided a quick lesson on the alimentary canal would be in order. As we went from throat to gut Ye Min Aung suddenly put his hands to his head and sang out, 'James, James! So sorry. No, no. Not monkey shit stew. Monkey stomach stew! From the stomach.'

Very heartening news indeed. Such linguistic embarrassments happened all the time. 'You are very lazy,' Cho Too might tell me with a wondering smile. Slightly ruffled, having thought I was putting in considerable effort, I would ask what he meant exactly.

'I think, you are very lazy,' he would repeat.

Then Kawn Sheim would rescue us. 'He says', he would announce, 'that you are very *tired*.' Oh well, that was different, that was OK, then.

Another time I would be talking with Ye Min Aung, keen to learn whatever I could from him. Then he would interrupt our conversation: 'But I think you are not very interesting?' He would say it like a question. How was I supposed to respond? I could hardly deny it if it was his opinion. A little later I discovered he meant, 'But I think you might not be interest*ed*?' Aha! OK. And I could refute it and ask him to carry on with the story.

One time Ko Min Aung looked me in the eye and said, 'James, you are a very simple man.' I did not misunderstand that. In Burma it is a great compliment. It means 'straightforward'. I felt honoured.

On another brief excursion to a nearby village we found ourselves with a severe bed shortage. I insisted that we could just sleep rough. Ye Min Aung told me it would be too cold. We gave it a try anyway and by the small hours realised that it really was impossibly cold. We made our way into a hut full of friends and looked for a space. There were two very heavy hardwood tables each serving as a bunk for a soldier. Another had lain down on the ground between and one more had slung a hammock over him, the ends attached to the tables. As Ye Min Aung and I blundered in, one of the guys on a 'bunk' woke up. He sat up to rub his eyes and have a short chat. Then, after a couple of minutes he made to stand up.

As he took his weight off the table, and as one had slung his hammock on to it, the far edge of the table began to rise. It was all in horrible slow motion where you just watch as the seconds unfold in paralysed horror. The hammocked chap fell to the ground, pulling the table right up on to the two nearside legs; the table, which was extremely heavy, teetered for a moment or two, then came crashing down on the slumberent body asleep on the floor. The edge hit him squarely in the chest. My God! It looked enough to break anyone's ribs, but to be woken up that way was catastrophe. His body seemed to jack up and his contorted face instantly turned a whitish blue. He was trying to suck some air back into his lungs and I cannot remember if he was making a sound like rending metal or if he was winded to silence, but the picture was horrible. I was in a flap and a panic, did not know what to do. Then I saw red liquid in his mouth and on his lips. He still could not breathe. I was a man of the world, had (half of) a university education, had been to great cities and the great outdoors in four continents, had an opinion on everything. And yet I stood there dumb. Ye Min Aung had spent the last ten years fighting in the jungle. He pounced towards his friend, hauled him to his feet and wheeled round behind him. Then he did a textbook but enthusiastic Heimlich manoeuvre, with his arms around his comrade's torso and his fists clenched below his sternum and began jolting the life back into him. Very quickly the chap was breathing, his face relaxed (even if his eyes still showed terrible alarm) and all was sweet. The redness around his mouth turned out not to be blood but just the ubiquitous stains of betel. The moment passed. Everyone else was laughing. I was feeling a growing respect for Ye Min Aung.

Other than a couple of other trips to nearby camps I had not been in any hurry to explore the general area. My intention was to stay in Minthamee for a few months and there to learn as much as I could about Burma from the students, to learn the language and to build up complete trust with my hosts. Then, when the time was right, I wanted to make my way deeper and deeper into Burma until there came an inevitable confrontation with the regime. I would have to be very careful about that; as long as I did not get shot in the first minute by some trigger-happy kid I was confident I would be detained in their company but not killed. It would be tough, of course, but I would find out for myself what the junta was really like. But events took over. Instead of me going to the front line, the front line came to us.

Every dry season the Burmese army launches an offensive against the Karen and Minthamee lay in Karen State. This year was to be a major one. In February rumours began circulating about the impending attack. Ko Min Aung left for Thailand to make arrangements for a mass evacuation there. We had grown incredibly close since I had come, eating together and many evenings staying up late to learn about each other's culture. He was a gentle, kind, tough, humble, intelligent, sincere, humorous man. The camp seemed half empty without him. Ko Ko Oo missed him too.

By mid-February people started packing up certain equipment: mostly paperwork from the main office and the few bulky possessions of the camp (there was one tailor with a Singer sewing machine). Then my English classes stopped. Students were called off for military preparations. Guard posts were increased and all the weapons were gone over: cleaned, oiled and made ready. There were AK47s, M16s, GPMGs, 60mm mortars, hand grenades and rocket-propelled grenades. But nobody denied that the armoury was wholly inadequate. There was very little ammunition and half the shells were duds (but you never knew which ones until you fired them). A couple of men even had Lee Enfields, rifles dating back to World War Two. Other equipment dated back to the Vietnam War. Most of it had come through China to be sold in Thailand.

We were in Karen-controlled territory. Informed observers reckon the Karen to be the best jungle fighters in the world. In World War Two they killed more Japanese per head than any other nationality fighting in that theatre. More than the English, Scottish, Irish, Welsh, more than the Gurkhas, the Indians, the Australians, New Zealanders, Canadians, West Africans, Americans, Chinese. Today, although underequipped, they have lost none of their courage and skill.

But the impending fight would be unequal. The Burmese army is 400,000 strong and has forty per cent of the country's GDP spent on it. The resistance armies are only ever a few thousand strong. The plan was a defensive withdrawal. Not to give the land away for nothing, but neither to aim to hold on to it.

I did not want to leave. I know from my diary that living there was hard, but I cannot remember the hardship. I remember only paradise and the most inspiring and wonderful company. People so brave and yet gentle, so tough and yet cheerful, so poor and so kind, and so genuine.

The primary school at least was not closed down. There were about eighty children in the camp, maybe fifty of them at the school. *Pyo Pan Wai* (nurturing luxuriant flowers) had been built in 1994. About half the children came from Minthamee's families. The others were local Karen. Some had been sent there by their parents who lived in areas too dangerous to keep their children and where it is impossible to run a school. Others were orphans, their parents killed or missing due to the regime's genocidal campaigns. I asked if I could start teaching at the school.

The kids were fantastic. There were three classes based on age, the youngest being four or five and up to a handful of teenagers. They were taught Burmese, maths, English, history and geography. I was supposed to teach English but for the next two weeks we just had a whole load of fun. There were a few counting and alphabet games, then 'I went to market and bought a . . .' ('. . . a *longyi*' '. . . a *longyi* and a chicken' '. . . a *longyi*, a chicken and a cheroot' '. . . a *longyi*, a chicken, a cheroot and a helicopter . . .'). I think we got up to a list of over twenty items. The children were undoubtedly smart. I got ambitious and began on grammar, then thought better of it and returned to 'San Says' ('Simon Says'). Imagine talking to a classful of nine-year-olds who have grown up in the jungle and saying 'San says point to Rangoon' or 'San says point to Bangkok' and then seeing the whole class do it right (although admittedly the majority were just following the lead of the brightest). Then saying 'San says stand up, San says touch your nose, San says turn around . . . now sit down' and then the squeals of laughter when half the class sit down, only to realise that San did not say it. I had never really mixed with children except growing up with those my own age. I was scared of children – how on earth does one get on with them? But in these 'lessons' they would not be the only ones nearly wetting themselves with laughter.

I picked up a shoddy strip of metal from the front desk, examined it with little interest and, thinking it was a bit dangerous to be lying in the classroom, I tossed it casually over my shoulder out of the window and into the scrub beyond. The girl at the desk shrieked with horror and looked at me in astonishment. I felt as if I had just killed her pet mouse or something. Much horrified, I discovered it was her 'ruler' and I immediately dashed out and round the back to retrieve it. In Burmese culture teachers are very respected figures. One does not really expect to laugh in the classroom and certainly does not expect to see the teacher doing anything undignified. But they were in fits as I waded into the brambles and brush, desperate to find the rod that I had so nonchalantly cast away. I got it and returned much abashed but with my conscience salved.

I do not know about the children but my favourite game was animal sounds. I would name an animal and they all had to make the sound of it. I was astonished how many we built up: dog, chicken, cow, cat, rat and mouse (yes, you could recognise the difference), toad, gecko, snake, crow, pig (much fun), mosquito, bird, elephant, monkey and best of all, *Jah!* – tiger. Next we went on to boat and car and finally finished with fish. That stumped us all.

Again I doubt the children learnt much English, but there are other things. A strongly-worded resolution by the United Nations, condemning the Burmese junta (as they do every year) means very little to a six-year-old in the jungle. In fact, it means nothing. But having a big white clown blundering around the camp is a sure sign to them that the outside world has not forgotten them. They can see that they are not abandoned, that they have friends from far away who care about them. Not words of sympathy, but the reality of sharing life with them because they are worth it. It is not true that the only thing the average Westerner can do to help Burma is to write to their government or lobby the EU and the UN to press for action. The average Westerner can go out and give the sort of help on the ground which our governments and huge institutions are not suited to giving. I was unqualified, unemployed, not aligned to any organisation or charity, no boss, no director, no resources other than what I had earned myself working in minimum-wage factories. Governments have a job to do, so do citizens.

I had been at Minthamee less than two months and it became undeniable that we would all have to leave. A possibility had turned to a rumour and a rumour had turned into reality. The *Tatmadaw* was closing in. For three weeks this had been clear to my hosts but I had not wanted to believe it. They stopped watering the plantations as they would have to be abandoned anyway. I started attending to a plot. For an hour every morning and an hour every night, slogging up a steep bank with great cans of water. It was good exercise but pointless. Soon all the vegetables were to be pulled up and scoffed, and what could not be carried would be destroyed.

A truck came to take away the heavy kit and the sick. About ten people left on it, making their way to Thailand.

The next morning I sat at a table outside the main office with Phoe Ni, Ye Min Aung and his brother, Soe Min Aung. Soe Min Aung was a gorilla. He always walked about camp in full combat gear, carrying at least two rifles (or else that is just my imagination) and never saying a single word. He was built like an angry tank and seemed to be scouring the area for lurking *Tatmadaw*. One felt very safe beside him. We were chatting, drinking coffee and then heard the thunder. It was too early for the annual rains. I listened in as the thunder rumbled, then looked to the boys. They grinned and gave a few cheers. It was artillery fire, quite close.

'Is that them or us?' I asked.

'It is us! It is the KNU (Karen National Union),' they declared. I am not sure how they knew, but it did not matter. The end was coming.

I began discussing with Ye Min Aung a plan for me to stay behind. In New Zealand I had decided I wanted to meet the *Tatmadaw*, but in such a way that they did not feel it worthwhile killing me. I managed to persuade Ye Min Aung that the idea was workable, but I needed to get permission from above. I went to see the military leader Ko Htay Aung.

He listened. He knew I was genuine. He was touched but not convinced. 'Thank you for your time here,' he said. 'This is our soil, we can die for our soil but you should not die for it.' I had no intention of dying but he knew the Burmese army better than I. He also felt responsible for my safety. There was no point in trying to come up with a workable plan, and none in asking whether I would be brave enough to do it. He had made his decision and I had to accept it. It was a strange evening. My body felt lighter; I would not have to face the danger. My heart felt terrible; I was leaving them to face the danger. My head had the last word; you are their guest, do what you are told.

I said goodbye to a couple of platoons as they headed off to meet the *Tatmadaw*. Half of them did not even have boots, just flip-flops. As Ye Min Aung's need would be greater than mine, I gave him my boots. I wanted camera film and Aung Than agreed to drive me up to Htee Htar on the camp's one motorbike. The ride was as crazy as the driver. He did not stop speaking and laughing, pointing out everything in the world and announcing to me every five minutes that he was "Merican, 'Merican. I am American.' We slewed about on the sandy road, nearly crashing into trees and riding over huge drop-away banks. He found this hilarious and it would have been rude not to be equally amused. We returned a couple of hours later to discover that Ye Min Aung and Kawn Sheim had been called away in the interim. We had not even had a chance to say goodbye.

I went to the river for a wash. Two boys from *Pyo Pan Wai* followed me. I was not in the lightest of spirits. When I started shaving they both picked stones out of the water and mimicking me, drew the stones across their cheeks and chin in synchrony with each stroke of my razor. I gave one of them, Bo Bo, my hat to wear. They seemed unconcerned that their world was being turned upside-down. They followed me back to the hut and I decided to get a photograph of us. Nobody else was around so we would have to use the self-timer. I placed the camera on a post and aimed it at the table we had been sitting at. Bo Bo and Maung Po were well in the frame so I pressed the button, then dashed over to get in shot. I sat in the middle and grinned at the camera, that awkward, goofy, fixed smile of someone waiting for a flash to go off. Meanwhile Bo Bo and Maung Po were looking at me like I was a nutter. They might have grown up in the jungle but they had seen ABSDF visitors use cameras before. They knew for sure you had to hold it to your eye and press the button.

'Argh!' I flapped. I gesticulated madly, pleading with the boys to look at the camera, certain that it was just about to go off and catch me in mid-flap. The boys seemed to consult as the seconds ticked by.

'Look at the camera! Look at the camera! There! Look there!' I shouted desperately. They looked at my pointing finger instead and then, at the very last moment both turned to face the camera. I whipped my arms down and tried to compose myself, the boys were delighted with the madness of it and Maung Po was trying so hard not to laugh he looked like he was about to cry. Bo Bo was happy with the hat (see photographs).

Eventually the boys left and let me pack. It only took a moment but I could not have kept a light heart with them so was glad to be alone. Those from the family village area were gathering their belongings by the roadside. I joined them. So much activity. At 4 p.m. the final word came. We would leave that night. The column assembled. At about 5.30 I took a photograph of Kyaw Htay. He was smiling broadly and behind him were knots of people ready to leave. I took another of him on the same spot one hour later. The column had set off. He was one of those staying behind to fight. He was no longer smiling. Look at his face (see photographs).

It was sunset when we set off. I started at the back of the column, then walked fast to catch up with the front to see if all was well. It was, so I began falling back again to the rear, looking for a way to be more useful. About halfway I met Tin Yu Shwe and Sein Sein Aye, the two female medics. They were struggling to drag along a very very reluctant pig. They had already abandoned its partner back at camp, as he had obviously decided that he was never going to leave. And now the other pig was desperate to go back. It was terrified and making a great deal of noise. We pondered the problem – as little as our shared language would allow – pushed the pig, pulled it, pondered some more and then with much regret, untied the rope and let it run. A few moments later we met a bunch of the armed escort party and as soon as they learnt there was a pig on the loose they charged off into the thickets to hunt it down. Meat was rare.

As the whole evacuation had been so well organised there was nothing I could really do except fall in line. I offered to carry some of the girls' baggage. It was a good excuse to walk with them. Along with four other women and two elderly men they had formed the third English class of each day. The lessons were very basic so I did not really learn much about them. They were also incredibly shy and for the first weeks found it almost impossible to answer questions in class. Whoever had to answer would stand up (it took ages for me to insist they could answer sitting down) and as their classmates all whispered the answer to them, they just wilted and giggled and hid their mouth with the back of their hand. If they then sat down and another stood up, the roles were reversed. So all were smart enough to know the answers, but to speak directly to me was a bit overwhelming.

On the evacuation, though, they lost their shyness; they were efficient, determined and in control. Over the next few days they kept me fed, found places for me to sleep and made sure I knew where we were pausing and when we were going.

A week earlier Kawn Sheim had said Tin Yu Shwe walked like an elephant. I could not believe he could say this of such a flower. 'No, no,' he explained, 'see how an elephant walks. Very gracefully. Very slowly. One foot in front of the other.' He paraded down an imaginary catwalk. 'And never looking to side or side, but to keep the head looking directly. Very beautiful.' Then he burst out laughing.

Alongside the tracks we would see bunches of bodies huddled up in the dark. Sometimes whole banks of faces, children's faces shivering and worried, their bodies hidden by blankets and blackness. These were the thousands upon thousands of Karen who were evacuating too.

At about 11 p.m. we came to a bottleneck. There were a couple of rivers ahead, and though with only a little water running, their banks had been turned to an almost impassable quagmire. Impassable that is for the few trucks that were taking out the heavy equipment and the sick (of the Karen). Thai loggers had made available, at a price I hate to imagine, a couple of earth-moving vehicles. These were dragging the trucks through one by one and having great difficulty with it. There were engines running, revving and grinding, horns going, headlights blinding in the darkness and a great number of worried and raised voices. Infants had to be carried across the muddy banks.

I was halfway across, great drops to left and right, trying to pick my legs over huge and high logs and branches which had been laid over the mud, convinced I was going to fall. The flatulent swamp would not admit flip-flops, so we had to walk barefoot. All this was no problem except that I was carrying a baby. Just then there was a roar from an engine under particular strain and the sound and confusion and lights alarmed the child. He began struggling in my arms, trying to twist around. His eyes flared wide open and there was such a look of fear in them. Until then I had not been worried about what was going on. But seeing the baby like that suddenly made me afraid. There was a massive and brutal force bearing down on vulnerable and defenceless groups. Terrible things were going to happen.

That night we slept in the forest. We ate some cold rice and vegetables, laid blankets on the leafy floor and tried to sleep. Sein Sein Aye and Tin Yu Shwe, the two medics, laid some blankets down and were joined by Aye Aye Mu, also beautiful. They would keep each other warm. Her husband, Hla Shwe, slung a hammock between two trees and built up a fire. I slept as close as I could to the fire, not caring if I cooked myself in the freezing night, thinking about the future for those of Minthamee and, in no small measure, about three women on the other side of the fire ten million miles away.

A couple of days later, when we were close to the Burma–Thai border Aye Aye Mu was speaking to me. She referred to Minthamee camp. News had reached us that the stay-behind party had just burnt it down. Aye Aye Mu looked right into my face. 'I think of our home, Minthamee, and sometimes I tear. Do you tear, Jame?'

I had to walk away before I did.

That night there was a funeral for a Karen boy. He was seventeen. There was a long church service, his mother and sisters weeping. If he had male relatives left, they were out fighting. His body had been washed and laid out under a cloth, and towards the end of the service the cloth was removed. There was a hole in his chest where the bullet had entered, the rough flesh clean and still pink. I thought then, when I saw his face and his long eyelashes and the peacefulness of his expression, that he looked like an angel. I am not searching for a word or cliché. That is how he looked. As the fighting escalated, few others would get such a funeral.

The next day it was time for me to leave. I was reluctant to go but Ko Tint Saw was assigned to take me into Thailand. He spoke good English and fluent Thai. He knew the border and he knew many of the Thai officers. Phoe Ni wanted to come part of the way too, to see me off. Although he had had his reservations when we first met, we were now like brothers. I could not take in the idea that I really was walking away from it all now, leaving them behind to be squashed up against the border until the Thais agreed to let people through. Only women and children would be allowed. Men over fourteen would be turned back, whether they were armed or not. We began climbing to higher and higher ground. After a couple of hours the time came to say goodbye to Phoe Ni. I remembered the freezing nights in the jungle and the sweaty nights in Bangkok – so I gave him my jacket. We shook hands and promised we would meet again.

'I used to hate the British,' he told me, 'now I do not.'

But we did not even get through the KNU checkpoints on our side. The border is not a distinct line. It is a wide strip of hills and jungle, mostly unmarked. Thai soldiers were in the area apparently patrolling for people trying to sneak across. In any case, it was not a good time to go over. Ko Tint Saw and I were turned back. My heart leapt. Hooray. Maybe they would not let me cross at all!

But no, the next day was goodbye for real. Once more I shook Phoe Ni's hand. 'I am sorry', I began, 'that I could not see Ye Min Aung and Kawn Sheim to say goodbye. Please say goodbye for me.'

'Never mind,' replied Phoe Ni. 'We never say goodbye. We say see you again.'

We parted, and I prayed that we would. When Tint Saw and I reached the Thai side a major of the Thai 9th Army looked me up and down. Tint Saw said I was just a teacher. I stood there looking as sweet and unmilitary as I could. The major decided I certainly was no mercenary and went back to his hut for a brew. No mention of passports or bribes.

I saw briefly the site at Huay Nam Rong that was to be the first refugee camp for the women and children who would be able to cross soon after. It was grim. There was a body of water nearby, which already smelt. With thousands of people about to descend on it for washing, cooking and drinking, it would become foul. And the site was far too close to Burma, not safe at all. Burmese forces have crossed into Thailand countless times. They abduct exiles from their homes, they rampage in refugee camps, mortars, machine-gun fire, burning entire camps down, killing women and children. The Thai army does not always protect the refugees.

Tint Saw escorted me to Bangkok. Within the first few kilometres our bus was stopped five times by Thai soldiers looking for illegal Burmese. Somehow they overlooked Tint Saw.

'There are only two good foreigners,' he told me, 'Mr Ted and you.'

'Who is Mr Ted?' I asked.

'British. He give us training. Soldier. Very funny. Very kind. Mr Ted very good.' Later I got Ted's address. I would certainly want to meet him.

I spent a couple of soulless days in Bangkok, then hitch-hiked to Singapore to get my flight, many months early, back to the UK. The Thais, Malaysians and Singaporeans I met on the way were outstandingly kind. So many offers (and insistences!) of food and places to stay. I remember thinking too, as a father of eight drove me south and addicted me to banana fritters, that nobody can ever think they know the meaning of 'green' until they have seen the forests of north Malaysia. Their kindness helped ease my pain – the feeling I had abandoned my friends to an unknown fate.

I made two resolutions which drove me for the following four years. First, as the regime had destroyed *Pyo Pan Wai*, our primary school, I would make sure it was rebuilt. And to compensate for the months and years it would take to rebuild, I wanted it bigger and better funded, and in a safer place. The second promise I made myself was that I would make known the story of Minthamee and of those who lived there. The regime is trying to rewrite history. It is important that the truth be told.

CHAPTER 5

All nature is but art, unknown to thee;
All chance, direction which thou canst not see;
All discord, harmony not understood;
All partial evil, universal good. Alexander Pope

O VER THE NEXT few months I did what I could in the UK, knowing all the time that it was far too feeble. I wrote to MPs and to the Foreign and Commonwealth Office (FCO). When replies eventually came they listed all the marvellous things the government was doing for Burma. But who can be satisfied with that while the problem persists? I gave slide shows at universities. Those who came were obviously affected by what they heard, but the groups were usually small. I wrote for a student newspaper:

> *. . . ABSDF's territory is in their hearts and minds, not on the ground. So although they have temporarily relinquished control over an area of jungle, they will never give an inch of their ideological territory. Their courage and sacrifice is inspiring.*

It was not published. Then I recalled how apathetic I was as a student and felt I had no right to be disappointed. Short letters to national newspapers were not published either.

I tried to visit oil companies investing in Burma. The Americans and French made themselves unavailable. The Japanese just hung up the telephone. Premier Oil of the UK agreed to see me. The generals in Burma have crippled the economy. They are desperate for hard currency to buy their weapons, to buy their ammunition, to keep their senior officers paid. Without foreign investment the regime would collapse. Premier Oil UK is one of their biggest financial backers. So I met a regional director and for forty minutes he spoke very plausibly and smoothly. He was a nice chap. As he walked me back to the lift he told me that Daw Aung San Suu Kyi could not even speak Burmese. Then he was either very ill informed or a liar. Was everything else he had said equally untrue?

The oil in Burma belongs to the people of Burma, and if Premier want to deal in it then they should pay the representatives of the people of Burma – the National League for Democracy. But to pay instead a group of armed thugs who use the money to oppress the country is wicked. From the legal perspective it is dealing in stolen goods. From the economic perspective it is idiocy. Foreign trade will thrive as freedom thrives. We could do great business with a democratic Burma. Perhaps by funding the dictatorship now we will make ourselves unwelcome in the future when democracy does come.

I was doing everything I could and getting absolutely nowhere. Meanwhile I was working as a temp in London, saving up money to return to Asia. London was fun, but 'fun' was no longer satisfying. On 22 May I received the following news in a letter from Ko Chit:

> . . . Now, 24 students are arrested in Ratchaburi province and they are in jail 23 students will free from jail before end of this month, only Moe Zaw Aung, he was arrested by the police with a bomb [shell]. Therefore, he will be in jail for 4 years.
>
> We have many problems on the border after fall of Minthamee camp but we will never give up our aims and objectives.
>
> Thank you very much for your volunteer cooperation for the revolution.
>
> Sincerely Yours,
> Ko Chit

That meant twenty-four of my comrades from Minthamee had eventually been able to sneak over the border into Thailand. They had been arrested and slung into a Thai gaol, and the regiment medic, Moe Zaw Aung, faced four years in prison. His wife and daughter now had a very tough time alone.

I met with Burmese exiles in the UK. We spent some good time together. And I contacted 'Ted', the English chap Tint Saw had told me about, legendary friend of the ABSDF. He was making a fortune in the city and seemed to send most of it to his Burmese friends. It was hard for me to believe that what had happened in Burma was real, but talking to Ted I knew that it was. It meant the world to me to be able to share our experiences.

Trying to fit in with the British way of life was not always easy. My twin brother was now an officer in the Royal Artillery. I joined him and some of his colleagues at a pub in Guildford. It was a balmy evening after a beautiful hot day and the atmosphere was very relaxed. We homed in on a group of girls and started chatting. The girls asked what we all did and, not in the habit of mentioning the army (for security reasons) and under the influence of many drinks, the officers said they were 'combustion engineers'. They said they 'looked after the pipes under the pitch at Wembley to make sure it did not freeze'. The girls must have been drinking too as they found this suitably impressive, especially when offered tickets to the forthcoming Michael Jackson concert at Wembley. I had kept silent about myself because the truth of it sounds too strange. But seeing the army boys get away with their prize piece of nonsense, I thought I could risk the truth. I was standing to one side with two of the girls. I told them that I had just got back from Burma where I had lived in the jungle with rebels and exiles teaching them English. The two looked at me, incredulous, snorted in contempt and then, 'C'mon Sally, let's go and talk with them nice combustion engineers.' It took me some time to find this funny.

I was not exactly satisfied with life. Campaigning from abroad for democracy in Burma is helpful. It achieves a great deal of good. But there are plenty of people doing it. What I really wanted was to take up the fight where extra people were most needed – in Burma itself.

I spoke with my family about returning. I could not give much detail as I did not know exactly what would happen. But I related the facts of the dire political situation and said I wanted to do something about it. I assured them that whatever I did I would be very careful. Mum and Dad accepted it; after all, none of us was a stranger to travelling in dangerous parts. They had been all round the world while in the army and Jeremy was doing the same now. Jonathan was living in Australia and Emma was spending months at a time in remote regions of India to complete her Ph.D.

By the beginning of August I was back in Thailand and fairly devastated by what I found there. The community I had known at Minthamee had been ripped apart. Some were living illegally in Bangkok or further north. Many were in refugee camps. Some were in Thai gaols and detention centres. Two families were missing. A few of the men remained in Burma fighting alongside their Karen allies. Eight were dead.

In Bangkok I met up with Cho Too. He and his wife lived in a 10 × 8-foot room with their infant daughter. Next door lived Myo Win with his wife and child Yo-Yo. Another student, Aung Myo Min, was visiting. He had left Burma after the uprisings and graduated in America. He then returned to Thailand to work as a journalist and support his friends. Out of his salary he paid for the rent for several families. Despite the poverty, the hospitality was never lacking. As there was not enough space for us all to sit together in an apartment we went up on to the roof. Yo-Yo was not quite two but she caused plenty of trouble. She broke a glass on the mat I was supposed to sleep on and shortly afterwards wilfully (?) kicked over a bowl of chilli sauce. We laughed about this and cleaned it up but she was not finished. Eyes dancing and knees trembling, she steadied herself against her father's legs, then urinated all over the mat. What fun! As they were there illegally it was dangerous to go out, even for a shopping trip. Cho Too spoke a little Thai so he usually made the excursions. The other families spent nearly all their hours in the room.

Aung Myo Min looked at Yo-Yo. 'She is lonely,' he said quietly, 'she has no companions. She needs a playmate.'

Aung Myo Min had won several human rights awards for his work and deserved them. He was dedicated, selfless, cheerfully generous and a great 'bridge' between the cultures of East and West.

Others were working illegally. The available jobs were classed as the 'three Ds – dirty, difficult and dangerous'. Thai employers like Burmese immigrants because they work hard and can be employed cheaply. Phoe Ni, my brother, was working with two comrades at a rubber factory. They were paid 3000 Baht per month (about £60) with food and accommodation provided. Local Thais earned several times that amount for the same work.

I went to visit. The area was a slum, one of Bangkok's poorest. Thailand has been called the 'Land of Smiles' and for the first time I saw this to be true. Local people were a little shy but if I smiled it would be returned in great measure. Among all this, the three students lived in one room, 12 × 8 feet, which had been turned into a shrine to Burmese democracy – pictures of Daw Aung San Suu Kyi and democratic flags adorned all the walls. I was worried that the employers might be cruel, taking advantage of the immigrants' vulnerability. But this was not the case. Their Thai colleagues were friendly and the owner of the factory, a Taiwanese man, was kind too. I went to meet him and sat in the reception with Phoe Ni. The atmosphere was uncomfortable. I was offered coffee or tea but the secretaries were distinctly uneasy.

At last one could stand it no longer. 'Are you the boys' immigration officer?' she asked with concern.

'No, no, no way, a friend, just a friend!' I answered. We could all relax after that. The joys of language barriers.

Other students lived in Maneeloi, or the 'Safe Area'. This was a camp, deep inside Thailand, where thousands of refugees lived while trying to be accepted for residence in a third country. First they had to be recognised by the UNHCR as having refugee status. That process is full of bureaucratic obstacles. In truth, people sneaked in and out of the camp regardless. It was rife with drugs – hash, heroin, amphetamines. A hell with drugs, a hell without them.

I was reunited with Ye Min Aung there, the man who had looked after me so well when I had stayed at Minthamee. If he were arrested by the Thais and repatriated to Burma he would be executed as a deserter. Still he was smiling. I asked him what had happened after Minthamee. He had been one of those who burnt down the camp and he spent the next few weeks on the run in the jungle. He had to carry 15 kilograms of rice, 200 rounds of ammunition and a GPMG. This with barely any water to drink or food to eat and for weeks. He told me his urine was red and he thought he was about to die. That was when he snuck into Thailand and made his way to Maneeloi. In Maneeloi there were a young Englishman and a German teaching English. Ye Min Aung was as keen as ever to learn. And wonderful thing, there was meat on the menu every day – 'chicken curry, as much as you like, yesterday I had eight plateful!'

Most of the students hoped to be accepted for residence in Australia, Canada or the USA. Europe also was becoming more accessible but the process took years. Once over there they could study, further their education and dream of returning to a democratic Burma. Ye Min Aung gave me a letter from Kyaw Kyaw Soe. The beginning is worth sharing – I blame his English teacher for the grammar:

James
I really remember to write a letter for you. I think, you will currently be fat and handsome . . .

How very uninhibited! Then he told me about those who had died. An extract from my diary.

. . . battalion commander Chit Ko Ko is dead. Killed with four others in the Mergui area, their boat unable to spot SLORC's [the regime's] through the darkness and mist. And 'Apollo 2' (!) (Pollo) is dead. Shot on the banks of Minthamee/Tenasserim river as he stuck his head forward to see the enemy. Shot dead. And the CSM, big drinker, shot

while boating up the same river. Ye Min Aung heard his boat while at
the top of a hill with five of his soldiers (whom he misses terribly) but
was too late in rushing down to warn the man who slept in the next bunk
in the barracks – he took the boat too far and I suppose was a helpless
target.

Eight men were dead. When it was time to leave I got on the back
of a scooter and tore off. It was not just the wind in my face that
made my eyes stream.

Kawn Sheim and two others had just been sprung from gaol
with a 10,000 Baht bribe. Ten other ABSDF had been released
by the police and rearrested on the same day by the army and
thrown back into prison for more months. I went to see them in
Ratchaburi gaol, taken there by Phone Kyaw, a student who
knew his way around Thailand and spoke the language fluently
(as well as English). Phone Kyaw's father was an elected MP
(NLD), now in prison. His younger brother was in prison for
handing out leaflets. And he himself had faced death a hundred
times in the jungle. Yet he was so casual, so humble. He did not
consider that he had a special story to tell . . . or was it that he did
not believe anyone would listen? He looked after me with great
kindness.

We arrived at Ratchaburi gaol and Phone Kyaw had a few
words with the police. They searched our bags, then waved us
forward to meet our comrades. The detention block was
desperate, dark and confused within the cell, difficult to see
inside, but I estimated there were about eighty men in the very
crowded conditions. The place reeked of urine and sweat, and
despite two ceiling fans it was stifling. There was water available
from a tap but not enough to keep everyone clean.

Our comrades came forward eagerly. It was so dark and filthy
that I could only recognise four out of the ten, and I felt ashamed
for it. They stood behind a dirty, waist-high wall with vertical bars
emerging from the top and reaching the roof. We stood two feet
away behind a waist-high metal fence and between us all was a
metal grille (two-inch square) with an awkward gap in it which we
could reach through to shake hands or pass food. All of us were

leaning forward, pressed against the walls or clinging to the bars. Kyaw Htay squatted on the wall, looking thin and troubled, but his eyes still shone. At least he was alive. Most of them were smiling but that is what they do anywhere. They also said it was terrible.

How sad it was trying to have a conversation, trying to learn about their conditions. They were allowed pens and paper but not books. For food they received two average-sized bowls of rice a day with a couple of ladles of curry. The police let us pass in six bottles of clean water and ten packets of cooked rice with a little meat and vegetables.

When the majority of prisoners are Thai there is violent extortion within the cell. 'Fortunately', at this time, most of the prisoners were Burmese (including Mon and Karen etc.), which meant they could defend themselves from assault. Originally there were eleven ABSDF here but one of their number was taken to hospital. I saw a picture of him later. He was an old, old man and his ankle was chained to the bed. But the sheets were perfectly clean and at least he was in hospital. For those who came to prison alone, for those with no outside help, sickness was fatal. Our friends told us that a few days earlier a Burman man had died in the cell from starvation/malaria. The authorities did not care to provide extra food/medicine/assistance and there was precious little the prisoners could do. He had been a porter for the Burmese regime and had escaped to the Thai border where he was arrested and lasted about six days in gaol. From hell to hell. Tragic.

The lads had been in this prison for two months and expected to be sent the next week to Kanchanaburi IDC (a detention centre with much better conditions). Their short gaol term was possibly a reprisal by the Thai 9th Army for ABSDF's writing articles criticising their methods.

That night, back in Bangkok, Ko Chit said to me, 'SLORC is our enemy, Thai authorities are our enemy and even the Karen National Union can appear to be our enemy.' Why is it, then, that when you follow a courageous, honourable path everyone seems to be your enemy? God knows . . . better than any of us.

To meet others, I had been praying to be able to visit Htam Hin refugee camp. It was well inside Thailand, safe from border attacks, and most of Minthamee were there. I managed to get a lift from an NGO worker called Harry. Arriving in the camp was, according to my diary the:

. . . moment of a lifetime – Win Naing and his falling jaw when he recognised me in Harry's utility yesterday. A face of ripping astonishment as he scrambled towards Ko Min Aung's shelter to hurl 'Mista J! Mista J!' by which time I was out of the vehicle and shaking hands & forearms like a madman. I was completely gobsmacked, uttering half grunts and 'Mingalabas' with a grin from east to west as well as a surreal breathlessness. Sein Sein Aye and Tin Yu Shwe came hurtling round a corner and semi-buckled as they shrieked with surprise. Otherwise most were calm as calm but with big grins. Ko Min Aung looks heaps younger (& not so severe) with longer hair and other than U Aung Myint's burst blood vessels in his left eye, everyone looked bloody healthy. Kyi Wai, Ko Ko Oo, Min Zaw Shwe . . .

The mark II Pyo Pan Wai opened that day (previously the Thais had forbidden it) so I gave four quick 'lessons' in each class. The younger classes laughed most. The older ones were more surprised. One dear lass ran to her mum and asked/told her to cook me up some coconut rice. Then she came and guided Ko Min Aung and me to their shelter where we sat and ate. Touching indeed . . .

There were countless moments of 'what the hell do I say?' with virtually everyone, especially me! Got a constant stream of letters to take back to Bangkok. Inside the camp there is virtually no contact with the world outside so it was a fiercely taken opportunity. At least information can come in (on foreign radio stations DVB, VOA, RFA and BBC) . . . We managed to pick up the old threads but it was a sad time too. Win Naing joked feebly that they still 'do much for our revolution' and there were rueful laughs from those about. Kyi Wai particularly. And what can they do when so isolated and repressed? . . .

Physically everyone seemed fine. There was sufficient food, water, medicine and shelter but only five basic foodstuffs so they are missing out on certain vitamins and micronutrients. This is damaging in the long term. Diplomatic and bureaucratic considerations outweigh humani-

tarian ones. Htam Hin is classed as a 'temporary camp for displaced persons'. Specifically they cannot be called refugees. This means they supposedly only need temporary shelter and thus the roofs are inadequate – blue plastic sheets which don't give good protection from the sun. It is intensely overcrowded with 7500 people. Most activities are banned. There is virtually no education or trading or cultural celebration or growing vegetables or foraging or excursions from the camp. Psychologically it is a terrible predicament – no need to record why. Children bear the brunt of the frustration and short tempers of adults . . .

Worst is Harry told me three weeks back some Karen National Union leaders met with SLORC representatives at Three Pagoda Pass. SLORC said that they cannot accept the refugee situation and all must return to Burmese soil but because of the disgrace that they have brought upon their country they must all be punished. God that sounds so evil. I am sure it means gaol, forced labour, execution etc. Another SLORC officer said, 'In ten years all Karen will be dead . . . you will have to visit a museum in Rangoon to see one' . . .

Every student who lived in the jungle had had malaria. Nearly all the males had scars from fighting. Three of those with the worst injuries were staying at the Student Relief Committee office in Bangkok.

When I arrived . . . and met Ko Moe Kyaw I was so pleased to see him I immediately stuck my arm out for a handshake entirely not remembering his lack of hands. He held out a stump and I shook that anyway.

Everybody laughed. Ko Moe Kyaw had had both forearms blown off and lost his vision completely in one eye and badly in the other when he tried to remove a landmine. In disdain for his injury he could still light a cigarette, use a spoon and I even found him typing a brief autobiography on a computer, using the bits of bone projecting from his stumps to type with. He is one of the most cheerful people I have ever met.

Another student there was Tin Soe, who had been in charge of the generator at Minthamee. He was dark-skinned, with luxuriant hair, and muscles hanging off his body like ripe fruits.

Diary:

> *Remember Tin Soe who lost three bits of his brain to a SLORC shell,*
> *it was only two days ago that I noticed it has disabled him. His right*
> *arm is limp (almost useless?) and his right leg is lame. I did not see this*
> *in Minthamee or for four days here. He had part of his skull blown out*
> *back in 89/90 (he let me feel it). Long shell from SLORC near Tavoy,*
> *other privates died. He was carried unconscious by Phoe Ni etc. as*
> *SLORC gave chase. They got him in a boat and headed to Minthamee.*
> *Boat sank! He survived somehow! Three bits of his brain left on the*
> *jungle floor but he's certainly smart enough now. Looks very strong. He*
> *is 'expert electrician' (Ye Min Aung quote), often taking shocks from*
> *generator while tinkering but 'that's OK 'cos he had rubber slippers on!'*

Another note from my diary:

> *Yesterday I talked to Yan Kyaw Aung. He was here in SRC having his*
> *dressings changed (three weeping 'growing boils') as I sat round the*
> *corner reading. When I heard his muffled screams (they hurt!) I recalled*
> *where I'd seen him before. Jan 2nd, Htee Khee, ABSDF HQ [my first*
> *day in Burma].*
>
>   *His legs are wasted and one arm almost immobile. He drags himself*
> *across the floor, constantly rearranges his legs with his good arm, he rests*
> *his ankle on a rag as he drags his leaden legs about to stop friction*
> *problems, but when he sits he sometimes rests his hip/thigh on it to ease*
> *the pain of the boils. He has terrible scars above each ear where none of*
> *his 4-inch hair grows. I read his brief biography and was so moved. He*
> *is not a cripple. He was a healthy young man, member of the ABSDF*
> *for 3 years. Then while (I think) in the Mergui Archipelago he was shot*
> *in the head. He recovered and fought on. Then on 7.3.93 he was shot*
> *again in the other temple. He spent 1 month unconscious. He is now in*
> *this way. He stays upstairs, half-hidden by a cupboard. He wants to*
> *walk but cannot. (I'm crying now.)*

This is what had become of Minthamee. Why was it happening?
I could not believe that there was a cartel of evil generals sitting
in Rangoon plotting how to make the lives of their people so

wretched. It is not that the regime planned all this; it was just that they did not care. All they cared about was power, about maintaining an absolute grip of control over Burma, and they would do anything to try to destroy whoever challenged them. Their justification for causing such horrific suffering was always that they were holding the Union of Burma together and they seemed to think that a price worth paying for that was the brutal suppression of millions of people who wanted a degree of autonomy and freedom of expression. I wanted to go to Rangoon to protest against this.

Whenever I stayed in Thailand, I would try to read as much as I could about Burma. There is a profusion of human rights reports documenting the injustices. The following information came from army deserters. There is no question of its veracity.

Child soldiers who die under SLORC's abominable movements are often not declared dead for months so that their senior officers (who could well be directly responsible for the death) can draw their pay! At Manerplaw SLORC used 100s/1000s of children in human wave tactics, drugged up on amphetamine/rum solutions. Frequently, injured SLORC soldiers are shot by their own officer rather than be looked after. SLORC sergeants tell the parents of dead soldiers that the soldier deserted, then the sergeant pockets the dead man's pension!

Reports like this made me even more determined to meet the junta. I had an idea of what I would do, but I needed to run it past the ABSDF leadership. It would be unthinkable to make any kind of protest in Burma without the approval of the Burmese themselves.

CHAPTER 6

If you can dream – and not make dreams your master;
If you can think – and not make thoughts your aim;
If you can meet with Triumph and Disaster
And treat those two impostors just the same . . .   Rudyard Kipling

RIENDS IN BANGKOK arranged for me to meet members of
ABSDF's CEC (Central Executive Committee) in northern
Thailand. There was a camp deep in the Thai jungle, on
the banks of the Salween river, the border with Burma. The
journey there was a long one. A group of about a dozen ABSDF
were making the trip and I joined them. It was the wet season, so
vehicles could only go so far. We went by truck to the village of
Huay Noi and after that we went on foot. The truck had great
difficulty. The road was a sea of mud and clay, with ruts in it
sometimes three feet deep. Every few minutes the dozen of us
would have to get down and dig the truck out of the mud and
push-start it. Just at the end of the journey the rain came down. I
have never known rain like it. Glorious! Magnificently torrential.
Two kilometres on foot. Scrambling up mud slopes and sliding
down the other side. Moving down to paddy fields and hurrying
along irrigation channels, all gushing so strongly. The thick warm
rain washed the colour out of everything: pale bamboo, slick
brown mud, but everything else was grey. No, that is not true.
Nothing could dim the gorgeous bright green of tender young
paddy. Exhilarating, though, to be so wet!

At Huay Noi I met Paul from Utah. He was a father of seven and had travelled to the border to instruct students on pre-hospital medical treatment (i.e. emergency first aid). He had come off his own bat, funded himself, donated medical supplies to the camps and was now on his way home. He had huge respect for the students. He warned me, though, that the way ahead was difficult. The rivers were swelling in the rain and almost impassable. They could grow terrifically in a matter of hours. We would have to leave early to be sure of reaching our destination before dark.

The following day I set off with a group of four men, three women and two babies. The women had just attended a meeting of the Burma Women's Union and were now returning home. Two of the men were travelling between various border camps to gather and deliver information; there were no postboxes or telephone wires here. We were all heading to the same camp. I recorded the journey in my diary.

After the first river crossing I took on a bit of an extra load as I still had room in my bag and the old chap carrying this box had a bursting longyi full of other kit. So on we went. Some river crossings were easy enough – others impossible. I would cross with one (pace-setting) chap, we'd dump our bags then return to carry the ladies' bags and give them a helping hand. After 1½ hrs we came to a very difficult crossing. In the dry season a 4WD can make the journey. In this, the wet, I doubt a tank could!

Once all the men had crossed we cut down some long bamboo to try and span the river but the current was too strong and the scheme failed (50ft bank to bank). The three women & two babies seemed to decide to go back to the last crossing, cross over there, and then make their way through the jungle to meet with us. It was not a workable plan and could have taken hours (see later). Instead the older chap urged me to go back and help the strongest of the three across. So I did this and as we made it safely he urged me to return for a baby. I was very very reluctant. This was more responsibility than I'd ever faced in my life. To cross this torrent with an infant as the mother watched on . . . but clearly we had almost no options so I had to give it a go.

The child cried like hell until we reached the other side and though I was nearly up to my neck at times he only got a wet arse. I felt truly happy and obviously had to return for the others. By now I'd crossed at this one point 9 times so when I went back for the 10th I got washed quite far downstream. I was beginning to lose it. Got the young baby across who had the insolent cheek to sleep through the whole thing! And then I returned for the last two mothers. Got washed heaps downstream and crucified against a semi-submerged bush. Took much heaving and rolling to struggle to the steep bank where I hauled myself back upstream with vines & roots & brambles. Altogether we did about a dozen river crossings and at this particular one I made 15 trips. By the last 4 or 5 I was staggering like a drunk once I reached the bank and struggling so much against the current. After that we took a ten-minute time out and had a single star fruit. Much needed.

The next crossing was impossible – it would have been a frantic swim, impossible with babies. So we climbed up the damned steep hill and for 50 minutes forced our way through the jungle with many a minor slip & scratch. Had we been able to cross to the track it would have taken less than 10 minutes. I began to admire Paul. Then we waded the river bank for 20 mins until we rejoined the track. A few more river crossings later (recall moment of mirth when I produced pair of dripping lady's sandals from my pockets after a very wet crossing) and they told me we were 10 mins from HQ.

We passed through a Thai/Karen plantation and I felt like asking for a drink. Some confusion to find the path, five minutes had passed. Then up up and up another terribly steep hill. I swore for the first time. This was too much. We reached the top and it was 4 p.m. (i.e. those 10 mins were up). Never mind it's downhill now but I'm beginning to crack up. At the bottom I am faced with one more uphill. I want to throw my bag down and give up. Throughout the 4½ hrs I have been the second in the column (i.e. following leader). I have not slowed anyone down (hey, there were women present). But now I'm nearly through . . . somehow I say to myself 'one more push' aware of God's help. I hadn't taken three paces but I heard the beating of bamboo and murmured voices. Another three paces and a surprised voice called out to the guy 20ft in front of me. We are there. We've reached HQ! Brilliant.

I sit queasily at a hut and confusedly take care of details of

71

unpacking. I'm worried but I don't know what about. I ask for water and drink two big cups. I visit with MT to UTS and I apologise as I ask for more water. It is boiling. Too hot to gulp. Probably safer like that as I pour it from cup to cup to help it cool then slowly sip. Just before I met UTS I went to the central well and met MMG. We chat briefly and then I apologise again. I must sit down. I must drink. I must sit down. I cannot see properly. Everything obscured by dark patches and lightening patches and they are all swimming in my eyes. I am having heat exhaustion. Just before I went to this well, after my two greedy cups, I stood up and steadied myself on the bamboo house post. Then I took maybe only five steps before I had to sit down on the muddy floor to get my balance. I think I am going to faint. I am shaking a little . . .

So, after much to drink, a wash in the river, a few cheroots, a bowl of rice, more to drink I am feeling good . . .

After that nightmare trek the other students seemed fine, suffering none of my knackardness. They're tough for sure. I'm lucky to have had such an early chance to gain a bit of trust.

Apologies if I cast myself as Burt Lancaster and recorded all that in rather too much detail. But it was about the first time in my life I felt I had been able to make a difference. Working hard at school keeps parents and teachers happy. Working hard in a factory keeps your workmates and boss happy and hopefully serves society. A lot of people can do that. But carrying a baby over a river so that he does not have to spend a night rough in the jungle with his mother, well that seemed to me to be the most worthwhile thing I had ever done. It was not that many people could not do that either, it was just that they *weren't* doing it.

On 31 August I met with two senior members of the ABSDF and outlined my plan to them: I wanted to go to Rangoon and make a simple demonstration in support of democracy. When arrested I could get a close look at the junta. They told me it was too dangerous. They told me it was not necessary for me to take such a risk. I insisted that I would accept all the consequences.

'What if you are shot?' asked Aung Thu Nyein.

'They won't shoot me. No soldier will shoot a white guy in Rangoon unless his officer orders it. And no officer will order it until he has received the order from his superior. In fact, the decision will have to go all the way to the top and then all the way back down. That takes days in Burma! But if we can arrange it so that word gets out as soon as I am arrested then the world press will know all about it and the junta will not be able to make me "disappear".'

Aung Thu Nyein nodded. He knew better than me how slow the regime was to make a decision, and how terrified they all were of taking initiative or responsibility. They had gunned down thousands of Burmese people in Rangoon but this was a different set of circumstances. 'What do you think will happen to you?' he asked me.

'I don't know. I want them to keep me for a little while so that I can see what they are like. I want to meet other prisoners. I think, no more than two weeks inside.'

Aung Thu Nyein agreed it could work. He told me to go to Chiang Rai in northern Thailand to meet Moe Thee Zun, ABSDF's vice-chairman. At last I felt a great weight off my shoulders. I had spent a month in Thailand trying to meet the right person and to convince them there was a workable plan. At times it had been very frustrating. Finally it looked as though it could go ahead.

That night I stayed with Myint Aung and his wife. 'He likes VOA. I like BBC,' Myint Aung's wife told me. 'Sometimes we argue, me and him.' She finished with a laugh, and once again it was clear how invaluable these foreign radio stations are for Burmese who want information of the outside world and of their own country. The military regime does not broadcast any news worth hearing.

My two hosts cooked up wonderful food out of nowhere and, with a few others gathered, insisted we drink some jungle juice, a rare treat out there. They absolutely would not let me pay for it. 'In Burma', explained Myint Aung, 'there is forced labour, forced relocation. Here in our camp, for you, it is forced drinking alcohol!'

A few days later I was sitting on a balcony in a northern Thai town finalising the plan. I had never been in Burma proper (central Burma, territory controlled by the regime rather than the border areas controlled by the ethnic groups) so was relying heavily on others for advice. Fortunately I met up with just the right people: an Australian woman, a Canadian, and Moe Thee Zun, all fully informed on Burma. Once we were agreed that this was not blind folly, but a safe and sensible project, the atmosphere was wonderful. No faffing around. The two Westerners had been to Rangoon recently so could keep us up to date. Ko Moe Thee had a feel for what would go down well with the locals and taught me some more Burmese history. Originally I wanted somehow to target the 'People's Desire', a disgusting tract of state propaganda, which reads as follows:

1   *Oppose those relying on external elements, acting as stooges, holding negative views.*
2   *Oppose those trying to jeopardise stability of the State and progress of the nation.*
3   *Oppose foreign nations interfering in internal affairs of the State.*
4   *Crush all internal and external destructive elements as the common enemy.*

It appears in the state newspapers every day, it appears in the flyleaves of religious books and architectural books. It is read out several times each day on state radio and television. It is ubiquitous. It is even painted in large white letters on huge, bright-red billboards dotted around cities and towns. You might have thought that the junta would be a little shy of exhibiting this bile to foreigners, but quite inexplicably it makes all these appearances in English as well as Burmese. The regime are trying to ram the 'People's Desire' down the people's throats. They will not accept that the people can articulate their own desire, and that they did precisely that in the 1990 election.

However, my fellow conspirators recommended another target. We agreed on the following: 16 September, midday, I would chain myself to the gate of St Paul's High School No. 6 in Botataung, Rangoon. There I would distribute a letter I had written (which Ko Moe Thee would first get translated into

Burmese). I should phone through on the 15th to confirm that all was in order. We devised a simple 'code situation' so that if changes had to be made they could be done innocuously over the phone. The Military Intelligence would certainly be monitoring international calls. In fact, the whole thing would be a strain to carry out because the MI monitor every move which foreigners make.

My colleagues agreed to organise the media side. Ko Moe Thee said he would make sure the whole thing was seen by people on the spot and as soon as I was arrested they would contact him in Thailand. He would then release prepared statements. I did not want to know anybody in Burma, I did not want to know who would be watching me. There is no point in knowing too much and the very last thing I ever wanted to do was put a local in danger. My white skin and dual nationality would afford me a protection that Burmese people do not have. Once the media responded, the British and Australian governments would respond. This was the most important aspect of our preparation. I was convinced that the junta would not resort to brutality once they realised the world was watching.

Originally I had wanted to spend about a month in Burma to see as much of this beautiful country as I could. My imagination yearned especially for Pagan, the ancient capital near Mandalay. Around Pagan were thousands and thousands of ruined pagodas, some dating back a thousand years. This idea was scrapped. My friends wanted me to demonstrate before 18 September, which was the ninth anniversary of the regime's blanket military crackdown (which followed the chaos and massacres of the preceding months). This would give me only a week in Rangoon to sound things out and get a feel for the atmosphere. I knew I was in for a hard time there, but the only sacrifice I felt I was making was the chance to travel more widely around a country I loved. Once I demonstrated, I would be blacklisted. After that, I would not be able to travel around Burma as a tourist again.

I wrote letters to my family explaining that I was going to Rangoon and that something unusual was going to happen. I indicated dates and told them it would look bad at first but they should not worry about what the press said. I asked them to trust me that nothing would get out of hand and I would see them all again soon. I did not want news of my arrest to come at them out of the blue.

Before leaving Thailand I watched a video of events in 1988. Burma's dictator since 1962 had just stepped down. His first successor was detested throughout Burma and lasted no time at all. The next one was Dr Maung Maung. As he walked past a video camera a journalist shouted out, 'Will there be amnesty for political prisoners?' Dr Maung Maung walked off laughing nervously. 'Not my business, not my business,' he said. If not the president's, whose was it? I had never in my life seen a face like his. It was one of irretrievable stupidity. He was panicking, full of fear. Shortly afterwards he had a nervous breakdown and was replaced. And journalists are no longer allowed in Burma.

CHAPTER 7

*Those who say that religion has nothing to do with politics do not know
what religion means.*   Mahatma Gandhi

A S THE AEROPLANE approached Rangoon my face was
glued to the window. I was trying to take it all in, the
paddy fields, the huts, the trees, and then a flash of gold
caught my eye. Standing in a sea of green was a tiny golden
needle. It was far far away but unmistakable. It seemed not just to
be reflecting sunlight but actually producing it. My whole chest
suddenly churned in exhilaration. It was surely the Shwedagon
Pagoda, one of the world's wonders, a hundred metres tall, many
hundreds of years old and a famous symbol of Burma. You are
here now. Magic land. Ancient land. Another world.

Why did I feel this resonance with Burma? Surely I should have
been nervous, scared? One Burmese man gave me his
explanation. 'James,' he said, 'I think you were Burmese in a
previous life.'

But by the time we had touched down and I arrived at
Customs, I was more than nervous. In my bag was a bunch of
over 200 letters asking for the release of political prisoners and
expressing solidarity with the people of Burma in their suffering.
There was also an ABSDF T-shirt with the symbol of the freedom
movement – a yellow fighting peacock on a red flag. Worst of all,
I had a great dirty chain and three padlocks. The chain was three
feet long and very thick. How on earth would I explain that if it

77

came up on the scanner? Say I was a keen cyclist with a mania for security?

But I got through without incident. Oh, Rangoon! How much I wanted to do there. How much I wanted to greet every man, woman and child, and tell them that the outside world knew what they were going through. I could not. I spent eight days sorrowfully exploring the glorious city. Every moment I felt as though I was betraying them by keeping my mouth shut, by being a tourist come to goon at their culture and yet be blind to their suffering. And every moment I felt I was going to be swooped upon by policemen demanding to search my bag. My great fear throughout was only that I would be kicked out of the country before I had the chance to protest. What a disaster that would be.

The three-, four-, five-storey stone buildings were a mosaic of decay: crumbling walls stained by pollution, streaked with rust, pocked with rot and bandaged by moss. The uneven pavements were as crowded as a busy market. Pedestrians struggled to squeeze through as shop owners spilt their wares into the way from one side, and hawkers with their stalls and cases pitched their goods from the kerbside. Vegetables were piled up and unknown foods fried there on stoves beside them. The minor roads were narrow and muddy, full of obstacles to avoid. The main roads, multi-lane highways tearing through town, were smoothly tarmacked and hoards of pedestrians played space invaders with the oncoming traffic. There were no rules. Cars were fitted with horns so that steering wheels would be unnecessary. Why steer a path when you can just use your horn to blast everything out of your way?

I checked into a downtown guest house and had a few tasks to complete. I needed to buy two cans of spray paint but without any awkward questions. I needed to reconnoitre the chosen site to make sure it was suitable. And I had to get rid of my passport, visa card and anything else that would identify me. I was worried that as soon as the junta got me they would put me on a plane back to Thailand. I hoped that if they did not know who I was, and I had no passport, it would delay the deportation.

I hoped to bump into a tourist to whom I could give my ID,

then I would be able to collect it later from an agreed address in Thailand. Despite the fact that it was 'Visit Myanmar Year 97' (the junta's attempt at attracting foreign currency) there was hardly another foreigner to be found. In the main this is good. It is sinful for sightseeing tourists to breeze around Burma pouring dollars into the generals' coffers. On the other hand it is vital that people who know about Burma and those who would learn more, those who are sensitive to the suffering, they should definitely come. If they spend their money wisely the junta need not see any of it; it can go directly to the people: for example, by staying in private guest houses rather than junta-owned ones. More important is to show the locals that we know about them and care. There are ways of doing this without courting any danger (for them or oneself).

One woman I met later in the UK told me how she had found an old man dying by the roadside. She washed him, fed him and took him to a hospital. They said they could do nothing for him. She paid for him to stay there a few days. The hospital staff said after that they would have to turn him out again. It was not that they were heartless, but that everything is under the control of the regime. Thank God that woman visited Burma. Quite apart from what it meant to the old man, her actions demonstrated a broader concern. Democracy can never take root in a country by efforts made on the outside. It has to grow from the tradition, understanding and desire of the indigenous population. Otherwise any system imposed from above or without will collapse. And if people are to desire and to work for their freedom, they need their self-respect. The junta aims at destroying this self-respect to make them subservient. Foreigners, like the woman mentioned above, can go to Burma and redress that. Tens of thousands of foreigners can, if only they would. Will they be arrested for feeding the hungry? Or clothing the naked? Or tending to the sick? They may be kicked out but they have nothing to fear. Deportation does not hurt. Being followed by MI does not hurt when you have a home abroad to go to. Why do we demand our governments fix the problem in Burma when there is so much we can do ourselves, as individuals?

But as I scoured Rangoon for such a tourist I had no luck. One Frenchman was working for the junta leading tours. No point explaining anything further to him. There was an Australian businessman who had no love of the regime but I could not ask him either. Finally I found a man in Mr Guitar Café, Mahabandoola Street. He was American, we were getting on well and I was sure I could ask him to take my passport out. As I began on the crux of it, he interrupted me. 'I'm not supposed to meet you,' he said tensely. Oh Lord! He was the eyes.

'. . .' I said.

'I'm a reporter. I'm supposed to film it all. We are not supposed to meet.'

How dreadfully embarrassing. I had not known that my colleagues in Thailand had organised a reporter as well as low-profile observers. It was vital that whoever acted as messenger should not be connected to the demonstration; it would be no good if the messenger was arrested too. We smiled and I assured him I would steer clear of him for the rest of the stay. Rangoon was a big place. We would be fine. I downed my drink and left.

In any case I would not be able to get rid of my passport until the day before the demo. To stay in a guest house in Burma you need your passport to sign in (these lists are sent to the MI daily). Although you only need it on your first day, I was moving around frequently, so I had to hang on to the passport. Once I was arrested and eventually identified, I knew that the police would find out from their lists where I had been staying. I did not want to draw attention to a particular place, as the police are a far too suspicious lot (and they might trouble the guest house owner). Best that I spread myself around, staying in different guest houses and keeping on the move. To that end I think I walked through every single street in downtown Rangoon and beyond. Dilapidated city? Gorgeous city! It was the wet season and everything but the trees seemed drab. Each day, when the rain came down, gutters turned to streams, drains sucked greedily away at the water, became full, baulked, then gave up. At this point certain roads turned into rivers and you did not need an umbrella to get across but a boat. Once the rains had stopped, though, the water subsided quickly.

To recce the spot outside the school where I would demonstrate I thought I would fly past in a trishaw, then walk back past it after an hour or so. If I were in a trishaw it would be difficult for anyone to follow me. A car would be too fast, by foot too slow, by trishaw they would not be able to see my face; I did not want them to see me scrutinising the front of the school. The street, Anawratha Street, was one way. This would make it that tiny bit harder for them to follow me on the walk back, but of course they could do it on foot. I think back on it now and cannot believe my level of paranoia. How ridiculous I was. But on the other hand it paid to be careful about every minute detail. I did not want to land anybody else in trouble. Unfortunately, this did not stop me being inexcusably rude to the locals.

I was in a flap when I got the trishaw for the 'fly-past' and regrettably picked one with a very old man on the saddle. As we set off he was obviously having great difficulty keeping up any momentum, despite us being on the level. I hated to see him straining like that and was even angry with him for picking me up (rather than being angry with myself for getting in). I had flagged the ride two blocks up from the school and asked to go to Sule Pagoda, which is at the end of the same road. There was no way he could avoid going past the school. But just as we approached he wheeled off leftwards and went down a side street. I was fuming. The old goat! I thought he was trying to prolong the journey, despite his creaking knees, so that he could charge me extra. Not so extraordinary but why now of all times? Old goat! You idiot, greedy, sick, sick old man! I was livid, but could not insist he go back or I would draw unwanted attention. The fact that he was nearly dying only made me feel worse. I thought I had to stay in until we got to Sule Pagoda or it would seem strange, but by the time we reached the GPO halfway there he seemed about to breathe his last.

'Stop, stop!' I shouted. I got out full of anger. 'How much do you bloody want?'

I paid him and stormed off. I am disgusted with myself about that. How shameful anger is, how foolish. And as it went, I learnt two days later that trishaws are not allowed on that part of the one-way system; they slow the traffic down. The old man was going the correct route after all. (And the following year in Indonesia I worked out the solution to the dilemma. Over there I asked the drivers to sit in the cab and shout directions while I pedalled the bike myself! Simple, lots of fun and very scary.)

I made a similar error with a taxi driver. The fixed rate was 150 Kyat (less than 40 pence). I had just got out of a cab and gave the driver two 100-Kyat notes. So many times in Asia I had been ripped off by cab drivers. Every traveller knows this. So I did not want to be ripped off. And I was in a bad mood from the trishaw diversion. I held out my hand for change but after a little searching the driver said he did not have a 50-Kyat note. I glared at him, not believing it. Very briefly there was a pained look in his eyes, then he handed me back one of my 100-Kyat notes and drove off. I stood there fairly dumbstruck. Anywhere else he might have been trying it on. But here in Burma there is truly so little greed. I think the junta have a monopoly on greed as well as power. The cab driver was not a rich man. For sure he would be working every hour of every day to struggle to feed his family. And I had quibbled over less than 40 pence.

A couple of other times I made mistakes like this. Later on it made me think about those who adamantly insist they are right yet are utterly blind to their own error. It does not matter that I say I respect Burmese. It does not matter that I think I make every effort to be polite to the locals and never offend their cultural values. It does not matter that I strive to be humble and calm. The fact is that I go around putting my foot in it, causing offence and hurt. What clumsy creatures we are.

When I made my recce past the school I was horrified by the crowds of kids. They were so young: eleven to sixteen. No way did I want to jeopardise their safety. Why had this spot been chosen? It was midday, they were all pouring out for lunch. The same time of day I would demonstrate. Oh brother. I had assumed that the schoolchildren would be safely confined to the school grounds, to the classrooms, not spilling all over the street. A knot of boys strolled past me and one whispered back mockingly: 'Yeah, I know, Visit Myanmar 97.' He was laughing at me for being the idiot tourist, for falling for the regime's propaganda. He was only fourteen. I wanted to chase after him and tell him I was on his side. I wanted to ask him everything he felt about the regime, about democracy, about life. But I had to walk on.

And see the very young children playing soccer in the filthy streets. They are running and shrieking and laughing like kids anywhere in the world. They look so happy. What else will they do? I asked two of them where I could buy a *New Light of Myanmar*, the regime's trash newspaper. They ran off delighted and returned out of breath with that day's copy. They did not want any money for it. I had to insist.

I visited as many teashops as I could. These are centre points of Burmese culture, where everyone who has a minute or a day or a month to spare comes to relax. In a teashop you chat, gossip, argue. Probably there is music – traditional Burmese or old Western pop – and certainly there are gallons of green tea to be drunk, virtually for free. If you have a little money, or it is a special occasion, you might pay more for coffee and perhaps some sweet bread, bagels or cake. In the more modern teashops you sit on bright plastic seats with your knees tucked under simple tables. In the older, outdoor shops, you squat right down on low wooden stools and, being a foreigner, fidget about in discomfort. In such shops I met and chatted with students, old men, families, workers and soldiers. The conversations were almost always innocent. Sometimes you just knew that you were talking with informers, men who were not necessarily paid by the MI, but who would run to them with any interesting information for the sake of the favours and protection which returned. As I left one such table I noticed a ten-year-old boy following me. No doubt the men had told him to report to them where I went next. He was only young and not very adept, not very inconspicuous. Funnily enough, I do not think he would learn how to be either. The MI in Burma see no need for subtlety or discretion. Even the adults are painfully obvious when they follow you. It is not considered undignified. I lost the little boy and was inordinately furious with the world.

That night I went miles out from the town centre to a restaurant on the edge of Rangoon. It was recommended in the travel guide and I did not want to bump into the reporter again. I walked in. It was empty except for one figure hunched over the bar. Surely not . . . but yes it was him again. My American friend. The owner had already clocked me so I could not just walk out, especially as this restaurant was so isolated. It was not as if I would have anywhere else to go. And it would have been strange not to greet the other customer. We introduced ourselves.

'Larry.' Larry sighed.

'James.' James sighed.

We felt a touch foolish, but what the heck, might as well share a few jars. Perhaps we should have used different guidebooks.

With two days to go it was time for me to ditch the passport and all the spare keys for the padlocks. I also acquired the paint. I thought a lot about friends from Bristol and our antics together. The only thing that made me smile more was the kids in Rangoon. But of course, they were not all laughing. There was a girl of no more than six years old walking around carrying her infant brother. She would pat his stomach and point to his mouth. Perhaps her parents sent her out to beg, perhaps she had no parents.

That night there was a sudden commotion in front of me. A crowd was reeling about and there was a great deal of excitement and shouting. But it looked wrong. I carried on over and saw a mob of twenty men dragging another man along the road and throwing in punches and kicks. 'What's going on!?' I demanded. 'What are you doing to him!?' I was trying to push my way to the middle of the crowd. The victim looked terrified. His lips and cheeks were bleeding.

'He is thief,' said a man who had turned to me. He was friendly and triumphant. 'He tried to steal someone's car.'

'You should not hit him,' I said quickly. 'Why do you hurt him?'

'He is thief.' And the crowd moved on, dragging their victim away. That is what happens, I suppose, when there is no police force to rely on. And where there are so many people living in poverty and still not stealing from anyone it must gall when somebody does. Surely the thief was desperate too.

By the afternoon of the 15th everything was prepared. I had the paint, I had got rid of my ID (passport and visa card), I had phoned Thailand to confirm all was well. I sat on my guest house bed and for the first time in my life tried seriously to meditate. For about an hour I just felt bored and frustrated and foolish. But very quickly that changed. I became at peace. Time vanished. Later on I felt utterly relaxed, not confident of the immediate future but accepting of it. What would happen would be right. Meditation is the same as prayer; it is to bring yourself into harmony with what Is.

My last night, where should I go? Mr Guitar Café was great, but I had assured Larry I would not go there. It was admittedly a bit of a tourist bar, too expensive for most locals. But the live music was fantastic. Cover versions of cheesy Western songs. I must have been feeling poignant about home too. I decided to go.

It was a fine, warm night. Many traders had disappeared with the sun but there were still plenty of people on the streets, still plenty of women selling food from hot, smoky fires on the pavement and plenty of others selling kitsch jewellery. I arrived at the Café and was delighted when the band played 'Country Road' which, as anyone who has been to the border knows, is an absolute Burma classic. It brought back all the memories of Minthamee. I was fairly knocking back the drinks, enjoying a last spell of decadence. Then a foreigner walked in. It was Larry. He shook his head in disbelief. What the heck. We shared a few more. But it was an omen of the farce to come.

CHAPTER 8

We grasped the truth that it was not rifles, not tanks and not atom bombs that created power, and nor upon them that power rested. Power depended upon public obedience, upon a willingness to submit. Therefore each individual who refused to submit to force reduced that force by one 250-millionth of its sum.   Vladimir Bukovsky

BEFORE I LEFT the guest house to make the demonstration I padlocked the heavy chain round my wrist and sellotaped the remaining length of it up my arm. I hid this under a long-sleeved shirt but it looked most suspicious. My arm weighed several pounds too much and clanked inexcusably if I moved it too fast. I would rip my shirt off when I reached the gate; underneath was the ABSDF T-shirt with fighting peacock. Then the moment I had been dreading arrived.

Ever since 4 September, when someone suggested I spray-paint a couple of slogans, I had been worrying about the cans. You need to shake them up to mix the paint, otherwise it won't spray properly, and shaking the cans is noisy. I was convinced that if somebody walked in on me to investigate the racket I could not possibly find a plausible excuse. I certainly did not want to leave it until I reached the school gates. I could not afford to stand in the open shaking up a can for two minutes and hoping the police would ignore me; every second there would count. St Paul's School was right opposite the government ministry building, so there would be plenty of soldiers about. Perhaps the most tragic event in Burmese history happened in that ministry building. Fifty years earlier independence leader *Bogyoke* Aung San, father of Daw Aung San Suu Kyi, was assassinated. His popularity remains tremendously strong.

So I had to shake up the cans in my room but still I thought the sound was deafening. I had a cassette player and blasted out 'Carry Me Home' in an effort to drown out the noise of the ball-bearings in the cans. It was also a favourite song from Bristol and reminded me once more of the good times there. Nobody interrupted. I slipped the cans into my bag and left.

I arrived at the spot a few minutes early. I should have waited for Larry but was too scared to delay any longer in case I bottled out altogether. With twenty yards to go I reached into my bag and pulled out a can of paint, ready to give it a last shake. Then I noticed with paranoid shock that there was a car parked in front of the gates, on the wide pavement, not on the road. The doors were open and the engine was running.

Oh goodness! (or something similar) I thought, *I'm rumbled.* I pushed the can back into the bag but did not want to do a hasty about turn. Try to be calm. A few steps from the car and a man leapt out from the school grounds. He ran round the car . . . then jumped in the driver's seat and roared off. Phew. Three teenagers were watching me as I walked past, then doubled back and began shaking the can again. They laughed at the odd sight and walked on. On the left and right of the school gate were two walls, which had just been repointed and even tiled. There was a beautiful big clean white space perfect for the slogans. I began painting the first word, *'metta'*, in Burmese script. It is a Buddhist term roughly translating as 'loving kindness'. The paint was coming out very thinly. I had to go over each curve two or three times to make it stand out. The seconds ticking by should have been tense, expecting to be arrested at any moment, but instead, a surreal calm descended. I was aware only of the paint going on to the wall, and that I was going to write every character fully and legibly and not be in a rush.

When it was done I dashed over to the other side of the gate to paint on the other wall. As the repair work had just been finished, there was still a tarpaulin propped in front of and over the wall, like a tent. It meant that nobody would be able to see what was written. But I had spotted it on the recce and in my mind's eye had practised the drill a hundred times. Paint 'metta', then 'freedom', rip down the tarpaulin, rip off your shirt, get chained to the gate . . .

I started on the second wall: F . . . R . . .

I'm doing these letters too big, I thought, *I'll never fit them all on.*

. . . E . . . E . . .

No, I'll be fine, dismissing my worries, *I could not be so stupid as to* . . .

D . . . O . . M.

'Damn!' The last letters were squashed up illegibly. I ran to the gate and flapped about. What's next? I threw my bag down and flapped about some more. Aha! I ripped off my shirt, buttons flying, and set about chaining myself to the gate. I had every detail worked out. The chain went round the gate twice, was padlocked tight, then the last few inches were wrapped round the short length between my wrist and the gate, and that padlocked into place too. I reckoned this would make it all the harder for them to cut me loose. As the last padlock went home I looked over to my left and in disbelief saw that I had forgotten to rip the tarpaulin down. No one would be able to see the 'freedom' slogan. Idiot! What was next? I had no idea.

I emptied my bag on to the floor and picked up a bundle of letters. I would hand them out to the . . . there were no passers-by! What had happened to the midday crowds? Turned out it was a full-moon day. Holiday. Everywhere was closed. Doh! There on the ground was my cassette player. I had it primed with the soundtrack from *The Mission* and pressed 'play'. Nothing to do with democracy but if I was going to go, I wanted to do it listening to a fine piece of music.

A couple of people passed. I threw some letters towards them. They grabbed a handful and hurried off. I was shouting out something or other about freedom and democracy in Burmese but I doubt anyone understood my appalling pronunciation. Then I spotted Larry. He had just arrived and was filming it all.

Made me feel dreadfully self-conscious about my poor Burmese.

I had two copies of the *New Light of Myanmar*. I read out an excerpt from the editorial of one. It said that people were like machines and just as machines had breaking strains and should not be overloaded, so people should not be overworked. I suspect it was a dig at some too ambitious entrepreneur who had failed to sweeten the military enough with a cut of his booming enterprise and hence had fallen foul of them. It was a smug nasty little piece and quite disgusting in a country where the regime uses forced labour, even to the death. I ripped up the paper and tossed it aside.

By now a small crowd had gathered on the far side of the road. A few more pedestrians took leaflets. Then I saw the little girl again, carrying her tiny brother, patting his stomach and pointing to his mouth. She was looking at me kind of scared but knew I was a soft touch from last time. I fell still and quiet.

Can't you see me little girl? I thought. *I am chained to the fence. I cannot come to you. I have a fistful of political literature which means prison. You don't want to be here, little girl. Go away, take your brother away.*

But she was looking at me and holding out her hand, and her face was full of worry. She knew something was wrong here but did not know what. I suddenly realised I had a pocket full of money and would have absolutely no more use for it. I grabbed a wad and stretched out to the girl. She was too scared to come forward and I was at my limit, and I was sure the police would be here soon and . . . she danced forward, took it and was off. Phew!

I reached for the spray paint again and began painting '8–8–88' on the pavement in front of me. It was to mark the uprisings of 8 August, 1988. I got the first three done then realised that I could not possibly stretch far enough to do the fourth. Damn! Never mind, it was palindromic. I could try at the other end. But I could not reach that either. I began laughing at the silliness of it all.

Then a plain-clothes chap arrived. He stood right in front of me and asked me what I was doing.

'*Khinmya doh ayey-ha, janore ayey bar beh!*' [your cause is my cause!] I shouted to the thirty-odd people over the road.

He shouted at me and then, quite ridiculously, grabbed my wrist and tried to drag me away. I took one short step before my arm jolted tight on the chain. He turned round to look and I raised an eyebrow, nodding my head towards the gate and waiting for the facts to sink in for him. How had he not noticed? He let go of my arm and started fuming: 'What you do!'

'*Shi-shi-shi set shi*,' I shouted back, which was not rude but meant '8-8-88'. Then I tried to paint the last digit again, forgetting that I could not reach. He decided he wanted the can and we had a bit of a grapple. It was pointing right in his face and for half a tiny moment I thought of spraying him with it. But that would have been daft. I only had one arm anyway so gave up the can.

A few of his colleagues arrived. They were mad. They tugged uselessly at the chain and tried to shut me up.

'*Than Shwe, metta, nar leh la?*' [Than Shwe [the head of the regime], do you understand loving kindness?] I shouted. Years later the MI reported this as me shouting obscenities about Burma's leaders to cause unrest. '*Khin Nyunt, lut lat yey, nar leh la?*' [Khin Nyunt [head of MI], do you understand freedom?]. Not likely with my accent. Perhaps I *was* saying something obscene.

By now the authorities were arriving by the carload. They had gathered up nearly all the letters I had strewn around. There was a truckload of soldiers. The soldiers came over, milling about with their guns behind the ring of MI and police.

'*Mingalaba!*' I shouted to the soldiers, 'How are you today? Have you been paid yet? Or does your officer keep your pay?' Then, to the crowd opposite, which had grown to about fifty people, '*Bogyoke* Aung San founded the army to liberate and protect Burma, but the *Tatmadaw* today is here to oppress and murder Burma!' The soldiers climbed back into their truck and withdrew to the background.

I was running out of steam and slogans. I had not eaten for twenty-four hours. Excuse the indelicacy but I had imagined the worst-case scenario of being chained up there for half a day and did not want nature to press. None of the officials seemed to know what to do. By then, neither did I. One was standing just in front of me watching the crowd on the other side of the road. I reached forward with my free hand and patted him on the head. That is a terrible insult in Burma and I should not really have done it. He wheeled around in fury and belted me in the face, sending my glasses skew-wiff.

'No fear!' I shouted out at the top of my voice, straightening my glasses, full of fear, 'No fear!' I was afraid. And tired. I squatted down, fairly exhausted. The music from *The Mission* was still playing twenty minutes on. Behind me Larry was sitting in the school grounds surrounded by police.

I reached out for my bag but the chain pulled me up short. An MI man glared at me.

'Cigarette?' I asked. He pondered, shrugged and passed my bag over. I pulled a cigarette out and sparked up. It was so unexpected. I think smoking is the one right which Asians respect.

The traffic was still going by but too fast to notice anything. Still, I thought it was bad form to be squatting down. It looked too miserable. I stood up and saw a monk striding along the other side of the road. 'Theravada Buddhism,' I shouted out, 'very good!' He looked alarmed and hurried on even faster.

There were two crowds on the far side of the road, maybe sixty people, mostly civilians. Around the gate was a larger crowd of assorted officials: police, soldiers, MI, plain-clothes, immigration and, at last, one handyman. I had been there for almost an hour. The handyman, thick-set and bandy-legged, began on the chains with his hacksaw. My free arm was handcuffed and the hostile crowd tightened around me. They were not going to let me slip away! Then the hacksaw blade broke. I gave a cheer and laughed. Maybe I'll be here for ever. But they had a spare blade and a few minutes later the chain was cut.

My arms were whipped behind me and cuffed together. The surging crowd swamped me through the gates, my feet hardly touching the floor. It was pretty scary, like doing a parachute jump and feeling yourself accelerating away. I emerged from the scrum being propelled by a very satisfied policeman. He was young, tall and trying to break my wrists by wrenching them up my back. I was not smiling at all. It had all become rather terrifying. I whinged about the pain and he seemed to relent a little. In any case we were soon in the main office of the school. It had been commandeered for the initial questioning.

There were various men around the edge of the room. I stood in front of a desk, waiting, until a fairly senior army officer arranged his bulk into a chair behind it. His dark-green uniform was bedecked with insignia and flashes and military ribbons, his peaked cap gleaming polished over his pouchy worried face. 'What is your name?' asked the officer through an interpreter.

'I will not answer that question. Let us talk about 1988,' I replied. They did not know how to deal with such a response.

'What country are you come from?' asked the interpreter.

'I will not answer that question. First you tell me why there are thousands of political prisoners in Burma.'

When they realised they were not getting anywhere they drove me off to a police compound. In there, I was locked up in a small, gloomy cell for a short while until an interrogator was found. I was nervous. How were they going to act? Would I be able to handle it? Eventually a man entered. He was fortyish and, for a bloke, good-looking. I recognised him as one of the MI men who had been at the school, and by sheer luck I had heard someone call out his name there. 'Good afternoon, Ko Myo,' I greeted him civilly. That spooked him for a moment. He began questioning and was pretty angry. He got nowhere. I still had the chain padlocked to my arm. Ko Myo went off to fetch the handyman.

This, I thought, is their chance to be really nasty. They had to cut the chain from my wrist with a hacksaw. It was very tight and the slightest slip meant they would cut me open. Ko Myo held the chain as the handyman began sawing. I was getting very nervous. I tried to explain that they should put two metal strips across my arm in case the blade slipped, but they would have none of it. As the job went on, my worry remained but my mistrust subsided. They were both concentrating very hard and being extremely careful. The chain was killing me as they twisted it into a cutable position. Both men seemed concerned about this. Especially the handyman. In his own way he was quite tender. By the time he had finished, without scratching me in the slightest, I felt warmly grateful. He grinned at me on his way out. Nice chap.

At length I was taken to another van and moved to the main police HQ in Rangoon – a huge, rambling colonial building is the accepted cliché, I believe. I shared the ride with Larry who was not at all happy. They had seized all his pictures. What did he expect? One of the police snapped at us to shut up and keep our heads down. We did so.

Inside the building I was separated from Larry and taken to the top floor by a bunch of a dozen police and MI. Over the following hours we had a long, long talk. We discussed religion, politics, war, family life and, of course, Burma. But I would not tell them who I was. There were jokes and anger on both sides. Some of them were reasonable, friendly and intelligent. Others were mad ogres, snorting with anger and unable to hide their contempt.

'Do you want to die for your cause?' spat one twisted man in a rage.

'Not at all,' I replied.

At 8 p.m. someone ran in, excited, with a note. They huddled around it and had a brief conference.

'We know who you are!' they announced in triumph. 'Mr Jame Mobsly, age nineteen.'

I did not know how they had found out but had hoped that the press would have been in action by now and that perhaps even an embassy had begun making enquiries. Indeed, they had got the news from the wire.

I agreed that was who I was and corrected them on the spelling and age (I was twenty-four). It would not hurt to earn a little goodwill. I was made to stand up, hands cuffed behind my back, and denied water. A couple of hours later I was sure I was going to faint.

'Give me water or I'll sit down,' I said for the sixth time. They snarled at me. I tried to stay up but knew I could not. I sat down on the floor. They glared at me but that was all. Damned idiot James. Should have done it hours ago. I was also very confused about the talk we had had. Much of what they told me was utter nonsense ('there is no fighting in Burma' 'there are no refugees'). But an awful lot of it seemed to make some kind of sense. We could agree, after all, that the conflict in Burma went back hundreds of years. This regime had not started it. And also, in every civil war unspeakable acts are committed on all sides. That is life. At midnight they handcuffed me to a bench and let me lie down on the dusty wooden floor. Not very comfortable but I was well ready for sleep. Sleep, of course, took an age in coming. At 3 a.m. I was woken again.

They had brought bananas, a beautiful honey drink and a packet of Marlboros. I tucked into them delighted; I had not eaten for forty hours. They would not share the food but were happy to accept a few fags. One of them seemed particularly genial. He was about fifty, said he was Indian, a businessman. He asked me to write out a statement of what I had done the previous day. Why not, I thought, good chance to make my point about political prisoners. But I was not too bold with it. In retrospect I should not have done it. The amiability of an interrogator is no reason to overlook due process.

Then, at half-five, we moved downstairs. I had to have a pee on the way. We went into a thoroughly unsanitary room and I had the pleasure of peeing into a urinal while the policeman handcuffed to me peed into the adjacent one, both of us with only one hand to manage the technicalities. How unique.

Then into a huge room and the only one I had seen that looked half decent. There were about twenty-five officials in there, fairly senior, right up to Ohn Gyaw the chinless Foreign Minister. I was pointed to a chair and sat next to a chap from the Australian embassy. The ambassador was there too and not at all pleased. They had been there since midnight, slogging it out, and had convinced the Burmese it was best to deport me immediately. I was embarrassed about causing the diplomatic staff a headache but it was unavoidable. Worse was this news of deportation. I told them my passport was unavailable. The Aussies said they would issue me with an emergency travel document. I whispered to the second secretary not to do it.

He looked at me like I was a loony. 'We have to do it,' he explained. Well, that was it, then. Next thing was straight to the airport with the police. Larry was put on a 7 a.m. flight, the American ambassador coming to see him off. I had to wait until

4 p.m. It was a strange day, chatting innocently with the six guards around me, getting as bored as anybody waiting for a flight, not quite able to believe that it was all over.

I had a brief meeting with Robert Gordon, the British ambassador (and the very personification of diplomacy!). He asked the Burmese if he and Tiffany White (the political secretary) could speak with me alone. Ohn Gyaw looked at me with utter disgust. He could not bear the sight of me. He flounced off but someone agreed to the private meeting. We had about fifteen minutes together. They were very kind and I was very upset. I was upset to be leaving Burma, upset that I had somehow betrayed the prisoners. If only I had been more defiant, if I had taken a harder stance, I might have had a chance to visit a prison. Robert Gordon suggested I could learn all about the prisons from UN files kept in Geneva. But that was not the point. I did not want to do an academic study.

Just before it was time to board the plane I asked to go to the toilet. I went in and a guard followed. He took my hand in both of his and shook it vigorously. 'Thank you for what you have done. I really never forget you. Thank you.' A stewardess on the plane said the same.

But I was in no celebratory mood as I left. I was sad to leave Rangoon, the unique atmosphere and teashops, and I was awed by the size of the problem. There would be no quick resolution to it. A problem which has taken hundreds of years to develop will not disappear in a day. And I really had not expected to be kicked out so soon.

CHAPTER 9

Success, like happiness, cannot be pursued; it must ensue, and it only does so as the unintended side effect of one's personal dedication to a cause greater than oneself . . .   Victor E. Frankl

I CONTACTED MY FAMILY from Bangkok to assure them I was fine. There was a brief flurry of press coverage, but the papers did not seem to be interested in what was happening to the Burmese. I wanted dearly to revisit Ko Min Aung et al. in Htam Hin refugee camp. Harry, the NGO worker who had got me in the last time, refused. He said it was too risky, that the Thai guards were not supposed to let unofficial visitors in. What a trash excuse! I would have gone crazy if I thought I could not revisit my friends. I phoned around and secured a lift in there with a group of Thai women. They took powdered milk into the camp for the mothers, knowing it was not ideal, but what else was there to do when the mothers' milk was drying up?

The student organising the trip, Pim, was suspicious of me. 'Are you journalist?' she asked.

'No, a friend.'

She considered it over the phone, then agreed to pick me up. The following day she told me that if I were a journalist she would not have taken me. Hours later we drove into the camp. This time we entered through the main checkpoint at the front (with Harry we nipped through the back). I was sitting in the back of an open Ute with five others, sticking out like a sore thumb being the only white. We had to stop at the checkpoints but the Thai soldiers ignored me completely, did not even ask the driver who I was. We went in. Easy! What the devil was Harry moaning about?

I was so excited as I paced down the dirt track towards the ABSDF's section of the camp. I saw a figure in the distance . . . it was Maung Myint, twelve years old, a pupil of *Pyo Pan Wai*. He recognised me from afar and vanished, emerging later with a crowd of Minthamee's kids. When I finally reached Ko Min Aung's hut I had a child dangling from every finger and a dozen others trying to grab my knees or arms or belt. I could hardly walk. It was magic to see them all again and a brief moment of happiness at an otherwise disturbing time. I thanked God for Pim and the Thai women, and that there is always a way in if you look for it.

The only other highlight in those days after the demonstration was having a burger with Phoe Ni and his colleague Tun Tun. Usually I ate Burmese food but Phoe Ni insisted on treating me to some Western crap. There was sadness that night too. Phoe Ni and Tun Tun were trying to get residency abroad and wanted me to write to the Australian embassy on their behalf. I agreed and started jotting down a few details of their backgrounds. I asked Phoe Ni to tell me about his family. His parents were dead and of his eight siblings, three were dead. He had been away from his family so many years that he could not recall their ages and not even all of their names. He was struggling to remember their names. So sad.

Some people expected I would come out of Rangoon all excited and happy to have got away with the demonstration. The reality could not have been more different. The following is from my diary.

Now, after four days of debilitating misery it is time to pull myself together. Why so miserable? I failed. My mission in Burma was to go to gaol and I did not, though I could, achieve this. On the 17th talking to the Brit. ambassador and right now I feel like it is a bloody good job I failed – it was ill thinking indeed. But since then I've felt so disconnected . . . save for the highlights of dinner with Lyndal, five more hours in Htam Hin and a burger with Phoe Ni & Tun Tun. The reason I feel better now (i.e. this half-hour) is reading a snatch of Václav Havel . . . I am with direction again, viz: '. . . directness can never be established by indirection, or truth through lies, or the democratic spirit through authoritarian directives.' (Summer Meditations) i.e. politics is based on morality.

I had just discovered the writings of Czech president Václav Havel, a man who had spent time in prison himself while resisting the communist regime. What an inspiration he was. What an encouragement. Press ahead with the truth, he was saying; it will overcome all cleverness, brutality and lies.

My brother Jon was living in Sydney, Australia. We had both gone out there four years earlier to visit Mum's side of the family. I loved it but itchy feet kept me on the move. Jon loved it and chose to settle. I flew out there from Thailand to stay with him. He was great company, best friend as well as brother. He read through all the newspaper articles that had been written about my demonstration and decided to compile one himself.

> *DROPOUT IS A VERY NAUGHTY BOY*
>
> *University dropout James Mawdsley was shackled to a fence outside a Burmese school and fed bananas by brutal enemy troops. He spoke only of his escape from death, after spending his school years confined to a hospital bed. His mother boxed his ears as a child and his sister called him crazy.*
>
> *Mr Mawdsley, forty-two, patted the enemies' heads as they used a hacksaw in an attempt to cut him off. However, as soon as his Uncle David got on the mobile, he was rescued by plane, narrowly missing a long stretch in Insane Prison, where no doubt more bananas would be waiting.*

It was about as accurate as all the others.

I had something to get off my chest but did not know with whom I could speak. It had to be someone who had an idea of the Burmese junta. Back in the UK I had caught up with Ted, the man whom Tint Saw had recommended as one of the few decent foreigners he knew. I wrote to him.

Dear Ted,

Excuse the lack of introductory pleasantries and the absence of a sense of humour but I am in a stunned state of hopeless pessimism as far as freedom in Burma goes. I fully expect this defeatist frame of mind to melt away over the coming weeks but at the moment I see no solution to SLORC's barbarity.

My main motivation for the protest in Rangoon was so that I could meet some of the authorities for myself and so judge how open they are to reason and appeal. I met and talked with a fair range of them and undoubtedly most are good blokes. Some were able to give very plausible reasons for SLORC's policies and others unmistakably indicated their support for democracy and Daw Aung San Suu Kyi (albeit very subtly). We were able to joke together and some went beyond the call of dissimulating PR in their kindness to me. So far excellent. This is how, naively, I'd expected all of SLORC to be. Despite all the reports of atrocities I believed that behind it all there were men with whom agreement could be found.

Tragically, though, it was the highest-ranking men who had the reptilian smallness of mind and the unconcealable contempt for those who stood for freedom and justice. The bloke from the Burmese Foreign Office [the Foreign Minister], the two highest-ranking military men I came into contact with and three MI men who clearly held most authority – these six men were indescribable in their idiocy. Perhaps that's why I find it so hard to write. Just as they found the very sight of me, the very presence of me, a revolting offence so my contact with them has chilled me and deadened the belief I used to have in mankind. For the main these men ignored me, but if they had to face me it was either with a very nervous 'laugh' as they encountered something they considered wholly alien, or it was with a face of twisted contempt spitting with fury. I hope I am not sounding too dramatic but contact with these creatures has really dislodged me.

I do not regret this at all. As I said my chief aim was to discover first hand what I could about the minds behind the madness. Unfortunately it was a burst of sour reality which my unrealistic romantic optimism had not prepared me for. My disorientation now is just me coming to terms with a more authentic reality than the wishy-washy one I used to inhabit. So, an unpleasant but necessary step . . .

I had to get a job. I joined my brother cutting grass. It was good hard work, physical and in the sun. We worked from park to park to botanical reserve in north Sydney. On the hottest days our lunch breaks were spent swimming in Sydney Harbour. Lovely. I was also thinking hard about Burma. From my diary:

6.10.97
   I'm certain that any political remedy imposed from outside Burma (i.e. not of the people's will and understanding) would certainly collapse. If they adopted another country's workable system then without the tradition, historical evolution, social understanding which delivered such a system, it would break down. So what, if anything, can outsiders do to help? I am by no means saying we shouldn't help.

Then I received a letter from Ko Chit.

   . . . 6 students were die in action in the front line on 16 October 1997 and three arrested by the SLORC including former battalion commander Ko Zaw Than. Many problem were staying with us right now.

Ko Zaw Than was executed two days after he was captured. His best friend Maung Maung Htay was killed too.

As I had done in the UK, I tried to organise slide shows and to write to parliaments. But again this was going nowhere. I wanted to be with my friends, to share their lives, to fight the injustice with them. I detested the argument that I should be lobbying governments. There were already millions of people doing that. Were the governments going to do any more because I added my two penceworth? I could be of more use back in Burma.

6.11.97
   . . . short-term goal: arrange another chat with SLORC, but a longer chat.

I was happy to be with my family in Australia but Burma called. I thought about my grandpa. He had been an ANZAC (Australian and New Zealand Army Corps) and for a while he served as a guard in a prison camp. A Japanese prisoner had made a cigarette holder from part of an aircraft wing (we still have it). My grandpa bought it from him. Other guards were incredulous. 'Why did you not just take it?' they asked. My grandpa did not bother answering.

I heard that story from his son, my uncle David. Grandpa himself would not talk about the war. Because words cannot explain the experience to one who has not had it, and what more than a look and a nod is needed by another who has. This is how I felt after Rangoon. Not that I had been through a terrible experience, but the futility of words. How could I explain to people in Australia about what I had seen in the faces of the regime's most senior? It is a frightening thing. You do not see faces like that in Oz or the UK. What was the use of discussing Burma? You cannot understand totalitarianism until you have seen faces like that. Or maybe I am just very slow.

I read a book that wheeled my brain around. It was *To Build a Castle* by Vladimir Bukovsky. He had spent twelve years in Russian prisons and psychiatric wards for defying the communist regime. Eventually he was thrown out because the regime could not break him. He seemed to me to be one of the most courageous, perceptive and humble persons who had ever graced our planet. His book introduced me to four key ideas.

First, that if you are engaged in defying a regime, being thrown into prison need not be the end of it. In fact, there is a great deal you can do inside a prison to fight for democracy and, after all, the regime has by then lost one of its main weapons against you (threat of incarceration). In prison you can confront the regime as often as you choose. By asserting values of truth, by defying the regime's wicked manipulations, and continuing to defy them, their power is brought into question. They begin to doubt themselves. Why can they not control you? And the broader population is encouraged. They too will recognise that the tyrants cannot subdue everyone. And if they cannot subdue a few prisoners, then how could they subdue a whole population? It is vital, though, that if the prisoner is not to become a martyr, he or she needs a high profile. That is where the international community can help. When the world is vigilant and vocal, prisoners can be protected.

Second, that it is very useful to fight totalitarian regimes through the legal system. It does not matter how corrupt and evil the system is, you are not fighting to win a pardon but to expose the illegality. No regime can cope with total isolation and all want international respectability. Otherwise why do they bother at all with the charade of courts, judges and legislation? Of course, they commit gross injustices but they will never admit that to the world. If you can show the world that they have committed a gross injustice, to the extent that the regime cannot deny it, the regime will be weakened (and probably back down).

Third, that underground/secret organisations cannot deliver freedom. The only way to bring justice, openness and truth is to be just, open and truthful.

Fourth, that your freedom is inside you. It does not matter if you are in prison or not. The regime has its weaknesses. If you can find them and exploit them, and if you are able to endure the pain the regime heaps upon you, you will overcome.

Cutting grass was pleasant enough work but it paid very little. I was not saving much at all. I prayed, quit, searched for a better-paying job, and within thirty-six hours of quitting, Jon and I were working on the Sydney Olympic site for up to four times the pay. Minus fixed living costs, that meant more than ten times the savings. Thank You, God. It was real hard work this time, a lot of hours, a lot of heat. I set myself the target of returning to Asia by 28 March and I ended up leaving on 26 March.

I discussed it with my family. They were not keen for me to go. There was especial warning of rape in Asian prisons: 'I'm warnin' yer, Jimmy-boy, you won't be able to hold a melon in yer arse when yer come out!'

I do not believe I had any intention of trying. But I did have other doubts.

19.03.98
   Perhaps gaol is folly. Can I really anticipate the discomfort, the

hunger, thirst, cramp, ordure, heat, loneliness, isolation, skin infections, dysentery, malaria, hepatitis, HIV, typhoid?

On the other hand what does it mean to say 'I have complete faith in God'?

I agonised over my motives for return. Why did I want to go to prison? What a lot of trouble it will cause the FCO, and what a lot of grief for my family and friends. I asked my uncle David how it could possibly be right for me to cause my mother such pain.

'James,' he reminded me, 'even Jesus put a sword through His mother's heart.' It was surely not easy for him to say that. He loved his sister, my mother. And for himself he did not want me to go back. But he knew that we are called to something more than family. That is true love; when you do not seek to cling, when you do not seek to restrict one you love, but are willing to let them go. My cousin Tania gave me similar strength, her faith and obedience an example to follow. And once again, what was the alternative? To increase awareness abroad?

20.03.98

. . . educating a thousand Aussies as to the situation in Burma cannot be more productive than educating a dozen Burmese guerrillas or a single member of the SPDC [the military regime].

I had still not spent much time with the regime. Perhaps God was protecting me, lowering me into it all gently? I was spending almost every hour of every day thinking about Burma. What was the solution? What could I do to help it? I could not really come up with a convincing argument as to why I should go to prison. But I felt drawn there, that I had to share something with the suffering inmates and insist upon our dignity. More obviously, if I wanted to be part of the solution, I needed to understand the problem. That absolutely required spending time with the regime and I could only do that as a prisoner. The consequent hardship was a price worth paying for the goal for which we were struggling: freedom. And I knew for sure that all arguments about me staying in the West and working from there were lame.

25.03.98

. . . what a tragic shame that on certain aspects of life children can see so much more clearly than adults and yet growing up is inherently a process of dimming that vision. All children know that war, starvation, forced labour, torture, arbitrary detention, restrictions on movement/ press/association/assembly, forced relocation, rape and extortion are wrong. *Children know this should not happen. Yet adults, in their 'wisdom', explain why in fact these things aren't so bad, and that they are how the world works, and that things aren't that simple.*

Really I think they are that simple but an adult is someone too weary and confused to attempt to change the situation, too comfortable and cowardly to risk losing their gains by getting involved.

Again, in my diary I was trying to work out the best approach to achieve democracy in Burma.

25.03.98

Were it an easy matter to resolve the conflict in Burma then folk would rush to do it . . . the reason governments/UN don't do more to improve the situation is not because of any selfishness/coldness but because it really is so very very difficult. If things are to change in Burma then there are 45 million people who have to will it and centuries of history to be overcome. This is a vast task.

All external means to shape the situation seem only to make it harder for the SPDC to perpetrate its brutalities, rather than making it easier/more attractive for them to take positive steps (i.e. spend money on schools rather than armaments, abolish censorship and promote free press/radio, have the courage to extend real degrees of autonomy to the ethnic groups with an open invitation for them to join a federation of states). So this indirect influence from abroad will never tip the balance towards freedom as there is little positive about it. It is not enough to 'oppress' the oppressor. We need to promote and establish channels of freedom. Not aim to destroy what we deem is bad; but to build up what we know to be good. Positive influences I think can only be effected inside Burma.

The regime operates in absolute contradiction to fundamental human values and therefore must ultimately fail. The desire for freedom is too strong to be perpetually suppressed no matter what threats are made. Countless Burmese have already proved this by their massive, dauntless sacrifice . . .

I do not see military means as the solution to Burma's problems. War can contain a problem, but it can never solve one. It is not just an extension of politics. It is a crude attempt at replicating the success which politics can bring but, as it has so little substance, the victories of war cannot last as long as political victory. The SPDC may make military gains, but they will lose them through political defiance . . .

The answer is education: education of the Tatmadaw *(to weaken the SPDC within) and education for the ethnic / Burmese groups who are suffering so much . . .*

The average villager is not too concerned about what happens in Mandalay or Rangoon so long as he is allowed to farm the land without having most of his rice stolen by taxes or his children press-ganged into 'meaningless' construction / development programmes / war. A vibrant student / town class with inevitable strong rural links would easily be sufficient to restart Burma on the democratic road. (Sounds like Ne Win's Road to Socialism!)

Recall the police officer in Rangoon who had spent one year of his job posted in Thailand. It had profoundly effected him and he was one of the kindest / warmest of the officials who dealt with my booting out . . .

One aspect of education is that given sufficient literacy (i.e. once taught *sufficient literacy) and an open market on ideas / information then people can read widely enough to work out solutions for themselves. That is (and is this too obvious to set down?) the ability to read opens one up to innumerable ideas so then it is a question of judgement rather than genius to find a solution to a problem and there is far more good judgement in the world than genius.*

And in practical terms (if not moral) a government is far more accountable to its people if they are well educated. They cannot be so easily fobbed off, intimidated or deceived.

But these mechanics of education are not really what I have in mind when I suggest that the solution to most ills in most societies is education. After all, as [uncle] David said on Sunday night, the heads of the Gestapo were undoubtedly very refined, cultured and aesthetically orientated men. And there's many a high-flying graduate who would not know compassion if it came and punched them in the face (!?). Instead I think of values, as in compassion, courage, humility, sincerity, honour (or as Tania says, Faith, Hope & Charity). One learns these by seeing them in action.

And where are the Tatmadaw *to look if they want to be inspired by such? To the leaders who utterly lack these qualities? Or to the people whom they are ordered to brutalise (and therefore surely block out their empathy to save conscience)?*

No wonder Daw Suu Kyi is such a beacon to the people of Burma. They know she is different from SLORC, they know that she cares for them.

Yet now that I have written it, it seems so utterly utterly feeble to say that I want to go to Burma in apparent disregard of my family's concern because the human rights situation in Burma is so appalling so, wait for it . . . wait for it . . . I'm going to go over there and try to be brave and good and kind . . . ! I mean, really! What is most ridiculous is not that courage, honour etc. might be the solution to the problem (that could get fair support) but the startling notion that I consider myself to have sufficient understanding / quantities of any in order to make a significant difference. Would I not also be importing my contaminating influences? Pride, impatience, romantic anti-realism?

Well anyway, I am not here to argue my way out of going. I don't think I could anyway. But it does seem that I don't have a public defence for going.

I knew I was in for a hard time in the months ahead. And while I had the best family in the world, and the greatest friends anyone could hope for, I was lonely for intimacy. There was not much room on my chosen path for a girlfriend. But I wanted a woman. I got drunk. Would I come back from Burma? Surely I would. But what if I didn't? What if this was the last chance to touch someone, to hold someone, to kiss them . . . ? With my brother Jon and our housemates I got even more drunk, fearfully drunk. There was no chance of finding someone now . . . except . . . a prostitute. I remember thinking to myself: if I can get into town then I can find a brothel.

Moral conflict? No problem Sir, have another beer while your conscience wrestles with it. Still unclear Sir? How about a gin to clear the head? Oh certainly Sir, a double for extra clarity. That's better now isn't it? Six more of those and you'll find there's no moral conflict at all. Well done Sir, that's the spirit.

I was in no state to walk, but that does not deaden the sexual imperative. I asked Jon to drive me to town but, good man that he is, he reminded me that he had been drinking. OK, I'd do it myself then. I didn't have a licence – I'd never got around to sitting a test. Oafishly I stole Jon's car keys.

With great concentration I managed to get the car to the top of our shockingly steep drive and then passed out at the wheel. The car rolled back down the drive and by some miracle slew round at the last moment, avoiding crashing into the house by inches. I don't remember that. I could have written off the car, myself and whoever was on the other side of the wall. Jon rescued me, but I was too drunk to be berated.

When I regained a little sense I stole the keys again. But this time I was accosted before getting out of the house and the keys, thank God, were confiscated for good. But I was not finished. I staggered to a near neighbour who I knew was good for a favour at any hour. He was sober as a judge and had the morals of a feral cat and was happy to drive me to town. I sought out a brothel: an hour of fun, the illusion of intimacy and a weight of shame in the morning.

CHAPTER 10

The man who has two tunics should share with him who has none, and the one who has food should do the same. John the Baptist

I STOPPED IN INDONESIA for a few days on the way to Thailand, knowing it would be instructive to see more of the region. Tension was building there as students massed to demand Suharto step down. I sat with a group in their 'strike camp' on a campus in Jakarta. What an outstanding bunch of people! We listened as the news came in of demonstrations in Solo, a town to the east. Two girls were shot dead and scores injured. Others went missing. Hospital costs were shared between the university administration and the police who committed the brutalities. Two things sank into me.

First, that had I not visited Indonesia I might have seen a small report in a newspaper about the two girls being shot and I would forget it immediately. But being there, it was a thousand times more real. Each time we read the paper and learn of a few imprisonments here, a few deaths there, it is too easy to forget that there are real lives behind it all, daughters, fathers, friends.

Second, these students were no anarchists. They were intelligent, peaceful people. When they demonstrated, the regime would pay a few thugs to join them and turn the thing into a riot by hurling missiles at the assembled police. Then the police would react with violence and claim justification. The thugs were mostly members of GOLKAR's (Suharto's regime) 'youth wing'. The same thing happened in Burma in 1988. Members of the state organisation USDA tried to turn peaceful marches into riots.

Sitting with a friend in London watching the news once, we saw protest marches by Iranian students turn into a rampage – looting, fighting, overturning and burning of cars. The 'security forces' responded with bullets and dozens of students were thrown into prison.

'They are fools,' commented my friend, 'those students. They had international sympathy and now they've gone crazy. Who wouldn't send them to prison?'

I nodded in reluctant agreement. Then it struck me weeks later that those Iranian students were just like the Indonesian ones, the Burmese ones. They had been stitched up and, despite thinking I knew about the subject, I fell for it too. How easily deceived we are. And how shallow our major news networks are to present the simplistic picture.

The following week I arrived in Thailand.

Now in BKK. On Tuesday will visit Ye Min Aung & Phoe Ni in a gaol near Ratchaburi – bloody unlucky but I am not overly upset. It is part of the picture and as Ye Min Aung reportedly said, it is 'new experience'. They should be released this week anyway.

I was becoming accustomed to the hardship. But my friend Ko Min Aung, leader of Minthamee, had something to show me. He handed me a pile of photographs taken when the camp was burning down. It had happened over a year before but I still had not seen the result. Of all the pictures the most distressing were of *Pyo Pan Wai*, its sign still visible, a beautiful bush of red flowers in the foreground, yet its upper storey engulfed in huge balls of angry flame. I felt my eyes smart and my throat tighten. My nose turned to gunk and I wept and wept into my lap. Ko Min Aung and Thein Saung left me for ten minutes to regain composure. I wondered what they made of such an emotional display. Their sadness must have been greater than mine yet I doubted there were any public displays of grief on their part. The regime in Burma says you can see that there are no human rights abuses in their country because the people are always smiling, they are happy. Ko Min Aung told me that the people smile because they have no tears left.

Again before I headed off for arrest I wanted to catch up with as many Minthamee friends as I could. Cho Too, Myo Win, Kyi Wai, Ko Ko Oo and many others were living in a new concrete block of flats. Most worked for the same boss, '(*maybe 5am–5pm/10pm 6 days/week @ 200Bht/day) delivering milk cartons.*' They said the boss was good. Kyi Wai's left hand was monstrously swollen and a deep purple blue after he crushed it at work. Although he was an illegal worker, he was given three days sick pay and time off. He laughed about his injury. I began to see the fall of Minthamee in a changing light:

> *Possibly the fall of Minthamee and subsequent predicament of so many students is not the utter disaster I assumed. That many are now in BKK, working (illegally), or studying English or whatever, it is a vast opportunity for them to learn about the outside world (to a degree) and may well be of advantage for when they return to a democratic Burma. After nine years in the jungle what would another nine add? Diminishing returns.*

I visited Ye Min Aung and Phoe Ni and six others in gaol. They were there for illegal entry into Thailand. Despite the circumstances, it was an excellent reunion. Twenty men crowded into a tiny room with one tap and one hole in the ground. But Ye Min Aung smiled. He said it was an important experience. Prison made him stronger. Not everyone looked so brave.

Next I went to see Moe Zaw Aung, Minthamee's medic, in the prison. He had changed beyond recognition. His curly locks had been shaved away, he looked thin and troubled. There was a shop in the prison but prisoners were not allowed to keep money. Instead visitors would pay it in to the office at the beginning of the day and prisoners would be issued with 'tickets' worth about eighty per cent of the value of the donation. They had to spend them the same day and before noon. After that the tickets became worthless. But worse, ordinary prisoners, and especially foreign ones like Moe Zaw Aung, were not allowed to visit the shop. They had to give the tickets to a trusty, a 'head' prisoner, and he would buy what they asked for. Of course, he would take a fifty per cent cut. It was a cruel system.

Moe Zaw Aung was suffering from a gastric ulcer and his gums were bleeding. He could diagnose his own problem but there was no way he could buy the medicine and foodstuffs he needed.

I am sure Than Shwe [head of the regime] did not plan on Moe Zaw Aung suffering from a gastric ulcer in a faraway prison and being unable to soothe it. But when you lust for complete control and will employ any amount of brutality to pursue it, the fallout is unimaginable and untraceable. Though was it just the dictators to blame?

> . . . I understand that there is no evil master plan/mind behind all this horror; no one/group has that much control. But the reality is more disturbing. It occurs only through the 'consent' & behaviour of millions of people, in and out of Burma. Each violation of justice is more or less an accident of circumstance but only because the people involved see the background conditions as acceptable.
>
> So what is 'unacceptable'? It is not enough to be moved to tears, not enough to protest & condemn, not enough to try and include some opposition to the regime in your life. 'Unacceptable' means that something must be stopped, and at great cost if necessary . . .
>
> OK, if folk don't want to sacrifice all then at least be honest. Stop talking about 'unacceptable terror' & 'gross violations of human rights'. More like, 'it's annoying, it's undesirable, it would be better if things were different'. But the strong-worded resolutions of the UN, the powerfully written reports by NGOs and the sensationalist press – they all smack of hypocrisy and falsehood. Of an indignation which is not true.

I had seen my friends but I was impatient to get into Burma and protest. It was not that I looked forward to prison, but I was scared that if I procrastinated I would bottle out completely. I took a bus up north and found myself sitting next to an American girl, Marci van Dyke.

111

She had spent several years in the Philippines working on aid projects and was now with an NGO on the Burma border. Her specific task was to give health care education. But the more we talked the more I felt she was giving a lot more than that. She was giving the Karen a degree of comfort and moral support that was rare from foreigners. When refugee camps further north were attacked, her boss decided they all had to pull out of the southern camp. Marci felt that this was precisely the time to be in the camp when help was needed most. But NGOs are frightened of tarnishing their image; where will they get funding if their workers are killed? What frustrated Marci was the unreasonableness of her boss's fear. These camps in the south were not actually at risk. And although the boss had thousands of Karen to ask about the border situation, and nobody understood the threats better than they, in fact he got his information from the *Bangkok Post*! A newspaper! How can a newspaper know more about a situation than the people on the ground?

What was the message to the refugees? We care deeply about your suffering and we are going to move mountains to help you . . . but just don't expect us to hang around if there is the tiniest hint of a shadow of a suggestion that we might be at risk from witnessing something nasty.

Marci was doing a fine job, but I was glad I did not work for an NGO. I valued my independence. My plans always had to be very vague, the details only falling into place at the last moment. It would be impossible to operate any other way in the infinitely complex situation of the Burmese border. Nevertheless, I tried my best to keep my family informed of the broad outline and what to expect in the near future. I wrote to my sister Emma:

> . . . *the place to apply pressure is to the SPDC . . . If I am arrested then I want to stay, one week, one month. Whatever I can. It is extremely difficult for me to reach a balance, to commit an act which gets me over one week in detention but less than six months. That is my aim. In this time of detention I can make my point. The SPDC has no mandate to govern Burma. They are a bunch of terrorists. Burma belongs to the ethnic groups and to the NLD . . .*

I do not expect to change anything on paper. I do hope to make a political point. The only laws I will break will be the SPDC's whimsical non-laws, not international law, not moral law.

I wanted to go deep into Burma, to a town in the central areas far from the border. After my last deportation I was certain to be blacklisted so a visa for Rangoon would be out of the question. But as I saw it, I did not need a visa or passport. The regime was an illegal one. They had no right to ask people for travel documents. It was up to the people of Burma to decide who was welcome and who was not.

I also wanted to make a graphic point to the regime that they were not in control. That people could get past their army and police checkpoints, even ones who stood out like sore thumbs – white guys.

But to get inside Burma I would need a great deal of help. The ABSDF already trusted me and agreed to sound out the Karen about a possible trip through their territory. Thu Rein acted as regional liaison officer between the ABSDF and the Karen, and he agreed to introduce me to them (as well as pave the way for my request). First he took me to a refugee camp and I waited there to see if I would get the chance to put my suggestion to the Karen. I spent the days in the camp mostly as a children's entertainer: card tricks, coin tricks, games with matches. Unfortunately I had to give up, as the kids were too smart, their eyes faster than my hands. But it was fun while it lasted.

One girl, standing holding her baby, asked me if I was married. I said no. They asked how old I was. Twenty-five. They all found that hilarious. Twenty-five and still not married. I went a little red. An old man, sixty-three, came and visited me. I was blown away when I tried smoking his pipe. It was the roughest shag in the world and he was delighted as I coughed and spluttered. Quite unlike the mild Burmese cheroots. He saw one of my American dollars and pointed to the portrait, fascinated. 'George Washington,' he said in wonder, 'American king.'

Despite the distractions, I was worried sick that Thu Rein would come back with news that the Karen did not even want to discuss the plan. The days were passing, but then at last he returned with a positive result: I would get the chance to speak with Brigadier-General Htin Maung of the KNU. If I could win his trust, he could arrange my passage deeper into Burma. Together, Thu Rein and I crossed the Moie river into Karen State, 7th Brigade area. Minthamee camp, where I first stayed in Burma, had been in Karen State, 4th Brigade area. Here we were further north. In all these places, the Burmese junta are afraid of the Karen. The junta's soldiers outnumber the Karen soldiers enormously. They outgun the Karen massively. But they cannot beat them.

Thu Rein had done most of the initial liaising. Now I had to speak for myself. Brigadier Htin Maung, tall and with bearing, came and sat with us. I paid my respects and thanked him for giving me a hearing. He asked what I wanted to do – to be escorted to a town deep in Burma and then left on my own. I would start giving out stickers calling for change.

Like everyone else along the border, like the ABSDF, the NGOs who helped me, the other ethnic groups, Brigadier Htin Maung alerted me to the danger. Nobody encouraged me to go. 'They will put you in prison,' he warned.

'I know.'

'They will beat you. They might torture you.'

'I know.'

'They could kill you.'

I paused. 'Sir, I don't care. I do not believe it will happen but it does not matter . . .' Then I began to tell him of my respect for the Karen. I knew a little of what they had done in World War Two. Formidable soldiers and dear friends of the British men who fought alongside them. Brigadier Htin Maung could remember the war. I asked him about Major Hugh Seagrim. Htin Maung looked thoughtfully into the distance, then softly told the story as he knew it.

Major Seagrim's nickname among the Karen was Grandfather Longlegs (as opposed to the Japanese 'shortlegs'). As the Japanese took control of Burma and the British withdrew, Seagrim stayed behind. He organised resistance groups so there would be a force

Above: Pupils of Pyo Pan Wai on Tenasserim River, Minthamee. 1995.

Above: Ko Moe Kyaw, Bangkok. December 1996.

Right: Ko Ko Oo, Minthamee. January 1997.

Ye Min Aung with ex-python, Minthamee. January 1997.

Below: English class, 1st of the day, Minthamee. January 1997.

Below: English class, 3rd of the day, Minthamee. January 1997.

Tenasserim River, Minthamee. January 1997. View from author's bed.

Tenasserim River, Minthamee. January 1997.

Hospital at Minthamee, January 1997. Standing, Moe Zaw Aung.

Grave at Martyr Hill, Minthamee. Died 8/8/93.

Karen Festival Day, Htee Htar, February 1997. In the background, traditional dress. In the foreground, modern dress.

ABSDF platoon prepares for front line, February 1997. Chit Ko Ko (centre with beret) was killed shortly afterwards.

Last day at Minthamee, February 1997.

Evacuation, February 1997. Pictures and stories of 1988 massacres left around the camp for Tatmadaw soldiers to find.

Evacuation, February 1997. The pigs did not make it.

Evacuation, February 1997. Kyaw Htay.

Evacuation, February 1997. Kyaw Htay one hour later. (Far right, U Aung Myint)

Evacuation, February 1997. From left: Hla Shwe, Tin U Shwe,
Aye Aye Mu, Sein Sein Aye.

ready to strike when the British inevitably returned. When the Japanese heard about these groups and about Seagrim, they went to terrible lengths to get him. They began arresting Karen civilians and torturing them to reveal his whereabouts. Teenage boys were hung up by their arms (behind their backs) and whipped for hours with bamboo sticks. By the end of 1943 they had killed 270 Karen in this and similar fashion. The majority of Karen gave nothing away. The Japanese vowed to kill 1000 unless Seagrim gave himself up.

When Seagrim learnt of the extent of the reprisals he told his dear friends that he would surrender himself to the Japanese, knowing it meant execution. 'But the Karen said,' continued Brigadier Htin Maung, ' "Never mind. Do not give yourself up. They will kill you. You don't die."

' "Never mind," Seagrim told his friends, "I must go. I cannot bear that they kill any more of you. I will go."

' "No," replied his comrades, "never mind. Do not go to them. You are our best friend. We won't have you die."

'"I will go,' said Seagrim finally. "If I have to die, never mind. And if anyone says I am a fool to die, never mind." '

He did go. The Japanese received him honourably, but he was sent to Rangoon. Throughout his incarceration, Seagrim had a profound effect on other prisoners and on the Japanese guards through his calm and strength. In September 1944 Major Hugh Seagrim, 19th Hyderabad Rgt. attd. Special Operation Ex. GC, DSO, MBE was sentenced to death with eight of his closest friends. There was no valid trial. Seagrim accepted his death but pleaded that the eight Karen with him be spared as they were only following his orders. The Japanese ignored the request and the Karen told Seagrim they were happy to die with him. All were executed.

A Karen soldier gave Grandfather Longlegs his epitaph, saying the words would not be found written on any gravestone, but were written on Seagrim's heart. Quite simply, 'He loved the Karen'.

I already knew the story but what bowled me over was to see Brigadier Htin Maung telling it. He was looking wistfully to the trees as he told it, and he was remembering it. He had not met Seagrim but he heard all the news at the time. And each time he said 'never mind', it was as if he was saying it all for real, for today. Would the Karen risk their lives taking me through to Moulmein? *Never mind.* Would I risk my life going to Moulmein so that I could protest against the regime's persecution of the Karen? *Never mind.*

We understood each other perfectly. The regime had to be fought against. The Karen army chose guns; I chose letters. But it had to be fought against and you cannot do that without risk. I had not tried to prove anything to Brigadier Htin Maung except that I understood the bond between Karen and British officers during World War Two. I understood that they died for each other, they fought together and they won.

Then British politicians who had too much on their plate abandoned the Karen. Betrayed them. Left them to the mercy of the Burman majority and the fifty years of devastation that followed. I wanted to apologise for that. Not in words but by action.

It may sound like madness to British people today who think the world has moved on. But it was not madness to the British fifty years ago. It was not madness to the Karen fifty years ago. And it is not madness to the Karen today. It is stark reality. Mankind is one body. We cannot move forward except together. We cannot leave parts of our body behind. None of us is free until we all are free.

We had spoken for less than an hour. It was time to act. Brigadier Htin Maung called for one of his captains, Mana, and began writing out his orders plus a sealed note to give to a major inside Burma. Thu Rein told me to get ready. Everything happened very quickly. Mana, stocky and youthful, assembled four of his men and we lined up ready to go. I was not sure if the journey would take one week or one month. Certainly it would be difficult, but failing to complete it would not be an option.

'Have you got a water bottle?' asked Mana. I did not. He gave me his. We set off.

'Have you got a hat?' called out Brigadier Htin Maung. I had my Akubra, but had left it with Thu Rein along with my passport and other belongings. The hat was a birthday present from my brother Jon. I did not want the junta to get their hands on it.

'Here!' he said, throwing me a baseball cap, 'you need a hat.' Ba Saw, one of Mana's four, was wearing a bandana. Another had a beret. Tow Nigh sported a great stetson. We looked like an odd bunch! But beneath the mixture of hats, all were first-rate soldiers.

We set off, travelling light, boating down the Moie river and before too long disembarked to begin crossing the hills. They were shockingly steep. Soon enough I needed to go to one side for a pee. I asked Mana if that was OK. Not that I was in the habit of asking to go to the toilet, but as an inexperienced person with a group of experts, I was not going to do anything without their approval.

'Don't go off the track,' Mana told me. 'Landmines.'

And there began two of the most magical weeks of my life.

CHAPTER 11

. . . I cannot swear to everything I have said in this argument – but one thing I am ready to fight for in word and deed, that we shall be better, braver and more active men if we believe it is right to look for what we do not know, than if we think we cannot discover it and have no duty to seek it.
                                                            Plato

WE CROSSED RANGE after range of hills and passed through the lushest and driest of valleys. Every now and then we would pass a village, deserted, rotting, dilapidated or even burnt down. Very occasionally we passed Karen civilians on the track. They were always hurrying. Often they would not even glance at us. Too much fear in that land for superfluous talk.

On the side of one hill we saw men with catapults shooting into the trees. They were aiming at tough-skinned fruits and knocking them down from fifty feet away. It was incredible. Then they cut down certain stalks of certain plants, held the six-foot length of it above their heads and let the water within drip drop by drop into their thirsty throats.

Towards the end of the first day we came to a large stream. We were all sweating like pigs. Mana bent down to scoop water into his mouth. Tow Nigh, so young and warm and welcoming, looked at me for a moment, I looked at him, then quickly we dropped our packs and raced into the water and jumped under. Glorious!

118

After pressing on we came to another village. In the centre were two ancient women and a tiny young girl. They were alone. Mana went to speak with them, then we continued to the far edge of the village. As we got there a knot of about forty frightened-looking men and women emerged from the surrounding forest. They seemed wary at first but soon relaxed. I asked Mana what had happened.

'They saw us coming,' he explained, 'they thought we might be *Tatmadaw*. They have to hide in the jungle.'

At first I was disappointed that our little column of six was moving so conspicuously that we could be seen from afar. But then I reconsidered. The fact was that it meant more to villagers around here that they get warning of any approaching soldiers than it means to any soldiers that they are not seen. These villagers had to keep constant vigilance, afraid every hour of every day that the Burmese army might arrive. Imagine trying to live like that. Deeper inside Burma the price of being appre-hended could be weeks of forced labour or portering. Closer to the border, the penalty is death. The *Tatmadaw* is ordered to shoot on sight anybody in these 'black areas', places where the resistance groups hold the upper hand.

Ba Saw, the youngest of our group at seventeen, asked me if I wanted a coconut. Why not? He disappeared for a few moments and then I caught sight of him shinning up an enormous tree. At the top he dislodged eight great hairy coconuts while Mana paid the villagers for what we took. Quite delicious.

We ended the next day in another village. There we met about a hundred Karen soldiers. There was also a Japanese soldier, Roki. He told me that he came to Karen State as often as he could. His boss in Japan, an elderly man, loved the Karen and was willing to pay for Roki to come out here and bring medicines, and also to fight for a month or two. Roki was not a mercenary, he did not want money, he wanted the Karen liberated. We spent the next week together. He was a man of outstanding courage and I was secretly thrilled that we were there together, Karen, Japanese, British, Burman, all on the same side. Certainly the world is getting smarter!

I also met the 'Padre with the AK47'. That is the title of the autobiography he intends to write when freedom comes. Like the other soldiers he wore jungle greens, but he surprised me with his bright-red football socks. 'I will have a house', he explained, 'on top of a hill, near a river. I will grow orchards, so many fruit. I will keep chickens for eggs and pigs for meat. I will not keep cows. Disgusting animals. They make the water all muddy; they churn the banks into mud and turn it green with their urine. I will have music and books. I will have a motorbike and a four-wheeled drive. You must visit me then. Oh, many orchards. This is my dream. I will have a young, beautiful wife. Visitors will come to me in my helicopter. Very wonderful . . . but no cattles, foul creatures.' He laughed throughout as he said it and was great company in the following days. He was forty, and most definitely felt ready for a wife.

We set off the following morning as part of the greater column. Patrols, platoons, columns of soldiers are constantly on the move in these areas. Depending upon your task, safety might be found in lesser or greater numbers. At this stage it suited us to attach ourselves to a larger group which was going our way. Again the hills were unbelievably steep. We passed an elephant on one, dragging giant logs on clanking chains. Soon after that there was an explosion of excitement up ahead, shouts and warnings, people running about.

Turned out one of the men had disturbed a snake. It was a beauty, about four feet long and apparently quite delicious. It was also deadly, hence the excitement. But you do not let food slide away, especially meat. So our man had grabbed a stick and was now doing battle with a terrified snake. There was more shouting and heckling and jeering than at the Derby. Sadly for the snake, the Karen are good at everything they do.

We passed a few villagers at an empty cattle station, a woman there too, and stopped at midday beside a beautiful pool in a river. The leader of the column decided we would stay there till the next morning. There is no point in rushing through the jungle. At least, not for them, even if I was in a hurry. Most of the men slung up hammocks and began preparing food. I went for a swim with Ba Saw. He brought a harpoon gun with him and had borrowed, from somewhere, a diving mask. It was a tiny little gun and the quarry, fish, were as tiny as they were fast. Neither of us caught anything, but it was a lovely swim.

An old man on the bank had a probe connected to a large battery. I am not sure how it worked but he was electrocuting the fish. I am not sure how successful he was either but there were always fish to accompany our jackfruit and rice. Perhaps it was the traditional net that came up with the goods.

After the swim we repaired to some rocks beneath shady trees to enjoy lunch. The snake curry was quite remarkable and complemented chef's choice of vegetables perfectly. April is the hottest month in Burma but our trees provided a cool shade far more pleasant than any air-conditioning system. Over lunch we had fallen silent, but the talk livened up again as we sipped our post-prandial cup of *cha*: green tea, fresh from the Shan mountains. Exquisite. The session would not have been complete without tobacco, and so out came the mild Burmese cheroots. We puffed away, watching the river tumbling off down the valley into the jungle, watching the baking sun cook the land from our shady retreat, and contentedly blowing out clouds of smoke as someone or other nattered about life and dismissed the hardship.

I had about three pounds of sugar with me. It seemed like a good idea just before I left Thailand, as sweeteners were hard to find in the jungle. Tow Nigh, helpful as ever, appeared with an armful of limes, just then plucked from the bushes. We got a few mugs together, filled them with the freezing river water and added a few good heaps of sugar to each. Next the limes were crushed and squeezed, their juice and pulp added to the drink, and I am sure you can believe that the result was the tastiest fruit drink I have ever had in my life. At least, this is how all the pleasures of life seemed: somehow magnified. Perhaps when you are thirsty all drinks taste good, and when you are hungry snake-flavoured rice is a treat, and when you are hot and tired it is a charm to swing on a hammock in the shade. And when you do not know if you will be alive the next day, it is a blessing to sit with men you respect and to talk and laugh and fall silent.

Eventually Tow Nigh beckoned me to follow him to the river. 'Brush your teeth,' he told me, and showed me how to do it using sand instead of toothbrush and paste. It worked, but I confess I do not nowadays keep a jar of sand in my bathroom. The West does have its benefits.

The ants were out in force. I did not have a hammock and was not going to ask for one. Instead, I would sleep on the rock.

'Tonight', warned the Padre with the AK47, 'you will be crying like a baby.' He smiled, full of delight and mischief. 'The ants will bite and bite, and you will sing out like a baby.'

I tried to look unconcerned but I was not looking forward to it. As it went, all the ants turned in to sleep as well. I was surprised that the Padre did not know they were not nocturnal. Maybe I just smelt bad. But I did not get bitten once. There was no need to tell the Padre that, though. He had a new respect for me in the morning.

Again we pressed on. Sometimes, as we moved down the valley, the rocky trail would become impossibly vague and then vanish altogether. We would leap from boulder to boulder, looking out for where the trail began again. But the ground was becoming flatter and flatter. Sometimes we could get up a belting pace on dark earth tracks, which sloped gently down through the woods. Sometimes the vegetation dried out, sometimes it became fruitier, lusher. We entered a lovely lime-green grove. There was grass on the ground and the light leaves on the shapely trees batted playfully in the gentle breeze. I noticed the soldiers in front of and behind me began filling their pockets with a pear-like fruit from the branches that surrounded us. I thought it best to copy and got about four or five. I was pretty hungry and decided to tuck in. The fruits were very green and very hard. They were not pears. They were bitter, too. Ba Saw started laughing at me. I threw the fruit away. Turned out they were mangoes, not close to being ripe and certainly inedible with the skin on! Dunderhead. But that night they tasted gorgeous, skinned, shredded and mixed with tea leaves and ground nuts.

In one valley we stopped to cook lunch. Damp rice was wrapped in great green leaves, then buried in shallow holes and fires lit above them. After about forty minutes the rice was cooked to perfection. The nearby stream was fearfully contaminated by cattle dung – I took the Padre's point – but the boys just dug holes beside the bank. When they got to about three feet they pushed baskets to the bottom to stop the sides from collapsing and soon water seeped into them. Dip your mess tin into that and it is ready to drink.

Mana was an excellent guide, thirty, solid and perhaps at first a little surprised by this assignment. But he made sure I had everything I needed. He had been to a Baptist missionary school and we discovered that the film about Kalahari Bushmen, *The Gods Must Be Crazy*, was a favourite for us both. He was very well educated, very well organised, very committed to his cause.

Another time we passed a decaying monastery. There was still a bowl of water out there, filled up by passers-by for the monks and the thirsty. Further on we could look back and see white pagodas gleaming on the dry hillsides. Surreal, these symbols of peace in a land of war.

We were getting close to a temporary HQ, where the local Karen commander was based, and our column of a hundred entered another camp. The first thing I saw was a circle of men, quite old, standing in their underpants and watching a pair similarly clad wrestling in the middle. Well what else was there to do? Good physical training. When we set off the next day I watched the whole column file past. I could not believe it: 100, 200, 300 very tough and very well-armed men. They needed so little to live on; got much of their food from the jungle and much of their hardware from their own armoury. I began to feel the awesome strength of the Karen. They will never give up their land. They will fight to the last. I pray that it does not come to that.

On the way up to HQ we passed a couple of Karen women, a little old, but attractive too I thought. The Padre stopped to chat with them and asked me to stop as well. The women were inspecting me and reporting their conclusions to the Padre. When we pushed on I asked him to translate what they had said.

'You are too tall, your head is too small, your nose is too big, your skin is too pale and you are covered in hairs like a monkey!'

We stayed at the HQ for a week. Mana delivered the sealed orders from Brigadier Htin Maung to the major (the local commander) who then set about finalising arrangements to get me to Moulmein. That week I spent mostly in the rock pools beneath a fifty-foot waterfall, climbing the granite falls, then jumping from height into the water below. The Padre had lent me his Gideon Bible and in the front was the hymn 'How Great Thou Art'. I relearnt the words and sang them out at the top of my atrocious voice every day at the falls. Fortunately the roar of water was so loud that not another soul could hear me.

We had eaten a little *jaggery*, a sort of chalky sugar, but one day a boy came in with a pot of wild honey. Ah! Nothing in all the world is so sweet! It still had furious bees fuzzing round it. The wax we chewed on was not discarded but kept to make candles. I had brought a cassette player with tapes of democratic songs for the Moulmein demonstration. Here at HQ I switched on the BBC World Service. There was a round-up of events in the world – twenty-two shot for Rwanda genocide, Tibetan exiles setting fire to themselves in Delhi, Serbs moving into Kosovo and massacring civilians, an Indonesian sorcerer murdering forty-two women, kidnappings and executions in the Yemen, trials demanded for the Khmer Rouge, trouble in Palestine. Next was announced a half-hour show on . . . garden gnomes. I wondered for a moment if the true purpose of the World Service was not to tell mankind that though there be war, earthquakes and persecution in every land, back here in Britain we are so civilised we just concern ourselves with garden gnomes, or the cricket, or church fairs.

We were based near the top of a hill. At night the wind used to rip through the bamboo shelters and through our blankets, and it was fearfully cold. Late one night I got up, trying not to wake the other three asleep on the springy platform. I left the shelter to squat by a fire and chat with Ta Roe, a Karen boy.

He shared his thoughts with me. 'I think the world will end soon,' he said quietly, 'it is the Book of Revelation, the time is come.'

'Don't say that,' I admonished, 'it is not so bad, there is so much hope.' But I regretted saying it. Who was I to interpret the Bible to him? He could read it himself and he could see all around him that the Book of Revelation was coming to pass. I considered my arrogance in thinking of Christianity as a European's religion. Come to think of it, which was closer to Galilee, Lancashire or Karen State?

For some reason the Major took a shine to me. He was short, bearded, and had a long-service medal: fifty years in the front line! He had been fighting for fifty years. Over the week we had eaten together, but he spoke no English and my Karen was worse than my paltry Burmese. He knew I spent all my time playing in the water but knew as well that I was dying for the order to be off. Every day waiting was an agony. I wanted it all over and done with. Just before I left he fairly insisted that I must come back one day and stay with him. I would be most welcome. And I should bring my girlfriend. One day I will, when the Karen are free.

I thought hard about my motives. I was sure that if my motives were 'bad' only ill could come from the whole exercise. The trouble was that I knew four things for sure: I could not possibly have bad motives, that I could not conceivably have good motives, that my motives were beyond a shadow of a doubt noble, and that my motives were undeniably base. In this existential quagmire I decided to ditch the question altogether. I no longer cared what my motives were; I just knew that the injustices had to be protested against. And if I had been wrong, the Karen would not have risked their lives to help me do it.

Everything seemed so pure: the people, the jungle, the rivers, the wildlife, the sun and at night the stars. Perhaps in anticipation of the hard times ahead, I was appreciating what is around us every day. It was time for me to go. Ta Roe would take me to the next village and there I would meet my escort for the final leg of the journey.

The Padre walked us down the hill and to the edge of the forest. 'Before you go, James,' he said, 'I want to pray for you.' He said a short prayer out loud and then looked at me. 'I have seen your scar. I think you are hard to kill.' We shook hands and were gone.

It was dark by the time we got to the village. I hid outside while Ta Roe checked we were all clear. The *Tatmadaw* had been camped there for the past five days. They had got word that there was a foreigner in the area and were lying in wait. The Karen had intercepted their radio transmissions. It turned out that the woman we had passed at the cattle station a few days earlier had tipped them off. One cannot argue with that. The deal for locals is that they either inform the *Tatmadaw* of everything they see or they be executed for withholding information. Perhaps the woman felt that if she did not inform, one of the other villagers would, and would also have to tell who else was present. Then this woman would be in trouble for being present but not saying anything. It is a horrible game of fear.

The village was clear. I was greeted on the outskirts by twenty well-armed men. They were in good spirits; it was quite a novelty to be taking a foreigner so far into Burma. Across the fields we could see by starlight, stumbling as we went on the rough ploughed ground. But when we moved through forest it was pitch-black. Still they did not slacken the pace. I had to keep no more than two steps behind the body in front, or he would vanish utterly. All I could see of him was that he made a slightly darker form than the blackness around. We were really clocking up the kilometres.

At midnight fifteen men peeled off. They were replaced by two villagers, unarmed, no military kit. At two in the morning we came to a large river. The rest of the soldiers turned back. It was quite a moment, saying goodbye. Ta Roe went with them. He was exhausted. He had set off with me at four o'clock that afternoon and had had little rest on the way. Now he had to get back to relative safety before dawn. The two villagers and I waded into the river. It came up to our chests but we got over all right.

Then we got lost. Until then I had been in awe of the Karen, regarding them all as supermen. It had not occurred to me that to ask a villager to walk from his home village in the hills to a town on the coast over a hundred kilometres away might cause him navigational challenges. A bit like asking someone from Putney to walk to Birmingham without using the roads, or a compass, or a map.

As we circled round and round the scrub I did my best to maintain my equanimity. But when we passed the same junction in the tracks for the third time I confess I became quite concerned. There was nothing to do, however, except keep following. At last we struck on with confidence, my two guides no longer having conferences of war every few minutes. We walked and walked until I thought I would drop. There was less forest and more open scrubland, as well as the ankle-twisting ploughed or stubbly fields. I was praying for the dawn, for first light, when we would have to find a spot to hide; it would be too dangerous to be seen in this area. At last it came. My guides took me to a clump of bushes surrounded by fields and I laid me down to sleep. They disappeared to find food.

Before nodding off I looked out across the fields. There was an excellent all-round view – I would have plenty of warning if somebody approached. But it meant that there was nowhere to run to. I would be out in the open. I just had to pray that no one would come snooping by. Nobody did.

The sun climbed up, the ants came out and I cried like a baby. The Padre was not there to see it, but I got virtually no sleep at all. I tried to reason with the ants, I tried appealing to their better nature. No good. I was in their way and they were going to make me suffer. Soon after that it was too hot to sleep anyway. One of the guides returned. He had three metal bowls, clipped together one on top of the other, and a bag of rice. The bowls held chicken curry, pork curry and prawn curry. It was gourmet; the prawns were the sweetest, juiciest, loveliest things on no legs. I marvelled that such food could be rustled up out here. What a paradise if not for the war! He had got the food from a nearby village. Burmese people are well accustomed to assisting passing strangers without asking questions.

Through the day I hid. At night we walked. I began to worry about my stamina, never renowned for it. I thought of Jeremy, my twin. He was back in the UK doing commando training, setting records for assault courses and endurance runs. I wished I had a bit of his athleticism. Fortunately the walking phase was over.

As I emerged from my hideaway one evening we made our way to a river bank. The final hours would be by boat; there were no army checkpoints on these rivers. A couple of lads from a nearby village were with us for the evening. They asked me if I wanted beer. How very astute of them. I gave them some money that they did not want and they ran off to get two big bottles. When they returned the two villagers and I shared the first bottle. I picked up the second and was alarmed when I saw the filthy label. It was port. My goodness! A litre of port! I ummed and ahed for a few seconds but decided against it. Sharing a final beer was all well and good, but this was not the time and the place to get rattled on port. With great reluctance we put it aside and made our farewells. One villager and I left in the boat, the other returned home.

I got to thinking about that bottle of port about two years later when I was in prison. It would have been beer after all, but just rebottled into an old port bottle, the label remaining. Damn, could have had the second one after all.

I lay down in the narrow wooden boat, not taking any chances of being seen, even though it was night. The villager paddled us downstream. He stopped by the banks at one point, clinging on to an overhanging branch as the boat swayed in and out of the current. There were lights and voices on both sides of the shore ahead. Was it a *Tatmadaw* camp? I became increasingly nervous. Twice I hallucinated, thinking I saw a huge soldier glaring at me from the murk, brandishing armfuls of guns. Twice I literally had to bite my tongue to stop myself screaming out. I really thought I was about to be shot. After an age we regained the current and paddled on.

The following morning the first rains came down. It was torrential but fortunately this meant we could not be seen. Just after dawn we pulled into some reeds. I scrambled in to shore and hid among them, the villager disappeared for twenty minutes. He returned with beef curry. We got back into the boat and the river widened dramatically as we joined the Salween. By keeping to the middle nobody on the shore would be able to see the colour of my skin. I could afford to sit up and scoff a little curry.

Nevertheless, we were taking no chances. After that I lay back down beneath a blanket with a bamboo hat over my head and an old sack partially covering my feet. The rain had stopped and I had one ankle exposed to the sun. It was being cooked. I was too wary of sitting up to straighten the sack. My ankle was in agony, I reckoned with third-degree burns (although I confess I do not know what that means). I was praying and praying for some relief, hardly able to breathe under all the covers. I could not speak Karen and the paddler could not speak English. I had no idea how long this would go on. Just as I thought I could not take another second of it, a huge dirty rain cloud came and blocked out the sun . . . thank You, God.

But soon we were ashore again. I asked no questions but took the cue to scramble into the bushes; on the muddy bank we were quite exposed. I leapt from the boat and sank to my knees in glutinous mud. What a disaster. I could hardly move, stuck there for all the world to see, my escort as alarmed as I was. I managed to haul myself along, leaving my flip-flops buried, and once again hid in the reeds and bushes.

My escort followed me and in a miracle of sign language he told me to wait there for forty minutes and then I could head off to Moulmein.

'Moulmein?' I asked, pointing around and then spreading my hands questioningly.

He pointed in four different directions; we were surrounded by it. Just as he turned to go I stopped him. He had walked with me through the darkness and then paddled me down the river. The last leg was sixteen hours of paddling with barely a break. You can imagine the tone of his muscles. If at any stage we had been caught he would certainly have been executed. We had made the trip almost in silence.

I had made a point of not asking people inside Burma about their backgrounds or even their names. What was the point of knowing this when you might soon be facing torture? But here was the bravest man I had ever met in the world. I wanted to remember him. I wanted to find him again when democracy came and see what on earth I could do to repay him for his courage.

People question whether what I do in Burma is sensible, they question whether the local people want it. The fact is that the local people have risked their lives to make it happen, and if after fifty years of war they judge that it is sensible I do not need anybody else's opinion.

'What is your name,' I asked in my best Burmese.

'Kublai.'

In fact he was not Karen, but along with a countryman of his I met on the border, he has made dear to me for ever one more of Burma's ethnic groups. We shook hands and smiled. Then he was gone.

It was a miracle that I found the centre of Moulmein. It is a huge, rambling place, the third-largest town in Burma (after Rangoon and Mandalay). I made my way through the forest and along the edges of paddy fields. I was covered in filth from the river bank, which would not help me pass as a tourist once in the town. I stopped in a flooded wood and balanced my kit on a tree stump. Then I stripped off and had a wash in the puddles around. It would have been a most awkward moment to be apprehended! The best plan I could come up with if it happened was to smile broadly and then ask, in the voice of an old colonial duffer, whether by any chance, 'You know the road to Mandalay?' I would still be grabbed and thrown in gaol but at least I would have a cracking after-dinner story to go with it. Better than flapping.

I heard the voices of children playing, so headed for them. Then I saw huts and the beginning of a track. I expected at any moment to be confronted by police or soldiers; foreigners were not allowed in these parts. I wandered down the track. Gradually there were more and more houses, the track began to flatten out, became a road and more and more eyes started following me. My boots were still covered in mud. I did not want anybody in town to notice that – tourists can only arrive in Moulmein by the airport. I stopped to clean them and a couple invited me into their yard to wash them there with a brush. They did not seem put out that I had emerged from the outskirts. But I did not want to draw attention to them so soon pressed on. By the time I got close to the end of the road, at the main street, there was a big crowd following me. They had worked out that something was up.

I was gasping with thirst and asked at a stall for water. They gave me a huge glass and would not let me pay. I asked which way the main market was. When the brightest one had deciphered my accent, they pointed in accord to the main street and off to the right. Just then a bus went past the junction. They shrieked after it and one man ran to stop it. I downed the remaining water, thanked them profusely and charged off after the bus.

It turned out to be just a few minutes to the centre and the bus stopped right beside the main market. I was terrified that someone would arrest me before I could begin demonstrating. How good was their MI? How alert were they? I made a quick survey of the market building: a concrete block, two storeys, and with courtyards within, quite busy but not quite right. I went out on to the streets and looked around the town. At last I had an idea of where to go: around the main block of four streets, then into the market for the last stand, waiting there to be arrested. I saw a couple of traffic policemen. They ignored me but it gave me a sense of urgency.

Deep breath. It had taken over seven months to bring myself to this moment. Beginning with hard work in Australia to earn the money, including the endless discussions to bring family onside, all the planning and researching to find out what was possible, the month in Thailand trying to make it happen and that fabulous but exhausting two weeks through the disputed territory. Ahead of me lay even harder months in a grim prison. This was my moment of freedom. To do just what I wanted to do.

CHAPTER 12

We may sometimes feel, in exasperation or despair, about ourselves . . .
that an entity so prone to error, so stuffed with illusion, is itself an
illusion. Iris Murdoch

I DUG THE CASSETTE recorder out of my bag, switched it on,
slung it over my shoulder with democratic songs blaring out
and took out a handful of stickers. The stickers showed a
picture of Min Ko Naing and called for his release. His real name
was Paw Oo Tun, but he had been given the legendary *nom de
guerre* 'Min Ko Naing', meaning 'Conqueror of Kings'. He was a
student leader, arrested on 23 March 1989 and sentenced to
twenty years solitary confinement for making 'anti-government'
(i.e. pro-democracy) speeches. He had won renown throughout
the previous year for his fearless stand against the military. In
public speeches to crowds of thousands he had said:

*Our brothers in the past sacrificed to topple this military dictatorship but
their demands were only met with violence, bullets and killing . . . We,
the people of Burma, have had to live without human dignity for twenty-
six years under an oppressive rule. We must end dictatorial rule in our
country . . . If we want to enjoy the same rights as people in other
countries we have to be disciplined, united and brave enough to stand up
to dictators. Let's express our sufferings and demands. Nothing is going
to stop us from achieving peace and justice in our country.*

Today, more than twelve years later, he is still in solitary confinement. In his words:

> *I will never die. Physically I might be dead, but many more Min Ko Naings will appear to take my place. As you know, Min Ko Naing can only conquer a bad king. If the ruler is good, we will carry him on our shoulders.*

The sticker I gave out also called for the release of all political prisoners, that the universities be reopened (they had been closed for most of the past ten years) and that the students be able to form a student union. One of the first things Ne Win had done in 1962 when he seized power was to dynamite the Student Union building, regardless of who might be inside, shoot dead an unknown number of protestors and lock up thousands. Ne Win could not cope with any kind of dissent. Only once in his life did he give a press conference. A question came that was not to his liking. The 'president' then overturned his table, stormed out ranting and never gave a press conference again.

At first I just dropped the stickers and cassettes on the floor, wanting to move quickly. If anyone wanted to pick them up they could. After a couple of minutes I began sticking them on lamp-posts, careful not to put them on the wall of a house or shop where the owner might be troubled for not immediately ripping them down. By the time I turned into the third street there was a crowd of delighted children skipping after me and begging for stickers. *Rather missed the point*, I thought, but I gave them a few, then decided I had to conserve the rest. Two disappointed children moped off, then started peeling the stickers down from lamp-posts behind me. 'No, no!' I shouted. They ran away giggling. I arrived at the market and did a few laps of the ground floor, saturating every pillar with stickers and handing them to locals who caught my eye. Half an hour after I had begun I started to worry that I would not be arrested. I sat down, shattered, in the middle of the central courtyard, music still playing, and hollered out a few things about freedom.

A large crowd was gathering but still no police. I spoke a little with the people around me and one man ran off to get me cigarettes and Sprite. I drank gratefully.

Then at last a grim character appeared. He looked dirty and exceedingly angry, dressed in plain clothes. I stood up. 'Give me one!' he demanded, pointing to the stickers.

'Sorry, chief, I don't have enough left.'

He scowled at me and immediately a gorgeous young woman appeared and put out her hand. She was so sweet, and determined to get a sticker. Young, fresh, playful, she was the antithesis of the obscene, joyless and politically constipated regime which sought to dominate her. I quickly gave her a sticker and smiled unapologetically at the nark. He fumed off. Seconds later uniformed police arrived.

The police wanted me to come with them but I refused. They tried to get the cassette player but I held it at arm's length behind my back. We had a minute's fun like that, then I signalled them to relax. I brought the tape recorder forward, ejected the tape, then tossed it over the heads of the crowd. The police grabbed the machine and tried to grab me. Their anger was very much tempered by a feeling of helplessness. For five minutes I argued: 'Am I being arrested? What am I being arrested for? What is the charge? What is the name of the arresting officer?'

'No, you are not arrested. Just come with us. Don't ask questions. You must come with us.'

Every now and then a couple of thugs tried to push the crowd back. They would hit the front row fiercely and the crush would reel back on all sides, seeming to go almost horizontal, then springing back immediately into place. What they were witnessing was more than unusual. Several jaws were hanging slack.

At last the police had had enough. They manhandled me out. The second-storey balcony of the market was ringed with 'spectators'. Altogether maybe 300 people had witnessed it all. Just as I left I shouted out 'democracy' at the top of my voice. I looked up and another girl caught my eye. She waved quickly, blushing and smiling. That really touched me. Just a small sign but it was enough confirmation that we were all on the same side.

Outside, I was surprised by the number of vans and motorbikes that were waiting, surrounded by milling police. I was directed to the back of a van and we were off.

CHAPTER 13

If only it were all so simple! If only there were evil people somewhere insidiously committing evil deeds, and it were necessary only to separate them from the rest of us and destroy them. But the line dividing good and evil cuts through the heart of every human being. And who is willing to destroy a piece of his own heart?   Aleksandr Solzhenitsyn

As SOON AS the police van drove away from the central market place, the smile disappeared from my face. It was important to look cheery while hundreds of Burmese locals were watching, but now it was just the junta and me, and I did not feel brave at all. There were four officers in the back of the van with me. None of them seemed to know what to do. I tried to enjoy the views of Moulmein – the sun setting over the sea, the houses and hills, the few people on the quiet streets – but my mind was elsewhere. Soon we arrived at the police compound.

I was taken to a crumbling brick building, made up of only two small rooms, and told to sit at a table. The bare walls were as dirty as the concrete floor, the wooden desk clear except for a couple of pens. On the other side was the smuggest-looking weasel I have ever seen, weak chin and sharp face. He was Than Nyunt, the head of the Thaton division of the MI services, thin, thirty-five and full of his own self-importance. About twenty other men were crowded around and outside the room. I was quite a novelty. Than Nyunt asked me who I was and I returned the question. He asked me where I was from and I told him 'planet earth'. He was not pleased.

One of the other officers had my kitbag. He emptied it contemptuously on to the filthy floor and he and several others began searching through my belongings. There was not much there. I had removed anything which might identify me, cutting the labels out of clothes and even throwing away a pen because it had 'made in Australia' written on it. They were surprised to find no passport. They searched me and then became more excited by the absence of any documents.

'How did you get here?' asked Than Nyunt.

'Who are you?' I responded.

'I am police.'

'Who made you a policeman?'

'?'

'Where do you get your authority?'

'I am police. You must answer my questions. What is your name and nationality?'

'Have I been arrested? On what charge have I been arrested?'

'No, you must answer *my* question. Where country are you from? You are American.'

'Have I been arrested?'

'I think you American.'

More and more men were coming and going. The atmosphere was uncertain but not yet threatening. I took out a cigarette and asked for a light. They let me smoke. I still had half a bottle of Sprite left and set about finishing it off, unsure of where my next drink might come from.

'Tell me your name,' Than Nyunt repeated. He was laughing, nervously and angrily.

'I am under no obligation whatsoever to answer your questions. You are not a policeman. You work for anti-constitutional terrorists. I will answer any question put to me by a police officer who has been appointed by Burma's elected government, the NLD. I need to go to the toilet. Can I go to the toilet?'

I did not need to go, but I wanted to find out what rights I still had. They led me out to the extremely dilapidated toilet. There were about twenty other buildings in the compound, all one-storey, getting more derelict towards the back. The toilet was filthy and the door would not shut. An officer was waiting outside, and kept peering in to see if I was trying to dig an escape tunnel. He hurried me up.

Back in the interrogation room Than Nyunt carried on: 'You are from South Africa, I know you are. Where is your passport? You are English.'

'Let's talk about human rights. Your soldiers are murdering thousands of Karen civilians. They burn down villages. They tell everyone that they have five days or even five hours to get out of the village and then they burn it down. If people are too old or too sick to move out, they burn them alive in their homes. Soldiers push broken bottles into the vaginas of young girls . . .'

'You must answer my questions. I am policeman. Where your passport? Where you been staying? What guest house?' He was more confused than angry.

'You are not a policeman. You have not told me if I have been charged . . .'

Than Nyunt raised his hand above my head to hit me. 'Answer!' he shouted. 'Where you from?' I flinched, but he did not hit me. 'You English. That is sure. You are an American. Where you from?'

'Let's talk about 1988. Thousands of civilians were shot by your regime. Housewives, nurses, schoolchildren, Buddhist monks bayoneted. . .'

'No! First you must to answer my questions!' His men were still bewildered, but he was beginning to get angry.

'No, 1988 happened before today, so let's deal with the first problem. Later we can talk about today. These were peaceful demonstrators . . .'

Than Nyunt grabbed a bottle and swung it down past my head as if to hit me. The bottle was plastic, which somewhat spoilt the intended effect.

'You are not a policeman. I have no obligation to answer your questions. I will answer an officer appointed by the NLD.'

Than Nyunt gathered his patience. 'Please tell me where you are from and how you arrived in Moulmein?'

'Do you mind if I smoke?'

'You can smoke.'

'Very kind of you.'

There was a pause to light the cigarette. Than Nyunt smiled. His men were searching my bag for the sixth time. They shook their heads – still nothing.

'Now, can you tell me to where you from and why have you cause disruption to our national peace and stability?' (His English was not very good but these were stock phrases from the regime's incessant propaganda.)

I smiled at him, took a long drag on the cigarette, certain that soon I would not be allowed to smoke at all. 'I will answer any question put to me by an officer who is appointed by Burma's elected government the NLD . . .'

Than Nyunt shot to his feet. 'Stand up!' he screamed, and for the third time drew back his hand as if to strike me. 'You must obey. I am government. You are guilty one.' He turned to his men and issued orders in Burmese. They surrounded me, told me to hand over my boots, belt, watch and anything else I had on me. I was surprised that they had not done this straight away. I had been grateful to keep my watch for that long. It was getting on for about seven o'clock, which meant I had to hold out for another eighteen hours if I was to give Kublai enough time to get away; I reckoned a day's grace would be enough.

Than Nyunt stormed off and the room emptied after him, and my kit too was taken away. A couple of guards stood outside but otherwise I was alone. So far so good. I had enjoyed making the point that the National League for Democracy was sovereign but I did not know how long the polite approach would last. I now had just my T-shirt and trousers. I sat there full of adrenalin and apprehension, but it was best to act unafraid. I put my head round the door and asked a guard for a smoke. He did not know what to do, but assumed that I would not have asked if it were not allowed. Should he hate me or be polite to me? He gave me a smoke.

Eventually the mob returned. This time a middle-aged, well-fed man sat opposite me. He was wearing very casual clothes. 'Good evening.'

'Good evening.'

Pause.

'Will you tell me your name?' He was very friendly.

'Who are you?'

'I am an NLD sympathiser. I have just . . .'

'A what?'

'I am an NLD sympathiser. I have just come from the golf course.' He beamed. His English accent was good. 'Look, you can see that I have just come from the golf course.' He waved his hand down his body to indicate the polo shirt and slacks. Certainly very casual, certainly fine golfing clothes, but was this supposed to turn me?

'What do you mean an NLD sympathiser?' I asked. 'Do you agree that the National League for Democracy won the election in 1990?'

He smiled uncomfortably.

'Do you agree that they won eighty-two per cent of the seats, that they are Burma's rightful government, and that since then the military junta have exiled, imprisoned and murdered hundreds of Burma's elected representatives?' He reminded me of the 'Indian businessman' brought in during my Rangoon interrogation: intelligent and civil, but utterly full of deceit.

'Look, I sympathise with the NLD. Many people do . . .'

'Are you a member of the NLD?'

'No, I am not a member. I am a sympathiser. I have just come from the golf course. I was playing a game of golf. They asked me to come and speak with you.' He seemed very pleased that he was a golfer. Golf was the favourite game of the generals, to show how modern they were. 'Where is your passport?'

'Do you sympathise with U Win Tin? He is an NLD member, has been in prison since 1989. He is an innocent man. He is now sick, very sick but is being denied proper medical attention. He could die. Do you sympathise with him?'

The golfer looked at me sourly. We carried on like this for a while and then again the room emptied for a conference of war. The Sprite was finished. I smiled at the guards. They looked away. I sighed, smiled again and they smiled back.

I wondered how long this would last. Yet another man came. He looked more unsure than the last, and a good deal uglier. He announced that he too was an NLD sympathiser.

'No, you're not,' I retorted. 'I saw you in the next room ages ago. You're one of them.' I hitched my thumb towards the bunch of police and other officials. I looked at him sternly, but I was half bluffing, not sure if I had really seen him in the crowd. The bluff worked, he plodded out, looking foolish.

Next time the mob returned they were triumphant. 'Stand up!' someone barked, 'hands behind your back!' I saw the handcuffs and my stomach churned. They were getting serious. The cuffs were put on painfully tight and I was led out to a cell in another building. There was a pithy sign above the cell door, for some reason in English. It said that the guilty man would burn whether he confessed or not and therefore he might as well confess. Strange.

Inside the cell there was nothing but a bamboo mat. I sat down on it and was relieved to see them all go. Would they leave me now? Of course not. Moments later they opened up the room again and half a dozen men poured in. I had already stood up, I felt too vulnerable on the ground. They told me to turn round and face the back wall. I did it and grew increasingly nervous. There was some activity behind me; one man had a stick. They were doing something, building something or maybe moving some equipment into the room. I could not tell what was going on, but it was accompanied by giggles and laughter. Eventually they told me to turn round and I wondered what terrible instrument of torture would await me.

In fact, there was nothing. One man had a ruler and – wanting to measure my height – they had been marking off foot-long intervals on the wall. I suppose they had started laughing when they got to five foot and then had to do another; Burmese, of course, are not generally so tall. The real fun would have begun when another wit suggested they mark off seven feet.

They worked out that I was six foot one and a bit, but before I could relax they produced a blindfold. That surprised me. Although extremely nervous, I was also curious to know what they would do. Ideally, they would sit me down with a judge and we could argue the toss about sovereignty. That would at least mean there was some sense in the regime; that they were willing to talk, if not to listen. But that was a far-off dream.

The blindfold smelt of petrol, which immediately saps your resolve. It was no longer the question of a dreamer wondering: 'Could I hold out under torture?' Now there was a stark choice: 'Shall I tell them my name or risk having my face burnt off?' I was led out to the front of the compound, sharp stones cutting my bare feet. There was a van with its engine running and as I was bundled into the back I heard the voice of some Igor-type creature shout 'Torture!' following it with a shamelessly melodramatic laugh, which began deep and ended hysterically. I tried to climb on to one of the benches, which I had felt down the side of the van, but was pushed to the cold metal floor. We set off into the night and I have never been so terrified in my life. There was no turning back. This bizarre situation was not a dream. It was real. And I had no one but myself to blame.

I prayed and prayed like a mantra, 'Dear God, please be with me now. Dear Jesus, please help me now. Dear God, please be with me now.' I wanted the journey to last for ever, but it was over in no time. Still blindfolded, I was taken into another compound. As we got out there were lots of voices and footsteps. I was led into what felt like a huge building, but I later discovered was the very poky reception area of Moulmein prison. We sat down in a side room and the blindfold was removed.

Old faces, new faces, too many for me to keep track of. A senior-looking man, who turned out to be the prison governor, asked me my name and nationality. I gave the usual response.

Then they brought out their trump card. He was an elderly gentleman, dressed in a *longyi* and collared check shirt, with very dark skin below his frizz of white hair. He was the best-spoken person I have ever heard. 'Good evening to you,' he said in perfect BBC English. 'May I have the pleasure of knowing whom I am addressing?'

I fairly laughed. 'Could you tell me who you are?' I enquired politely.

'Certainly,' he answered with a smile. 'My name is U Maung Maung. I am party secretary for the National League for Democracy in Mon state.'

That was most unlikely to be true. It was not that I would have to answer his questions anyway; so long as I was taking the constitutional line I would say I was still waiting to meet a proper policeman or judge. But if somehow this chap really were NLD I did not want to offend him, indeed, I would want to worship him. So I dragged out the conversation a bit and the situation became clear. He was getting terribly confused between 'them' and 'us', did not know where he stood and had absolutely no interest in anything except my name and nationality. He was working for the regime alone, so I told him that I did not believe he was NLD.

They were getting increasingly exasperated but were obviously wary of physically hurting me. They would have no such doubts over a local, but interrogating a foreigner was uncharted territory. An official who makes a mistake in Burma is cruelly punished, unless, of course, he can pass the blame on to his underlings and cruelly punish them. Usually both things happen: a storm of rage from the top causes punishments to rain down right to the bottom of the hierarchy. They decided to have one more try.

This time they brought a young man to me. He was dressed in a white *longyi* and shirt. This was prisoners' uniform. As a nice touch he was also wearing handcuffs and I was told that he was NLD Youth and yes, indeed, a prisoner. They seemed to have missed my point about introducing me to someone with authority from the sovereign government, but I was keen to learn as much as I could and to drag things out for as long as possible. It was now approaching nine in the evening. I had to give Kublai sixteen more hours.

I was immediately suspicious because this 'prisoner' looked so clean and healthy. He was wearing immaculate clothes and the handcuffs on him were not tight like mine or fastened behind his back, but were two jolly dangling bracelets out front. Supposedly he could speak no English, so U Maung Maung translated with his usual eloquence.

The 'prisoner' wanted to impress upon me that he had been foolish to believe in the NLD and that now he saw how the junta were truly the loving leaders of Burma. I asked him what subject he had studied at university. This shook him; he had certainly never been to university, but wanting to maintain his NLD Youth cover he eventually said history. I thought of asking him a history question to see what he knew, but the syllabus in Burma has been destroyed and twisted by the regime anyway. I asked him what university he had gone to. U Maung Maung had noticed his stumbling on the last question and, not realising that I understood some Burmese, translated, 'What university did you go to? Say Rangoon.'

I clapped my hands in delight and told them they were all frauds. It might have been more professional to carry on talking, but I wanted to come across as a straightforward guy. The two sloped out and immediately I heard the handcuffs being removed and the 'prisoner' launching into an excited jabbering of what had happened. His demeanour had changed completely; he was obviously talking to colleagues rather than to his gaolers. I could not believe they had even tried such feeble ruses, never mind having botched them so completely. Anyway, they were tired of it too. It was time for harsher methods.

The blindfold went back on. I was told to stand. I could hear them circling round me and questions came intermittently from different directions, sometimes right in my ear, sometimes far away, slightly disorientating. 'What's your name?' 'Where are you from?' 'How did you get to Moulmein?' 'Where is your passport?'

From now on I answered only, 'I am sorry, I cannot answer that question.' The British army recommend that you add 'sir'. The idea is to hold out for twenty-four hours so that the military situation on the ground has changed sufficiently and all information you have is out of date anyway. Although I was not a soldier and Kublai had asked me to give him just forty minutes to get away, I was determined to give him twenty-four hours.

One of the men had a towel, which he twisted into a rope and began flicking next to my cheeks. Then he hit me in the stomach with it and then the genitals. Blindfolded and with my hands behind my back, I felt totally vulnerable, at their mercy. I was not allowed to sit, not allowed to eat or drink. I was already exhausted from the two-week trek from the border. It did not take long before I began to get dizzy.

Whispered questions and accusations continued. 'You are CIA,' which surprised me. 'You MI6.' Did they really think that possible? 'You CIA, I know you CIA.' Later on it got even more ridiculous. 'You KGB, MOSSAD. Sure, you are KGB.' I laughed, but it was a real worry that they could be so stupid as even to think it.

Occasionally one of them would kick the back of my knees to see how weak my legs were. I would gladly have fallen over and pretended to sleep, but I doubted they would stop there. Still not sure if they should hurt me, one of them found a cat and wiped its anus down my arm. This caused them great amusement. I told them to let the poor animal go. Each time the towel flicked into me my body jumped. I wondered what would happen if I fell and soon found out. Fists and feet came from everywhere and I was hauled back up. They were not vicious blows, but they were frightening.

One guard then took a pen and started probing with it between my knuckles. My whole body tensed since I knew what was coming. Torture does not require elaborate medieval apparatus. An accomplished torturer does not even need a pen. I squeezed my fists as tight as possible but eventually the pen was prised between two of my fingers. The guard gripped my fingers in his hand and began slowly to squeeze. I do not know how painful that sounds but the reality is excruciating. Your knuckles are in agony and certainly feel as if they soon must break. And when you are blindfolded you do not want to take one step from where you are, not knowing what will happen if you do. I was rooted to the spot.

As the pressure grew I began talking about why I had come, slamming the junta for human rights abuses and insisting that I was under no obligation to answer their questions. I began shouting louder and louder and just as my fingers were about to break I hollered out at the top of my voice, 'For justice and FREEDOM!' Suddenly the pain stopped. They had become nervous. I had probably woken up a quarter of Moulmein. The pen was removed.

Unable to stand any longer I passed out. Kicks and punches woke me and again I was hauled to my feet. More blows in the genitals and the guard with the pen kept prodding it into my knuckles to remind me what he could do. He was enjoying it. Later he would just click the pen by my ears so that I could not forget it.

There were light moments. The blindfold kept slipping down. I could feel it loosening and would warn them that it was about to go. Strangely I felt sorry for them that they could not even get that right. Fortunately it meant that I was frequently able to look at the clock so could focus on how long I had to last. Sometimes I would roll my head around as if in terrible distress but in fact I was glancing out of the bottom of the blindfold at the clock. I was hoping that the BBC would have broadcast news of my arrest and that they could get my name that way. Then I could begin talking to them, having made the point of not volunteering my name.

Handcuffs make you feel defenceless. With your arms behind your back every itch becomes a problem. You cannot scratch yourself, you cannot wipe your runny nose, you cannot wipe the sweat from your brow. Not at all brutal, but distressing; you feel helpless.

The night wore on and I passed out again. The next thing I remember is sitting cross-legged. Again I could just see straight down below the blindfold. There was a huge cockroach on my leg. This caused much merriment for the one who had put it there. He was trying to urge it up my trouser leg. I wondered if I should shake it off, but then they would know I could see. In any case it flew away.

I asked for water and they refused. I was not allowed to go to the toilet. Then began the 'iron road'. This is a favourite tactic of Burma's MI. The victim sits or lies with his legs straight out and an iron or bamboo rod is rolled up and down the shins with increasing pressure. Done long enough it will strip you to the bone. In my case a senior officer must have signalled them to stop before it went too far. After that they tickled my feet for half an hour. I could not believe it. Here was the brutal and heartless Military Intelligence torturing their victim . . . by tickling his feet. But as the idea was sleep deprivation it was completely effective. My left foot was being held down and tickled, my right foot was being stabbed with a bamboo cane.

I asked again for water and this time a cup was brought to my lips. I sucked at it greedily but they would not tilt it back, I was gulping only air. Ever so slowly they tilted it back and I sucked away until it was horizontal – still no water. This was just their little joke.

When you are being tortured it is not so much the pain that beats you as your own fear. I was uncomfortable and exhausted, but only rarely in pain, and then not often excruciating. But I began to wonder: what if they extinguish a cigarette on me? I could bear it on my body. But in my ear? On my eye? What if they spread my legs and one of them grinds a testicle under his heel? What if they make me squat naked and light a candle under my scrotum? Surely it was not worth keeping back my name in the face of that – after all, the BBC was bound (I prayed) to be broadcasting it soon anyway?

But I did not want to give in. I really wanted to make the point to them that they had no authority, that the junta were illegal and that no one on earth has the right to torture another.

I do not remember how often I passed out. One time I was kneeling down and asked for a cigarette. It was nearly morning and to my great surprise a cigarette was placed between my lips. My heart leapt as I thought they were changing tack again. Perhaps someone in Rangoon had ordered a softer approach. I waited for a few moments until it dawned on me – no light. I considered eating the cigarette just to annoy them, but spat it out instead.

The next thing I remember is waking up in another room. I had insisted on being allowed to go to the toilet and I thought to myself that perhaps this was where I had been taken next. In the toilet there was no water or paper to clean oneself – with pretty unpleasant consequences for one's clothes. I was lying on the floor covered in sweat and grime, my trousers soiled with blood and shit. I felt utterly awful. As I opened my eyes I saw two men looking down on me. They were in civilian clothes, MI officers, probably sergeants. As they caught my eye I was filled with dread. I so much wanted to sleep and now I had let them know I was awake. But they did nothing. They let me close my eyes again. They let me sleep a while.

But I had to get up before the sun and was again made to stand up although there was no strength left in me. I wondered if it would really hurt for me to tell them my name and nationality. A soldier should give name, rank and number, but again, I was not a soldier, I was trying to make a political point.

How does torture work? It is not all brutality and pain. Half the task of a torturer is to make you feel irrational for holding out. And sure enough, when you are thoroughly exhausted and desperate for food or sleep, it is hard to think clearly. Sometimes they would sigh and pout, bring in a reasonable fellow who said that all they wanted was my name and nationality and then they would give me all the food and sleep I wanted. They complain that you are making their lives difficult, that they are tired too, that they have wives and children to go back to.

It was approaching midday. Since dawn they had not really hurt me. They seemed content to just let me stand there, handcuffed and blindfolded. Probably I spent a lot of time sitting down as well. The situation began to seem silly. I began to feel silly too. I was wiped out, I felt alone. Had news got out to the outside world? Did the British embassy know about my arrest yet? How long would it be before they put someone more cultivated than Than Nyunt in charge?

If I could wait just two more hours I would have given Kublai his time. I would be disappointed that I had had to back down on my principle of not giving my name. I would have preferred for them to get it from the media like last time and then I would have said, 'OK, let's talk.' After all, we had much to talk about and I could not argue the case for democracy with my mouth shut. But my principle now seemed irrelevant and petty. I just wanted something to drink, somewhere to sleep. I could start talking now and easily delay two hours before mentioning how I had got to Moulmein. That was my way out. I began to cry, only for about one or two minutes, but the kind of tears you just cannot stop or control.

I would tell them my name, I said, I would tell them my nationality, if only they would promise that I could then immediately contact my embassy in Rangoon. Certainly, they said. I asked again and again for confirmation. It came from the top. Of course I could talk to my embassy, only first tell them . . .

'James Mawdsley, dual citizenship, Britain and Australia.'

Everyone sighed.

I was wrong to start speaking. I should have held out, been less fearful. But I had forgotten God, I had ceased praying. It was to be – however – perfect training for the next time.

CHAPTER 14

The crucible is for silver and the furnace for gold, but the Lord tests hearts.

Proverbs 17:v:3

A NINE-DAY INTERROGATION began. I told them enough truth to be plausible; after all, I wanted them to believe everything I said about the human rights atrocities along the border. But I was always vague over details, or else changed them. The last thing I was going to do was give them names other than the three people who said they did not give a hoot. Brigadier Htin Maung could not care less if they knew we had met, and Thu Rein, who introduced us, actually wanted me to mention his name to raise his profile.

To cover all the rest I invented a character called Naing Gyaw who was supposed to have arranged everything for me in all my involvement with Burma. (Later on the *New Light of Myanmar* vilified the 'terrorist usurper Naing Gyaw'.)

I was inspired by the memoirs of a British officer who had been there during the war. A Japanese interrogator demanded: 'You are an officer. You must know. What towns and villages did you come through?'

The Brit responded, 'We avoided all towns and marched on a compass bearing all the way.'

In his awe of these hardy folk, the interrogator swallowed the story. But if he had spent any time marching through the jungle he would know it was absolute nonsense. Wingate, the visionary

British officer who established the Chindits, might have planned that his men would never use roads or tracks while moving behind enemy lines. But when they met the reality of the Burmese jungle they thought bugger that, we will walk on the roads and if we meet the enemy then we meet the enemy. They had guns and were, after all, some of the most outstanding soldiers in the world.

The point was, you should not ascribe intelligence to interrogators that they do not have. You can get away with a remarkably vague memory.

The interrogation had stalled when they began asking about my friends. I refused to speak, so the handcuffs went back on. But relations cannot have been too bad because I remember that I was sitting down and allowed to smoke.

A young man with a huge mouth and a stylish tuft of hair sprouting from a mole on his chin sat beside me. He was extremely nervous. 'I am English teacher,' he explained. 'I am here for translate.' And it was probably true. 'You must answer their questions,' explained the English teacher.

'They are a terrorist regime,' I told him, 'I don't have to answer their questions.' The poor interpreter was terrified. How was he supposed to translate these unspeakable things? He was more afraid to talk than I was and he was just the interpreter!

'Can you tap my ash?' I mumbled, twitching the cigarette conspicuously. My hands were cuffed behind my back. The interpreter reached out for my cigarette to knock the ash off. His hands were trembling even more than his voice. I was shocked.

He left after about half an hour. He gave a great nervous laugh to the assembled MI and asked them if he might be able to put up a few posters in town advertising his tuition classes. Silence ensued. The poor man laughed even louder and scuttled out. So strange how business works under that regime. Do them a favour and maybe they will let you advertise your business . . . but not this time.

I protested against the imprisonment of Min Ko Naing. I said he was an innocent man who loved Burma, and he was one of Burma's bravest.

Than Nyunt laughed. 'Min Ko Naing is die,' he said with

venom and all his colleagues joined in the laughter. That unbalanced me. It was terrible to see. They were laughing about the death of one of their country's most exceptional men. It turned out to be a lie.

'Why do you hate the ABSDF?' I asked Than Nyunt in gentle desperation.

'Because they are anti-government,' he shot back immediately and very satisfied. But that means nothing. It has nothing to do with truth or justice or what issues and rights people are fighting for. Than Nyunt only thought in terms of power: 'us' who have power, and 'them' who would take it off us. He did not conceive of the students as oppressed people fighting for a chance to live with dignity and liberty. They were just enemies. Anyone who challenged the regime was an enemy, and therefore to be destroyed. But to destroy innocent people one has to be capable of hating them and that is why Daw Aung San Suu Kyi says: 'You cannot fear people you do not hate; fear and hate go hand in hand.' The regime are frightened of the people, so desperately frightened that they hate them and in hating them they are blind to the inhumanity of their actions. Their own lust for power is destroying not the people of Burma, but themselves and anybody else who joins them in hating.

They also boasted 'the NLD is crush'. I am not sure how sinister that sounds; perhaps we are all too jaded by Hollywood. But these men were insane. They were laughing and bragging about the imprisonment and murder of Burma's elected representatives.

Sad, also, that many of them did not mean it. They were following the lead of Than Nyunt, and he was just falling into line with what his superiors expected. Surely they had to be terrified of something in order to sacrifice their souls like that.

My interrogators also asked a great number of questions about my background, such as which primary school I had been to. I was happy to tell them. Igor – whose demented voice I recognised – the major with the mutilated jaw and love of torture, had been questioning me for some time. I decided to ask him a few questions. 'Are you married?' I asked.

'Yes.'

'Any children?'

'Yes.'

'How many?'

Without pausing and in an absolute deadpan monotone he responded, 'Seven thousand.'

He did not look at me to see how I reacted, he was not joking, not boasting – he just stated it. It was one of the scariest moments of my life. I was already very wary of this creature and did not like being alone in a room with him. When he said that I felt for sure he was a loony. I was grateful when others came in. But their news was distressing.

'Immigration,' said one, 'that's what you in for. Minimum of three years.' I did not want to do more than six months and here they were telling me the statutory minimum was three years.

Eventually, on the third day, I was taken to a cell in the prison. It was about 8 × 15 feet and perhaps twenty feet high. There were no windows, no escaping through the roof. Beyond the barred door was a small courtyard with a wooden door so that one's isolation was complete. Inside the cell was a wooden pallet to sleep on, a pot for a toilet and a jar of water just outside the door with a cup for drinking water.

The heat inside was unbearable, the dirt and smell more than uncomfortable. If ever I lay down on the pallet bedbugs would start on me and mosquitoes joined them. There was no way I could sleep. By morning my whole torso and arms and shins were covered in bites, my skin more red than white. On one wall was a set of three iron brackets, two spread apart for one's ankles and one at waist level. I thought with horror of how it must be for Burmese prisoners who are chained up in their cells and for extra punishment chained to the wall. I was going frantic even though I could pace around my cell! And I had taken to heart the jibe about three years. The idea of that was terrifying.

When food came it was brought by a guard and another prisoner, the cook. There was rice with some oily vegetables and low-grade *ngapi* (fish paste). Later, when the cook found it uneaten he was upset. 'You don't like my cooking?' he asked sorrowfully, bowing his shiny bald head. I felt dreadful. As if his life were not wretched enough already and here was I giving the impression that I was too good for his food. The truth was that I was too scared to have an appetite.

I did manage to keep a brave face in front of my captors, but inside, and when I was alone I was devastated. Two incidents helped me. The first was an MI guy. He came to my cell to check up on me, and whether or not he knew what effect the news would have on me he said, 'Everyone in Rangoon and Moulmein is talking about you.'

I held my hand to my ear as if holding a radio and asked, 'BBC?'

He nodded. This was a massive relief. It meant that the ABSDF had done their good work and made sure that there was someone in Moulmein who witnessed what had happened, had relayed it to Thailand and the ABSDF could make press releases. It was too late, then, for the junta to pretend I did not exist, or to claim that I had disappeared in the jungle. It meant they now had to keep me alive and in one piece.

The second incident was at the dead of night. A guard came into the courtyard outside my cell and produced a steaming cup of coffee and four slices of sugared toast. He was nervous, his movements shaky. I could not eat the toast as my mouth was too dry. If it was found the guard would be cruelly punished so I had to give it back to him. The gulped coffee, though, was delicious. I showed him my arms, which were red with bites.

'I am sorry,' he said under his breath, hanging his head. He sounded as if he was about to cry. He was ashamed for what his country was doing.

That show of sympathy went a long way. I cannot say how far. It restored me. I could focus again on why I was here and recall to myself that I always knew it was going to be hard; I should not be surprised now that it was. After he left, still unable to sleep, I began singing 'How Great Thou Art'. My voice got louder and louder until I was belting it out. I could feel strength coming back to me; I was not going to bow yet. A gaggle of guards came running and told me to be quiet. They were excited and afraid. I sang to the end of the song, congratulated myself on my defiance, then crumpled back into bleakness.

I cannot catalogue the lies and dirty tricks they used during the interrogation. It really was shameless. They refused to let me have any contact with embassy staff or notify anybody as to where I was, saying that the telephone was not working!

On day four they brought in the top judge of Mon State, of which Moulmein is the capital. He was a weedy little man and clearly rich – his robes were good quality, his hair was neatly styled and his face was pampered. He had brought along his obese spoilt son, dressed in Manchester football strip, to gawp at the subversive foreigner. 'I will be the judge at your trial,' he told me.

'I want to speak to someone who understands Burmese law,' I replied. 'I want to speak to a lawyer.'

'I will be your lawyer,' he told me.

'But you're the judge.'

'Yes,' he said happily, 'I will be the judge *and* your defence lawyer.'

'You cannot. That is illegal.' I could hardly believe that I had to say it.

A policeman interrupted, there was a brief consultation and the bemused judge left. I never saw him again.

Shortly after that, as I sat in the prison office, it seemed that they had run out of questions. They said I was free to go. What were they on about?

'C'mon,' said a senior policeman, 'let us go into town and enjoy some coffee and cake in a teashop.'

I was somewhat perplexed but sure enough the door was open and they were indicating that I walk out. About twelve men followed, but they kept a few feet away from me. They pointed to the prison gates. 'Go on. Come on, let's go into town.'

As we approached the gates a photographer took some snaps. Just before we reached them one bright spark shouted out in Burmese, 'Hold on, chaps. No need to go to town. We've got coffee and cakes inside!'

The boys blocked off the gates and indicated that I should turn round. How bizarre I thought. Then I saw the photographer again. He was snapping away and a huge grin appeared on my face as I realised with incredulity what they were doing. They just wanted a photo of me walking free. What were they going to do? Put a caption in the paper: 'Brit Prisoner Has Tiffin with Gov'nor'?

Then I laughed and smiled even more as I realised how stupid I was to be laughing and smiling at the camera. What would the next caption be? 'Brit Prisoner Laughs at Suggestion of Maltreatment'.

In any case my time in Moulmein was over. I had tried never to be hostile to them. I wanted them to trust my word so that they might believe the democracy movement was honourable. They did not have to admit it, but I wanted to colour their hearts. In the beginning they repeatedly called me a 'fool' or a 'liar' or a 'coward'. By the end, some of them would find quiet moments to tell me I was 'brave' and 'intelligent' and even 'good man'. But now Rangoon wanted to deal with this. On the morning of day five I left Moulmein handcuffed in the back of a tiny car with four guards. One of them bought me two boiled eggs on a ferry over the river. Wonderful! I could have eaten 200. Although we were fearfully cramped in our tiny vehicle, Than Nyunt drove ahead alone in a spacious estate. He was showing everyone who was boss. I was delighted when our car broke down and we could get out to stretch our legs. Soon after we were in Thaton, about fifty kilometres north of Moulmein. Here we drove into Than Nyunt's compound. He was the district head of MI. His compound was large with a big black satellite dish for communications. I was not expecting what followed.

Than Nyunt had radioed ahead and organised a banquet lunch. I was guest of honour. Before eating I said I wanted to change my clothes – the same ones I had been wearing since the banks of the Salween. I was given my bag and tipped it on to the floor. There was little there. I picked out the least offensive *longyi* and T-shirt (smellwise) and noticed my phrase book was missing. 'Where is my phrase book?' I asked. Surprisingly, Than Nyunt sent a man back to Moulmein to get it.

For lunch Than Nyunt sat at the head, I sat at his right and three of his buddies crowded round the far end of the table. We ate on a veranda with people in attendance to bring more dishes and one personally to waft the flies from my food. There was an abundance of it, top quality, many varieties. I did not want to lose my dignity so tried to restrain myself. Maybe I should have turned my nose up at it altogether but I got stuck in. I am afraid my hunger overtook my disgust with the way everyone fawned about the man with power.

'My wife,' said Than Nyunt appeasingly, and nodding towards one of the attendants. I smiled civilly. We set off again for Rangoon, this time in Than Nyunt's chauffer-driven brand-spanking-new air-conditioned four-wheel drive. My heart was aching as I saw the landscape go by, so beautiful. In Pegu was a tree with astonishing bright orange blossom. I have never seen anything like it, before or after. We drove through small villages and I got my first glimpses of central, rural Burma. Mostly the ground was flat and I do not remember many trees. The roads were almost empty and the land looked dusty dry. If the regime had not worn the landscape out, then the hot season certainly had. Nevertheless, I sat transfixed, glued to every scene and aware that I was glimpsing forbidden views. We passed through several army checkpoints as well as construction projects and road-widening schemes; women and children breaking rocks or carrying steaming baskets of pitch; soldiers standing about as we went past. Every time I saw a person I felt a rush of excitement. *There* was someone who knew so much about this regime, someone who could explain so much to me about living in Burma, except that I still had not learnt to speak Burmese and of course I was being whisked through the country by the police and there was no way they would ever let me mingle with the locals.

The driver believed he was king of the road, racing down the middle and forcing oncoming traffic to swerve on to the dirt. At one stage, though, we got stuck behind a huge rumbling truck. It was mulling along at about thirty and our driver was livid. He could not go to the left, he could not fit round the right. He hammered on his horn. Eventually the road widened and we could overtake the heaving mirrorless truck. I tried to catch the driver's expression, hoping he knew we were there and that this was his little piece of political defiance. Who knows?

Our driver knew his place, though. A massive army lorry, bristling with soldiers, came hurtling towards us. Our driver yanked us out of their way. The MI might be more feared than the army, but none of them argues with brute force.

As we got closer and closer to Rangoon Than Nyunt became more and more placatory, more and more nervous. He was gripping the sides of his seat in tension, sweating buckets in the cool car, and twisting his body round to look at me from the passenger seat. Eventually he came out with it.

'What will you tell your ambassador?' He was terrified of the punishment he was going to get for torturing a foreigner. He looked so weak, so afraid.

'Don't worry,' I assured him, 'I will tell the truth, but I will not get you into trouble.'

I had enjoyed the drive. I wanted it to last for ever. But by sundown we reached Insein prison, Rangoon. We passed through several gates and checkpoints, the prison itself set hundreds of metres back from the main road. I was led from the vehicle and for one short moment abandoned, no one beside me. I looked off to my left and saw a prisoner shuffling towards me. He was dressed in the white prison *longyi* and shirt, his legs and waist in chains. His back was bent, his head to one side and eyes lowered. Then he noticed me. He stopped shuffling. There was the most painful question on his face. Yet his eyes seemed to have died. There was no life in them, no brightness . . . and I was whisked on into the main building.

I was told to sit on a chair in the middle of a large empty room and left alone for a while. Eventually a dozen men filed in, pretty senior ones judging by their spangly uniforms. They formed a semicircle in front of me and just gaped. They did not have a clue what to do and they looked on me with incredulous distaste.

'*Mingalaba!*' I said cheerily to break the ice. Straight away half of them broke into smiles. One of them offered me a cigarette. I took it.

'*Say leippya khwep shi day la* [Do you have an ashtray]?' I asked. They were delighted that I could speak Burmese. I was showing off, really, no intention of telling them that I knew hardly anything else. But neither did I want to give the impression that I was a complete alien, or utterly ignorant of their country. I had been expecting something more to happen, perhaps someone might tell me what was going on, but that was it. They all filed out and then I was taken, with a hood over my head, for a 640-step walk to my cell.

Over the next four days the interrogation continued. Often it went on all through the night, sessions ending after dawn. The officers conducting it used to complain to me that they were tired, that they had families to go to, could I not just answer their questions? But when it came to names of people I knew, again I drew the line.

'Do you know Aung Thu Nyein?' asked an MI major.

'Who is he?' I asked, feigning ignorance. 'A Burmese general?' They had a chuckle at my mistake.

'Tell us who you know in Thailand,' the major persisted.

'I am afraid that if I tell you then you will hurt them,' I said.

'Oh!' they protested jovially, 'we will not hurt them!'

'Oh yeah? Look at me!' – referring to the blood on my wrists from the handcuffs and the torture in general. Oddly enough they took the point and did not persist. Had I been Burmese the sticks would have come out. On the eighth day they were finished and they told me my trial would be coming up.

The British and Australian embassies were pushing for consular access. For the first four days the Burmese authorities denied they even had me, or knew anything about it at all. Then, up to day seven they claimed that I was still in Moulmein. When a British consular official insisted on boarding a plane to Moulmein to see me the authorities finally admitted that I was in Rangoon. Still I did not have any contact with them until day twelve, seconds before my trial began.

I had been wearing the same clothes for a week and had not been allowed to shave, so did not exactly cut a dash in the courtroom. The two ambassadors had insisted they be allowed to speak to me before the trial began. We were given two minutes. Their expressions were fairly grim. I think they were not at all pleased to see me again or looking forward to the headaches ahead.

They asked if I had been maltreated. I told them about the pens stuck between my fingers and the knuckles squeezed until they nearly broke. Unfortunately, perhaps because we were so rushed, the British officials misunderstood. They thought I had had pins pushed under my fingernails and they sent that message back to my family. Very distressing.

I had time to shake hands with a lawyer who accompanied them but no time to talk. The 'trial' began. What a load of nonsense. There was a crowd of about forty uniformed goons watching, with one white face in it. Reportedly this was Burma's first open trial in ten years. Open to whom? Only those hand picked by officials.

There was a woman from the Ministry of Foreign Affairs translating. She was pretty and sweet and absolutely full of lies. Initially I faced a charge of being a mercenary, which meant twenty-five years in prison. As all my involvement with Burma had been utterly non-violent and as I had never been paid a penny for it, this was ridiculous. Behind the scenes diplomatic pressure convinced the junta to drop that accusation. The embassy staff were very kind, they were concerned and they were very professional. But we had completely different agendas. I believe them to be the best in the world at their job – protecting British interests abroad – but that did not extend to democracy, at least, not enough.

The junta lessened the charge. A couple of policemen from Moulmein testified that they had seen me there and arrested me for illegal entry. How were they supposed to know I was there illegally? They could not possibly find that out just by looking.

I was given the opportunity to ask them questions. 'Do you know the Karen have been on their land for over 2600 years?' I asked. 'Much longer than the Burmans, and as they welcomed me into their territory I did not need a passport.' It was for the benefit of the court rather than to get an answer.

The next chap said something about me giving out stickers in Moulmein market and I was told I could question him. What was there to ask? Was I supposed to try to deny it? It was why I had come. 'Are you aware,' I said, trying to make my statement sound like a question, 'that the National League for Democracy won eighty-two per cent of the seats in the 1990 election and are therefore the rightful government of Burma? As far as I know the National League for Democracy does not require visitors to get entry visas.' Again I was trying to make a political point rather than get anywhere with my trial. One of the diplomats hung her head in her hands. They wanted as little fuss as possible. I began to feel exceedingly alone.

'I want to speak with a lawyer,' I said. Crazy to be thrown into a trial with no chance to find out where it was all going. The judge nodded (only because diplomats were present). The lawyer who had accompanied them came and had a word with me. He could not tell me anything until I engaged his services. That would cost about US$1000. I did not have it and did not want to send a bill to my parents for what would be a waste of time. Just before returning to his seat the lawyer told me that what I had said about the Karen and the National League for Democracy would not be entered on the court record. The junta want trials to go exactly as they have planned. The defendant is not supposed to say anything except 'guilty'. I turned and shrugged to the Australian ambassador. She shrugged back. The lawyer had been incredibly brave just to offer his help to me. Certainly the regime would try to victimise anyone who challenged their plans. It is not a waste of time to fight a case you will lose; it is essential to justice that people fight for the truth regardless of whether they may win or lose, even in dictatorships. You must fight. But I could not do that alone and it was becoming clearer that nobody was even going to give me advice on how to do it.

The session lasted about an hour, then I was permitted to see embassy staff for a longer meeting.

'Do you want to make an official complaint?' asked the British ambassador regarding the maltreatment in Moulmein.

'What would that entail?' I asked.

'Well, you would need to undergo a medical . . . these things build up a momentum of their own . . .'

Medical? There was nothing to show from Moulmein except scars on my wrists. I could see that a complaint would go nowhere, my word against theirs. I also remembered assuring Than Nyunt that I would not drop him in it. 'I am not bothered about what happened to me,' I answered, 'but I am angry with a system that allows that to happen . . . no official complaint.'

What an error of wording that was! A junior minister back in London then began responding to letters from the public by saying, 'Mawdsley has not complained of maltreatment.' How devious.

The British embassy staff were strained but sympathetic. They brought biscuits and soap for me to take back to the prison. The Australian ambassador was quite formidable, not taking nonsense from the Burmese and telling them we would not start the meeting until they got rid of the inevitable video cameras and photographers (the MI chiefs who pretend they are too important to get involved like to watch it all later). The cameramen left and the meeting started.

'Stop!' said the Aussie ambassador. She pointed to a guy filming through the half-closed window. 'Tell him to disappear.' He did. Brilliant! At least there was someone willing to stand up to them.

They told me that the immigration charge carried a penalty of between six months and five years. Well, at least the minimum was not three years.

Two days later the trial continued. Embassy staff were there again but the single white face from the crowd had disappeared. Perhaps the junta did not want anyone else to see me asking defiant questions. They need not have worried. I was rapidly running out of defiance. The only opportunity I got to speak that day was to plead.

The interpreter, Ni Ni, began reading out the charges. '. . . when you were questioned in Moulmein . . .' she said.

'Tortured,' I interjected.

She resumed. '. . . when you were questioned in Moulmein . . .'

'Tortured!' I said again, quite angry.

She gave me a baleful look and then carried on: '. . . admitted to working for terrorist insurgent groups in the border areas to destabilise the Union . . . and illegal entry . . .'

Then I was asked how I pleaded.

'I reject all that about terrorist groups. I know no terrorists. The Karen National Union are defending their land . . .'

'OK, OK,' said the interpreter, flustered.

'But I do not plead regarding any terrorists. Is that understood? Just the illegal entry charge?'

I was asked to plead to the illegal entry charge and said 'guilty'. Great. Day over.

The *New Light of Myanmar* had me down as an insurgent terrorist. An editorial in that paper was headlined JIMMY THE MERCENARY. It told of how I had been 'nabbed red-handed', which was a bit odd considering I had been sitting in the main market with a tape recorder blaring and waiting impatiently for the police to arrive. It also said 'he made no secret of his covert or overt activities'. Quite how someone is to make a secret of either I am not sure.

Another two-day wait for the next court session, the sentencing. The night before I got on my knees and prayed. I was terrified. 'Dear God, dear God, please please get me booted out tomorrow. I cannot face six months here. I know I cannot do six months. Please please get me booted out tomorrow . . .' It was a pretty one-track prayer. And it began to dawn on me that I was saying all the wrong things. I had come here looking for trouble. I had come expecting hardship. Now I had got it, why did I want to back out? And why was I suddenly taking the nonsense of the trial so much to heart? My incarceration had nothing to do with the law and when, eventually, I was kicked out, that would have nothing to do with the law either. I had been unnerved by the embassy staff's apparent acceptance of the corrupt legal system. But surely I knew that people went to prison in Burma whenever the junta felt like putting them in, regardless of all legality. So why was I hoping for justice at the trial? And surely I knew that the regime were weak and cowardly, and when they saw that they gained nothing by keeping me in prison, but in fact that I was an embarrassment to them, then, with a bit of external pressure, they would throw me out. I prepared myself for the worst possible scenario – that they would sentence me to six months.

My prayers began to change their form. Instead of praying for release, I began to ask that He give me the courage to face the situation I was in and the strength to endure it. *But don't worry*, I told myself, *you won't have to complete the six months. Only be sure that when they say it you do not show any signs of shock or distress. Be hard as a rock. Pretend you could not care less. Do not show the junta your fear.*

The next day the judge gave an excessively boring preamble to the sentence. They had learned a little about PR and had let me shave, but I was still wearing the same clothes as eleven days before. I was standing up, waiting for the sentence.

'Five years and a 50,000-Kyat fine,' concluded the judge.

Bollocks! I thought without flinching. It was a shock to hear it but in the first split second I just thought it could not possibly stand. The next moments I spent trying to work out how much the fine was – £100, £1000 or £10,000. Phew, it was only £100. Good-o. The junta-friendly press present reported that 'Mawdsley showed no emotion as he left the court.'

I had a second hour-long meeting with embassy staff (and, of course, a dozen Burmese officials). I was not so composed as it began, I was angry about the five years. The Australian ambassador snapped at me to shut up, which I obediently did.

I still had not been allowed any exercise outside my cell over the two weeks. The ambassador brought up the matter with the officials, asked if I could have time outside my cell to stretch my legs.

'What,' asked Ni Ni, the translator from the Ministry of Foreign Affairs, 'does he want space to run and jump and play?'

She was quite serious. We all looked at her like she was from another planet.

'I think somewhere to walk will be sufficient,' said the ambassador evenly, taking the thought right out of my mouth.

I asked for a Bible as well. It was not that I wanted to read it – as far as I could remember from school it was the most random,

THE HEART MUST BREAK

boring and irrelevant book, though admittedly with some cracking good plots. But I thought it would be difficult for them to refuse me one – after all, on what grounds could they refuse? It was not that they allowed Burmese prisoners to have books, but then they did not have to explain themselves to anyone on that. And I thought that once I had the Bible, I could start pressuring them to give me other books. One step at a time. The British ambassador persuaded them to agree that I could have it.

The consular staff were in regular contact with my parents. They sent back the following message:

> . . . *When we spoke with James on Friday 15 May he looked and sounded fine. He had been allowed to shave and was composed in the face of the sentence he had just received. He asked that all the family be reassured about his condition and was adamant that you should not worry about him* . . .

But I did not look so calm when I was alone in my cell. The cell was 10 × 8 feet, concrete floor and a low ceiling of barbed wire with a tin roof above it. There was an iron barred door and a tiny barred window. The cell contained just a wooden pallet, a bamboo mat, an urn of drinking water and a toilet bucket. I was allowed to keep a toothbrush, toothpaste, bar of soap, and spare shirt and *longyi*. It was only now, on day fifteen, that they issued me with the white prison clothes and a blanket and pillow to sleep on. The blanket was too filthy to use. I laid it over the edge of the short pallet to stop my ankles getting splinters but the nights were too hot for a blanket anyway. The pillow was rough and filthy but quite a luxury in prison.

The building I was in was just three cells in a row, me in the middle one and the other two empty; they wanted me to be completely isolated. I could see very little from the cell. Through the high window I could glimpse the top row of bricks along the compound wall and the crown of a tree behind it. Through the door I could see only the empty corridor. If I pressed my face to the bars of the door I could see out of the ends of the corridor, left and right, and so strain to see small sections of the paths and vegetable patches beyond. If I waited like this patiently I might be lucky enough to see a prisoner or a guard walking by – that is about as close as I got to company. Next to the building, out of sight from my cell, was a small *paya*, built by Galon U Saw, the man who assassinated *Bogyoke* Aung San. Beyond that was a building for the prison guards. The whole compound, about 100 × 150 metres, was full of vegetable plots and a few trees. Round the edges were solitary confinement cells and larger compounds. This was the special ward for political prisoners. Student leader Min Ko Naing had been kept in one of the solitary cells before being transferred away from Rangoon, away from his family.

I was now allowed out for forty-five minutes a day to exercise. I was taken to one of the 50 × 50-foot compounds. They were against the main compound brick wall and their other sides made from a mess of corrugated iron and barbed wire. There was a wooden hut in the compound and an enormous mango tree. Oddly enough, the guard used to sit outside during my forty-five minutes. Ripe mangoes had fallen from the tree and were rotting in the mud. I was so desperate for food, for sugar, that I thought nothing of greedily eating them. Over the next week I ate them all and there were none left on the ground. I searched around and found a couple of half-bricks. I hurled them up at the tree, aiming at bunches of fruit thirty or forty feet above. It was made more difficult by a barbed-wire net which had been strung over the compound. I recalled what I had read about Burma: this was where U Tin Oo had been incarcerated during the 1990 election. In the 1970s U Tin Oo had been Chief of Staff of the Army and Minister of Defence. He had been gaoled then for opposing the regime. Now he was the NLD vice-chairman and while he was detained in Insein the regime were paranoid that the USA were going to send in helicopters and airlift him out. Hence the barbed-wire roof. U Tin Oo is a remarkable man: full of courage, full of humility, full of great wisdom. Yet he rose to Minister of Defence for the regime in the 1970s. I wonder if there are more like him in the regime today, ready to stand against what they realise to be a system of lies and cruelty.

The unripe mangoes were most reluctant to come down early. Over three days I scored about two and, were it not for my ravenous hunger, they would have been inedible. Occasionally the brick would come crashing down against the corrugated-iron walls. The guards became alarmed and investigated. When they found the bare mango skins they reported it to their seniors and I was never taken to the compound again. Instead for exercise periods I was permitted only to pace the twenty-eight-foot corridor directly outside my cell. (It was not twenty-seven feet, nor twenty-nine feet. One has an awful lot of time in prison to attend to the details.) When the prison authorities tried to explain the changed arrangement, they told embassy staff that they did not want me to walk in the mud in case I caught a cold. Pathetic.

Each morning at about seven o'clock I would be allowed round the back of my cell for a few minutes to wash from an urn of water. Food would be brought at ten o'clock and four o'clock. There would be a large plate of low-grade 'red rice' with a small cup of spinach or sour beans to go with it. Sometimes the vegetable option was just leaves and grass boiled up, exceedingly bitter. In the afternoons I would also get three or four morsels of meat in chilli sauce. The rice often included ants, sometimes weevils, but after a while you eat them too. At first the guards seemed afraid even to open my cell door, as if I would leap out and escape. The cups they could pass through the bars of the door but the plate of rice they would push under it, through a tiny gap so that the rust, detritus and spiders' egg sacks on the door frame would be scraped into my food. For the first few weeks the food made me retch. I could hardly stomach it.

One day I pushed the food back to the guards. It was too foul even to look at. '*Khwep ma ho bu!*' I snarled angrily, thinking I had said, 'I am not a dog.' Actually the Burmese word for 'dog' is '*khwey*'. '*Khwep*' means, 'cup'. The guard left a little confused, wondering why I was protesting, 'I am not a cup'!

But I *was* like a dog, one of Pavlov's dogs. As the ten o'clock and four o'clock feeding times approached I would become restless. I would start squashing my face to the bars of the door to see out of the ends of the corridor left and right and maybe spot the food coming. Then I would stop breathing so I could hear better – could I hear the buckets and plates clanking? I would pace around my cell becoming increasingly agitated. If I heard a footstep or any noise outside I would fly to the door like a pin to a giant magnet and strain to see if it was the food. I had no watch, but my body clock was well tuned to feeding time (a new prisoner counts not just every day but also every hour).

After one month I collapsed from lack of nutrition. I had finished eating the foul meal and stood up. Immediately I felt dizzy and tried to grab the bars of my door to steady myself. Instead my arms and legs started working up and down uncontrollably. I was marching on the spot and pounding my arms. I tried to call out to the guards but no sound would come from my mouth. My vision started darkening to a narrow tunnel and my hearing turned into a low buzzing. I could feel myself falling backwards. Just as I was about to go over I accidentally kicked the metal plate on the floor. It made a clattering din which cut through my confusion just enough so that I could stick my arms behind me to break the fall. I came to on the floor.

I called for a doctor. The authorities did not know what to do. It made no sense to them that a prisoner had rights. If I was starving to death, that was my business. The fact that they had locked me up did not mean they had responsibility for feeding me. If I had a complaint, I should have thought about that before getting arrested. Prisoners do not have rights. If you have broken their 'law' you are fit only to rot away. They were not angry that I asked for more food, they were just completely bemused. Why should they give it?

On the next consular visit, which occurred every three weeks, I brought the matter up. Only when the diplomatic staff complained did the prison authorities agree that I could have extra food. From now on I got a hunk of bread each morning and a boiled egg in chilli with my morning rice. Supposedly prisoners are allowed a 'prison account' whereby they use money paid in by family to supplement their rations. The authorities agreed that I could give an order to the guards every two weeks to get food from the market. In reality, because I refused to pay bribes, this never really got anywhere. I got to spend about 800 Kyat (£2) every three weeks and the food they brought would be rotting. Bananas which were liquid inside their skins, and me so hungry that I ate them, with the inevitably unpleasant consequences.

The exception to this was noodles. One packet of noodles seemed to last for ever, and each night at eight o'clock a guard would come with a steaming cup of them, garlic and bits of leather (maybe it was meat) added. What a highlight that was every day!

I had one jar of drinking water in my cell, which would be topped up every two days. Algae used to grow in it. I had to use the same supply to clean myself after the toilet (no need to use paper in that part of the world). Burmese prisoners often did not even have enough water for that. They would have to use the stumps of cheroots to clean themselves, tearing the stub open to get the crumpled bamboo and newspaper that acted as a filter.

It is customary to use one's right hand for eating and left hand for ablutions. At first I thought that this sensible measure was designed to prevent one from contaminating one's food. After a procedural lapse I learned to my cost that perhaps it was the other way around – to stop you getting chilli on your sphincter! Most alarming.

But usually after eating there would be no chilli left on my fingers anyway. I would lick them spotlessly clean so that I did not miss the slightest stain of nutrition. I would lick up to the top knuckle and then find myself licking my palm and the back of my hand right up to the wrist and beyond on to the forearm. It was an animal-like compulsion, which I was almost unable to stop. It reminded me of our dogs at home who would sometimes lick our hands in a similar way, apparently to get salt. And so, then, was I, taking back the salt from my own sweat. Licking myself like a dog, my arms and even, I confess, my knees. It was bizarre. You do it without quite knowing why but underneath your consciousness your body is *screaming* for salt. I reflected on that later. The body knows what it needs and will hijack the rational part of our being to get it. In the same way, when one is in darkness and hell, the spirit knows what it needs and it screams out for God. Do not ask a comfortable man whether or not he believes in God. Put him in hell, threaten him with an awful slow death and you will see that he calls out for help from above, then will his spirit assert what it has known all along.

Why is prison so terrifying? It goes beyond the unpleasantness and discomfort described. It is because the MI can do whatever they like to you and nobody will help you. Time and again they have tortured, raped and killed, with no apparent comeback. So fear grows. And in my case, it was not even that they would come to do terrible or brutal things. Just that they would leave you to rot and that they did not conceive of you as a human being, as something which could suffer, as something which had a right to dignity and autonomy. You were a prisoner. You had crossed them. As they had the power to lock you away and leave you to rot, they also had the right to do so. As you had no power to fight back against it you had no right to do so and, when you tried appealing to them, it was absurd. What was your appeal based on? You have nothing to threaten them with so why should they do anything for you? Might was right. Nothing more to it.

I thought about Westerners doing time in Third World prisons for, say, smuggling drugs. Though they might at first curse their stupidity in taking such a risk, I had heard of many who came to terms with their awful predicament by recognising the wrong of their crime. Well, I did not even have that comfort! My incarceration was my own fault, just as theirs was, but I had no excuse at all – I was in from the purest stupidity! What had I been hoping for? But then I saw it a different way. It was true that I had committed no crime and therefore deserved no punishment. Like everyone, however, I was a sinner and so, like everyone, I would suffer. What did it matter when and where? I do not claim there is a shred of logic in this paragraph, but the ideas gave me a measure of peace in prison.

Occasionally, if I were out of my cell for a wash, I would see the MI major who oversaw the Rangoon period of my interrogation. I would always smile at him and wave, pretend to be cheery. He would be a little embarrassed – surely I was supposed to be afraid of him – but he would wave back, sheepishly. In truth I was afraid of him, or at least afraid that my interrogation would recommence. I had spun a cover story to account for all my time in Burma and Thailand, and although it held up to their scrutiny I was convinced that a sharper mind would see the holes in it and then demand the real facts. So almost every single day in prison I had to go over the whole story in my head. All the dates, and places, and people. Much of it was true but any details that could incriminate a friend had to be changed. I was paranoid about how thorough their investigation might be. It was mental torture, the fearsome pressure of feeling the need to be constantly on the ball, frightened that if I did not hold together I might be exposing others to risk: people who would suffer from it far more than I. The incarceration felt crushing because it was relentless. There was no rest from it, nowhere to go for a break, no end date, no reprieve, no place to recover one's energy.

Physically, I had almost nothing to do in my cell but to pace around it. Each circuit took eleven single steps to complete. I got to know the cell exceedingly well. There were marks and stains on the walls, all sorts of shades and shapes from various bodily fluids. TB sufferers held there before me had coughed their lungs on to the walls, there were mucus, faeces, urine, blood, filth. The stains used to take on specific shapes. One was the back of a herd of cattle, another was an owl and another a kookaburra. I do not just mean that if you squinted and tilted your head you could make out the shape of a bird. It *was* an owl and that one *was* a kookaburra. There was one which I christened 'Shakespeare's spaniel'. It had the body of a cocker spaniel, the beard, mouth and moustache of the Bard, the sunglasses of John Lennon and the wild hair and forehead of John McEnroe.

You do not just see things that are not there in prison, you are full of wild imaginings . . . the crows! Perhaps this is the most insidious method of the Burmese MI to break a man's spirit. Every morning between about six and seven the prison authorities would command half a dozen or so specifically trained crows to land on the corrugated iron roof of my cell. They would then proceed to hop about, jangling their talons and scraping their toes along the roof, backwards and forwards making a dreadful noise. Jumping up and down. They even trained them to drag sticks across the roof. The terrible thing was the pauses, the silences. Thinking, or desperately wanting to hope, that it had finished for the day. But no. It went on. Stupid bloody crows! And each morning the horrible certainty that the peace was about to be shattered. It is so cool around 6 a.m. You are so tired. You can have beautiful sleep . . . but for those damned clanging crows! How much I wanted to negotiate with them. But the diabolical creatures were not open to talks. Oh, the maddening purpose-lessness of it.

Every now and then guards would give me a cheroot, usually when I asked. But getting a light for it was a different matter; it depended who was on duty. If I called out for a light I might have to wait two minutes or two hours to get it. Sometimes they refused altogether. I recalled Vladimir Bukovsky and his heroic and successful efforts to light a cigarette. Everything is possible. So with a cheroot in my teeth I climbed up the iron door and then grasped the barbed wire netting on the ceiling. I leaned myself further and further back until I was at a terrible angle but had the cell light bulb in front of my face. I hated the light, glaring as it did all night, but maybe for once it could be useful. I pushed the tip of the cheroot against it and began sucking furiously to get a light. Alas, I was not up there for as long as I should have been, my arms and legs and hands were in an agony of strain, so I jumped down unlit. Pesky 40-watt bulbs!

The next day when the light was off I unscrewed it and hid it in my cell. Five minutes later I had a reality check and just laid it by the door. That night when it failed to come on I enjoyed two hours of darkness before the guards noticed. They rewired the fitting so that it hung out of reach just beyond my door. Oh well.

(I e-mailed Bukovsky on my release and was thrilled to bits to get a reply. He said he was flattered that I had tried his light bulb method but that he doubted he could repeat it now at his age. I was dancing!)

At nine o'clock each evening there would be an hour of propaganda blaring out from a speaker outside my door. I detested it.

It was supposed to be Buddhist teaching but was no such thing. The self-satisfied orator would shout abusively at his audience, hysterically losing control and then lapsing into conceited little giggles. If there was an audience they responded to his chants like zombies, no life, no belief in their voices. Or they were children being brainwashed, their infant voices pathetically agreeing to everything they were told. It was in Burmese; I could not understand it. I am sure some of the language of it did come from Buddha but the hypocrisy was sickening. Why every night, so loud, so aggressive, in a language I could not understand anyway. Nothing to do with Buddha's compassion, tolerance, wisdom and truth.

Three weeks after the trial I was taken outside my cell for a shave. My own razor had given up the ghost halfway through the pre-trial shave. Then, as now, they brought another prisoner to shave me. He used just a bare razor blade, pinched between his fingers in a tiny metal clamp, and of course no such thing as shaving cream. I splashed cold water on my face and he set to work. Not once did he cut me, not the slightest scratch. After that I was given a very clean set of prison whites. Something was up.

'Your mother come,' said the MI major who conducted my interrogation, 'and your brother.'

Blimey! I thought. 'Which brother?' I asked him. He did not know. A hood was put on my head and I was led back to the main building. If I had had any gumption I would have refused to wear the hood. But I had not yet taken to heart the truth that 'no one can humiliate me but myself'.

I was taken to the huge prison office and waited there for twenty minutes. My mother and brother Jon (who had been made to wait twenty minutes in the adjacent room for no reason at all) entered the room, followed by the British chargé d'affaires and an entourage of assorted prison officials, MI, MFA, policemen, immigration and cameramen.

It was magic to see my family. Big hugs, big smiles. We assured each other we were all fine and fired off thousands of questions at each other. It was impossible to take any information in. Apparently my mother told me that Suharto had fallen, but I do

172

not remember hearing it, even though I had been in Indonesia only two months earlier hoping for it to happen.

Jon had brought in a four-pack of Aussie beer. I declined to join him, perversely proud of my five weeks of abstinence. Also there was the unspoken understanding between us that under the eyes of the authorities we would not treat this meeting as a special event. We would act as normal as ever. No need for me to celebrate anything with a drink. Nonchalantly, Jon offered the beers to the assembled crew. They were slightly alarmed and refused. He tucked in alone.

Mostly I wanted to know that everyone at home was OK and to give them the impression that I was coping with it all. Certainly none of us shed a tear or pleaded with the junta for anything. No point in showing weakness, though it was an agony to hide it.

I asked again for the Bible. The chargé d'affaires pointed out to the prison governor and to the MFA officials that they had agreed three weeks ago that I could have one. Why had they not passed it on. They assured him they would do so forthwith.

Mum had brought an embarrassment of food and medical supplies for me. She spread them out on the table. But I did not want to be singled out for such special privilege. I was acutely conscious of the 8000 men and women in the same prison who had scarcely any medical facilities available. I picked out a couple of items, toiletries I think, and pushed the rest away.

'Ask them to give it to the other prisoners,' I said. The chargé d'affaires began remonstrating with me. We talked a little and he persuaded me to accept the vitamin pills. After that we donated the rest to the prison. Mum tells me that the prison governor was astounded. And I doubt the other prisoners saw any of it anyway. It was not that I was being a martyr. I felt instead that if I had a serious medical problem they would deal with it or not, regardless of who had supplied the medication.

Jon told me that Dad had tried to visit me back in May, a month after my arrest. When he had arrived in Rangoon the authorities refused to allow a prison visit. Apparently the Sultan of Brunei was on a trip to Burma and so the Ministry of Foreign Affairs was too busy to deal with anything else.

'Will you appeal, James?' asked Mum.

'What? Through court?' I responded. 'What is the point?'

'No, I mean will you write a letter to this *creature* Than Shwe?' Mum said the word 'creature' with such feeling that it thrilled me to bits. Obviously she understood the regime perfectly.

So we discussed a gaol appeal letter. Every prisoner supposedly had the right to send a letter to the authorities regarding their sentence, to give reasons, perhaps, why it might be lessened. We were all agreed that an appeal through the courts was useless. A letter might be worth a shot, though, if I cut out my belligerence. I was told that I would be given a copy of the court transcript and one of the criminal code to work with when framing the letter.

Meeting family was stressful for me and stressful for them, but without it I do not know how I would have got through the following weeks. Their love was vital, knowing that they would stand by me whatever happened – but it would have been a bonus if I could have been sure that they also thought that what I was doing was sensible.

To cope with all the difficulties I had to be disciplined. It is reassuring to feel in control of your life and as a prisoner you cannot control the big picture, so you must focus on details. As for food parcels and cigarettes, at first I was hopeless. If it was there I wanted to consume it *now*, not ration it. It was too much pain to sit in the cell with it untouched. And why not? Will my pleasure in consuming be any the greater for delaying it? Every three weeks the embassy staff would visit and leave a food parcel – biscuits, noodles, bananas. I shared them out a little with guards and on rare opportunities with other prisoners. But often they were too scared to accept anything from me. I confess that I did not push the matter. Instead, I made myself sick and in agony from gorging on the food, unable to make it last more than three or four days. I once received four lemons. I decided to eat one lemon every other day and promptly tucked into the first. I ate the whole thing, skin and pips included. A few minutes later I decided to speed up the timetable because the last one was not likely to be fresh after a week. So I ate another there and then, and agreed to save the others for the following two days. Ten minutes later I ate the third and before the evening was out I had had the fourth.

The embassy staff had pressured the prison authorities to increase my food ration, but it was still meagre. Yet after nine days of this (with no other food) I realised that I was not going to starve to death. In fact, even a little food was enough. And, most important, all food, no matter how rotten or contaminated or unpleasant, is a wonderful blessing. Food is life. It is magic. It grows from the soil, we put it in our mouths and we stay alive. How wonderful! It took me a long time to conquer the lust for food but the regime gave me no choice. After that I made much more effort to share out my food parcels; giving is more satisfying than eating.

After the incident with the light bulb I decided to give up smoking; relying on the guards for a light was undermining my defiance. It made me vulnerable and dependent. It was remarkably easy to quit, despite numerous failed attempts prior to prison. I think I managed it so easily because it was not for reasons of saving health, or money, or 'kissing like a dirty ashtray', but because I connected it to the cause that was my life. I could not defy the regime if twice a day I had to beg for their indulgence with a light. By successfully giving up smoking I felt a little stronger.

But it was discipline in sleep that was crucial. I cannot describe the torment I used to feel at night. The oppressive heat, the bedbugs, the mosquitoes all making it impossible to fall asleep and these as nothing compared with the mental turmoil I was in. Nights were spiritual tempests where all my fears would crowd in and try and try to rip me to pieces and yes, sometimes I cried out in distress. But there was one thing I felt I could cling to, one pillar which I would never let go of, no matter how vicious and diabolical the winds around me – that God existed, that He was Love, and that it was He and nothing else who was in control of the universe. If I was in prison it was with His knowledge and His consent. I had to trust Him.

I would fall asleep exhausted at about three or four o'clock, utterly worn out. When I woke in the cool dawn it was indescribably sweet. Only slowly would I come to realise where I was and

only slowly would I remember the spiritual battle of the night
before and only slowly would I come to understand that I was not
dead, that I had survived it, that I had won yet one more day. It
was a beautiful thought. The morning was gentle and soft, cool
. . . then the crows would come! But I did not have the energy to
go on fighting like this.

I decided that each day, after the early morning wash, I would
not lie down in my cell even for one second until the 9 p.m.
propaganda began. It was difficult; so tempting during the day,
when you are wilting with tiredness, to put your head down for
just a few minutes. So tempting to lie down and rest when there
is nothing, nothing else to do but sit and think or pace the cell. So
boring to be awake when you could just nod off. But within a few
days my body adapted to the rhythm and no matter the heat and
mossies and bugs and fear, by the time nine o'clock came I was
pooped. I began having some of the best nights' sleep of my life,
if only for five or six hours, very sweet all the same. Very regular.
Very refreshing.

It was strange in prison that however much I yearned to be out,
even just to be out of the cell to stretch my legs, whenever
opportunities for that came I was in fact reluctant to leave my cell.
Part of me was secretly pleased when I was no longer allowed to go
to the distant compound for daily exercise but could only walk the
corridor outside my cell. When you spend over twenty-three hours
a day in a room, for weeks on end, you become attached to it.
Sometimes I would hate to leave it and when exercise finished I
would be relieved to get back. The cell was a place where I could
be alone, unseen. When I was outside I had to appear strong and
happy. When I was inside I could be sorrowful. My cell was my
own space in a very unfamiliar surround. It felt safer there.

Each afternoon after three o'clock the sun would be in a
position to throw a little ray of sunshine into my room. It fell on
to the wall and slowly moved up to the top, fading and becoming
more orange as it went until it vanished with the sunset. Listening
to the prison gongs, I could be fairly accurate about what time to
expect it. It was a most welcome companion. But the prison gongs
frequently did not sound during the day, so once I had the wall

calibrated, I ended up using the sunray to tell the time. Most important, I could tell by it how long until food would come, as food was due at four o'clock.

But something weird started happening. I was aware that each day the 'sun clock' would need a small readjustment due to the sun's progression between the tropics. But even taking this into account it seemed that my food was coming to me at irregular times: not just five or ten minutes out but getting later and later and later. I became more and more worried over the days; were they playing games with me? You have so few events in your prison life that the small things that do happen, which do break up the day, take on an extraordinary significance.

After a few weeks of paranoia and distress a thought struck me. In Lancashire and in New South Wales we are accustomed to having a shortest day in the year and a longest day in the year. But between the Tropics of Capricorn and Cancer things are slightly different. The sun passes directly over Rangoon *twice* a year: once in April on its way north and once in August on its way south. This means that Burma has *two* longest days in the year and *two* shortest days (although the shortest day at the summer solstice is much longer than the shortest day at the winter solstice). So the prison authorities were not up to the most devious of mind games at all. The erratic timer was a consequence of beautiful cosmological clockwork. I doubt I would ever have had time to think about it if it were not for prison.

One night a beetle fell from the ceiling into my ear. I had heard all the urban myths about travellers in South America who cut their heads and then had insects lay eggs inside. The traveller would return home and weeks later suffer increasing headaches and agony and then be able to *hear* their own brain being munched away. Or the Frenchman in a Thai prison who heard the guy in the next cell screaming and screaming in agony. After much effort the Frenchman persuaded the guards to let him go next door and help. He found the prisoner sitting exhausted, looking like death, and on his throat a great lump that was wriggling and moving. He slit it open with a razor blade and a heap of fat maggots spilled out . . . I could hear this beetle going

177

frantic in my ear. It was stuck, did not want to go backwards but was burrowing deeper and deeper in, sounding on my eardrum like a helicopter. I was going crazy. I tried to dig it out but only pushed it further in. I shouted for a guard and, seeing my predicament, one reluctantly gave me a narrow but blunted knife. I tried to dig it out with that but to no avail. I was really distressed, thought it would be through my eardrum any second. Each time the beetle panicked my ear ached unbearably. The guard retrieved his knife and ran off to call the prison doctor.

Quarter of an hour later he came. About four men entered my cell and the doctor told me to lie on my side. He peered into my ear with a torch, spent a moment thinking, then sent a guard off to fetch something. A few minutes later the guard returned and I heard a fizz as the doctor opened up a bottle. He poured a liquid into my ear and it was the most bizarre feeling. The liquid was warm and effervescing, bubbling and crackling in my ear. Seconds later he fished the beetle out. The liquid was soda water. The bubbles had fixed to the creature and it floated out. Wonderful. He gave me the beetle. It looked like it had had a harder time than I. I felt sorry for it, all was forgiven. I laid him gently on the ground and he scuttled off to tell his mates.

I looked at the doctor with the most profound gratitude in my eyes. I had a hero! He had a nice smile on his very wrinkled face. From then on, whenever I saw him, we joked about the 'beetle-in-ear' while everyone else tried to look grim.

In my cell I had all day to think. If I focused on the comfortable life I used to know, of friends and good times in England and Aus, it brought temporary solace but I was always gutted on having to face the present reality. Reminiscences of family and fun would not save my brain. It was just like a drug, with the inevitable payment of comedown and hangover. But when I considered the democracy movement and, to cut a long thought short, that I was there to fight so that Karen children did not have to lose their parents, their homes and their lives to this regime, it gave me grit to continue.

On 22 June I was given a single sheet of dirty, very poor quality paper and told to write my gaol appeal letter. No court transcript.

No criminal code. I am not at all proud of what I wrote. I was thinking back especially to the meeting with my mum and my brother. While I had plenty of personal support from my family and close friends, I did not feel any support for my course of action. There was not much fight left in me.

I wrote I was a fool, that I was wrong to enter Burma.

I wrote I was utterly non-violent in my involvement with Burma and had never been paid for any of it (i.e. not a mercenary).

I wrote I heard of a Frenchman who got two weeks' detention for a protest in Myawaddy and I did not expect such a harsh penalty.

I wrote I co-operated in the interrogation – I told them the truth because I wanted them to believe me about the human rights issues. I pleaded 'guilty' in 'court' and promptly paid the fine.

I wrote I did not come to disrupt or disturb but to appeal to the authorities to open dialogue with the democratic groups.

I wrote I taught English to refugees and it broke my heart to see the school burnt down and some students killed.

I wrote I was young, that my family were suffering so much too because of my actions.

I wrote I would never return to Burma.

I wrote I was a fool but my intentions were noble and compassionate.

I wrote it was my most earnest wish to go and settle down in England, to get married perhaps.

I was not defiant. I felt I was alone, that my idea to come here and confront the regime must have been wrong; nobody else seemed to see any sense in it and nobody was going to encourage me in it.

There was another consular visit. I was shown a few letters from friends that the authorities had just vetted. I stared at them, read them, could not take a word in. It was impossible to concentrate. An Australian friend wrote that they would try to visit me 'after Christmas'. What on earth! It was June, I was still clinging to the idea that I would be there for less than six months and here was someone candidly talking about eight months down the track.

But there was another line that was a jewel. My dearest friend from Bristol, Tom, had written, 'P.S. Don't let the bastards get you down.' I was particularly pleased that the MFA and MI had read that. They needed to know.

Again I asked for the Bible. Again the prison governor assured consular staff that I would get it immediately. I was saddened that the consular staff seemed to accept that.

I returned to my cell, though, thinking about the suggestion that I would still be there after Christmas. Then Insein prison really became hell. It was not the physical things that made it so, it was not the psychological difficulties – isolation, communication barriers, the prospect of a wasted life. What was absolute, unbearable, devastating hell was facing my conscience.

I had put myself in prison and I had absolutely no one else to blame. I had put my family into unspeakable distress. I could feel their pain inside me. Family friends like Christine Glover who I knew would never hurt anybody, who had not the tiniest suggestion of malice, and I had gone and put them through this. I was hurting the people who loved me most, and hurting them with a pain that left them numb. Whatever grief they felt for me I felt the same for them. It was devastating. And what tore into my conscience was the idea that we have one life, just one short life, and yet what did I do with mine? Use it to hurt the people who loved me most. I had to face my every folly and every sin. It was not just the low things I had done in my life that pricked the conscience. It was every missed opportunity to do good. I had one short life. I could use it to love. What else do we need but love? What else was I missing so sorely in prison? But I had not spent my twenty-five years loving. I was too busy, or too greedy, or too distracted by trivialities.

When we die we will see all of our life in the true light. We will see that we could have loved, fully, freely, completely. And we will see that we did not, but we will no longer understand any of our excuses. Our excuses will fall away like chaff. Millions of men and women and children are living today in inhuman conditions.

They are starving to death while we throw food away. They are dying of curable diseases while we plough money into cosmetics. They are living in soul-destroying fear of brutal men with guns, being thrown into prison and worked to death while we do trade with their oppressors. Hell is realising that one did not help when one could have. Hell is realising how little one truly loved.

Whatever excuses we think we have for turning our backs, they will melt like breath into the wind. We will be left naked. Our souls will stand alone before God, before His almighty and absolute love. Will our souls reflect His love? Will they find a home there?

I cried before God, 'You help me! Please please show yourself to me. I cannot go on. I am nothing. I have nothing. I have no strength, no courage. My Lord I am full of terror. I am sorry for what I have done. I am sorry for the hurt I have caused. I am sorry for the wrong I have done. Lord, the pain of the wrong I have done is killing me. Lord, all the times I have turned my back on my brother, because I did not want to see his suffering, because I was too scared to help, because I was too greedy to share, because I was too pompous to care, Lord my God, forgive me and help me. I know now what it is to suffer. I know now what it is to be completely alone, to be persecuted and terrified and have no one to go to. Lord, I know now what it is to be shown no love and I cannot live. Lord God, I have asked to serve You and I have got only silence. I know You are there, but You do not come to me. I know You exist, but You do not show Yourself. I am finished. I am nothing.'

How crazy to have ever thought that I had anything of worth to offer to Him. I laid me down and I died . . .

CHAPTER 15

You shall know the truth, and the truth shall set you free. John 8:v:32

HELL TURNED INTO heaven. I was taking a wash one afternoon. Guarding me was a man I had reason to despise and despise him I did. He had given up, bowed completely to the regime. The very sight of him made me sick at heart. The thought that he might be the one to bring my food would make me angry. Then this day, as I was taking a wash, I looked at him as he crouched on the ground ten feet away. He was gently picking out weeds from the earth, utterly absorbed in his task, his mind a million miles away from prison and his job of guarding me. In that moment I saw the man, stripped bare of all the superficial trivialities by which we judge each other. He was born as innocent as me, he wanted peace and rest and freedom just as much as me. He was not so much a guard as one of millions of prisoners in Burma. My heart went out to him. All I wanted to do was to show him that we were brothers. I smiled as I was filled with this tender compassion. Ever since that moment, whenever I saw him again I felt glad. The tension between us had vanished and he was as glad to see me as I was to see him. He was called Thu Nyein.

I received the Bible. I had had nothing to read for nine weeks so I read it with a thirst. Certain verses burned into me:

1 John 3:v:17–18: Whoever possesses the world's resources and sees

182

his brother in need, yet closes his heart against him, how does God's love abide in him? Little children, let us not love in word or tongue, but in deed and in truth.

James 2:v:15–16: If a brother or sister is poorly clad and lacks the day's nourishment, but one of you says to them, 'Go away in peace; get warmed and get fed,' without supplying them with their bodily needs, what is the use?

Psalm 94:v:20: Can a corrupt government be allied with Thee, one that organises oppression under the pretence of law?

Micah 6:v:8: He has showed you, O man, what is good; and what does the Lord require of you but to do justice, and to love kindness, and to walk humbly with your God?

God is a God who loves action. He does not want words, or sentiment. He wants us to do what is so plainly obvious: to love our neighbours as ourselves. St Paul tells us to rejoice in suffering. How can that be? If we seek suffering for its own sake no good will come of it. We are told only to 'follow Me', and whatever suffering we encounter as a consequence of that, never mind. It will be to everyone's benefit.

I fell in love with the Jews, with their tradition, their struggle, their wisdom. I was not just comforted by the Bible, not only glad, but fulfilled and even in rapture. All creation seemed wonderful: blades of grass, a ray of sunlight, the concrete floor in my cell. It was as if God had put me through the most terrible devastating time so that I could realise my own helplessness, my own nothingness; appreciate that He was everything. And in that absolute despair, when I had utterly given up in myself, God smiled because I had finally seen the truth.

Psalm 144:v:3–4: O Lord, what is man that Thou dost regard him, or the son of man that Thou dost think of him? Man is like a breath, his days are like a passing shadow.

Days earlier I had been in hell. Hell was to face one's failure full on, to stand without excuse beside the fact that one had failed to love. The truth of that is terrifying. But now God blessed me with its resolution. He is merciful. He is perfect love. He forgives. He takes away our iniquities. He makes us complete. And this is the most wonderful realisation of all. That *we* are not expected to do anything because we cannot. We cannot do good. We cannot conceive truth. We cannot love. We are utterly weak. All that is required is that we give ourselves to Him and let Him do everything. And the feeling of giving oneself to Him (not saying it, not believing it, but doing it) is heaven.

It did not matter that I was in prison. I felt God's love, over-whelming, terrifying, everlasting love bubbling up within me and overflowing. What glorious joy. 'For now we see in a mirror darkly, but then face to face. Now I know in part; then I shall understand fully, even as I have been fully understood.' I felt like I had been touched, pierced, filled with the briefest hint of *then* . . . 'even as I have been fully understood.' I submitted my will to His. To forget myself, and to seek with all my heart and soul to serve His will, that was what it meant to be free.

The concrete floor became pastures green, the painful pallet now restful waters. I was in wonder, rapture. I was aware only of love. There was literally nothing else in my mind. Beauty.

When I came back down to earth I thought yet again about democracy. What was it Burma needed to deliver and sustain democracy? Education. And not just education in Burma but education in the West too, so that we all come to understand our dependence upon one other. So what could I do to this end?

I decided that when I was released I would write a journal about the situation in Burma and about human rights more generally, with a touch of political philosophy and religion. If people in the West read that, it would be one tiny step in helping us to see our brothers' plight, and the money raised from it would be used to build a school for exiled Burmese children: *Pyo Pan Wai* III. So over the next few weeks I thought and thought about what exactly I would write. I felt I was using my time, not wasting it, taking advantage of the unique circumstances. If the journal was a flop it did not matter. At least I was fully occupying my mind.

Apparently, when people get old their long-term memory

improves; they begin to remember incidents from decades ago, from their childhood. The same happened to me. It was as if the mind is like a barrel of water, and the events we experience are like apples thrown into the water. So long as we are rushing around and busy there is a constant bombardment of new apples, which push the others down deep and are themselves submerged by the next. But when you pause, when you stop bombarding your being with new sights and sounds, the water settles and the old apples come floating back to the top. I could recall in vivid detail pictures of childhood which I did not know I had even forgotten – catching minnows in the overflow channel of the canal at Rufford, belly down on grey stones and green grass beneath the great black-and-white-painted beams of the lock. Such peaceful fun. Or boating down the flooded river which runs through Glenridding into Ullswater, my brothers and I paddling furiously to no effect as the torrent spins us round and throws us against the rocks, half an hour of mayhem until we are spat out, dripping and panting, into the calm of the great lake. Such terrifying fun.

I did not have much opportunity to speak with the guards, and barely any with other prisoners. But one time a young guard was parading himself outside my cell. It was the wet season and he had just been issued with a new pair of shiny plastic Wellingtons. He was exceedingly pleased with them. He was swinging his arms, marching back and forward, and trying to hold his head high but unable to resist glancing down at his new boots. This is a problem with the generals in Burma. They put on a peaked cap, a smart uniform, a chest full of medals and they really do think they are god.

The prison governor came round on his monthly whirlwind inspection tour. His entourage stopped outside my cell. 'How are you,' he asked me in Burmese.

'I am fine,' I answered, regardless of how I felt.

'Have you eaten today?' he continued in the traditional Burmese greeting.

'Yes,' I answered thinking the question a bit odd.

'What curry?'

This was the natural follow-up from the previous question, but under the circumstances I thought it particularly inane. I looked at him with slight disbelief. 'Every day the same!'

The governor's jaw dropped, he shuddered, then stormed off in a temper. The two armed guards following him were straining their eyes towards me (but facing straight ahead) and trying desperately not to laugh. I don't think they had ever seen anybody giving the governor lip.

Much of the time I spent wrestling with quantum physics. Einstein was one of my childhood heroes. He conceived of a most wonderful thought experiment called the EPR paradox (Einstein–Podolsky–Rosen). To understand each step of the experiment is not so difficult if you have time to concentrate. But to hold all the steps at the same time, which you need to do to appreciate the paradox, is a terrible challenge. It is perhaps like standing with your back to a mirror and then wheeling round as fast as you can in the hope of glimpsing the back of your head – to see your rear-view reflection before it has time to turn with you. Or else it is like juggling. Each step is easy enough to understand on its own (each ball is easy enough to throw and catch on its own) but try keeping nine of them in your head at the same time (or nine balls in the air). So many times you can get eight balls up but by the time the ninth is up too three of the others have fallen away. So I sat in my cell for hours doing battle with particle physics and those hours just flew by. I swear that two hours by the prison gong lasted only ten minutes for me. There is a glorious instant, it is like seeing heaven, when just for a moment you have all nine balls in the air and suddenly the universe is turned on its head. Our everyday perception of reality becomes impossible and the impossible becomes essential. Then suddenly all the balls come crashing down and you cannot remember what you have just seen but you know that it was exquisitely beautiful and you are left breathless, in awesome wonder . . .

Until of course you are brought back down to earth. Both my ears became infected. It was excruciating. According to Shakespeare, 'There was never yet philosopher could endure the toothache patiently.' I might add Insein ear infections. I sat there for hours with my head on fire, as if I had been whacked in the face with a brick. When the doctor made his twice-weekly rounds he would rarely even open the door of the cell. No time. No point. I had to raise hell to get treatment. When they realised I was not prepared to sit quietly, they eventually came up with a stack of pills – painkillers, antibiotics, anti-inflamatories. Even then the trusty who issued them wanted me to bribe him and wanted to give only half a course of antibiotics.

I got scabies as well. It is an allergy to the eggs or droppings of almost invisible mites that burrow under your skin. My back and chest and arms and legs itched frantically. During the day it was no problem but by evening my skin would be burning. The embassy staff had dropped off scabies cream but the authorities refused to hand it over. It got worse and worse every day, but the doctor just recommended I drink three cups of water each morning. Bedbugs and mosquitoes are like nothing compared with scabies.

Thu Nyein, the thin old man who had guarded me washing, came quietly with some advice. He told me to pour water over my shirt and keep it damp. Quite simple, but it had not occurred to me. It relieved the pain greatly, but I got a chest infection from the cold. Never mind, it was better than scabies.

Again when I was on my forty-five-minute exercise period, supposedly just in the corridor outside my cell, another guard indicated to me to stand out in the rain. It was bucketing down and the warm rain cooled my burning body most soothingly. The forty-five minutes were up but the guard just winked at me. He let me stay out, long overdue, taking a great risk on himself.

The guards were kind. They were becoming less wary of me, figuring out for themselves that I was not a 'mercenary terrorist'. Could I carry on with prison? Not on the stark faith with which I had entered – that bare belief in God as the just, omniscient creator. This was sufficient to draw me to search for meaning, to end up in prison. It was not sufficient to carry me through.

But now, the absolute confirmation of God's existence, knowledge of His love, plus explosive expansion of Biblical detail, richness and fullness, meant I was equipped to proceed. It makes no sense to say, 'God give me resources and I will act.' One must go the other way round. 'God, I will act because I believe that if it is Your will then You will grant me the resources to carry it through.' I knelt down and prayed. 'Dear God, I do not care how long I have to spend here, be it one more week or one more year. Only let Thy will be done and I will be happy with that.' I meant it. I was no longer afraid of prison.

I still was not sure that what I had was scabies – the doctor had told me it was not. But I demanded the cream anyway. Eventually they gave it to me and I wondered what to do with it. Maybe apply a small amount of it to one arm and see what happened.

Before I had the chance I was summoned from my cell to the main office. 'We have some good news for you,' said Ni Ni from the Ministry of Foreign Affairs. 'We are going to release you.' She looked at me, hoping for a reaction but I was too distrustful to get excited. Perhaps they meant they were going to reduce my sentence from five years to three years and wanted me to be grateful for that.

'When?' I asked, feigning indifference.

'Today. Tomorrow. You must sign this.'

There were six copies of a form detailing the conditions of my release.

'I cannot read Burmese, what do they say?'

'Firstly you must not enter Burma illegally again. Secondly you must not break any law in Burma. Thirdly you must not do anything in the future which is anti-government.'

Well, how was one supposed to interpret that? I did not believe the SPDC had the right to make law and as the NLD were the rightful government of Burma there would be no way I would try to do anything anti-government. 'Do you mean I can return to Burma again if I have a visa?' I asked her.

'Oh yes,' she said sweetly.

'I am not blacklisted?' I asked in disbelief.

'Of course not,' she lied.

I was quite pleased by that, though, even if it was a lie. I signed the forms adding, 'cannot read' after each signature, as this would nullify them anyway.

Before I left I looked at Ni Ni and softened. 'I hope . . .' I began. 'You know I am not an enemy of Burma. I love Burma. I want all the best for this country. I hope you have good luck in solving the problems.'

'There are no problems!' She glared. 'We are doing fine.'

I was to leave the following day. I walked back to my cell that night without the hood on my head. The central watchtower was bedecked in gay little fairy lights. Most incongruous, but with the *paya* next to my cell it all looked somehow magical. Inside my cell I did not feel elated. I felt exhausted. I looked about it, conscious that I was even going to miss it, and tried to remember each tiny detail. And I thought of God. 'Lord, if You wanted me to read the Bible You would have to lock me up in a tiny room with nobody to talk to and nothing to read for weeks on end, then give me the Bible. That is just what You did. And this afternoon, when I felt I had finally and absolutely overcome my fear of prison, when I said I did not care if I had to do a week or a year, You chose to release me. Were You waiting for me to overcome my fear? If I had overcome it three months ago, would You have released me then?'

But we humans are slow learners. We need the message beaten into us.

I picked up the scabies cream, then demanded the instructions. It had not occurred to them to pass those on too. Turned out that what I had most definitely was scabies and that you do not apply the cream piecemeal but cover yourself in it neck to toe. It would take a few days to be effective. The warnings on the packet made it sound like DDT. Well, I probably needed an acid bath anyway. It was about the last thing I did in prison.

My father had come to Rangoon for a prison visit. When he landed the embassy staff told him I was to be released. Quite a moment. The next day he came with embassy staff to take me to the airport. I was giving the authorities stick about them not returning my belongings – glasses, watch, the tape recorder. I was advised to let the matter drop and be grateful that I was going. But I saw no reason to let the authorities think they can steal from prisoners. I got everything I wanted and we left. The new, colourful, bustling surroundings were obviously strange but the strongest thought lining my mind was that the task was incomplete.

'Have you had enough then, now? Is that it?' asked my father as we stepped on to the plane.

'Dad,' I replied, 'I have only just begun.'

CHAPTER 16

We forget that the Bolsheviks worked in conditions of relative freedom to establish tyranny, and not the other way round . . . How can grown-up people seriously believe that revolutions are the result of the activities of some underground organisations . . . How impossible and unnecessary illegality was . . . We grasped another and more important truth: you cannot achieve democracy by going underground. The underground produces only tyranny, only Bolsheviks of a different colour.

Vladimir Bukovsky

'HAVE YOU EVER had scabies?' I asked my twin and my sister as we hugged at Heathrow airport.

'No.'

'You have now.'

Three days after that I was in hospital for a week. I had passed out at home and was briefly paralysed. My temperature was up to forty degrees. Jeremy was with me at a Guildford hospital as the doctors examined me.

'Isolation ward for this one, nurse,' said the doctor.

'Don't you mean solitary?' I asked. I was not interested in TV or radio or reading. Journalists ask what do you crave most now that you are free, a meat pie, a game of football or a pint of beer? But the fact is you have just spent an agony learning not to care for those things at all and now that you are surrounded by them you could not care less. The best thing was company, silent company.

In the paper I read that eighteen foreigners had been arrested in Rangoon for handing out messages of goodwill. This was encouraging. They were sentenced to seven years' hard labour but released after six days. That too was good news. But I was not a happy man. I felt I had been on to something in Burma and it had all vanished so suddenly. I had to get used to life in the West.

Dad had surprised me on the plane by telling me Mum was in Thailand. She was on the border working in Dr Cynthia's clinic. Dr Cynthia, a Burmese woman, had established the clinic some years before to treat anyone from her country who came in need of help. I was dying for Mum to come back and immensely proud of her too. And as much as Mum wanted to return home immediately, her interest in Burma did not disappear just because I had come out of prison. She stayed on for another two weeks until her visa expired.

At the clinic she had seen some of Burma's problems first-hand: malnutrition, beriberi, tuberculosis, landmine victims. She gave a pint of blood and before it had even cooled down in the fridge a man came in with his leg blown off. He used it.

When Mum came home she said, 'I have seen it James. I understand why you went.' That was the greatest line I had heard for a long time. It really is difficult to understand the urgency of the problem without witnessing it first-hand.

Of course people were curious about what life is like in a Burmese prison. And if they ask you thoughtful, original, detailed questions then it is very easy, even comforting to answer them. But too often you get that most awful vague whine: 'Erm . . . you've been in prison . . . what's it like?' Is there a more effective way than this pathetic question to illuminate the gulf of under-standing? It isolates the released prisoner even more, sending signals that they are from a different world, that they have been an alien. And it shows that the questioner has never given prisons much thought, and that they have never bothered to read about the subject. That is fine as far as it goes, but it would be pleasant if such people did a bit of homework before venting their vapid curiosity on real souls.

Eight weeks after being released I went back out to Australia and began working on the Olympic site with my brother Jon again. But this time I started resenting the work; I no longer wanted just to 'dig for freedom'. I was keen to be doing something more. I had learnt a little from my attempt to approach the junta on terms of '*metta*' and 'freedom':

> *It is far more effective to empower people to resist exploitation than to appeal to the exploiters to cease. Empowerment comes from education. There is a trend, with many exceptions I admit, but in Burma from villager to student to group leader it seems that it is always the least educated who suffer most. Then the best thing I can do is perhaps to make available the resources for those on the border to educate themselves . . . The reality indicates that education is an immunity to exploitation.*
>
> *Does one ask if one's actions are likely to bring democracy or not? No. How ridiculous. No single person's activity will deliver democracy. All you can do is contribute to that direction. And democracy is not the goal. It is merely a label, never achieved entirely, always to be improved upon. It is not about elections. It is about accountability, the Rule of Law and maximum distribution of power. So conditions can improve under the junta, a transition will be made to democracy, and the struggle continues to establish and develop it. A matter of action, not time.*
>
> *In the move to democracy there must be millions of participants with millions of approaches. Certain approaches are armed struggle, diplomatic pressure, political defiance, increasing awareness, DVB/BBC, protests etc. Now whichever approach one identifies with most, which takes up most of one's time, effort and imagination, one may then be fooled into believing is the solution. Hence ———'s insistence on warfare, ———'s focus on BBC/CNN, or ———'s on press releases or folk in England who think it is only about writing to MPs, giving slide shows and fighting for a job in Amnesty.*
>
> *All approaches are essential. They support and reinforce each other. Media work helps recruitment, recruitment helps fund-raising, fund-raising helps weapons supply, fighting secures bases for political defiance – it all intermeshes. And if all worked with one approach the movement would collapse. We can't all be journalists as sure as we can't all be soldiers.*

As I thought about Burma by day I also dreamt about her at night. I had had a couple of nightmares about Insein, which I noted in my diary:

> *Scores of people were buried to their waists in rubble and 'crucified' in steel cages which fit around torso/arms/head. I refused to go to work. I fell asleep again and dreamt of torture — sledgehammers, claws, knives. Very disturbing.*

But I would not accept that the regime could remain just by scaring people off, by intimidating us so we would not criticise them. I wanted to go back.

> *I rarely have any fear of the SPDC but this is only because it is hidden by a greater anxiety. How do I justify the effects my return will have on Mum, Jon etc. I could die there, I think. As in when will enough be enough? When will I stop? And how can it be right that I hurt family so much. When I think what the authorities might do I can disregard it — there are more important things at stake. I have no debate here. But when I think of family then I debate indeed, in fact, I quake.*
>
> *I have a million good arguments to support my return. Is it laziness which prevents me committing all those arguments to paper — or is it the tragic premonition that whatever I write will never be good enough for those who don't want to understand? . . .*
>
> *I sometimes wondered whether the junta's cruelty was born of a lack of resources, lack of competence, or lack of caring. One is tempted to dismiss their wickedness as backwardness, their brutality as ignorance. But they must be condoning the murders, torture and rape in regions of forced relocation because there exists no system of redress. A villager has no one to complain to, there is no procedure or body to deal with these violations of human rights.*
>
> *And this is the reason why democracy cannot come merely with a change of government. Because it takes years to establish such channels, to change the minds of millions so that such are possible and understood.*
>
> *Also it will take years for people to nurse their sense of innovation back to health. That is that civil servants can take the initiative at a low*

level instead of the crippling inefficiency of ever awaiting one's superior's answers (done in fear*).*

Talking of which, I found out in my first month of detention just how terrifying that fear is. It is paralysing [don't want to leave cell]. It withers almost all before it. I cannot now remember what it was like, but I will never forget the realisation that one can never expect of anyone that they overcome this fear. It's too huge.

Nobody deserves to suffer oppression, however 'good' or 'bad' one perceives them to be, whether collectively or as individuals. There is good and bad in all of us – to try to defend the good (people) is impossible as there are none (just as there are no 'bad' people to defend them against). But one can surely stand up for good (the principle), oppose bad (i.e. lies, violence, exploitation, cruelty, deceit).

Within three months of being released from Insein I was back on the Burma border making plans.

On the way through Bangkok I caught up with Yan Kyaw Aung again. He was teaching his wasted legs to work. Not only was he now walking about the office (very unsteadily and with the aid of a stick) but he was also able to use an exercise bike. He had been getting treatment from a physiotherapist funded by the International Red Cross. Now he could walk again. He was getting stronger and stronger every week.

Kawn Sheim, Ye Min Aung and Kyaw Htay were no longer in prison or working illegally. They had finally been granted refugee status by the UNHCR and had won bursaries to study at a university in Bangkok – which meant a much better class of English teacher than the one at Minthamee! Ko Ko Oo and others had got married and had babies on the way. The orphans of *Pyo Pan Wai* had been smuggled out of the refugee camp (where schools were frequently banned) and had been taken in to a school run by an Italian nun. They mixed with local Thai children, had uniforms, full board, desks, books, everything they needed.

All this was good news, but for the Karen the situation was worsening. I went back to 7th Brigade area to give my heartfelt thanks to those who had helped me through to Moulmein. The

Thai bank of the Moie river was heaped high with sacks of rice. From the Burma side groups of Karen were appearing to collect it. There had been two years of poor rainfall. Ordinarily this would not have been a disaster for the rice harvest. But the *Tatmadaw* in that region do not carry rations; they steal rice from local farmers, or even just burn their stocks. In certain areas the locals were starving. Young boys had walked for days to collect as much rice as they could carry back to their families.

Thank God for the NGO that supplied the food. I had never seen such dire need for relief, never seen how graphically an NGO can save lives. And thank God for the Karen National Union who organised it, who did all they could to protect their people.

I met Mana again and the Padre. It was great to see them. Our previous meeting seemed like years ago. They told me everyone who I had met last time was well; none had run into any trouble. They asked about my time in Insein, keen to hear what the radio did not tell.

The next morning I went to see Brigadier Htin Maung. We were pleased to see each other. He asked me about my imprisonment and could not believe I had taken the torture passively. 'I would fight them with my fists,' he declared, pounding one fist into a palm, 'until the death!' And he would have, I have no doubt. 'Do you hate them?' he added.

'No. I don't hate them, I hate what they do.'

I talked with members of the ABSDF about returning to Burma. No one encouraged me to go, it would be my own choice. There was the tiniest chance I could get a visa, if not for Rangoon then a one-day tourist visa to enter the border town of Myawaddy. I recalled Ni Ni saying I could return if I had a visa. Undoubtedly I was on the blacklist after my two previous detentions but the Burmese authorities are not efficient. Maybe I would slip through their net. I did not have any plans to demonstrate or make any kind of scene. I just wanted to be back inside, to test the junta's reaction. If I made no disturbance, how long could they justify holding me, if at all?

I travelled to Hoauy Xai then boated to Vientiane, Laos. There

I applied for a visa to Rangoon. It was a long shot. After the stipulated three-day wait I went to see what had happened.

'Please sit down,' said the consular officer. 'Why do you want to go to our country?'

'I have read a lot about Burma. I like it. I want to meet the people there.' Surely he knew who I was?

'Have you been to Burma before?'

'Yes, a couple of times.'

'Where did you stay?' he asked.

I began to smile. 'I think you know where I stayed.'

'Yes. You are very famous man in my country. You cannot come there again!' We were both smiling. I shook his hand warmly and wished him all the best. One last try then, Myawaddy.

Of course I was worried about my family, but I reckoned that if I refused to return to Burma on those grounds I would have absolutely no right whatsoever to expect anyone, Burmese or not, to stick their neck out for freedom. If I would not do it, for whatever reason, I must accept that everyone can claim their personal interests are more important than freedom. But we have no personal interests without first securing freedom.

Who stands with me? Who on earth is there who won't say, 'don't go back'? I have to go back. Previous to this has just been dry runs, learning curve. In fact, if folk encouraged me to go back I'd get cold feet. So though the 'don't go back' line leaves me increasingly isolated and alone (am I, after all, wrong to return?) the 'do go back' line would be even worse. The best thing would be to meet somebody else willing to go in with me. In fact, someone who wants to go in alone but who would be prepared to make a joint effort. How wondrous that would be.

. . . I do not have to keep returning to Burma indefinitely. But there is something I must do before I can turn my attention to a less direct approach – I have to voice the truth without fear. This is something I have not yet done, and until I do it I cannot settle in England. And the truth is simple: that the SPDC hold their control over Burma only by violence and engendering fear. That the NLD were freely and fairly elected to power in 1990 and therefore they are the rightful government.

Once I have said this I must absolutely refuse to take it back (neither verbally nor through my actions). If I take it back to improve my conditions or to try to get an earlier release it has all been an utter waste of time and cause of massive unnecessary grief. Does this make sense? That if one fearlessly voices the truth and stands by it, one can do no more.

On 28 November 1998 I wrote out a statement.

I hope to enter Myawaddy on a one-day tourist visa. It is not my intention to be detained. I will cause no disturbances, carry no democratic literature (except for the Bible!), make no protests, no demonstration.

However, if the opportunity arises I will talk openly and truthfully with any of the locals who are happy to have a chat. I would like to hear their opinions and maybe to tell them about my previous experiences in Burma. This is by no measure a crime.

Ideally, the Burmese authorities will have no problem with this. They will be reasonable and sensible. I would welcome this response – it indicates that progress has been made. After all, we want democracy, not conflict.

On the other hand, if they choose to make an issue of it then I am willing to face the consequences – whatever they may be.

I am convinced that our thirst for freedom is stronger than anybody's thirst for domination.

As for my hopes (which surely cannot be a crime either!), there are three things in particular I wish to see.

1 *That the SPDC release all political hostages (Article 9, UDHR);*
2 *That the SPDC cease their interference with schools and universities such that they have had to close (Article 26, UDHR);*
3 *That the SPDC cease their harassment of the elected government of Burma, the NLD, and open dialogue with the aim to transfer power (Article 21, UDHR).*

The night before I went in I was on the phone to my brother Jon. He swore an awful lot. He did not think it was right for me to go back in. He gave me a very hard time, which was unusual, but succeeded in putting a rein on my impatience. He did me the biggest favour of my life.

I entered Myawaddy, scarcely believing I had scored the one-day visa. The regime blacklist so many people that it is impossible for the men at immigration checkpoints to read through the list for every visitor – they do not have computers at the border yet. It was an uncomfortably hot day. The town was fairly small, a few minutes by bicycle from end to end. Main roads were empty but side streets were full of people, hoards of grubby children playing or groups of men gambling on a game which, played on the dirt road, looked like a cross between snooker and marbles. Packs of soldiers lay lounging in some buildings, obviously extremely bored. I passed a long low structure surrounded by copious defences of barbed wire. Inside, tired-looking sentries leant against the walls. I asked a pedestrian what the building was and he told me it was a school.

What was I here for? However thrilled I was to be back on Burmese soil, I could not stop thinking about the telephone call with my brother. He had tempered my aggression. I felt sorrowful, not interested in confrontation. I chatted innocently with locals and did a bit of touristy sightseeing. There was a fantastic but decrepit monastery in the form of a huge crocodile. But mostly I sat quietly in teashops unwilling to speak about anything. I left after seven hours.

Maybe I needed to prove to myself that I was not afraid of another arrest. Certainly I wanted the junta to know that they were not in control and that they could not scare off opposition. The fact of my visit would be on their records. But the effectiveness of the trip ended there. I was too impatient. I had not done any of the necessary groundwork. I would spend the next months doing that.

CHAPTER 17

No one has ever measured, not even poets, how much the heart can hold. Zelda Fitzgerald

I RETURNED TO BANGKOK with prison no longer on the immediate agenda. Having spent so much time in Insein thinking about education and the possibility of writing a fund-raising journal, I decided to go ahead with it. It took me four days to write the thing, called 'Real Freedom', and another forty to edit it. I returned to the UK for Christmas and set about getting it printed and distributed.

The plan was to raise £20,000 by December 2000. I went into debt for the first time in my life to get 5000 copies printed. Money trickled in: first of all £1 or £2 a time. I persevered: then £5 and £20 donations: I persevered: then £100 or £200. A lawyer donated £2000. I had broken even, covered the set-up costs. Later a businessman donated £20,000. By mid-2000 the foundations of the school were laid in a safe place in Thailand and the whole project took off, overseen by the ABSDF education committee.

How happy that made me feel. I am not so sure the other side of the project was so successful – increasing awareness of Burma's situation through those who read the journal. I had ended up giving most of them away for free. Fortunately the wonderful generosity of people in the UK saved me from a marketing nightmare! I did not have to flog many copies before the target was reached.

But the journal was a distraction from what I knew I had to do. The trip to Myawaddy was a damp squib. I should prepare properly for a return to prison.

In Australia before Insein I had prayed for a job that would provide large savings. This time I was not so concerned about money but prayed for a job which would give me access to the Internet and plenty of time off when I needed it. I was blessed with a job as a temp clerk in London where the boss was happy to let me surf the net and take off any time I had to. It was difficult though, trying to ignore Burma while I had to work:

> *There is no joy in philosophy nor insight, none in music, fresh air or walking, none in food, beer or . . . Even the Bible is bland and meaningless – in fact, it only ever really held for me in prison. I want to go back to that, to that understanding.*

There is an argument for absolute secrecy, for keeping one's plans to oneself before springing them so that the 'enemy' can be caught by surprise. It did not apply here. To go without warning loved ones would be a betrayal and also folly. In any case I did not care if the junta were expecting me. Let them prepare for it, let them waste resources worrying about foreigners so that the locals have an inch more breathing space. It did not matter if they knew; that was not going to stop me.

On my birthday, 14 February, we had a few friends round at our flat in Kentish Town. I did not want to spoil the atmosphere but I had to warn them I would be going back to prison. I said I would be arrested around August to September 1999 and estimated I would spend six to eighteen months inside. I did not feel that the stipulated length of the sentence would be relevant; I would be detained on a whim without reference to law, and I would be ejected on a whim without reference to law at the time when the regime realised that they were gaining nothing by keeping me and losing a great deal. If I gave out letters I would probably get five years for it. I also expected to be there without a passport – another five years. And there was my suspended sentence to be rejuvenated. Around fifteen years altogether . . . maybe.

The main struggle in the next few months was to get support for returning from my family and friends. If they would not sanction it, it would be suicide. We talked much about the issues at stake. Mum had seen for herself what was happening on the border, Emma already knew all about political inequality in south Asia, Jeremy was no stranger to danger, having done tours with the army in Northern Ireland and Bosnia. I asked them to trust me.

When God calls one He does not necessarily do it with visions of angels or voices in one's head or with divine dreams. No apparitions. No lightning or fire across the sky. I am not a lunatic to say God calls me. He does it through our conscience and my conscience screams *at me that I cannot stand back while my sisters are brutally assaulted across Burma. To those people who can look themselves in the heart and truthfully say that they feel no such outrage, fair play. Their mission is different in detail from mine and I won't argue for a second. Allah loves variety. But when your heart screams at you every day and every night, and when you cannot talk about Red Bridge or Pyo Pan Wai or U Pan Kyaw or Van Sui Chin or Rangoon general hospital without tears coming to your eyes then . . . then who on earth still asks me to stay here in England?*

And my fortune is this. That when I wake up on the floor of Moulmein prison with two of my torturers standing over me and my filthy trousers marked by shit and blood, and my body covered in grease, dirt & sweat, when I look up at them I have this childlike love and trust, I have this inexhaustible feeling that we can get along, learn to understand each other. I do not fear them. No strategy. No plan. No subterfuge or fear. In an unusual way, I love them. There is an indomitable childlike trust. Why does the infant still love the parent who beats her/him? . . . The James you know is not one abounding in metta. *But that is why I keep wanting to go to Burma, because in Burma I am a better man.*

It was easier for me to tell right from wrong in Burma than it was in the UK.

Was I being unfair to the regime?

The devil without *horns is the worst. The most wicked can seem so soft, so welcoming and genial, so accommodating and reasonable. And you feel such a fool for challenging them – you must have been crazy. Here is this man trying his very best to help China/Burma, which is such a very difficult job that cannot we expect some milk to be spilt?*

Was it true that I could do more campaigning in the UK?

What, anything, is the most effective action to help Burma? Political change is magnified by proximity. You don't really change hearts and minds with rallies so far away in convoluted 'chains of influence'. If I have to convince a [British] government minister to convince a civil servant to convince a Burmese official that XYZ is beneficial, then I have truly set myself a gargantuan challenge. Much more obvious to go direct to the Burmese officials.

We can be deceived by noise & activity. If I rushed up & down the UK giving 3 talks/week and wrote 1 article/week for a newspaper and wrote to 2 MPs per week and sold 150 journals/week and visited Premier Oil every week and Lord knows what else . . . well, what a lot of activity! And how would all this change the real-life situation, day to day, of a Shan villager? Or a political prisoner? Or the mindset of an MI captain? By trickling through a long chain where the original intention is distorted and damped to mean virtually nothing. And if one wishes to claim the (very valid) 'drop in the ocean' theory, then surely it is clear that the drops need to rain in Burma, not England.

Democracy is not black and white, not just present or absent. It is an ongoing struggle for society's enrichment. It does not only require citizens being enfranchised with a vote, but also with the means to get things done, with power. We have reached that stage in the West. We, as citizens, have money, information, associations and a voice. We can use this power to act for ourselves, not to ask someone, or some government, to act for us . . .

One person may indeed make little or no difference. But that is not *a reason to avoid trying, it* is *a reason why others must join in if progress is to be made. But if I am to wait for a significant 'gang' to assemble for the off, then I will wait for ever.*

In my ignorance then, I did not realise just how many millions of people were doing great amounts of work, but doing it quietly. After all, our main task, our chief work, is to love. That generally does not make a lot of noise.

One day in March I had picked up a copy of the *Catholic Herald*. There was a large article on Lord David Alton and his new book *Citizen Virtues*. Lord Alton was a man committed to justice. I had had little luck with politicians or government previously, but wrote to this man of integrity on the off chance that he would agree to meet me. I read *Citizen Virtues* and was even more inspired. He had himself been to Burma and crossed the border to see the situation with the Karen.

I was astonished when he agreed we should meet. I had sent him a copy of the journal 'Real Freedom' and he had managed to ignore the worst aspects of it. We trusted each other before we had even shaken hands. I outlined my plan to him and asked if he would be willing to support my family in whatever they chose to do while I was inside. His voice would carry weight and authority; Lord Alton is respected in both Houses of Parliament and on all sides.

He agreed to do that and, in fact, did much more. I am forever grateful for his courage in backing me. Not every politician is willing to associate himself with an unknown, and particularly one who is about to do something which many people would regard as naive and foolhardy, or even selfish and stupid.

I read a human rights report. It told of Karenni women having boiling hot wax dripped on to every inch of their bodies by Burmese soldiers and being left to die. They survived. Christian Solidarity Worldwide had helped produce the report. I contacted them and Baroness Cox agreed to meet me. She also gave invaluable backing in the months ahead. I remember apologising that my plan might sound crazy.

'Don't worry about that, James,' she said, 'a lot of us here [House of Lords] are crazy!'

I was not so fortunate with everyone I met. One fairly well-connected woman I met in London could not see any point in my going to prison. She was particularly struck by the idea that trying to help people in hellish Burmese gaols was a waste of time; surely they were so wretched already that it was best to forget them altogether, that giving rays of hope to them would only prolong their agony. Besides which, she did not feel it could be a priority to help prisoners – they were, after all, criminals who only had themselves to blame.

At first I was shocked. Not just that someone believed people went to prison in Burma because of their own wrongdoing, or that anyone, however criminal, could possibly deserve to be denied their legal rights and kept in conditions which are designed to destroy their dignity. But shocked by the idea that it was pointless to give hope to those who are suffering worst. We do not ask ourselves what is the point of giving comfort to people on their deathbeds. Compassion does not ask for a purpose. And I knew myself that when one is in terrified misery the slightest restorations of hope – a bit of extra food, a piece of information from a prison guard or a smile from another prisoner, just signs that you are not disregarded – go a huge way in keeping you alive. You are not yearning for death but for freedom. Warmth from other people affirms that desire.

But I could not take offence at what the woman said. In my own imbecility I used to think that refugees should be turned back at the border so that they are forced to confront their political problems! I thought aid and camps only encouraged the flow of refugees. As if anyone wants to leave home! Or wants to live in a camp! How blind and cruel my thoughts.

I gave a short talk at a Rotary dinner. A Geordie, Alan McKenzie, heard about it and we met up. He showed great hospitality to students visiting the UK from troubled countries. My mum put on a beer and sandwich spread for a few of them. Our company that day comprised people from the UK, India, Sudan, Uganda, Ethiopia, Zimbabwe, China and Burma. We were getting along famously and the subject of my intended return came up. Some family friends were adamant that it was better to campaign from home.

After an enthusiastic debate that was getting nowhere, Moses spoke up. He was about thirty-five, a Ugandan, and he had enough experience of dictatorship to know exactly what he was talking about. Until now he had remained largely silent. 'Wait a moment,' he boomed in that classic African bass which shuts everyone up, 'if you are thinkin' that you can get rid of a military dictatorship without suffering bloodshed' – he had all of our attention – 'then you are *dreamin'*!' He was not advocating violence, only saying one should expect hardship. There was no painless way. The debate ended on that note. I was deeply grateful for what he said. It is hard for us in democracies to understand totalitarian regimes. We need to listen to those who have lived there, been born there, if we really want to get it.

Diary:

> *I am frequently shit scared and tearfully terrified by the thought of returning to prison, but that is not a valid reason for not going.*
>
> *In prison I will not be setting my hopes on any government to get me out; such is the path to speedy despair. I will not be relying on the people of Burma to rise up and overthrow the SPDC – I could wait until disappointed. I most certainly will not be depending upon my own strength and courage to face the deprivation – I wouldn't last a day. Really, my hopes lie with no mortal; mortals are frail. My Hope lies with Him and He will prevail.*

God does not regard the UK as more important than Burma. Then neither should I. God does not regard my family as more important than a family in Burma. Then neither should I. God does not regard me as more important than a prisoner in a Burmese gaol. Then neither should I. Of course I can love myself, my family and my country more than any others. But I think God wants us to broaden that vision as much as we are capable. When all things are equal we can give ourselves to our own. When things are not equal, when there is abominable and frightening injustice, then we should give to those most in need.

And I had learned this in Burma. There is no strong man and no weak man; no strong nation and no weak nation. Every one of us has areas of strength and areas of weakness. God wants us to use our strengths to help those who need it and in turn to accept help from the strong in the areas where we are weak. Throughout my time in Burma I had not felt that I had given anything but it had been returned tenfold. I did not give but received. I did not teach but learnt. Every time I had been to Burma I had benefited. And I had no reason to expect that to change.

My family had given me their blessing to return. As my mother said, they may have done it reluctantly but it would have been unthinkable for me to be sitting in prison thinking that my family back home was unsupportive. I could have done nothing without them.

Lord Alton had spoken to Jubilee Campaign, a human rights lobby group with much knowledge of Burma and excellent connections in Westminster. They were prepared to take up my case. Baroness Cox did the same with Christian Solidarity Worldwide, a group that truly is worldwide and was to make a crucial impact on politicians while I was incarcerated.

I had prepared a seventeen-page set of notes for family and friends, attempting to explain what I was trying to achieve and what was likely to happen. This included four open letters (see appendix). I hoped that they would explain to interested parties why I had returned to Burma. A lawyer had kindly set up a website for me which took extracts from 'Real Freedom' and explained about *Pyo Pan Wai*. It would also follow the progress of my case. And with Lord Alton's help I was able to speak to a couple of respected journalists before I went, so that they might give support once I was in prison. Almost everything was prepared. Then I was hit by a bombshell and all the plans were in danger of being derailed.

The bombshell was Kerstin. I met her at my twin brother's wedding, less than a week before I was due to leave. Jeremy married Nicole, a German woman, and Kerstin was a childhood friend of hers. The very second I laid eyes on her I went deaf and dumb. I could see her lips moving as she spoke to me but I heard not a sound. The background behind her head and shoulders was spinning, *literally* spinning round. I was pole-axed. I was in awed wondrous dread – *why was this angel talking to me?* This was more than a reaction to physical beauty. It was about big open eyes holding no secrets, bright wide smile signalling the most genuine goodwill, and a whole body radiating warmth and tenderness and strength. The following days were unreal.

On auto-pilot I told Kerstin that I was off to Burma, off to prison, but wondered now if that was true. How could I leave? How could I not? Why, oh why, oh why, in the name of the seven mad gods of the sea, does it have to be like this? Please tell me the difference between loving somebody and causing them pain.

CHAPTER 18

God seeks you more assiduously than you seek Him.
                                    Richard Wurmbrand

ONCE AGAIN I arrived in Thailand. My father would have preferred me not to return, but nevertheless he had driven me to Heathrow and wished me more than good luck. As for Bangkok, the city which had at first been a nightmare of the unfamiliar was by now a welcome friend. Ko Min Aung was fit and well at the Student Relief Committee office. He continued in his duty of looking after those from Minthamee. Although the families, students and orphans were dispersed now, he knew where they were and worked on behalf of those who needed his help in improving their conditions. He gave me some excellent news. Tin Soe, Minthamee's generator mechanic who had been injured by a *Tatmadaw* mortar, Moe Kyaw, who had lost his hands to a landmine, and Yan Kyaw Aung had all flown out the night before to Canada. Ko Min Aung showed me a photograph of Yan Kyaw Aung just before he left Thailand. He was in a safari park, standing up and needing no crutches, he had each arm draped around the shoulders of two bare-breasted Papua New Guinean women. It was a far cry from being half paralysed in the jungle. The Red Cross had done excellent work and so had he. Living in Canada or elsewhere abroad is not the dream of exiled Burmese students; they want to live free in a free homeland. But at least Canada offers them opportunities to work for that.

One of the Burmese students at the SRC office had a Thai girlfriend, Ju. She had driven Yan Kyaw Aung to the safari park and was constantly finding ways to volunteer her help. Gentle Thai, loving her neighbours and changing the world.

There were the customary visits to Bangkok apartments for Mekong, Krung Thipp and company with comrades.

Like the others, Ye Min Aung tried to persuade me not to return, but accepted that I would. 'This time, James,' he warned me with a smile, 'they will keep you in prison until Burma achieves democracy.'

'That should not be too long, then.'

'OK, my brother, I'll see you on the day at Rangoon airport!'

I did not believe I would be fortunate enough to get a visa again, even a one-day one from a border town. I headed north to sound out the chances of an escorted trip deep into Burma. My heart was on Mandalay, but it was very distant. Although it would be a symbolic blow to the junta for me to penetrate that far, it would entail unnecessary risks for whoever escorted me. We would try for something a little less ambitious.

My contact to arrange this was Ko Kyaw Kyaw. I wish he were our Prime Minister: what diligence, diplomacy, realism and hospitality! The planned trip went through Karenni State, northern neighbours of the Karen.

He introduced me to a Karenni general who would decide whether I could go with soldiers of the Karenni National Progressive Party. 'Have you used a rifle before?' he asked, Ko Kyaw Kyaw translating.

'Yes,' I replied. I had used SA80s, GPMGs, even the old 303s before that. And hunting in Australia – shotguns and high-powered rifles.

'Will you take one?'

'No, I don't think I should carry a weapon,' I answered.

'Surely you want to defend yourself?' he asked further.

'I would rather not.'

'Not even a carbine or something? You might get in a tight spot.' He could not understand why I did not want a gun.

But I knew myself. Confronted with a man pointing a gun at me

210

and me one at him, I would lower my weapon and say, 'Hang on, old chap, let's not be silly about this . . . I am sure we can talk it through . . .' Except, of course, that I would never finish the sentence. I would be dead by then. 'What if I shoot the wrong man? One of ours,' I asked him.

He thought about this for a very short time. 'OK, then,' he agreed, 'you don't have to take a rifle. I will let Ko Kyaw Kyaw know when we can take you. Be ready any time.'

We already had everything prepared – the letters, tapes and stickers I would distribute had been well packed. Nothing to do but wait. I should have tried to keep fit as well but I was more interested in eating as much as I could. Once we were inside there might be very little food.

Waiting was terrible. I could not concentrate on anything, just wanted to get the ball rolling. I spent many hours in a room next to Ko Kyaw Kyaw, fairly climbing up the wall with tension. *If this is how well I cope waiting for one week in a comfortable room,* I thought to myself, *with freedom to come and go, in good company, with fine food to be had and books to read and the Net to surf . . . if this is driving me mad, how will I cope with prison?*

Around that time I met Dr Naing Aung, Chairman of the ABSDF. He was committed and intelligent. Talking with him was an inspiration. If only men like him and Ko Kyaw Kyaw were in government!

Finally the orders came. I went close to the border with a friend and there met five ABSDF members, led by Soe Kyaw. They would be my personal escort within the greater column. Soe Kyaw was very accommodating, giving a warm welcome from the very first moment. Other soldiers like to weigh you up first, though. They want to see how you cope with hills and hunger and hardship, before they let down the barriers. To get right to the border we had to avoid a couple of Thai checkpoints, circling round them through the jungle. As we walked down the muddy road that sometimes looked more like a river, we had to keep an ear and an eye out for anyone else on the way. It would not do for them to see a white man here. Sometimes both sides of the road were bordered with steep embankments and cuttings, making it impossible to hide if a motorbike or vehicle approached. Fortunately there was little traffic.

Then the inevitable happened. Soe Kyaw heard voices ahead and signalled to me to disappear. I was terrified that the Thais would kick me out of the area. Everything had taken so long to plan, so much effort, I so much did not want to be thwarted now, even if it was just temporary. I hit the bank beside the road like a missile and launched myself up it. It was covered in thickets of bamboo but I crashed through them like a wounded boar. The earth was loose and muddy, giving way beneath my hands and feet. I drove my hands into it like spikes, up to the wrist, to give myself a grip. My legs were wheeling like something from a cartoon. After seconds of blind panic I realised I was about forty feet up the slope. I dived down and lay in the mud, trying to calm my breathing and nearly wetting myself. Had whoever was on the road heard my wild crashing?

Eventually they passed. Soe Kyaw called me down. He had to call me about five times before I was sure he was talking to me. We regained the road and continued.

Beyond that we used just forest paths. Up and up, steep but wonderful hills. At last we came to the thin red line of Karenni camps right along the ridge that formed the border between Burma and Thailand. It was a disturbing sight. There were trenches half silted up. They were impossible to maintain during the wet season. There were picket fences around the main points of defence; picket fences in an age of heavy artillery and fighter jets. The numbers on guard were few, their weapons old. But what is there to match the courage and dedication of the men defending this line? Thousands of their people behind them in refugee camps and only them to stop the Burmese army making raids across. The soldiers were calm and strong. They were not going to give up.

The situation here was worse than in Karen State. There are about 6 million Karen. Of their northern cousins the Karenni, there are perhaps 150,000. Karenni State in north-east Burma straddles the Salween river, but a huge strip of it, that section sandwiched between the Thai border and the river, has been taken by the Burmese army, as part of their *pya ley pya* (four cuts) campaign. The idea is to cut off supplies of food, money, information and recruits to the ethnic resistance armies. The junta do this by forcing the entire population of vast areas to abandon their villages and move into massive 'relocation centres'. They then destroy all the villages and crops in the chosen area and declare it a free-fire zone – anyone spotted there will be shot on sight. Those in the 'relocation centres' are dying of disease and starvation. As we stood on the ridge line forming the border, and gazed out west over the endless waves of ridges and valleys, green fading to grey, we were looking at stolen land. From one point alone we could see three 'fortresses' of the *Tatmadaw*. They had been built on strategic hilltops, conspicuous white surrounded by the cleared red earth. Built by forced labour of local people who were then herded to massive relocation camps beyond the Salween or taken for portering tasks. Many die in the process. They are used as human minesweepers, forced to walk at the head of columns and thus to detect mines by stepping on them.

In this vast section of land there was not one Karenni village left. They had all been destroyed, burnt down and overgrown. This genocidal campaign is at its worst today. To get supplies into Burma, to their friends beyond the Salween, or to get information out of Burma, the KNPP had to run the gauntlet between these *Tatmadaw* camps, engaging with any patrols they met on the way, ever alert for ambush.

On the hilltop a boy brought a sackload of honeycomb. It reminded me of being with their allies, the Karen, over a year earlier. But this time the comb was full of larvae, and not a few holes still had groggy bees in them, hung-over from the smoking they had had. Soe Kyaw bought a large section from him and the lads fried up the larvae and bees. It took me a few moments to psych myself up – the grubs were fat, slow wriggling gobbets of pus – but tucked in none the less. They were highly recommended as a source of protein. Delicious, I pretended. Anyway, the grubs were nicer than the bees.

Two days later the Karenni were ready to set off into Burma. We took our position in the middle of a large column which assembled at dawn. Over a hundred men, mostly unarmed porters carrying food, they were aiming to cross the Salween some thirty kilometres inland. There they would resupply their comrades, take over from those due leave, swap information.

The column snaked along the border ridge for a couple of kilometres, then wheeled left into Burma. Immediately we left the ridge we lost the vista too. Now we could see only the trees and slopes close around us, and only when we regained ridges deeper inside would we be treated again to the grand views of wave upon wave of green-to-grey hills. Every now and then a soldier from the vanguard would halt beside the track, directing the rest of the column to avoid him. Or, more accurately, to avoid the landmine he was standing over. Dangerous to walk round here without friends. In fact the guerrillas along the Burma–Thai border have learnt an important lesson from other countries with landmines. The mines they now use expire after six months. When this time is up, the home-made mine will not detonate. This is very significant for the future.

When on the move we walked fast, striding out hard. But there were frequent rests; no point in being exhausted if you have to fight. Sitting on the slope of one hill we all became aware of an extraordinary noise. What was it? A train? Impossible out here. A plane? No, too much of it, too close, all around us. It was humming louder and louder. Was it rain on the leaves above? But we were not getting wet.

Soe Kyaw rumbled it. 'Bees!' he said, excited. And then sure enough we were engulfed in the most enormous swarm. It was huge. Thousands and thousands making an incredible racket. They were buzzing just above our heads, only a few round our bodies, and the cloud of them drifting north. I looked around hastily to gauge the general reaction . . . which was to do nothing at all. Nobody was concerned; in fact, the men looked quite pleased.

'This is a good sign,' explained Soe Kyaw, 'we will have no trouble today. If you see bees, it is a good sign.'

Well, I thought, it was a darn good sign that the bees were not rabid monster killer bees and that not one of us was stung.

We continued, passing by destroyed villages. Sometimes I hardly noticed as they were so overgrown. A couple of tall charred pillars were graced with ivy. 'A church . . .' mentioned Soe Kyaw, '. . . before.'

It was warm, very humid and sticky, but not unbearable. Sometimes the vegetation was so thick that you could not see two feet in front of you and definitely could not see the path that your feet were on. Still we raced through it, myself aiming for the part of the leafy bushes which was still swaying from the man in front, because although he was only a couple of steps ahead, I could not see him.

At another rest point Soe Kyaw offered to fill up my water bottle. We were near the top of a hill so I did not know how he would do it but was not going to miss the opportunity. He returned shortly afterwards and gave me two puritabs to drop into it. I was used to the crystal-clear water of the Karen hills, conscious too that supplies here (including puritabs) were hard to come by, so I declined his offer. 'I'll just drink it straight,' I suggested.

'Erm . . . no . . . I think you really should use the pills.' He gave me the puritabs and fairly insisted. I dropped them into my bottle, had a swig or two before the necessary half-hour and we set off.

We passed a large scrape in the ground, a pond, except there could be nothing but algae living in it. It was brown with green scum and it stank. 'Blimey!' I said cheerfully, 'I am glad we don't have to drink that!'

Soe Kyaw looked blank for a moment. 'That is where I filled our bottles,' he said earnestly.

'You're joking,' I said gaily.

'I am not.' He was not. My smile vanished. Ooew. But never mind, if it was good enough for them it was good enough for me.

Further on, below the crests, the trees became magnificent. On the hilltops they seemed stunted and in the valley bottoms they were so lanky. But here on the slopes the great hardwood trees stood with sturdy majesty. They were too big to feel you or see you and you yourself could rarely see more than their hard dry shins and lower branches. Besides these famous teak trees, I had also heard about the legendary impassibility of northern Burma. The Chindits, the Allies who fought behind Japanese lines in World War Two, wrote all about it. Now I found out what they meant. I must apologise if I have ever used the word 'steep' in my life before we walked these hills. I must have been exaggerating. Perhaps there is no such thing as steep outside Karenni State, or perhaps they need to coin a new word. Coming down one hillside we literally swung from clump to clump of bamboo. If you did not grab hold of something within about eight steps of the last clump your momentum would build up too much and you would go flying. We were not really swinging from clump to clump but falling into each one and letting it break our descent. I made an error of judgement, trying to grab hold of an overhead branch to slow myself down. Instead, the whole rotten thing came crashing with me, twenty ploddy feet of it following me down the hill. How I laughed when I was impaled upon the thorny bamboos below, and how all the boys laughed with me!

The air down here was dark and dank, and most of the ground was bare wet earth or mossy rocks, rather than being carpeted in undergrowth like the ridges or else covered in dead leaves like the bowls. There was a large stream at the bottom. Enough to get underwater and cool down, and to refill our bottles with the silt-brown water. Then we faced one of the world's most ridiculous climbs. I am not sure I should call it a hill; it was more like a cliff, but made of mud. The column broke up into an ordered swarm. We were using every part of our bodies to ascend it: feet and hands were kicked or spiked into the earth to get a purchase, knees and elbows gripped whatever root or ridge there was to be had, the whole body pressed as close as possible to the sliding soil. I even grabbed vines and low branches with my teeth for extra hold while a hand or foot sought the next one. It was mental. When we passed the worst of it there was still an incredible endless climb.

'You are very strong,' suggested Soe Kyaw as we caught our breath.

'Not really,' I answered. 'I am not carrying anything. You guys have packs and rifles.' A porter had been assigned to carry my pack and I had not argued. I remembered carrying my own bag through Karen State and nearly being exhausted by it. I hated not to pull my weight, but it would have been far worse for me to collapse on the trip and expect these men to look after me. Forget pride and etiquette, I was not in their league and I was not going to pretend that I was.

'Yes, but', Soe Kyaw continued, 'we have had French and Americans here. Mercenaries. They are crying by this stage.'

I felt extremely flattered, not realising how soon I would be crying myself.

Before we reached the top of the hill the commander gave the order for us to bunk down. Now that we were out of the bottom of the valley there was much more light and much more vegetation. The fat, feathery bushes all around us were ideal for construction. Dozens of shelters sprang up in no time at all. Branches twisted and tied to make frames for the plastic ponchos, which everyone carried. They were not tailor-made, just rectangular sheets of green plastic used as waterproofs. Inside these tents leaves and foliage were laid down and another man's poncho placed over them to complete the 'mattress'. Very comfortable.

There was to be no cooking that night, no fires. The light might be spotted by the *Tatmadaw*. We could not even smoke cheroots unless under cover. We ate cold rice and tinned fish. It rained like a queen. Never mind. The morning was bracing cold.

We were off at first light, over the top and along the next ridge, soon warm again. This day we saw no bees.

'Dah . . . dah . . . dah,' said something up ahead. It was a strange noise, I could not think for the life of me what it was. '*Dah! . . . Dah! Dah!*'

Soe Kyaw had turned round to look at me.

Oh, gunshots, I thought nonchalantly. It was bizarre how that second stretched out, two and two being put together ever so slowly in my syrupy mind.

'DAH!DAH!DAH!DAH!DAH!DAH!DAH!'

Fighting, jungle, guerrillas, army, gunshots, automatic fire.

'Blimey! It's happened!' I finally twigged on. I had been

preparing myself for this moment for almost three years. What to do if you are attacked in the jungle. I never imagined I would have a gun and I never imagined I would have a plan of action. All I had drilled myself to do was to stay as absolutely calm as I could and copy exactly what the man beside me did. If he went to ground, I would go to ground. If he moved forward, I would move forward. If he turned and ran like a rabbit, I would turn and run like a rabbit. The two things I did not want to do was to start asking questions or to distract our soldiers (for example, by panicking).

Soe Kyaw crouched down, I copied. A second later everyone I could see jumped off the track and down the hillside a few yards. Soldiers ran forward but Soe Kyaw grabbed my shirt and pulled me a little further down the slope. The noise ahead intensified. The porters moved back as one and Soe Kyaw took me with them. We would trot back through the scrub for half a minute, then all crouch down again to reassess. Explosions started going off.

They were surreal. I would hear the initial explosion somewhere just ahead and it would echo off the first hill, then the next and the next. The sound seemed to be getting louder, building up a rumbling crescendo, circling round us perfectly from left, to behind, to right, to back in front. Still it got louder. It was like a jumbo jet coming in to land, spiralling around your head at an impossible speed. The gunfire picked up, and more and more explosions went off.

'RPGs,' explained Soe Kyaw. Rocket-propelled grenades.

'Who?' I asked quickly.

'Them and us.'

Every now and then we would move further back. The soldiers, those men with guns, were utterly calm. They looked intense, their movements were quick, but there was not the slightest sense of panic. I took my cue from them. I sincerely believed that there was not a better bunch of men in the world to be with in this situation. They had all been through it a hundred times before. And whatever my emotions might think, my brain had a single simple overriding dictum: there is absolutely no point in flapping, just be calm and follow Soe Kyaw. Whatever tasks the five ABSDF had deeper in Burma, their detail here was to look after me. Bodyguards if you like. They were not supposed to rush forward to the fighting. The Karenni soldiers would look after that. Meanwhile I was not going to try anything independent or idiotically heroic. When Soe Kyaw grabbed my belt and pulled me back some more, I followed immediately.

He pointed to a soldier's waist. The soldier grinned at me with a kind of sheepish relief. His water bottle had been blasted away from his hip. A twisted heart of metal strips hung on the clasps. He was unhurt and knew to receive the incident as a blessing – the only explanation for such a near miss was divine protection. I noticed then with great surprise that my own water bottle was hanging from a single hook – the rest ripped out: I had probably walked into a tree.

The porters, though, were not as calm as the soldiers. They were unarmed. I do not for a moment want to question their courage, but they all knew what this fighting meant too. They moved through the scrub like a startled flock. One or two would suddenly rise and gallop back a bit, the rest of the flock swarmed after. They were nervous, frightened eyes looking everywhere, sounds of distress. It is more difficult to be cool when you do not have a gun.

Usually these firefights last only a few minutes, not more than ten or fifteen. But the rifle fire and explosions had been going on for twenty, twenty-five. I began to worry. Was it an ambush? Being ambushed is a disaster on an utterly different scale from bumping into an enemy patrol, encounter warfare, where both sides surprise each other. We were moving back in considerably larger jumps.

'Two men shot,' said Soe Kyaw, as the news filtered back. Everything changed for me then. Whatever the danger, it had also been quite exciting. As the minutes went by and the noise continued I was pleased to find myself not panicking, but following the boss. But news of casualties took it all on to a new level. This was real, very very real. If we had been ambushed it could turn into a disaster. There might be another party of

Tatmadaw waiting behind us to block our retreat. We were now moving back at quite a hard pace.

I began thinking of my twin brother, now a captain in a commando unit. I remembered him telling me how important it was that the British army had the best equipment available. The soldiers needed the best kit so they could go into battle with confidence. And I was frightened by the idea that our politicians might let them down on that.

This thought ran parallel in my mind to the reality around. No soldiers would be braver than these Karenni, none in the world knew the land better than they or had more reason to fight for it. Man for man they were unbeatable. But as they are so grossly outnumbered, and as they have so little ammunition, so few guns, what can they do? It is one thing to debate the rights and wrongs of armed struggle. It is another to see underequipped men fighting heart and soul for their land against a monstrously powerful enemy. And the *Tatmadaw* used its troops as cannon fodder: young boys, press-ganged, brainwashed, abused, drugged, sent in to fight with a rifle *in* their backs. These soldiers are victims of the regime too.

An hour after the shooting started we paused to take stock. Here the trail had widened considerably, doubled, trebled and split again. The effect was to produce a kind of clearing. Occasional firing could still be heard. More men took position around the clearing, news came in.

'Not ambush,' Soe Kyaw assured me. That was a massive relief. The *Tatmadaw* column had been carrying sacks of rice to one of their strongholds. They had not expected to be attacked.

'How many of us shot?' I asked.

'Two men,' he answered and as he said it they appeared. They were being carried on stretchers, each one made from two or three *longyis* that were slung round a single bamboo shaft, a thick strong one, and the body lay in the *longyis*. Two porters carried each stretcher on their shoulders.

The first casualty had been shot only in his ankle. He was in obvious pain. Immediately a soldier began giving first aid, although I could see there was a dressing already on the wound.

The next man had been shot in the thigh, the leg swollen massively around his shattered femur. The *longyi* round his middle was covered in blood. He was laid down and Soe Kyaw began on first aid. Others helped him clean the wound. Antiseptic powder was sprinkled around it, a new field dressing wound over the bullet hole and morphine shot into his leg. This man was almost unconscious.

The column commander paused beside us. He was speaking into his walkie-talkie, sweating like a pig and slightly ruffled, but the expression on his face was one of intense determination. He had to decide our next move.

'Two more,' Soe Kyaw told me and I felt a crack in my heart.

When the next stretcher came in it was carried straight past us. A porter was on it, his head and shoulder exposed, and his left arm hanging out, hitting the thorns and branches as he was taken by. His face was white, he was moaning in deathly fear. He knew, as we all did when we saw him, that he would soon be dead. The two previous casualties were in distress but controlling it, their faces dark with blood and pain. This other man was wearing a death mask.

The fourth body I did not see. He was a porter. When the shooting began and we had all ducked to the south side of the ridge, he ducked down to the north. He was machine-gunned, shot in the knee, waist, chest and head. Still his friends picked up his body and brought it back. It was hastily buried close to the first aid spot and shortly afterwards the third casualty was buried next to him. Both were porters. Both unarmed.

'How many *Tatmadaw* killed?' I asked.

'Don't know,' replied Soe Kyaw, 'many bodies.'

The two injured soldiers needed to be taken to Thailand. There was nowhere here for them to recover. The commander decided that as we were so close to the border, only one day away, we would all go back with them. Soldiers had already been detailed to go point, to clear the way ahead. We followed ten minutes later, back past the previous night's camp, back down the cliff of mud, back over the large stream, back up the bamboo-covered slope.

Sometimes, instead of going up and down the hills we would

contour along the sides of ridges. The path might be no wider than the breadth of your foot, the seventy-degree slope falling away to one side. It was hard to keep balance. I cannot count the number of times I slipped, but fortunately each time I was able to steady myself. To fall down the slope would mean going twenty or thirty metres out of control before a suitably large tree broke your back. On advice in Thailand I had brought a torch with me, but was relieved when Soe Kyaw had told me that we would not march at night; it was difficult enough during the day. But darkness came and there was no hint we would stop. It began to rain, the tiny paths now becoming impossibly slippery. And as the rain seeped into and trickled over the hot earth a mist thickened in the air on the hillsides. It became harder to see ahead, even when the mist brightened from the moonlight.

If I thought I was having a difficult time keeping on my feet, I marvelled at the porters, the stretcher-bearers. Where I had walking shoes they had flip-flops or bare feet. Sometimes the path would twist with hairpins, studded by sudden three-foot drops and trees, boulders and overgrown undergrowth, making it impossible to stray from the track. The stretchers would be shifted from shoulder to shoulder, then lowered to waist height as the forest demanded, rested on knees or barged into bushes as the track became vindictively awkward. The porters did not seem to tire, their bodies tough as . . . incredibly tough.

For a couple of kilometres we went at a half-run down a stream bed, sometimes jumping from rock to rock, sometimes the water up to our thighs. The banks of the gorge were near vertical – an unpleasant place to be trapped. There was little time to think as at such a pace all your attention was devoted to spotting where your foot would go next, avoiding the low gnarled branches which hung green across the way and being sure that you were not losing ground to the man in front.

'Not long now,' said Soe Kyaw softly, 'not long now.'

The pace was fast. I was rapidly becoming exhausted. We walked for nineteen hours that day, reaching the border after midnight. For the last hour I was moaning with every step. I wanted to stop, I wanted to cry. I was finished off, worse than anything I had known before, yet I had been carrying nothing but a water bottle. These men carrying their brothers were strong throughout.

Back on the border in a hut, I could hardly move. Sleep was the most blessed thing in the world. At dawn the next morning I went with Soe Kyaw to a Thai town. Our two injured soldiers had been taken to a hospital there during the night. I asked Soe Kyaw if I could visit them and he told me it would not be a problem.

In the hospital only one was awake. The other was unconscious. But neither was in danger. The soldier shot through his ankle limped about. We could not really talk. He only spoke Karenni and I did not. I made a donation for food, but there was nothing I could really do to show my respect for them. They face this sacrifice every day.

I contacted my twin brother by e-mail. He gave me good advice. Told me it was the reality of fighting. He asked me if I had visited the families of the two dead men. I had not even thought of it.

The next day I met Ko Kyaw Kyaw in central Thailand. I did not want to ask anyone to take me in again through the jungle. They did not need any extra baggage. So Ko Kyaw Kyaw and I had just half an hour together to come up with a new approach. Although I had got into Myawaddy the previous November on a one-day visa, I hardly believed it would be possible for me to do it again. Surely it was an unrepeatable fluke that I had got in while blacklisted. And Ko Kyaw Kyaw had told me the SPDC had been expecting me for two months. A radio message to the MI on the border, warning that I planned to return, had been intercepted. I was not surprised that they knew as I had been making no real effort to keep it a secret. But however unlikely it seemed that I would get through immigration, it was one of the last options available.

Ko Kyaw Kyaw and I did not muck about. Within the half-hour we had a new plan. I would go to Mae Sai, opposite the Burma border town of Tachilek, gateway to the Golden Triangle. The following day I was there and the morning after I miraculously scored the visa. By evening I was in prison.

CHAPTER 19

'So-and-so! Article 58-1a, twenty-five years.' The chief of the convoy guard was curious: 'What did you get it for?' 'For nothing at all.' 'You're lying. The sentence for nothing at all is ten years.'

The Gulag Archipelago, Aleksandr Solzhenitsyn

I ENTERED TACHILEK ON 31 August 1999 and for the third time gave out letters calling for the release of political prisoners and the reopening of the universities. Strange that while some prisoners in Burma spend years detained without having a trial or even learning of the supposed charges, I was 'arrested, tried and sentenced' within ten hours. Remarkably swift injustice.

It is wrong to use words like 'arrest', 'trial', 'judge', 'appeal', 'law', 'authorities' in Burma because no such things exist. We need a new vocabulary to describe the fraudulent system of dictatorships.

I was not arrested in Tachilek, I was taken in. I was not informed that I was arrested. I was not informed of the charges against me. I was not told the name of the arresting officer. At no stage did I have my rights explained to me. I was not allowed to have any contact whatsoever with the outside world. I was not told that what happened at four o'clock that day was my trial. I had to guess halfway through. All this is in stark violation of Burma's laws.

I asked the judge if I could speak with a lawyer. The request was declined. Yet this right is stipulated in Section 435 (1) of the Burmese Courts Manual. And also, Section 340 (1) of the Criminal Code states unequivocally: 'whomsoever is charged with a crime in any court *shall have the right of defence by a lawyer.*' And further: '. . . it is not a question of indulgence that the counsel for the accused should be heard before judgement, but one of right. It is an elementary principle of law, that no order should be made to a man's prejudice especially in a criminal case without hearing him and the very object of the Legislature in allowing parties to be represented at trials by counsel is that counsel must be heard before a final opinion is formed by the Court . . . *And the conviction will be set aside if the accused's lawyer is not heard.*'

On this point alone my whole conviction should have been overturned. The Burmese legal system is based on what the British left behind in 1948. It looks like law, it sounds like law, but the entire current structure is vacuous and corrupt.

I was accused of distributing anti-government literature yet at no point was any of the literature produced or read out. No evidence was shown in court for the simple reason that there was nothing objectionable about it. Section 14 (4) of the 1962 Printers & Publishers Act notes, 'should the . . . Court judge that some or all of the . . . materials are in violation of the law they can order their destruction. Should the Court judge that the said materials do not violate the law . . .' Clearly, then, the materials had at least to be examined. But eleven months later, when the case was finally taken to the highest court in Burma, my lawyer was still not allowed to examine any of the evidence. This was of course because nowhere can it be considered a crime to say 'Treat People as Human Beings' or anything else that I distributed. I do not think even the judge saw them.

And finally on this charge, the 1962 Act provides for materials, which *can* be freely distributed, for example, material relating to social matters. Again there was never an opportunity to argue the case in court.

On the immigration charge they broke the law with abandon. One of the conditions of obtaining a visa is that you undertake not to break any of Burma's rules or regulations. You are not informed of this when applying, but it is common sense anyway. Once I was deemed to have broken the 1962 Printers & Publishers Act the court claimed that I had therefore, under Section 4 (2) of the 1947 Immigration Act, broken my entry conditions. That is true enough if the first charge could be substantiated.

But the *maximum* penalty stipulated under 4 (2) is *immediate deportation*. Of course the MI wanted none of this. So quite arbitrarily, with no explanation whatsoever, they changed the charge to Section 13 (1). This refers to people who enter Burma *illegally*, with no passport, papers or visa at all. I had been given five years for it in 1998 and now they added five more here.

The court transcript (when it finally appeared) recorded that I entered Burma *legally*. After seven months they even showed my passport to British consular staff, which confirmed this. Yet I was sentenced to five years under Section 13 (1) for *illegal* entry.

In effect – and the mind boggles at this – they said 'you broke the Printers law so seven years in prison, and breaking the law is illegal so five more years for that'. Laughable from the outside; wicked from the inside. I had been charged twice for the same offence, yet this violates Section 403 of the Criminal Code, which states that a person tried for a crime shall not be charged or tried twice for the same crime.

In any case no evidence was shown as to the immigration conditions. Now I was no lawyer but I knew this smacked of lunacy. I asked again and again for the court to try to explain it but they could not. Section 341 of the Criminal Code states that '. . . if the accused . . . cannot be made to understand the proceedings . . . the proceedings shall be forwarded to the High Court [which] shall pass order as it thinks fit'. But nothing was passed to the High Court.

Paragraphs 34–5 of the Courts Manual stipulate that the court diary may be taken in English if the accused does not understand the Burmese language and in 1958 it was ruled that the proceedings should be 'explained to the accused in the language he understands'. This was not done.

As for adding on my five-year suspended sentence, that was an utter joke. It was not even mentioned to me until two weeks later! And then I was only forewarned because a consular visit was due. In 1998 I signed a bond of three conditions for my release. It was done under duress after torture and ninety-nine days' solitary confinement, so I would argue that the bond was not legally binding. In any case I did not break the conditions of it. At least I had the right to argue it out in court.

It may sound silly for me to want to argue these things through when they would be rejected out of hand but it is one's right to defend oneself in court and furthermore the court is obliged to write it all down in the diary. I complained in court that whatever I said was not being recorded by the diarist. I could see him sitting idle. But it was still not recorded.

Finally, and in my opinion most despicably, the court disregarded my plea and fabricated it. I did not plead 'guilty' and I did not plead 'not guilty'. I refused to plead. I said that I did not recognise the authority of the court. In this instance the legal procedure is for the court to make its judgement but refer the case up to the High Court. They did not do this. Instead they wrote in the court diary, and it makes me sick to see it, 'After explaining the meaning of the charge till he understood it fully, he was asked as to whether he pleads guilty or not guilty, James Mawdsley pleaded guilty.'

The whole court transcript was a fabrication. And what I hate about this is that there are tens of thousands of innocent men, women and children suffering beyond description in Burmese prisons and they have been put there under this wicked and corrupt system, which knows no justice, no truth, no hint of reality. It is not just lies from mouths and pens, but it is a whole life of lies. The court is not a court, the judge is not a judge, yet they are dressed up as such. And merciless men sit behind it all saying they have a judicial system.

What am I supposed to make of members of my own government, members of the Houses, members of the Cabinet, some of them trained lawyers, some of them QCs, who spout the same degenerate nonsense that we must respect the SPDC's 'judicial system'? Shame on them.

That, then, was the trial: utter mockery of law. Thanks to my friends, though, I was quite safe. The ABSDF had done marvellously. Within three hours of my arrest the news was in Bangkok and put on to the wire. The junta had no chance to make me 'disappear'. So my first moments in the Tachilek cell were moments of relief. Months of preparation had come to an end and the interrogation was over as soon as it began.

The cell, although large, was the filthiest I had ever seen. The dusty floorboards were pitted with woodworm and around the edges of the cell they were moist and rotten. In one corner was a low concrete wall around a hole-in-the-ground toilet. That whole space was so disgusting with unidentifiable filth that I would not go near it. The rest of the cell was completely empty. At night the guards handed me a ruined mat to sleep on. I woke up in the small hours with a huge wet black rat pawing at my thighs. Most unsavoury. The guards did not know what to feed me so they went and bought dishes of noodles from a nearby café. About four of them lounged and slept on the other side of my cell bars. Beneath the formalities there was a good rapport between us – smiles, co-operation and a little laughter. Had we been in a free country we would have had a fine old time. But here they had to act like guards and, for their sake, I had to act like a prisoner.

Before making the demonstration I had stuck a few stickers on my back in case everything else I had was confiscated. Despite being searched one of these stickers had eluded them. I was delighted to have it in my cell. 'No More Arbitrary Taxes' it read in Burmese. I showed it to one of the guards to see what he would make of it. He seemed interested and held his hand out. I gave it to him. Evidently the bright-red writing on the bright-yellow background pleased him greatly. He peeled the back off it and stuck the sticker along the biro he kept in his breast pocket. Very attractive. I was somewhat amazed. I thought he would screw it up and complain to his boss that I was *still* giving out 'terrorist propaganda'. Instead he put it on proud and personal display. I had just got seventeen years for doing that!

I found yet another sticker on the inside of my sock and could not believe how inefficient their searches had been.

The guards were quite friendly, although also very wary. They told me I would be taken up to Kengtung, a town some hundred kilometres to the north-west. I was glad to be leaving Tachilek gaol; any cell would be better than that filthy hole. The junta were afraid to keep me in Tachilek, afraid that there would be a cross-border rescue mission launched by fearsome insurgent groups (I do not think the junta realised that I would have hated that kind of folly too!). Kengtung, though, was isolated, far more secure.

We flew there. I would have preferred a drive for the views but so it goes. On the plane I was not only handcuffed to the police officer on my right, but also to an officer across the aisle on my left. This meant his arm was stretched across the aisle and the stewardesses could not get through. We sat at the back of the plane and the rest of it was full of civilians. They ignored us completely. Nothing curious about seeing a Westerner handcuffed between two policemen on your domestic shuttle.

The guard on my right was rather too friendly. After twenty minutes or so he laid his hand on top of mine. Paternalistically? Homosexually? My blood froze. He was a bit of a dear old man so I did not want to cause offence. I pulled my hand back out (it could not go far because of the handcuffs) and gave him a disapproving Paddington stare. But it unnerved me about what might happen in Kengtung.

When we came to disembark, one policeman had the genius idea of laying a handkerchief over the cuffs so that nobody would see we were handcuffed! How bizarre. We walked down to the tarmac, almost hand in hand, with a handkerchief miraculously floating between our wrists. His superior snapped at him to remove it.

There were photographers and video cameramen to record it all. They always appeared when I was being moved or 'interviewed'. I very much doubted they were for broadcasting within Burma – why would the regime want to admit there were protestors. Instead, they would be for the benefit of MI chiefs who were too scared or too 'important' to show their faces in public. With this in mind, whenever I saw a camera I would grin at it and stick up two fingers in a gesture of victory, not sure what I was victorious about but better than looking downhearted.

Then we travelled in the back of a paddy wagon to the prison. I could see hardly anything out of the van. Kengtung is a beautiful town and I was missing it all. At the prison I was searched again and spent a good hour sitting among huge piles of papers and files while the authorities sorted out my admin papers. They were disappointed when I refused to sign anything. They could not understand why.

'You must obey our rules in our country!' they kept repeating.

'*You* must obey the rules in your country!' I protested.

The escort from Tachilek left to return there. I was very glad to see the over-friendly policeman leave. After that I was taken to my cell. I could hardly believe my luck; it was huge.

I learnt later that Kengtung prison has only four cells, or more properly, wards. Each one holds about a hundred men (outside was the women's section with a hundred women). There was no way that the prison 'authorities' wanted me mixing with other prisoners so they had to find me a room of my own. To this end, they kicked the officers out of their resting quarters and designated that as my cell. It was 27 × 23 feet, a high roof, freshly plastered walls. These walls were a blue/green pastel colour. At home they might be distasteful. In prison they were positively cheery. No blood, vomit and pus stains here.

The floor of the cell was concrete but almost half of it was taken up by a wooden platform, averaging two feet from the ground. It was seven feet deep and stretched from wall to wall. That is to say, my 'bed' was 27 × 7 feet! Unheard of.

Although the door was boarded up there were also five very large windows. The two at the back of the cell had shutters locked over them so I could not see out. But still there were two looking out east and one looking south for the winter sun. Admittedly the view was somewhat impaired by the nearby twenty-five-foot perimeter wall, which my cell was just a boulder's throw from, but at least I could see whoever was walking around the edge of the prison. Far better than Insein where I could see only a treetop and a few blades of grass. If I stood next to the south window and looked out to my right I could see through the barbed-wire fence into the corner of the main prison compound. This would be invaluable for communicating with other prisoners who happened to pass by, accidentally or otherwise. We 'spoke' in 'international sign language'. This spontaneous semaphore is entirely improvised and it is astonishingly comprehensive, universal and innate. From the two east windows I could see the gate to my compound (useful to know when someone is approaching) and off to the right I could see the resting shelter (once it was built) of my guards (also useful for keeping tabs on them). Were it not for the perimeter wall, I would have been able to see the sunrise too.

One small detail with significant consequences was that the floor of my cell was a good foot higher than the ground outside. This meant that I could look from side to side through the gap between the window frames and the shutters (which were always open) and thus see the feet and legs of any guards or officers near my cell. However, from their point of view, they could not see inside my cell unless they stood directly in line with the window, and if I was standing to one side they could not see me unless they pressed their faces against the bars. Basically it meant that I knew when someone was approaching my cell long before they knew that I had spotted them. This was invaluable when I was planning some kind of mischief as well as an important psychological advantage. They were very rarely able to surprise me. I got to recognise every trusty, guard and officer just from their feet!

The cell was furnished too. There was a mat, a tiny sheet and a blanket to sleep on. In one corner there was a pot of drinking water, in the other a bucket. What more does one need? I was not allowed to keep my toothbrush or toothpaste, nor a spare T-shirt or even a pair of socks, not allowed to have the Bible I had brought. But who needs all that? I had 27 × 16 feet of ground space to walk around and three windows to look out of. What a gift. I had plenty of time to fight for the rest.

I was delighted that the interrogation was over though I could still hardly believe it. I spent my first week waiting for a summons from the MI for further questions. But it did not happen. One week after I was arrested I decided that I would have to begin the 'dialogue' myself. If they did not want to come to me to 'discuss' the situation, I would have to get their attention.

9-9-99 was approaching. It was a potentially important date. Not only did it resonate with the unforgettable day of 8-8-88, but nine was a special number in Burma. Ne Win, the dictator from 1962 to 1988 was paranoid about the auspicious implications of the number nine, its astrological connotations. In 1987 he abolished, without even warning his colleagues, the currency denominations of 20-, 50- and 100-Kyat notes. Without explanation the notes were suddenly no longer legal tender. Millions of people lost their life savings overnight. Inflation soared as people were desperate to spend the worthless notes. Ne Win replaced the lost currency with 45- and 90-Kyat notes $(4 + 5 = 9, 9 + 0 = 9)$. What a crazy economic policy! In his early days as dictator he used to have his own special chair carried around from building to building. It was nine inches taller than the other chairs and he allowed nobody else to sit in it. The 1990 election was held on 27 May $(2 + 7 = 9$, the fourth Sunday of the fifth month). For whatever reasons, the number nine was a very significant number in Burma. I did not want to let 9-9-99 pass by without acknowledging this.

However, I did not want to make a scene on that day either. Political prisoners are sometimes accused of overestimating the impact of their actions. It was not that I ever dreamt I could stir up a wider disturbance, but I would die of shame if I gave the junta a pretext for accusing me of trying. If the Burmese people are to rise up, they will do so of their own volition and only when they judge the time to be right. It is wrong for any outsider, foreign or Burmese, to try to encourage those inside the country to begin protesting. We can protest ourselves, but let us leave the population to decide for themselves what they want to do. In any case no person or group in history has ever been able to orchestrate a successful and just mass uprising. If the will is not there among the crowds they will back down after the first few casualties. Those deaths would have been avoidable. If an uprising is to carry through it must build up its own momentum, over months and years, and will erupt spontaneously beyond anyone's control. This is what happened in Burma in 1962, 1974, and 1988. The 1988 uprising was tragic in the loss of life, but it was extremely successful. The people made great sacrifices to demand change – up to 10,000 civilians killed – and they terrified the junta by their numbers, their discipline and their courage. The junta were so scared that they promised the elections. The elections came and the NLD won eighty-two per cent of the seats. Now nobody on earth can deny that the people of Burma have expressed their desire, that they want democracy. And again it was proved that the junta was an illegal body, anti-constitutional. The Burmese people achieved a great deal by their tremendous courage. Can the outside world match their courage by recognising the sovereignty of the NLD? Britain, or any country, can raise this in the United Nations. The General Assembly can vote to reject the SPDC's delegation and accept one from the NLD. This measure cannot be vetoed by other countries. It is simply a matter of a majority vote. And as Daw Suu Kyi said: 'Is the United Nations General Assembly meant for the lawful representatives of the people of various nations or is it just meant for any old government that happens to have come to power?'

Some claim that Burmese people do not actually know what democracy is, saying to them it is nothing more than a slogan. Well, who in the West can define democracy? And more to the point, as Lord Macaulay said:

Many . . . are in the habit of laying it down as a self-evident proposition, that no people ought to be free till they are fit to use their freedom. The maxim is worthy of the fool in the old story, who resolved not to go into the water till he had learnt how to swim.

As if people do not know what they are calling for when they want to be treated with dignity and to live with freedom from fear and freedom from oppression!

With all this in mind, I thought I would make my own little protest to mark the occasion but a couple of days early. In any case the junta were well prepared for 9-9-99 and might have a trick up their sleeve to make it more difficult to protest on that date.

Each evening at around six o'clock all the prisoners would line up on parade in front of the four wards and sing the national anthem. They would then be marched into the wards and the doors locked for the night. Of course, throughout this I would remain locked in my cell but I could glimpse a few of their faces from the south window. The first time I looked out at them we regarded each other with grave expressions. I was worried that it might be insensitive to smile and no doubt they felt the same. Then I remembered a lesson from the refugee camps. Foreigners on fleeting visits to the camps tend to walk around with an understandably grim expression on their face. They are either genuinely shocked by the deprivation they see or else they think it appropriate to maintain a sombre bearing. But if you stay a few days this no longer seems right. Life must go on. Honest cheerfulness is quite welcome. And so, catching the eye of one of the prisoners, I risked a smile at him. The whites of his eyes grew a little and then he smiled back. He elbowed his companions and pointed at me. They all saw me smiling and immediately the whole bank of faces lit up in big grins. It was as if a floodlight had been switched on and I felt a surge of happiness. We beamed all the more. We were here together, we knew it was hard, but damn the junta if they thought they could beat us. No way. OK then, how would I share the message with the whole parade, not just these few prisoners on the end?

Burmese men sing well. I had heard beautiful Buddhist chanting in the prison. But on the parades the men sang awfully. They were so out of time with each other and out of key or tone or note (or whatever someone with a musical ear would say) that the performance was laughable. They mumbled and slurred or else a few individuals would shout it out at the tops of their voices in a parody of enthusiasm. I am certain that this was done on purpose to show their disrespect for the regime (but not the country). It was about the most outright way they had to protest without earning a beating. Well then, I could disrupt the parade as a sign of solidarity with them.

So on 7 September as the afternoon wore on, I psyched myself up. I was undoubtedly scared stiff. As the moment came closer I looked at my hands as they shook and could not stop them. I prayed and prayed for God to be with me and to give me the courage to carry it through, and to have the strength to face the consequences. I had no idea how the prison officers would react. But if they thought they had shut me up by putting me in prison they were mistaken. The anthem began and I faced the locked door towards the main part of the prison.

'Your cause is my cause!' I shouted in Burmese, '*Koe lay lone* [four nines], build on the spirit of 88!'

I did not want to say anything special about political prisoners (as if anyone would understand my pronunciation anyway). We were all suffering here.

'DEMOKRASI!' My repertoire of slogans was pretty paltry but I tried to make up for it in volume. A couple of guards ran to the window to signal at me frantically to shut up . . . and then the parade finished. I waited in my cell, bracing myself for the authorities' reaction but nothing came.

Oh well, I thought, *glad that is over. At least the other prisoners know I am on their side . . . next time I will have to do a little bit more than just shouting.*

But the delay was just because the officers had to have a council of war to decide what to do. Early the next morning a troupe of them, led by the prison governor, Maung Lo, barged into my cell. They circled around me. Maung Lo had a bamboo cane in his hand. He was a short, dumpy man, fifty years old, blind as a mole.

There was a brief exchange of views. The governor was furious that I seemed unrepentant. 'You must be disciplined!' he screamed, thwacking the bamboo cane against his boots in anger. It was the only time I ever heard him speak English. I looked at the cane, somewhat alarmed, but with that they were done and all filed out, firing back sour looks and withersome stares.

A few minutes later a group of men appeared outside my cell. Previously there had been just two guards assigned to me. An old man with two stripes on his shoulder and a young one with no stripes. They wore the brown prison uniform and changed shifts with other guards around the clock. But this new group of guards looked different. It was not just their uniforms, which were a sort of sandy-green colour and made from a canvas-type material, much rougher than the other guards' clothes. Nor was it only their size that was different as these new men were big, some really big, and covered in muscles unlike the thin old man and his partner. But it was their faces that were most strikingly different. They were hard faces. These were tough men and their faces showed that they had had hard lives. I wondered if they might be soldiers, if I were to be moved to another prison where I could be totally isolated. There were five of them and they did not smile. I looked out at them and they glared back without a trace of softness in their expression.

It turned out that I was not going to be moved away but these men were just there as an extra guard in case I caused any more trouble. The authorities did not want me disrupting their routine. They were meant to control everything. Nobody was meant to challenge them. So although at first the extra guards were a bit of a worry, as time went by some of them became very very dear to me indeed. I had wondered about shouting out on the 7th. What was the point of it? But the main result of it was this increased guard and they turned out to be one of the greatest blessings.

The prison authorities also changed the parade time from evening to morning. Then back to evening sometimes. And then morning again. I cannot think why.

CHAPTER 20

Where caution is everywhere, courage is nowhere to be found. Our ancestors were not quiescent; we shall die of prudence yet, you will see.   A bishop of Poitiers

I HAD BEEN WONDERING what tightened security arrangements the authorities might make for 9-9-99. The generals were fearful of a nationwide uprising. I could never have guessed their plan for us. From 8 September, and for the next three and a half days, instead of taking prisoners out on work details, all were confined to the wards, except a skeleton crew of prisoners who carried the rice to them twice a day. And then, over the speakers that were dotted around the prison to blare out the junta's propaganda, the authorities played . . . music! And what wonderful music. Not just Burmese classics and traditional Eastern instrumentals, but also pop stars singing cover versions of Western songs, mostly ones from the 1970s: the Bee Gees, John Denver, ABBA, sung in Burmese. What a wonderful plan! The idea of this three-and-a-half-day music fest, without break during daylight, was, I suppose, to pacify us all. Confined to barracks there would be no sudden uprising and breakout, and with music to soothe us we would all be gentle as lambs. If they thought that a little music was going to distract everyone from the significance of 9-9-99, if they thought the melodious atmosphere would soften us up and make the notion of protesting seem like a foolish one . . . well, they were absolutely right! For myself, anyway, it was

237

enchanting. There was one piece in particular, played about three times a day, which I adored. It was done on a sitar, sounded more Indian than Burmese, and it was incredibly skilful. The speed at which the player plucked the strings, the wonderful rising and falling scales and repetitive theme building up on itself like Ravel's *Bolero* had me dancing every time. Well, I did not quite dance but shuffled around my cell in a quickstep, trying to take one step for every dozen notes and failing, fingers clicking to the rhythm and head wobbling from side to side with the beat. Fantastic. I do hope the guards did not see me. Each time it finished I would call a guard over and beg him to tell me the name of the music and the artist. I dearly wanted to get a copy whenever I was released. But the communication barrier was insurmountable. I did not find out.

When democracy comes to Burma I will go to every music shop I can find and ask to listen to every sitar song they have, and I cannot wait to dance to it again!

Sometimes a guard would stand right by the south window of my cell and watch me. They soon moved a chair over to make the position more comfortable. In fact, as the ground sloped away the cell floor was considerably higher than the ground outside so they had to stack one chair on top of another to see through the window. The guards took it in turns to sit there. Naturally I detested this close observation; it is a horrible invasion of privacy. But I noticed a difference between the guards.

Most would sit there and after watching me for a couple of minutes, they would turn round and stare into the void, occasionally firing glances back. Two of them especially, of those five hard-looking men, would make a point of scarcely looking at me at all. They knew that to watch me was an invasion of my privacy and indeed it was a loss of their own dignity. As if they wanted to stare at the zoo animal! There was nothing special about a foreigner. I respected them for this. Every now and then we would have a short chat.

It turned out that the five men were prisoners too. In Third World prisons the regimes cannot afford to pay for enough prison guards. Instead, nearly all the work done is by prisoners themselves. Not just cooking and cleaning and laundry, which you would find done by prisoners in any Western country, but also the admin of the prisoners: sorting them out for work details or prison visits, counting heads, leading the parade and even doing guard duty. These were the trusties. In exchange for co-operating with the regime they could reduce the length of their sentence and also gain considerable privileges. The actual guards were there just to see that all was going smoothly and only those outside the perimeter or in watchtowers were armed (in case of real trouble).

It was an odd hierarchy. It meant that five per cent of the prisoners lived quite well. They were richer than low-ranking prison guards, better fed and for practical purposes much more powerful. Above all these were four lieutenants who were responsible for managing the system and above them the prison second-in-command and the governor.

When I realised that these five men were prisoners too I felt a great excitement. Surely we would get to know each other very well. Did their faces look hard? Well, they had suffered years in prison and before that some had been soldiers in the *Tatmadaw*. About 300 of the 500 male prisoners were deserters from the Burmese army. And once the prison authorities disappeared and left the trusties to guard me their expressions did soften.

I was not receiving adequate food. Twice a day I got a plate of rice with a small lump of *ngapi*, fish paste. In the mornings I would get a dribble of yellow bean mush on the rice and in the afternoons some spinach or perhaps four morsels of pork. My appetite was returning as I was settling in and I became voraciously hungry.

I asked the authorities to let me pay for extra food. I had money on me when I was arrested and I knew from Insein that prisoners are allowed to set up an account to buy extra rations/tooth-paste/cheroots. But the authorities said no. I complained that the food was insufficient. Two of the lieutenants brought me noodles on a couple of evenings. I gobbled them down.

'But not every night,' explained the middle-aged Lieutenant Smo Ki, 'I buy this with my own money.' He was lean, unkempt and perhaps a touch concerned that his amiability towards me should not undermine his authority.

'Thank you, they are delicious!' I answered, 'but please, I have money, let me buy them myself.'

'Oh no. Not possible.'

The other prisoners noticed my predicament. Chindithe, one of the five, came to my cell one evening. He was very tall for a Burmese and bald as a monk (most prisoners had their heads shaved but trusties could grow their hair long). He tentatively offered me a couple of dry biscuits. I was starving. I thanked him deeply and scoffed the biscuits before anyone else might notice.

The next day he brought me an apple. Wow! A whole apple. It was in fairly manky condition. You would complain if you saw it in a Western supermarket, but I was too hungry to care. I ate the whole thing, core, pips, bruises and all. A couple of the other guys began giving me food: bread, biscuits, bananas, *a kyaw soe* (fried vegetables in batter – outstandingly delicious!). I would eat this either in the toilet corner of my cell, which was not visible from any window (every other part of the cell was) or else hidden under my blanket. I was determined not to get anyone into hot water. Bananas were a problem because I was left with the skin. I would have to smuggle it back to a friendly guard for him to dispose of.

Soon there was such a flow of food coming to my cell, at all times of the day but usually at night, that I actually had to start turning it down. It was incredible. And on top of all this I had to keep up my protests to the authorities about getting extra food. Although the generosity of the other prisoners kept me fed, I did not want to rely on it for ever.

I was concerned about where the food was coming from. Surely there were hundreds of prisoners present who needed it more than I did. Chindithe told me not to worry. The prisoners were actually having whip-rounds to get the food for me. Back in the wards dozens of prisoners were involved in it. I had not explained to any of them why I was arrested but news filters down from the guards anyway. In fact, in such a closed and bored community there are few secrets. Everyone knows everything of interest within twenty-four hours (except me of course). They knew darn well that I was no terrorist, but that I was there for calling for democracy. And if they could not overtly show their approval they would find other ways.

I cannot overstate how much their kindness meant to me. If I had not felt their warmth I would have been desperately alone. When I shouted slogans on the 7th to the other prisoners it was because I believed that solidarity is worth showing. To an outsider, perhaps to the reader, it appears quite futile and even ridiculous. But I know this as a prisoner: physical isolation is hard to bear. Much harder is emotional isolation: when you are made to feel like a criminal for following your beliefs; when the authorities do all they can to cut off the slightest signs of approval for what you have done. So small gestures help. You do not need praise or back-patting, but to be reminded that there is truth and a truth worth suffering for. When the guys gave me food it was a great delight to the stomach but a much greater joy to the heart. Shouting slogans of defiance in prison will change few outward things but it is a signal to the other prisoners that we are all harbouring the same thoughts within us, that the repression is out of order. No man is an island. One who is treated as an island will die of despair.

Even more than food I wanted news and the guys began giving me that too. One of the trusties, Anawratha, spoke particularly good English. He was powerfully built and his eyes showed a depth of compassion. He told me a British girl had been arrested in Rangoon for singing pro-democracy songs. At the time it was very good to hear. Again it made me feel less alone. Sentenced to seven years, she was kept in Insein prison. She was released after two months.

I also learnt that a group of Burmese dissidents had taken over the Burmese embassy in Bangkok and shot at the portrait of Than Shwe with an AK47. Nobody had been hurt. Again, this was most encouraging news, although I knew very few details. They also told me that British consular staff were due to visit me on 15 September, two weeks after my arrest. Excellent.

On 14 September Lieutenant Soe Lin came to see me. 'You have not twelve years,' he explained. Twelve years was the

sentence handed down by the judge on the day of my demonstration. 'You have seventeen years.'

'Aha! Is that my five years from before, from Insein?'

'You have seventeen years now,' Lieutenant Soe Lin repeated.

'Yes, I was wondering about that. Is that my suspended
sentence from 1998?'

'Please, yes, you have not twelve years. You have seventeen
years.' He was smiling nervously and then trying to straighten his
face to look grave. Lieutenant Soe Lin was thirty years old, very
tubby, very polite.

Well that was that. I could not get any details out of him, I am
not sure if he knew any. Not twelve years, seventeen. No trial. No
judge. No examination of the previous conviction or whether the
conditions of my release bond were broken. Just a lieutenant to
tell me twelve years was now seventeen and I was supposed to ask
no more questions.

Never mind, I thought, *God willing I will see consular staff tomorrow and
I can ask them about it. Besides, seventeen years sounds much better than
twelve*! I had wanted to defy the junta, to show them some real
cheek by returning the third time. To show them that they cannot
break our spirit and that their lawless decrees deserve respect
from nobody. Frankly, twelve years had been a mild disappoint-
ment. But with seventeen I felt I must surely have riled them. The
more ridiculous the sentence the better it would be for me, the
more likely I was to get out early.

My mood before the consular meeting was a good one. Over
the past week I had asked/demanded to get my Gideon New
Testament and had received it. I had also managed to get a pair
of socks from my belongings, very important as mosquitoes love
our ankles! This was done in only my second week. In Insein it
had taken more like two months to win these concessions. Things
were going well.

Had it been my first time in prison I would have been terrified
by each passing hour that I was not able to contact the outside
world. But in Insein it had taken twelve days before I was given a
chance to speak to embassy staff. It was not unduly worrying,
then, that it took a little longer here. I learnt later that Tiffany

White, the British political secretary who had seen me off from Rangoon the first time, had arrived in Kengtung on the 7th. She had travelled 400 kilometres north and spent many hours in an office outside the prison requesting to visit but was not allowed. This is contrary to the Vienna Convention to which Burma is a signatory. Why would the authorities not permit us to meet for even one minute, just so that I could say I was OK? I do not believe the main motive was cruelty. It is just that they have tiny paranoid minds and they want to control everything. Nothing can go ahead except at their arrangement.

And while I spent those two weeks trying to settle into the prison my family were going through terrible anguish. The FCO (Foreign and Commonwealth Office) was speedily in contact with them but did not have many details to give. My family could not find out what had happened, whether I had been tortured again, whether I was dead or alive. It is natural in these circumstances to fear the worst.

CHAPTER 21

Hope, in this deep and powerful sense, is not the same as joy that things are going well, or willingness to invest in enterprises that are obviously headed for early success, but, rather an ability to work for something because it is good, not just because it stands a chance to succeed. The more unpropitious the situation in which we demonstrate hope, the deeper that hope is. Hope is definitely not the same thing as optimism.

Václav Havel

As IN INSEIN, the first certain sign that a visit was imminent was when a set of clean clothes appeared. I would be told to get changed. It only took two seconds to change but they brought the clothes an hour early. This was good preparation time.

Visits were conducted in governor Maung Lo's office. It was about fifteen foot square and, remarkably, they would leave me alone in there for ten or fifteen minutes before the meeting. I was able to study the huge map of the prison and environs, which covered one wall, and also a bank of photographs opposite. I got to look all round the prison thanks to those photographs. I saw inside the wards and outside the prison walls. I learnt where the guns were posted (watchtower and outside) and saw prisoners on work details: crop plantations, pig farms, chicken farms, road-widening, quarrying, so many tasks. Then the embassy staff arrived, one British and one Australian. I had entered Burma on my British passport and therefore should be represented by British embassy staff. But the Burmese authorities had not mentioned in Rangoon that I had entered with a passport and so both Britain and Australia sent a member of consular staff to the meeting.

They were followed in by five officers who sat down in a row uncomfortably close to us. There was the governor, the prison 2 I-C, an immigration officer and two others. One of the others would act as interpreter. Over the months the panel changed, but always included MI. Two or three of them furiously took notes throughout the meetings. The immigration officer shamelessly placed a tape recorder on the table in front of him. Other guards milled around the edges of the room, some taking photographs, some toting guns. Those who had nothing to do stared intently at the proceedings. It was a most intrusive atmosphere.

The consular staff tried to be sympathetic but could not really conceal that they thought I was an imbecile. We established quickly that I was OK and had not been tortured. I asked about my family and was assured that they were well. Although it was vital to get to the nitty-gritty of the charges, I knew that the whole legal thing would take an awfully long time. It was important as well to try to establish better living conditions. For example, I had not been allowed any time outside my cell for exercise, only five minutes daily at noon to wash. The governor assured the consular staff that I would be allowed regular exercise.

I complained about the lack of food. The consular staff had brought a few rations up, as well as two much needed blankets. Only because they insisted was I allowed to set up a prison account for extra food. There may have been some error in translation because I explained that in Insein I could buy food every two weeks. Here in Kengtung, however, they agreed to let me buy food every two days. Wow. I was not going to object.

The consular staff wanted to know if I wished to appeal and showed me a list of lawyers working in the country. Of all the Burmese lawyers only one had said he was willing to represent me. I knew nothing about him and had no way to find out. In any case I did not really want Burmese lawyers to be involved because I thought it would endanger them. As for the foreign lawyers working in Burma, every single one of them on the list had told the embassy that they did not want to be involved. Foreign lawyers in Burma are there to make a packet by rubber-stamping the regime's trade/shipping contracts. They are not at all interested in justice. If I were to appeal, it would need a lot of expertise and a lot of work from people outside the prison. That was not yet available. I said I did not want to appeal.

The sentence was a mockery of law; an appeal would be just the same. I asked, though, that they obtain a copy of the court record. I did not realise that this was the first step of an appeal anyway. I was sure, however, that once the court record was obtained the junta would not be able to detain me for much longer, as the illegality of my detention would be so manifest. And if the regime refused to produce a copy of the court record that would be an admission of the illegality and the FCO would have justification to demand my release. It is every defendant's right to ask for the court record. Even in Burma the process usually takes only five or six days. For me it took over eight months.

I rarely spoke directly to the authorities. It was too difficult for me to keep my temper. Instead, the consular staff would talk to the interpreter, he would ask the governor and the governor would make a note to consult with the MI later. He was not allowed to make any decisions himself.

'My toothbrush and toothpaste are kept outside the cell,' I reported to the consular staff. 'I have to ask for them each time I want to brush my teeth.'

Apart from the irritation of this I genuinely hated asking one of the guards to have to get up to pass them to me. The guards would lounge around half asleep and by no means did I want to interrupt their reverie. If the man wants to sleep let him sleep. I detested having to ask them to do everything for me: to bring my toothbrush over, to take it back when I was finished, to repeat that in the evening, to put my shorts out on the wire to dry after I had washed, to pass them back if it began to rain, to pass me the mossie repellent in the evening, to fetch Lieutenant Soe Lin if I had a matter to raise with the authorities, to take down my food requests every two days . . . what a lot of unnecessary bother.

The consular staff asked if I could keep the toothbrush and paste in my cell.

'No,' was the reply.

'Why not?' asked the consular staff.

'We will consult with higher authorities,' was their final answer. Each exchange took considerable time. Nothing could be done quickly.

I wanted my family to know I was OK. I sent back the following messages:

> Psalm 4:v:7: Thou hast put more joy in my heart than they have when . . . grain and wine abound.

> Psalm 31:v:7–8: I will rejoice and be glad for Thy steadfast love, because Thou hast seen my affliction, Thou hast taken heed of my adversities, and hast not delivered me into the hand of the enemy; thou hast set my feet in a broad place.

And after detailing the court proceedings:

> The trial was a blast. It would have made Skippy blush. I did not have a lawyer (though I asked for one) but then neither did they . . .

It meant the world to me to see embassy staff, to hear that my family were OK and to pass on the message that I was too. But I was puzzled by some of their comments. After explaining what I had done in Tachilek, one of them admonished me: 'This is a military dictatorship. There is no freedom of speech here.' It was about the most crass thing I had ever heard. Any law that prohibits healthy and non-violent expression is not, in fact, a law. It is a baseless decree worthy of no respect. Freedom of expression exists everywhere because everywhere there are people who will exercise it.

The meeting lasted about one hour. The next one would be in four weeks' time. As soon as I got back to my cell I tore off the clean clothes and put on my good scruffy prison wear. The governor, of course, had lied about the exercise. I was not to be allowed out of my cell for the next month either except for the daily wash. They also made buying extra food as difficult as possible. Every two days I could get a couple of apples and a packet of biscuits, or some bananas and a bag of noodles. This, however, was a great start.

My prison rations improved too. On the morning after the meeting Lieutenant Soe Lin arranged for me to be brought a cup of steaming sweet milky coffee and a few slices of lovely fresh bread. I do not know what he was thinking. 'Soe Lin,' I said to him, 'thank you very much for your kindness here. But when I say I am starving I do not think a cup of coffee is the answer.'

Soe Lin looked confused.

'You have the coffee,' I said and pushed it away. There was no way I wanted to accept cups of decadence from the regime. 'And thank you for the bread. Bread is good. But please don't give me three dainty slices each morning. Let me buy a loaf.'

'No, you cannot buy.'

'In the meeting the governor agreed with consular staff that I could have a prison account. Let me buy a loaf of bread each day.'

'Yes. You cannot buy.'

These conversations were painfully slow. The authorities saw every request as a trap and were scared to give a straight answer.

'OK. Never mind. I see consular staff in one month we try again.' My English was beginning to deteriorate. 'Please, no more coffee. It is better that you give the prisoners some meat. And the bread, let me buy a whole loaf. In Insein I was allowed a big piece of bread every day.'

Soe Lin smiled and blushed. 'Yes, OK then,' he agreed, 'you cannot buy bread.'

You have to be very patient! After a couple of days the bread and undrunk coffee were replaced by *san byo* and a boiled egg. A whole egg every day. Inconceivable. *San byo* is a loose term. Basically it is a rice porridge but depending on the mood of the authorities it could be either milky water with a few floating shreds of pulped rice, or else it could be so thick that you could stand your spoon up in it. On good days it was salty enough to have a flavour. Soon afterwards I was also allowed to buy bread.

Noise in the prison did not stop. I will not even go into what happens during the day, constant roll-calls and barked orders, shouting and clanking of chains, metallic pounding in the workshop. This background din was virtually constant. But it was at night too. Every fifteen minutes the guard in the main watchtower would bang a gong, once for every fifteen minutes past the hour. On the hour he would bang it four times and then bang it for however many hours had passed. So at one o'clock it would be struck five times, at midday and midnight it would be struck sixteen times. And, once he started dinging the dong, four others would echo it back from other strategic points around the prison. That is eighty bangs at midnight.

At about 6 p.m. over 400 prisoners would knock out the national anthem and be filed into their cells with chains clanking and bars rattling on doors. Then they would sing out twenty minutes of beautiful Buddhist chants. At half-seven there would be half an hour of traditional Burmese discordant music, which admittedly I grew to love. But one of the loudspeakers was attached to the outside of my cell and it was horribly loud. The sound quality was dreadful. Right after this would be an hour of propaganda, supposed to be Buddhist teaching but corrupted and an agony to endure. This began at eight o'clock and so did the 'banging of the bamboo'. About eight guards were stationed around the prison with two pieces of bamboo each and had to bang them together *non-stop, without any interruption* until four the next morning. Absolute lunacy. The idea was that the boss could lie down on his bunk and so long as he could hear the bamboo banging he knew the guards had not been overcome in a mass breakout. Or more probably he knew that the guards had not fallen asleep at their posts. Fortunately they frequently did. But this was the least of it.

Worst was that every fifteen minutes when the gong went off, between 8 p.m. and 4.30 a.m., the four guards assigned to the four ward entrances would each have to sing out as loud as they could: 'Ward One and all is well!' then 'Ward Two and all is well!' then 'Ward Three and all is well!' then 'Ward Four and all is well!'

You prayed each evening that the duty guard (or trusty) would be a sensible chap who called it out with the minimum volume he could get away with. But there were always one or two of them who were a little bit keen, out to impress the officers with their enthusiasm, and they would shout it out at the very top of their bursting lungs. Imagine that: ten feet away from your head, with just one wall between you, and every fifteen minutes some goon screaming at the top of his voice. I could picture him throwing out his chest and head raging with strain, coming up on to his toes as the final syllables flew from his mouth and then he would rock back down, deflated and puffed out, with a naughty smile on his face for being such a good little guard.

It did not end there. Twice a night at least, or if there was trouble, half a dozen times, an officer would do a lightning tour of the prison and each time he passed a guard the guard would have to again shout out his position and that all was well. And on these occasions nobody could get away with a medium voice. They had to try even harder to hit the decibels to prove that there was no disobedience in them. It must have deafened the passing officer – no wonder he rushed.

Outside my cell I had eight men, at least two of them up on night shift. Most of them were trusties but there would always be two or three guards too. Until midnight they would be chatting or talking or arguing or singing. Almost every night an older guard would rock over blind drunk. He would be asserting his power, causing fights and shouting at anyone inferior to him. Through the small hours whoever was on duty would pace furiously round the compound to keep warm, even jumping up and down. I could feel the vibrations through the floor, amplified by the wooden sleeping platform. The nights were full of noise. Sleep? Forget it.

The strip light in my cell was kept on all night. There were rats pattering around the cell, along the platform, over my feet. I was foolish enough to keep an apple overnight. The rats took chunks out of it. I would have got on much better with the rats if they had not made so much noise at night: exploring, fighting, mating. The consular staff once brought me an airline eye mask to help me sleep. The rats got that too. It took me a long time to work out how I could have lost a mask in my virtually empty cell. Sleep? No chance . . . unless you are called Ramon.

Ramon was the guard who seemed to be most often on duty in the main watchtower. To me, at that distance, he was just a name and a silhouette. It was his job to ding the dong every fifteen minutes, and thus set off the cacophony of echoes and voices that followed. But Ramon's job was so irretrievably tedious that he could not stay awake. As the minutes ticked by and it became apparent that he had missed his moment, guards on the ground would start shouting at him to wake up and strike the cursed bell. But Ramon remained slumberent. The calls became louder and louder, and angrier and angrier. They would start hurling clods of soil way up so that they would crash down on the tin roof or smash against the steel grille around the tower. Still Ramon slept. At last someone would dig out a catapult and fire huge dry clay pellets at the tin roof. They were rock hard but shattered on impact, making a sound as if they had been fired from a gun. At last Ramon would wake up . . . and then I would wait in excited silence for the comedy moment to come.

All of us on the ground knew it was, say, quarter past one in the morning because we had been following the progress of the night. That meant one bong. But poor Ramon had just been rudely awakened and, half in a dream, he scrambled up to grab his gong striker and cast his head back to look at the clock and perhaps he had knocked it over in his rush or had his head sideways or perhaps he just had difficulty telling the time because he read it as ten o'clock and launched into four bongs for the hour followed by ten for the ten. How we giggled! And how the officers snarled and snapped. The other gongs in the prison would leave a tactful pause before striking one solemn note each.

Around four in the morning the clanking bamboos and the shouting guards would stop, and straight away the propaganda would start again, blaring oppressively loud right outside the cell for half an hour. After that there would be a few moments' peace. Glorious silence for fifteen minutes until it was time for more Buddhist chanting.

Each morning at about six Lieutenant Soe Lin would come to

my cell to see that I got the *san byo*. The doors were opened for him, he would step over the threshold and be followed by four or five others. One, a prisoner-cook, would be carrying the food. 'How are you today?' Soe Lin would ask each morning. He was short, round-faced and his uniform was always immaculate.

'Fine, thank you, very good,' I would invariably reply. The food would be laid down on the sleeping platform and a prisoner would take away my latrine bucket to empty it. It was not the most glamorous of jobs and it was a task he would repeat at midday while I had a wash. (Burmese political prisoners are left to defecate on their cell floors and some days, if they are lucky, they are allowed some water to sluice it out.)

The prisoner who did this was called Brother Sid, but it took me a few weeks to learn his name. He was just a year younger than me and very short, thin and deferential. At first he would not enter my cell without taking his flip-flops off. In Burma one always removes one's footwear when visiting a *paya* and more generally might remove them when showing respect (for example, when visiting a friend's house). Most prisoners were indoctrinated into taking off their footwear whenever they went indoors, because as they were supposed to be so worthless they had to show respect to everything. After a little coaxing I assured Brother Sid that he could wear his sandals in my cell. Lieutenant Soe Lin did not object.

As Brother Sid was on latrine-emptying detail, no one seemed to think they owed him respect. Twice daily he would be hovering near my cell ready to take the bucket out. The guards, keen to demonstrate their authority, would shout out at him aggressively. Even if Sid was only a few yards away they would shout at him. Even if it was patently obvious that Sid was waiting there ready to do his task, the guards would bark out at him as if he were idle, or late, or miles away. 'Shit bucket!' they would holler in Burmese. For the first few weeks I thought that was Sid's name. They would not only shout it out, but do so with contemptuous anger, which meant, 'Come here at the double, you worthless shit bucket and be grateful if I don't kick you!' Visitors to Burma say that the Burmese are gentle folk. They should wait until they see a

Burmese addressing their subordinates before deeming them gentle or humble.

If Lieutenant Soe Lin decided the cell should be swept out he would signal his intention to one of the guards. 'Hurry up, shit bucket!' they would holler, 'get the broom and start cleaning!'

Brother Sid would hurry to the main latrines a hundred metres away, empty my bucket, wash it out using a splash of water and his foot, then run back to start sweeping. Meanwhile Lieutenant Soe Lin would stand in the middle of the cell either staring at the ceiling or engaging me in pleasant conversation. We might chat about local customs or British ones, about local food or else pass comment on how unseasonably clement the weather was. Beneath this I was trying to probe for information about prison affairs and conditions. The other guards would stand around aimlessly, occasionally making a pretence of searching the cell. They might bang the bars with keys, listening out for a dull sound, which would indicate that I had filed through the bars during the night with . . . with . . . with my flip-flops perhaps. Or they would walk over the sleeping platform kicking the hardwood boards to see if I had loosened any in an attempt to tunnel out. Sometimes they flicked the corners of my blanket over to make sure I was not concealing a cache of weapons. But mostly they were idle. If they tried to look busy it was to impress the lieutenant.

By this time Brother Sid was busy sweeping away. He would do most of the floor but obviously could not ask anyone to step aside; he was, after all, too low to address a superior. I watched painfully.

Lieutenant Soe Lin would be lost in a dream world as Brother Sid swept the floor around his feet. Unable to clean the spot the Lt was standing on, Brother Sid would move off to sweep the detritus out of the door. Lieutenant Soe Lin would take a few steps to one side still lost in his dreams and then would suddenly notice the spot where he had been standing had not been swept. 'Hey! You lazy good for nothing!' he would rasp, 'come here and clean the muckin floor!'

Brother Sid would hurry over, head bowed, to finish the job. Lieutenant Soe Lin would cluck and pout, and fume at the uselessness of the prisoner. 'Honestly! You can't get these worthless criminals to do *anything* right unless you watch them every step of the way!'

The trusties would spot their chance. The boss was angry, best try to appease him. So two or three would crowd round Brother Sid and snarl abuse at him. One might grab the brush angrily and give a few fierce strokes of the floor in a demonstration for Brother Sid to see how sweeping was done. They would glare at him for the rest of the job. But Brother Sid was not allowed to decide when the job was over. His superiors were in control of everything, and if Sid stopped sweeping it would be tantamount to telling the boss that he did not know what was going on. It was not up to prisoners to make any decisions. Brother Sid would start re-sweeping the clean bits.

Eventually the Lieutenant would come to again. 'Enough!' he would snap in a rage. 'Now wipe down the platform.'

Brother Sid would look helpless for a moment. He did not dare to point out that he had no cloth and it would be impertinent to ask for permission to get one. He would stand, helpless, waiting to be shouted at again.

The trusties would start to get angry. 'Go and fetch a cloth!' one would shout at him, earning points with his boss for his enthusiasm. Sid would run out.

'Back here now!' another would demand as soon as Sid was out of the door. Then a trusty would storm off to get the cloth. Sid obviously could not be trusted to do anything right. The cloth would be flung on the platform and Sid set about polishing the whole 27×7 feet of it. Yet again he would be instructed on how to wipe the wood and yet again Lieutenant Soe Lin would fail to notice when the task had been completed. So Sid polished on until Soe Lin woke up again and ordered him out in a fury for wasting everybody's time.

Often there would be an MI chap present too. They would remain silent but be watching everything. Lieutenant Soe Lin would be too distracted to realise when it was time for them to go. The *san byo* had been brought which I would not eat until they all left the cell. The latrine bucket was emptied and returned. Once or twice a week the cell would have been swept and the platform polished. But it was all such a strain to poor Soe Lin that he would forget what came next. Brother Sid had made his escape and now the trusties had nobody to bully. They did not dare to suggest to their boss that he should go now.

I would not say anything either. I found it hugely amusing just to stand there and smile at him while he beamed back. He would rock on his heels, hands clasped behind his back, smiling back at me genially and wondering if there was anything else we could talk about. My eyebrows would get progressively higher until he suddenly registered. He would collect himself in a funk and bid me good day, then march smartly out of the cell followed by his team.

Once he confided to me while the MI were not present that he hoped to be transferred to another prison. A bigger one. It was his reckoning that if he kept me sweet, if he made sure I was well behaved, he would get a gold star on his record and the transfer would come his way.

Most officers wanted a transfer. Kengtung prison was a small one and not great for opportunities. The more people who are under you in the regime, be it soldiers, prisoners, workers or whatever, the more you can extort from them; the richer you will be.

Actually Lieutenant Soe Lin was not a greedy man. His tubbiness was not extreme. Neither did he lust after power. One day a prisoner told me that he had a good heart. And it was true. He did. But he wanted to please his superiors: he wanted to do the job to the best of his ability; he wanted everything to work smoothly; he wanted to be praised and promoted for his diligence. This was no kind of vanity, just perfectly healthy ambition and a feeling of satisfaction from a job done well. He loved his country, he wanted it to thrive, and he felt that if only everybody would just obey the regime and stop causing trouble it would all come up roses. Unfortunately he did not realise that what the regime wanted was not a free and thriving nation but absolute power. That corrupt goal poisons everything. And it meant that people lower down the hierarchy like Lieutenant Soe

Lin could mistakenly think it is possible to love one's country without loving the people who make that country. It meant that in the name of progress and development and stability of the union, he was willing to see innocent men imprisoned and good men starved and beaten. He was willing to tell any lie and be blind to any injustice. Just obey the regime, he thought, and all will be well.

The other officer I saw most of was Lieutenant Smo Ki. He was about forty-five, thin but strong, wispy balding hair and a hard expression. Maybe once upon a time he had been as keen and green as his colleague Lieutenant Soe Lin, but he knew better now. He knew that the prison service was a dead end. You were not promoted in Burma unless a relative promoted you or else if you showed an unwavering disposition towards obedience and ruthless cruelty.

'Lieutenant Smo Ki,' I complained to him once, 'I want to speak with the prison governor.' I did not, but it seemed only fair to approach them through official channels.

'Why?' he asked.

'Because I am still not allowed out of my cell for exercise. It is not good, all day in one room.'

'I am sorry,' he said, 'I cannot give you permission for exercise.'

'No,' I replied, 'I am not asking you for permission. I am asking to see the prison governor so I can ask him.'

'It is not my decision.'

'I realise that. Thank you. But will you tell the governor that I want to speak with him?' It was only fair to give them every chance before making a protest.

'I cannot decide.'

'I am not asking you to . . .'

'OK,' he lied, 'I will tell the governor.'

I did not want him to think I was a whinger. I wanted him to see where I was coming from. 'Lieutenant Smo Ki,' I said, 'you know it is no good to keep anyone in one room all the time. I need exercise. I am here for seventeen years!'

'Mawdsley,' he said to me levelly, the only Burmese person who ever called me that, 'I am here for thirty years!' And he went.

What a statement. This was a prison officer. He regarded himself as a prisoner there, that his thirty years' service was harder to bear than my prospective seventeen years. And the fact of it is that he was right. Burma, the whole country, is a prison. Life for Lieutenant Smo Ki was tough. Did he have time off? Hardly. There were no weekends, no clocking-off time. Duty was often around the clock, sometimes days at a time. Once or twice a month there might be a festival day. Perhaps then the officers would wear *longyis* instead of their uniform. It was a constant struggle for these four lieutenants to manage the prison. Their superiors were ineffectual, dim and incompetent. The guards below them were so jaded that they did nothing unless ordered. And the MI were constantly about, watching for the slightest slip or error. Lieutenant Smo Ki had no enthusiasm left for life.

I was sorry, then, for all the trouble I was about to cause for these men, sandwiched between the immovable regime and the irrepressible foreign terrorist who demanded such outrages as exercise, or books, or freedom.

CHAPTER 22

Man is ultimately self-determining. Man does not simply exist but always decides what his existence will be, what he will become in the next moment.
                                                          Victor E. Frankl

TOWARDS THE END of September rumours began in the prison of an imminent visit from the International Committee for the Red Cross (ICRC). The preparation for the visit took days. Everything was cleaned, brushed, whitewashed, polished. Prisoners had to pick their way along the top of the twenty-five-foot-high perimeter wall to pull out the huge weeds which had grown there. I watched in agony, dreading that one might fall. Bamboo poles were strapped together to extend brushes so the whole wall could be whitewashed. Those who did the job at ground level had no brushes, they smeared it on with their hands. Vegetable patches were weeded and hoed and raked and brushed. Blades of grass were plucked out individually from the paths. Stones alongside the paths were whitewashed and, quite extraordinarily, so was all the barbed wire in sight.

Prisoners were kept in their wards during the days for lessons in how to respond to any questions they might get from the ICRC. They learnt by rote to say that all was well and that they had no problems. Also sinister was the clanking and pounding that went on all day and all night. Of the 500 prisoners, 200 wore shackles around their ankles, knees and waists. These were removed for the visit.

My own cell was repainted outside and mercilessly swept inside. The wooden platform was not just wiped with a cloth but polished with wax so that it gleamed. My water pot was changed to a big bright plastic one from the market and they knocked up a wooden frame to go over the latrine bucket – it was just something to squat on. Mysteriously the ICRC reported this as a Western-style toilet. I am not sure how many Westerners squat on a frame of wood over a bucket when they need the loo. Also a packet of sweet pink tissues and a bar of soap were put in my cell, as if I had had them all along. I did not actually give a cuss for these pleasantries. When in Rome . . .

The inspection tour began. Lieutenant Soe Lin told me to sit at the back of my cell and not look out of the window. I stood right by the window and waited to greet the ICRC party. Eventually they came by.

'Good day to you,' I said as cheerfully as I could. There were about four white faces there and a dozen uniformed Burmese following them. Lieutenant Soe Lin made frantic gestures at me to go and sit down. I waved back at him amiably and he pulled himself together.

'We will look around,' said a French accent, 'and see you later.' And that was that for the day. The following morning they returned and we had the chance to talk.

The mission was led by a Swiss man. He took a long time over his introductory speech. The ICRC had been trying for over twenty years to get into Burma and only in June had they finally got permission from the regime for prison visits. I chose not to comment that this was done without consulting the NLD. He said they had strict procedural procedures, or something equally impressive. They would cancel the whole mission unless they were allowed access to every part of every prison, unless they were allowed to speak with any prisoner they chose, unless they were allowed to speak with them in the open air and confidentially, and unless they were guaranteed the right to return visits.

And here we were, sitting outside in the sun, my first time, and not a guard or trusty or MI man in earshot. They were allowed to watch from a distance. The Swiss man told me a little of their teething troubles with the regime and it seemed that yes, he was no fool, and he was not going to let the regime pull the wool over his eyes.

But in exchange for the regime's co-operation the ICRC confirmed that its findings would be strictly confidential. They would not talk to the press. In his long soliloquy the Swiss man told me that the ICRC had been the first people to visit Nelson Mandela on Robben Island. They were very proud of that. Later on I read Mr Mandela's autobiography. He reported that the ICRC visitors, who came exceedingly rarely, were terrified of upsetting the South African regime and did not dare to make significant protests about the injustices they saw. White and coloured prisoners were allowed to eat bread. Black prisoners had almost nothing but maize to eat. Mandela asked the ICRC rep to raise this with the prison authorities. The rep was reluctant. Instead, as he was leaving, he shot back:

'You know, Mandela, bread is bad for your teeth.' And that was that.

The team included other Westerners and Asians. The Swiss man was very professional. The rest were not. They were patronising and did not hide their scorn for me. They thought I was worse than a fool, worse than an irretrievable idiot. I was dangerously irresponsible. I was a retarded troublemaker.

I had been really looking forward to their visit. I thought I could get a message to my mum that I was still OK. I hoped also for a little bit of non-hostile company. I was wrong.

'How have you been treated, have they hurt you at all?' asked one of them.

'Nothing too bad. Physically it was just the handcuffs. They cut my wrists with them,' I answered. 'Look, you can still see the marks after four weeks.'

I was about to put my wrists out but was dismissed. 'So the handcuffs were a little tight,' was the startlingly contemptuous reply. 'I mean, have they tortured you?'

'No. I was not tortured this time.' I was a little surprised by his brusqueness. 'But they do do it, you know. I was tortured last time . . .'

'I am not interested in what happened before,' was the snapped response, 'just this time.'

'Well, I do not think it is right that I am not allowed out of my cell for exercise. I have been here a month.'

No reply but they took notes.

'How about the food?'

'The food is OK. But there is not enough of it. Officially I am supposed to be allowed to buy extra fruit or whatever, but they make it difficult.'

A Burmese woman chipped in. She was lovely as any, but unfortunately, despite being Burmese, despite being part of the ICRC's prison visiting team, she did not have a clue. 'Why don't you get oranges?' she asked sweetly.

'Excuse me?' I responded.

'You can get oranges from the market.' I was quite dumbstruck. Did she think I was allowed out to the market or something? Or did she think I could just ask the prison officers to get them and they would? Did she not realise that everything was a fight in prison and if I asked for oranges they would tell me there were none in Burma and then they would tell me I was not allowed them and then they would tell me that they had to ask the higher authorities and then they would stall for months?

'How can I get oranges?' I asked her, aghast.

'They're in season, silly!' she giggled. 'The market place is full of them.' She shook her head at my unworldliness. Did I not know that September was the season for oranges?

I told them that since the consular staff had visited I was allowed an egg every day.

'An egg!' repeated one of the Europeans and began scribbling down. 'An egg,' he repeated to himself, impressed.

'Look, I was not expecting a hotel you know,' I said a little annoyed. 'I realise it will be hard here but . . .'

'I have to go now,' announced one of the team, 'I think you . . . I think you . . . I think you talk an awful lot.' That was this one's farewell line. Never mind at all that I had been in solitary confinement for a month and was yearning for a healthy open conversation, a chance to listen to intelligent people speaking without fear, a chance to tell them of what I had seen and heard in the prisons. No, I talked too much.

I had told them about the great whitewashing campaign but assumed they expected that. I told them about prisoners being forced to chant the answers they were supposed to give, that 'everything in the prison is OK'. The ICRC did not appear interested. I hope that was just professionalism – poker faces. 'There are 477 male prisoners here,' I said. 'I don't know about women, maybe 100. Of the prisoners, 300 are army deserters, including officers, commissioned as well as non-commissioned. They get two to five years or, if they took their rifle with them, they get twenty years. About a hundred prisoners are here on drugs charges.' My information came from the prisoners. Admittedly there were different versions. But the ICRC seemed convinced that the vast majority of prisoners here were in for drugs. Not many army deserters. I asked them if they had seen prisoners with shackles on, 200 of them.

'Oh no, silly,' came the reply, 'there are not 200 of them. Only a few, who go out to work every day. About forty or fifty wear chains when they go out to labour.'

'Have you looked at all the other prisoners? Have you looked at their legs? Have you looked for the scars?'

They had. No, there were no shackles in Kengtung (except for the work party who had them taken off once they were safely home).

Although I had expected to be inside for six to eighteen months I could not afford to voice this too clearly. If the junta got wind of it I was sure it would only encourage them to keep me longer. But the ICRC gave me to understand that I would be in for many years.

'Well.' One sighed as she left. 'I guess we will be seeing you many more times.'

'What?' I was startled. 'Why, how often do you think you'll visit? . . . Annually?'

'Maybe,' she replied. How utterly insensitive. I did not think I would see them ever again, once more tops. But it was tempting to believe that they might know what they were talking about,

JAMES MAWDSLEY

given their privileged access to the prison system. So they suggested that I would be there for many years.

I tried to be patient. No doubt it is not in the mission statement of the ICRC to give sympathy to prisoners, especially not idiot ones like me. I tightened my psychological belt.

One offered to give me a medical but explained that he was not a doctor. He had just inspected my cell and was so impressed with it that it only took him a few seconds. I think he must have been the one to report that I had a Western toilet.

The greatest boon was that I was able to write a letter, which they would then show to the authorities and, if there was no objection, pass on to my family. I hated self-censorship but I wrote a non-political letter to say I was fine. Later on other prisoners told me what they thought of the ICRC. It was not positive.

When the team left I felt utterly deflated. Whatever they thought they were there to do, and whatever their opinion of what I was doing, I do not believe it is excusable or humane to laugh at a person facing seventeen years' solitary. I pray and hope that the Swiss man's leadership will carry the team through to achieve something for prisoners in Burma. They cannot fail to do some good. But at what price? If they are too timid to confront the regime they will provide a stamp of legitimacy with little in return.

As the sun went down that day I was taken to the main office again. I had no idea why but it turned out to be another visit. Unbelievable. Anything to break the monotony. The office had had all the furniture removed and much smarter chairs moved in. The table was covered with a white cloth. There was one man sitting in the room. I sat down.

'How long were you in Thailand before you came here?' he barked menacingly.

I could not stop myself smiling. Was the interrogation to start again after all? 'Excuse me,' I asked politely, 'do you mind if I ask your name and the purpose of this visit?' Instantly his manner changed to civility.

'I am Colonel Kyaw Thein,' he said in a friendly voice. 'I am here to . . . assess you.' He worked as an assistant to Khin Nyunt, the head of Burma's MI. They wanted to see how my morale was holding out. Could they get me to co-operate? 'I was just passing through Kengtung,' he lied with a dismissive wave, 'and thought I would pop in to visit.' Pause. 'Whom did you see in Thailand before you came here?' he asked.

'I don't want to talk about that.' Remarkably, he accepted this and there were no more interrogatory questions at all. 'I came here to ask', I continued, 'three things. That the SPDC reopen the universities, release political prisoners and hold dialogue with the NLD. Why do you keep the universities closed?'

He was more open than any other MI I had met. 'Look,' he explained, 'of course we want the universities reopened. How can we talk about developing our human resources if the universities are closed?' He was well up on the jargon. 'I have two daughters myself of matriculation age. Of course I want them to go to college.'

'And if you do open them,' I responded, 'you know that after a few months the students will begin demonstrating again. They will start demanding the right to form a student union and to elect their own leader for the union. Why do you not just let them? They are not terrorists. They are not trying to destroy Burma. They love their country. They will ask to form a student union. Is that impossible for you to agree to? Do you have to shoot them for this?'

We moved on to political prisoners. 'All prisoners will be released at the right time,' explained the colonel.

'What is the right time?' There was a sudden blackout but we were both playing a game of gentlemen so we pretended not to notice.

'When we decide it is time to release them.'

'But these are innocent men and women who should not be there at all. It is not good enough to say the right time.'

A lad came in to place candles around the room. The tone of the conversation remained amicable.

'What about Min Ko Naing?' I asked. 'He has been in solitary for over ten years. His sentence is for twenty years. It is not right to do that to anybody, no matter what they do. And Min Ko Naing is not just an innocent man, but he is a hero, one of Burma's best and bravest.'

'We have an expression in Burmese,' interrupted Kyaw Thein, 'he who would reach for the big bamboo must be prepared to be bitten by the red ant.' He paused while it sank in. 'Do you know the red ant?'

I had been bitten by scores of them on the way to Moulmein. But I did not answer. I was shocked by his rationale. He meant that Min Ko Naing was after nothing else but power and that those who entered the arena to fight for power should be ready to pay a heavy price if they lost. I was distressed that he only saw political struggle as one for personal gain, rather than for truth. And I despised the analogy between being bitten by a red ant and spending a decade in solitary confinement. This colonel was intelligent. He could recognise the truth if he chose to, but that instinct had been all but killed off so that he would not let himself question the propaganda he swallowed and regurgitated.

A young guard walked in with a tray of glasses and bottles of cola but Kyaw Thein waved him out again. Our conversation was not what he had hoped for.

'Why do you refuse to hold dialogue with the NLD?' I asked. 'They won the 1990 election. They are the government.'

'The transition will take time.' It was interesting that he was even bothering to give me answers. No other member of the regime I had met would have tolerated so many questions.

'Take time? It has been nine years and you still are not even speaking with the NLD! Elected MPs have been imprisoned, exiled, murdered. You always promise to make change but you never do.'

It was also remarkable that Colonel Kyaw Thein and I were remaining amicable. We were playing a game, trying to assess each other.

Then I tried a new tack. I had scarcely ever mentioned Daw Aung San Suu Kyi's name to the authorities. I did not even want to suggest that I had heard of her. I thought they might twist it all and accuse Daw Suu of stirring up foreigners to interfere in

265

Burma. The last thing I wanted to do was cause a headache for a woman I adored. But I had begun to see things differently. There was really nothing I could say which would harm Daw Suu. She was in control of her life and she was never shy of the truth. She would not expect others to be shy of the truth either. 'What do you think of Daw Aung San Suu Kyi?' I asked him. He was silent. 'Do you know that the people of Burma love her? Do you know that they trust her and that they voted overwhelmingly for the National League for Democracy in 1990? Do you respect her as the Burmese people do? Do you love her as they do?'

Throughout this little speech Kyaw Thein had become increasingly agitated. At last he lost his composure and snarled out the bile that the junta's leaders felt for Suu Kyi. 'She is a foreigner! . . .' He was livid.

'She is your independence hero's daughter!' I corrected him.

Colonel Kyaw Thein vented his anger for a few moments, then finished with, 'She is a stubborn woman!' And so, stubborn woman, six years' house arrest, four more years of relentless persecution, hatred from the junta, public calls by senior officials to have you murdered, guns aimed at you ready to fire . . . because you are a stubborn woman.

I asked him about the Karenni, told him about the genocide on the border, about the vast tracts of uninhabited land.

'Do you know how many Karenni there are?' he asked me.

I was silent, not wanting to show my ignorance. Was it 100,000?

He answered for me. 'Less than a million!' he said with confidence. And therefore, he meant, they are not worth considering. Diabolical.

We had talked for about forty minutes, most of it amicably. When I stood to leave we both extended our hands to shake them. I do not like his 'politics' at all but he was more of a man than any one else with rank.

'I hope you have a nice stay . . .' he began, then checked himself, slightly embarrassed. 'Well, I hope you are OK here, as well as can be expected. I will see what I can do for you . . . but I cannot promise anything.'

'No worries. Nice to meet you.'

We stepped out of the office where a dozen others were milling about. It would have been quite a conversation for them to eavesdrop on. If I was reluctant to whimper and ask for favours, I was doubly reluctant to do it when the prison gossips would get wind of it.

'I have brought you some biscuits and some Sprite to drink,' he said somewhat sheepishly. He pointed to a couple of bags. I rather ungraciously ignored them. I was keen to get back to my cell. Deep down I would have loved to have spent the whole night chatting away with him, or anyone, just to be in new surroundings. But it does not do to show need. Better to pretend you are coping just fine.

There is a problem here. One can flatter oneself as being quite the diplomat after having a seemingly progressive conversation with a tyrant. How tolerant, hard-nosed and worldly you are! But nothing, nothing will change. And my God I pray that the UN Rapporteurs and EU Commissioners and US Senators and ICRC reps are a million times tougher than I am. I hope they have no vanity, no folly. I hope they will never be beguiled by the junta.

I reflected later on his first questions about my time in Thailand and my refusal to answer. What is truth? Immanuel Kant believed that you should always speak the truth no matter what. If an axe murderer asked you the whereabouts of his intended victim and you knew, it was your duty to tell him. But how absurd is any extreme philosophy which is a gateway to cruelty. Truth is more than speaking. It is a way of life. It is better to lie than to betray your comrades. You can claim ignorance or give false information. That is better than betrayal but is still perhaps cowardly. It is braver still and more honest to tell the interrogator to go to hell. That is not lying, yet it is not quite right either. One step closer to living truthfully is to tell him that you will not answer his questions because he cannot be trusted with the information, that you believe he will hurt your comrades if you say where they are. And it is legally as well as morally correct to tell him that he has no authority to ask, that sovereignty comes from the people, that in Burma they have bestowed it upon the NLD and therefore the SPDC has no right to appoint government officers or to interrogate people. That was how far I got with the truth, but our leaders show us how to go yet further.

The Lord Buddha was a man so in harmony with truth that he knew how to rebuke somebody, even an enemy who hated him, in such a way that they would not only take no offence but would leave more enlightened than when they came. He would tell them something that made them consider the error of their question. No human being can live completely in truth because no human being is perfect. But we have a duty to strive to improve, to try to become more like the Buddha or like Jesus Christ, to aim at living truthfully. In fine, truth is never simply a matter of words. It is more than just the facts. It embraces sincerity, humility, courage and compassion. When one's actions are steeped in these, one is being truthful. So it is a constant struggle.

Consular staff had asked the authorities if I could write to my family. I had never been allowed to do this in Insein but, perhaps in an effort to impress the ICRC, the prison authorities agreed. Once a month I had the opportunity to write on one piece of paper. With censorship, indefinite delays and the general obstructiveness of the authorities, this would not be a reliable way to get messages to them. I could do that in consular meetings. Instead, the monthly letters were a rare chance for me to tell the MI exactly what I thought of them.

What I wrote was extremely frank. It was not abusive but I reiterated all my reasons for coming to Burma and also my 'assessment' of prison conditions and procedures. If I were in the mood I would include more philosophical assaults on the regime. The trusties would read it first as they took it to the prison officers, then the officers would read it before passing it to the MI. The MI, I suspect, binned the letters despite their fanaticism for filing and recording everything. The letters would have been regarded as far too treacherous to keep on file.

In the October consular visit, Karen Williams (the British vice-consul) brought a few letters from friends and family. The prison authorities agreed that I could have them in one or two weeks, but of course they were lying. Karen also told me that the British embassy had made an official application for the court record through the Burmese Ministry of Foreign Affairs. I felt that my freedom hung on that court record but was willing to be patient.

'Will James be allowed exercise outside?' asked the vice-consul.

'We will ask the higher authorities.'

'You said that last time.'

Silence.

'Will James be allowed to keep his toothbrush and toothpaste in his cell?'

'We will ask the higher authorities.'

I also wanted to clean my own cell out instead of having Brother Sid treated as a slave.

'Will James be able to brush his cell out himself?'

'We will ask the higher authorities.'

In spite of this lunacy, I wanted to show my parents that my morale was still strong. I sent them the following messages:

> *It is not lack of resources or of development which is causing the deep suffering, but it is because the military regime does not regard the people of Burma as human beings.*

> *Min Ko Naing has been in solitary confinement for more than ten years. I would like every foreigner who comes to Burma to ask the State Peace and Development Council when they will release Min Ko Naing.*

The words themselves were not so important, but it was a sign to my family and the authorities that I was still in fighting spirits.

On most visits I was able to dictate a couple of pages of notes to consular staff. I would have preferred to write them myself but the authorities would not allow it: not even if I wrote it in front of them, not even if I gave it to them to censor, not even when I offered to write out an exact copy. I wanted to show respect to the consular staff and was uncomfortable with this arrangement. I was not a very good dictator (bit like Than Shwe, then . . . boom! boom!).

CHAPTER 23

A million surplus Maggies are willing to bear the yoke;
And a woman is only a woman, but a good cigar is a Smoke.

Rudyard Kipling

WHEN THE PROMISED letters did not arrive two weeks later I thought it worth protesting about. I got up long before dawn and twisted my blankets into ropes. The double doors on the north side of my cell consisted of vertical iron bars with wood panelling nailed on to the outside so that I could not see out. I threaded the blankets between the bars and tied the doors together. There was no way they could open the doors from the outside, other than by pulling them down. Next I alerted the guards and asked for my letters.

The guards and officers went into a panic. They pleaded with me to undo the blankets, saying that they would be punished if this came to the governor's attention. I bargained with them and was promised that I would receive the letters within two days. I could not really believe that they would be punished (for what I did) but in Burma anything is possible. After an hour of haggling, and much to their relief, I undid the blankets.

They confiscated my blankets and of course the letters did not come. Well, I had learnt a little lesson. They also thought they might stop me repeating the trick by boarding up the inside of the doors with plywood. This, though, had the effect of turning the doors into two great big drums, which was to come in very useful later on.

A few nights afterwards I heard raised voices behind my cell. The evening propaganda was blaring so I could not quite make out what was happening. It sounded like someone was in trouble, a fight perhaps. I looked out of the front, the east side, of my cell and saw the guards lolling about in oblivion. *Well, it can't be anything too serious*, I assumed, *or else the guards would intervene*.

Half an hour later the propaganda stopped and I heard clearly that someone was being beaten up. I took one step back from the shuttered windows at the back of my cell, then gave them a mighty kick. The shutters flew open and I saw a prison guard reaching through the bars of Number One Ward door and, gripping a prisoner by the hair, slamming the prisoner's head against the bars.

'Oy!' I shouted at him furious, '*a jintha, pye ta na shi day la*?' (Which I hoped meant, 'Prisoners, do you have a problem?' – limited vocab for expression!) The guard swung round to me and made the most threatening of gestures. Half a dozen prisoners stared wide-eyed at the scene.

My own cell guards had run round to investigate and were politely insisting that they shut the shutters. The guard who had been beating the prisoner looked wild and ran off, either to hide or to come and give me some trouble. But instead I heard the furious voice of an MI sergeant who intercepted him on the way. He was angry not because this guard was drunk, not because he had been beating a prisoner, but because he had been seen doing it by the foreigner. There followed the most gruesome smacks and screams I have ever heard. I felt mighty sorry for the guard despite what he had been doing seconds earlier.

The MI sergeant stormed into my compound. 'Are you all right?' he asked me, flustered.

'I am fine, but why do your guards stand back and do nothing for half an hour while a prisoner is being beaten?'

'Never mind that. I will sleep here tonight.' And he went to sleep on the little sheltered platform that had been built for my guards a month after I arrived. He meant it in a paternalistic way. He was sleeping there to protect me from any retribution from resentful guards.

The next day the shuttered windows were secured with planks and nails. I would probably break my foot if I tried kicking the windows open again. But what a lesson for the guards. Perhaps for the first time in their lives they had seen a guard punished by the MI for *beating a prisoner*. It must have been unheard of.

I had the occasional toad visiting my cell. One of them hopped around the whole perimeter, pausing frequently to ponder. Then he made his way to the centre of the cell and sat staring mournfully at the ceiling for a long time. He was oblivious to me, ignored me when I waved, even just inches from his sad face. I wondered if he was not a prison governor in a previous life and was now stuck in the prison, unable to hop over the twenty-five-foot surrounding wall.

I also had birds, butterflies, crickets and all manner of flying beetles as visitors. Sometimes they swarmed literally in their hundreds, plagues of tens of thousands across the prison. And there was a creature which I could not identify. It was flying round my room at such an incredible speed that I could hardly follow it with my eye. It was way too fast for a butterfly, way too big to be even a monster insect, far too agile and manoeuvrable to be a bird . . . what the devil was it? Then, at last, it flew smack into my head and got stuck in my hair. Oh, then, it was a bat. Tiny thing, actually, once it had landed.

The weather was getting colder just as the rains were about to stop. One morning I was standing shivering in my cell thinking how cold it was when two prisoners walked round the prison perimeter carrying a massive barrel of sewage. They made this trip several times a day, emptying out the latrines. I had a roof over my head to keep off the rain; they did not. I had a blanket over my shoulders to keep warm; they had just a thin cotton shirt and a *longyi*. I had flip-flops to keep me from the icy concrete; they had bare feet. I could stand, or sit, or lie down, or pace around; they had to work.

Kept in one room, one has plenty of time to examine every detail of it. My feet knew every rut and ridge in the concrete floor and my back knew every misalignment in the boards of the sleeping platform. On one inspection round I noticed that a screw in the hinges of a window shutter was protruding a touch. With a bit of effort I was able to loosen it up and unscrew it completely. Brilliant! A screw! Bound to be useful. I screwed it back in, content with the knowledge that it would be there when I needed it.

A few days later I took it out again and, checking that no guards were looking in, I scratched a few words into the window frames and walls. 'Democracy', 'Release Min Ko Naing' '*Metta*' 'Please please reopen the universities', this sort of thing. Over the following days the guards did not notice them so I thought something a bit more eye-catching was in order. I wrote out the words of Matthew 18:v:6: '*Whoever causes one of these little ones who believes in me to sin, it would be better for him to have a great millstone fastened round his neck and to be drowned in the depth of the sea.*'

And a verse from John on another wall. The guards did notice these and actually quite liked them. Moshi, the trusty who held the most power, was a Christian. He was a strong guy but also gentle. His arms and neck were covered in tattoos. The ink was all one colour – greenish-black – and the designs were magnificent: abstract patterns, birds, boars and tigers. Later on he brought a Bible to my cell window. It was written in Lahu and he spoke almost no English but I had my version to hand and we had a whole conversation just by exchanging verse references. It was glorious. I confess we concentrated on particular Psalms, taking encouragement from the mighty blow awaiting the persecutors. Moshi smiled when he pointed to Matthew 28:v:20: '*I am with you always, to the end of time.*' He did not doubt it.

Prison was grim, but the religious man, Buddhist, Muslim (there was one Malaysian) or Christian, had a way to cope. It seems odd to me that some people argue religion is no more than a human construct, a crutch to help those weaker people who cannot quite cope with life as it is. They have rather missed the point. Belief in God is not there to help you when you are weak; it is recognition that you are *always* utterly weak, helpless, doomed to failure. A human can achieve nothing at all of worth on his or her own. God is everything. He is the source of all hope, all life, all goodness, all strength, of the entire creation. He is the Love which we were built solely for. There is no purpose to our existence apart from Him. To liken religion to a 'crutch', then, is rather too feeble. It is everything. It took me a spell in Insein to realise that. Blessed are those who do not require such torment to be convinced!

Still the authorities did not respond to the writing on the wall. I hated graffiti but if I was not allowed a paper and pen to express my views to the regime then what did they expect me to do? Shut up? No way.

So I wrote in huge letters in the middle of one wall a fierce eighty-word passage of outrage at the tragedy of Red Bridge, where students were most brutally killed in 1988, and there had been no redress since. On the contrary, the head of the riot police who was responsible, Sein Lwin, was soon afterwards made president of the whole regime. I did not mince my words.

When the prison officers saw it they did . . . nothing. Well, actually a trusty was sent to come in and copy it down but it was not plastered over until *eight months* later. I was delighted that the message was being copied down, though, along with the Bible verses. I even corrected his copy (my handwriting is bad, never mind etching with a small screw into plaster work). I hoped whoever read it later would take the point.

One night a very senior prison officer came to my cell. We chatted through the bars of the window about nothing in particular and then, after furtively looking around over his shoulders, he slipped his arm through the window. Quickly and firmly he shook my hand. 'We are on the same side,' he whispered and was gone.

I had become quite an expert assassin of mosquitoes. I was so accomplished in fact that I no longer descended to just clapping my hands on to them. Instead I would prowl around my cell imagining I was Bruce Lee or suchlike. Then, with dramatic blows or roundhouse kicks, I would pin the wretched mossies to the wall by one wing, deliver an eight-punch combination to their vulnerable abdomen and finish them off with an almighty uppercut. But the sport began to lose its edge. The mossies in

Destruction of Minthamee, February 1997. Pyo Pan Wai Primary School.
(Photo: Aung Myo Min)

Destruction of Minthamee, February 1997.
Author's bedroom on right of picture.

Destruction of Minthamee, February 1997. Family village area.

Temporary camp at Huay Nam Rong, Thai side, March 1997.

Temporary camp at Huay Nam Rong, Thai side, March 1997.

Htam Hin refugee camp, August 1997.

ABSDF Battalion Commander Zaw Than (left) and Maung Maung Htay. Both executed by Tatmadaw in October 1997.

Left: Daw Aung San Suu Kyi, Rangoon. (Photo: Richard Vogel/ Associated Press)

Win Maw Oo, killed on 18th September 1988 by SLORC. Two of her friends were left dead in the street behind. (Photos: Steve Lehman)

'The People's Desire', billboard in Kengtung. October 2000.
(Photo: David Mawdsley)

ကျောင်းသားခေါင်းဆောင် မင်းကိုနိုင်နှင့်

နိုင်ငံရေးအကျဉ်းသားများလွတ်မြောက်ရေး

ငါတို့ကျောင်းတွေ ပြန်ဖွင့်ပေးရေး

ကျောင်းသားသမဂ္ဂတရားဝင်ဖွဲ့စည်းနိုင်ရေး

ပညာရေးလွတ်လပ်ခွင့်ရရှိရေး

တိုက်ပွဲဝင်ကြ

ရှစ်လေးလုံးစိတ်ဓာတ် စိုက်ထူကြ

(ဗကသများအဖွဲ့ချုပ်)

Sticker author distributed in Moulmein in April 1998. The picture is of imprisoned student leader Min Ko Naing.

Below: In Karen State, April 1998. Far right, Mana. Four from right, author. Five from right, Tow Nigh.

Left: Jeremy, twin brother, and his wife Nicole.

Below: Jon, brother. Kengtung, April 2000.

Above: Emma, sister, on field work in Bihar, India.

Above: Mum and Dad, outside Burmese embassy, London. 14th February 2000.

Left: Major H. P. Seagrim, G.C., D.S.O., M.B.E.

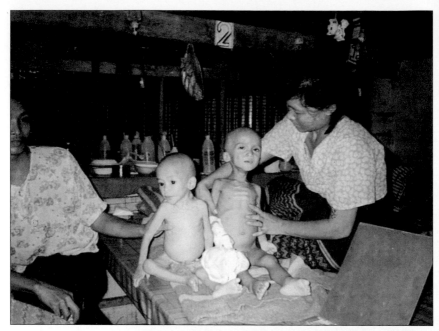

Above: Dr Cynthia's Clinic, Thailand. August 1998. (Photo: Diana Mawdsley)

Right: Soe Che, (left) 15 year old soldier escapes to Karen State. April 2001.

Kengtung were far too slow and dozy to be worthy enemies (unlike their formidable cousins in Rangoon). I began to feel a bit like a bully. Besides, I had just read the Lord Buddha's *Mingala Sutta* and realised my actions fell far short of enlightened. So with great goodwill, I invited the mosquitoes' representatives to a round-table conference and we negotiated a ceasefire. Remarkably, it worked. For many months I kept my side of the bargain – blessing the little creatures instead of murdering them. And for many months they agreed not to bite me – perhaps only one offender per week. But sadly, they were SPDC mosquitoes. The peace treaty had always been fragile. They began violating it far too frequently and my vengeful thoughts spoilt the *karma*. The armistice broke down and once again we warred with each other. Fortunately there is no risk of malaria in urban areas.

In mid-November the barbed-wire fence and a bamboo screen being built around my cell were finally completed. The regime were terrified of me mixing with other prisoners. Given that the compound was now out of sight from the rest of the prison I was allowed out for ten minutes' exercise a day. I had been in the cell for over seventy days.

'Hey Mista James,' whispered one of the trusties to me, 'your mother.'

'My mother?'

'Yes.'

'My mother what?' I did not dare to believe that she was here.

'Your mother, hotel.'

'Kengtung?'

'Yes. Tomorrow.' Excellent news.

So I saw my mother. This is something you long for and die for and then when it happens you are in such a stress to take in everything she says and in such a stress to give out all your messages to loved ones and such a stress to demonstrate that you are unstressed . . .

I had asked my parents not to campaign directly for my release. It would not make sense for me to get myself locked up and then expect a whole load of people to work to get me released. Instead I asked them that if they campaigned, please do so for the points raised in my letter to the junta (see appendix, D). Basically, if a campaign built up around my case, which was for an end to the genocide of the ethnic groups and recognition of the NLD's election victory, it would reach a stage where the junta felt so much pressure that they would choose to kick me out anyway. Parallel to this I wanted the gross illegality of my imprisonment to be exposed so that release would be a matter of justice and not the result of ridiculous requests for clemency.

My family's reaction to my imprisonment took many people by surprise. They were so solid, so strong, so united in the cause for democracy and human rights. I love them for that. What a strain for them, but how they carried it off. In the UK, and especially in the FCO, many people assumed I must be irresponsible or naive. But when they met my family, or saw them on TV, or read of them in the papers, slowly attitudes began to change. There was respect for their dignity, strength and commitment to the wider cause.

In all the prison visits I had, despite the difficulties, none of us ever cried. My mother was allowed four visits that week. Amazing. She dropped off a pile of books and the authorities (I think to impress the British ambassador who came for the third visit) even let me *have* some of them. One was *August 1914* by Aleksandr Solzhenitsyn. I loved it, a most wonderful piece. Mum and I spent much of the last meeting keenly discussing the Prussian front in World War One and the great need for courage and truth in all situations . . . and the junta looked on absolutely bemused. My mum was outstanding: unruffled, not in the slightest bit intimidated, disarming the governor by wishing him a very happy fiftieth birthday.

Mum told me about a letter she had received from Australia. Her own mother, Del Ekman, was a bit of a political animal and had been campaigning (in the most civilised way) for Burma in the 1960s when the dictator Ne Win began strangling the country. So an old Burmese man wrote to Mum to say he had been following my case but, for a long time, '*I had no idea James was the grandson of my old friend Del Ekman.*' Once again I felt glad to have such a family, a family to show that this was no reckless fling.

'Can I brush my own cell out now?' I asked during the first

meeting. The authorities were embarrassed to say no in front of my mum so the prison governor said I could.

The next day, when I asked for a brush, they said no.

When the ambassador came on my mum's third visit we tried again. Recently appointed, Dr Jenkins was resolute and (it gave me great heart to learn) a Catholic.

I was pretty frustrated with the prison staff. 'Why did you agree to give me the brush and then withhold it?' I asked.

'Headquarters say no,' was the eventual response. It was best for me to shut up. I was getting exasperated.

'It does seem to me unreasonable', said the ambassador coolly, 'that James is not allowed to clean his own cell.'

The authorities squirmed in their seats. The trouble was that despite their rank they hated to make the slightest decision. They wanted to consult the MI. Their orders were that I was not allowed *anything* new in my cell and not allowed out for exercise. But how could the authorities justify this? They could not. So, ever so slowly, we won concessions.

I was having trouble with my eyes. I could not always focus and often they ached. When I spoke with the MI my eyes would begin to shut. Not out of tiredness but pure stress. And my stress was compounded because my mother was there and I could not control it. I could not keep my eyes open. Imagine that for a mother, seeing her son perhaps going blind in a prison 8000 miles from home. But Mum was strong.

The ambassador persisted with the necessary details. 'Can James keep his toothbrush and toothpaste in his cell?'

'It is too dangerous,' explained the interpreter, 'he might eat the toothpaste to make himself dysentery. The toothbrush he might make as weapon.'

'?'

'He might sharpen it on the floor.'

It would seem sensible for us to spend these precious moments trying to sort out the legal side of my incarceration, or giving messages to loved ones. But you had to spend much of the meeting time just trying to sort out the most basic admin of your life. You only had one chance a month to bring the debate on one line further.

In the last meeting my mother asked, 'Is there anything else you need, darling.'

'Erm . . . not really.' We had discussed the most important things. 'Actually, I don't mean to be silly but . . . oh, never mind.'

'Go on.'

'Well.' I was very embarrassed. 'Do you think I could get a couple of cigars for Christmas? Could you ask the consul to bring them up for the December visit?'

'Of course. No problem.' It was not that I needed cigars, but it would be a fine gesture. Let the authorities think I had no more pressing personal concerns than fine tobacco for the festive season.

Mum asked me what I thought of the ambassador.

'Best man for Britain and for Burma.'

She thoroughly agreed.

After that meeting I was allowed to brush out my own cell whenever I wanted (and I would take an hour over it twice a week, very therapeutic distraction). I was also allowed to keep my toothbrush and exercise time was increased to twenty minutes per day. I decided to keep the toothpaste too. When my cell opened at noon for the exercise period the guards would come and take it away again. But I would get it back at 5 p.m. and keep it overnight. They would come in at 6 a.m. with the *san byo* and take away the toothpaste, and five minutes later I would ask for it back again and keep it until midday.

These are not pointless games. It is impossible to fight for abstract principles like 'justice' or 'dignity' or concepts like 'democracy'. The junta *say* they run a just and free democratic Burma. What do you say to that? Call them liars? They will call you a liar. So you have to come up with specific cases rather than general causes. I wish we were at the level where we were fighting for an extension to the prison library, or greater wages for prisoners, or their right to form a union . . . but actually we are still at the stage of fighting to get food and exercise and to keep a toothbrush (or, more fundamentally, the right to a fair trial, to free speech, the right not to be beaten).

Of course, the authorities tired before I did because, frankly, I had nothing better to do than to fight for every tiny right. So I got to keep my toothbrush and toothpaste. What could they do? Withhold it for ever? How would they explain that to the FCO? And books started coming now as well. My mother had dropped off about thirty. Originally I was allowed to keep only the Bible in my cell. Then supposedly I could have two other books to read but had to hand them back in before receiving replacements. But I fought them constantly to get more books and by the end of my stay I had up to a dozen in my cell at any one time.

I wanted, though, to fight for other prisoners' rights as well as my own. This was difficult as I was so isolated but I felt that my own fight with the authorities would give the prisoners heart. Some of them were astonished to see me winning concessions; they had believed that the authorities would answer to no one and now they saw them being beaten back. If I were alone I would have got nothing but beatings for the trouble I caused. But with the British and Australian Foreign Offices keeping a close watch, and with media interest around the world intensifying due to my family's efforts, the junta felt afraid.

On 16 December I refused all food. The following day I did the same and the next day I did it again. Lieutenant Soe Lin became nervous. 'What do you want?' he asked.

'Paper and pen,' I replied, 'let me write a short note to the junta.'

'Impossible,' he said.

'OK, then I do not eat.'

Not long afterwards a dozen officers filed into my cell, led by a senior policeman. 'Please sit down,' he said, while they all stood glaring around me.

'After you,' I answered. I was not going to sit down on my own. We both perched on the platform.

'In our country, you must obey our rules. You cannot go on hunger strike.'

'But you have no right to make rules. You are not the government. The National League for Democracy is sovereign in Burma. Ne Win's regime took power illegally and by force.'

'Aha,' he said with a twinkle in his eye, 'I think you are talking about constitutional matters.'

'Exactly so,' I replied.

'But it is not my place to discuss the constitution. I am a policeman. You must obey our rules.'

'Not at all. First we need to recognise where authority comes from. When this regime begins respecting the Burmese people, and respecting their own law, and respecting international law, then I will begin to respect the regime.'

The policeman stood up angrily and I stood up with him. He should not have done it because now I was a head taller than everyone else in the room. These things matter to totalitarians. He began walking out and tapped his watch angrily. 'I do not have time to talk with you,' he said and his entourage followed him out. I found it odd that twelve men made time to come to my cell and do nothing at all while one of them just exchanged a few lines. Perhaps if they did not spend so much time watching each other they might find a moment to get on with their jobs. But I got the paper and pen, and wrote my note to the junta.

Min Ko Naing has been kept in solitary confinement for over ten years. He is an innocent man. He has committed no crime. He should be released immediately.

I was learning in prison that when you raise another prisoner's profile you do not put them in danger. This is difficult to explain. If the junta think nobody is watching them they will do unspeakable things to the helpless. They will murder them. When we make it clear that we are interested, that we care, that we are angry, the junta become afraid. Orders will start flowing that so and so should not be harmed – the world is watching. The argument that such complaints only antagonise the junta is ludicrous. They have kept an innocent man in solitary confinement for ten years. There is nothing they want more than for the world to ignore him. They will keep him there until he dies unless we make them afraid to do so. It is close to wickedness for us to neglect these cases on the nonsense premise that 'we might antagonise the junta'.

The next day Lieutenant Soe Lin told me that the message had been delivered to the Ministry of Foreign Affairs.

I was very happy about that and British consular staff later confirmed it. 'OK, I will eat again on 23 December, after one week.' I had not wanted to put any time limits on the hunger strike as I was not sure I could even last one day. And I did not want to end it immediately because I did not want to pretend that I was making any demands, such as that the note be passed on. I was not. I just wanted to go a week without food to mark the injustice of Min Ko Naing's detention.

During this week I had two wonderful books to keep me strong. One was *Signs of Contradiction* by David Alton. He had sent it himself and it was an inspiring collection of short biographies of people like C. S. Lewis, Edmund Campion and Maximilian Kolbe. They were a light to me.

Also Steve Rhodes, a friend since Bristol, had sent *The Imitation of Christ*. It was written by Thomas à Kempis in the 1400s in what is now Germany. He wrote:

Without love the outward work is of no value; but whatever is done out of love, be it never so little, is wholly fruitful. For God regards the greatness of the love that prompts a man, rather than the greatness of his achievement. Whoever loves much, does much.

All men are glad to live at peace, and prefer those who are of their own way of thinking. But to be able to live at peace among hard, obstinate and undisciplined people and those who oppose us, is a great grace, and a most commendable and manly achievement.

I fell in love with the book and would not give it back to the guards. It was in my cell almost every day and night of my incarceration.

The vice-consul came on 22 December. I was happy that by the time my family learnt of the hunger strike it would be almost over and therefore they need not worry. The report sent back stated:

James . . . was feeling strong and in good spirits . . . [he] showed no signs of stress/tension when [the vice-consul] visited.
. . . [he has] cats, rats, bats and toads in his cell but [said he does]

not mind as they are good company compared to some of the other
creatures round here.

The rats were no surprise as every place on earth has them. The
cats were there to catch the rats but, sadly, after I gave this
message the cats disappeared. I asked the trusties what had
happened.

'Cat die,' one answered.

'Oh no!' I could not believe it. The regime had decided to
remove the cats because of my light-hearted complaint. How
imbecile. The rats began breeding prolifically.

'I think cat released,' I told the trusty, 'he finish seven years and
now he go.'

'Ah yes,' he agreed, eyes gleaming, 'cat is prisoner no more!'

When I finished the hunger strike the prison officers gave me
only *san byo* to eat, because it would be soft on my now tender
stomach. I did not object at first, ate once on the 23rd, twice on
the 24th, twice on the 25th. Great Christmas dinner – rice
porridge. At least it was thick. When I got it on Boxing Day
morning I thought they were taking the mickey. Never mind
turkey sandwiches for a week, this was even more monotonous.
When it came again in the evening I kicked up a stink. I had just
been on hunger strike for a week and they seemed to think I could
go for days on rice porridge. The following day I got solid rice
again with vegetables.

The vice-consul had also brought a large food parcel sent by
Val and Barry, long-time family friends now living in Bangkok, as
well as buying fruit herself in the market. The parcel included the
requested cigars. The prison authorities tried to hold it all back. I
went berserk. I most definitely wanted it for Christmas Day. I
dearly wanted the chance to give something back to the other
prisoners and guards who had been so kind to me and this food
parcel was an excellent chance. I would not back down and last
thing on Christmas Eve Lieutenant Soe Lin agreed to give it to
me.

On Christmas morning I psyched myself up to sing a carol to
the prison during the brief quiet period after the 4 a.m.

propaganda. I was not afraid of punishment, I was just afraid that my singing voice was too appalling to put on show. Anyway, I sang 'Silent Night' to the whole prison and it sounded not too bad.

It was cold enough then, but when dawn came it got worse. Kengtung is well over 5000 feet above sea level. December is the coldest month. On Christmas morning the weather did something ridiculous. It was just impossibly cold. It made you breathless. This put us all in a queer mood. Maybe for a few moments the regime was forgotten, the lack of freedom was forgotten, the political struggle was forgotten. We all suddenly felt that there was something bigger than humanity and humanity's fights.

After morning parade the prisoners were kept lined up and drilled through a session of exercise to warm up. No one objected and it seemed like a sensible idea to me. Never mind if the orders were sometimes barked out with contempt. Looking out of the south-side window I could just see the end of the line-up. The prisoners and I exchanged grins and gestures, joking about the cold.

That day I also sat down and read all the Gospel Christmas stories and relevant prophecies. Never before had they seemed so sweet and human, and never before so real and so majestically awesome. Rejoice, a King had been born, and the increase of His Kingdom would know no end. This was a real Christmas.

One of the guards gave me a cake. The night before I had given the eight of them around my cell either cigarettes or cake from the market. Today I was determined to get as much food as possible out to other prisoners. An MI man was standing there watching and I challenged him to stop me. But it was Christmas Day, it was so cold that we all felt like small vulnerable creatures and the MI man turned a blind eye. If any prisoner came near the compound, to work on the vegetable patches, or to carry the latrine barrels, or to fill up my wash bucket, or to bring my rice, I passed something to him. I was able to reach twenty-two people. Really it is better to give than to receive. The food was insignificant as nutrition, but as symbols of solidarity it was important.

I gave the choicest food to Brother Sid. Since I was always so polite to him, and showed respect to him, the other guards stopped giving him such a hard time. He began sitting with them in the compound, smoking their cheroots and occasionally their cigarettes. They started calling him by his name instead of 'shit bucket'. Then he would even join them for meals. It was a wonderful transformation.

Lieutenant Soe Lin was still in a huff about me demanding the food parcel the evening before. On Christmas morning he arrived at my cell and gave me a big cake, all pretty in pink and white icing, with 'Merry Christmas' written on it. But he was in a grumpy mood. I gave him a mince pie (M & S, courtesy of Karen Williams, the vice-consul) and he stomped off.

At midday when I was let out for exercise, he was sitting in the compound sulking. For exercise I would just walk round and round the outside of the cell, within the 50 × 50-foot perimeter of the barbed-wire fence and bamboo screen. I saw Soe Lin in a sulk and as I disappeared around the back of the cell I thought to myself: *Darn him! It is Christmas Day. There is no way I am going to let him spoil my mood. I am going to be happy!* What was he doing sulking anyway? Sulking is a tactic used by children and it only works when you sulk at a person who cares about you. You sulk to say 'look at me, I am miserable and it is your fault, so you had better come and cheer me up'. If the person you sulk in front of does not give a hoot about you they will just laugh. Not only was this thirty-year-old debasing himself by trying out a childish ruse, but did he really imagine that I cared for him?

But as I emerged around the cell and saw his sour face I felt stricken. One lap later and I could stand it no longer. I went over and squatted down before him. 'Lieutenant Soe Lin,' I began, 'I am sorry that I cause you difficulties.'

He pouted.

'You know the governor agreed with Karen that I could have the food parcel, and then he withheld it. I have the right to demand it.'

Silence.

'Thank you for the cake you gave me.' I had not touched it yet. 'And I hope you liked the mince pie.'

No reaction.

'It is from London.'

'Mm.' He sighed inaudibly.

'Anyway, have a Merry Christmas. See you again.' And I started lapping the cell again. Lieutenant Soe Lin got up and left. The next time I saw him he was all smiles and bubbles.

I was concerned about the court record. I knew that the junta would be reluctant to hand it over, and would certainly have fabricated it anyway, but it was important to prove that by getting it. Having gone through a week's hunger strike without too many problems, I thought I could do a longer one for the court record. I would give myself a couple of months to fatten up and ideally I would start on 16 March.

This would be the twelfth anniversary of Red Bridge, one of Burma's most painful massacres. I nearly cry every time I think about it: dozens of students shot, young girls clubbed to death or drowned in the shallows of Inya lake as they sought to escape from the riot police. What horrifies me every time is trying to imagine a man who is fit, strong, well-armed and surrounded by colleagues, who is backed up as well by one of the world's largest armies, charging after helpless young girls and clubbing them to death. What is he thinking of as he smashes his baton into her face? When she screams in the water and goes under does he reach down to pull her up by the hair so he can break her skull? She will not die with one or two blows. He must hit her on the arms and back and chest before getting a few good shots in at her face. They are floundering in the water and he cannot get a good clear swing. But blows to the face will not kill her either. They just mash her into a pulp. At last he gets one on the back of her skull and suddenly she is still and her face sinks below the water. He has got one. And now look! There is another one. She is trying to escape but she cannot swim so she is stuck. Her wet clothes are sticking to her body so she cannot move her arms freely to defend herself, and crack! crack! crack! the blows start falling and her cries of terror change to cries of pain . . . What is he thinking? What has happened to his humanity, where and how was it destroyed?

285

I have talked to Burmese men in the UK who witnessed this. I spoke with one man who saw the dearest sweetest love of his life, a Karen girl and his neighbour since childhood, shot dead. She was sixteen. She saw the soldiers levelling their guns and she walked forward and stuck her belly against the barrel and asked them 'Will you shoot? Will you shoot your brothers and sisters?' And her neighbour's heart died because he knew that they would and he ran forward to grab her, but the soldiers opened fire and blew away her stomach and she arched backwards so far and fell and bled, and he could not reach her body because the bullets were flying and he had to run away and leave the one who was like his sister. I see him now in London and I understand why he went through six years of hell in Insein prison but never gave up his will and never gave up the fight.

Another Burmese man in London, just twenty-five years old, told me how in 1988 they opened fire on him and his friends and he had to run for his life. For three minutes he had to run for his life, bullets coming, his friends falling dead. He asked me if I knew what it was like to be thirteen years old and have to run for your life. And I did not.

So it was like nothing to go on a hunger strike for the court record. I did not want to surprise my family with another fait accompli or they might start worrying that I was not keeping them informed. It was also sensible to let consular staff know what would happen at the same time that I let the junta know. This way there could be no disputes about the facts. The question was, though, did I set a time limit or did I do an open-ended hunger strike, which would end only when the court record was supplied? Well, I knew two things. One was that it would be a terrible mistake to make a threat and not carry it through. If I quit a hunger strike early I would lose credibility for any future protests. The other thing I knew was that I did not want to die. I would die if death came to me, but it is wrong to seek death out. However well I thought I knew the psychology of the junta, or what might galvanise the FCO, I could not tell whether or not I might be left to die on an open-ended hunger strike. I would be if I was demanding the release of Min Ko Naing. But what about demanding the court record? Never mind that it was my legal right.

Basically if I were not prepared to die on hunger strike it would be a mistake to take the chance. And the whole purpose of it was limited to getting the court record. Not that the action would prompt the regime into submission, but it might certainly bring pressure to bear on them from the outside. They would be forced to answer the question as to why they were still holding it back.

I decided to do a twenty-day hunger strike. One day for each year of Min Ko Naing's sentence. I knew of Zen monks who had lasted ninety-nine days on hunger strike. I knew of a Russian prisoner who died after only sixteen days. I guessed I was in better shape than the Russian and twenty days would be fine.

That was for March though. Meanwhile my plans for Millennium Eve were understandably modest. Basically they centred around the cigar, not so much for the pleasure of the smoke itself, but as a gesture to the prison authorities that I was not despairing. The implication of the cigars would be that I already had everything I needed and that I was treating myself to a touch of decadence.

Early on New Year's Eve the Count sauntered into my compound, smug as ever, bubbling with laughter at other people's misfortune and his own wonderful wit. The Count was perhaps Kengtung's most privileged prisoner, if not the relative of some general, then an unconscionable crook in his own right. He always dressed for the occasion, sometimes changing his clothes as often as three times a day. This was remarkable considering that other prisoners would wear the same filthy *longyi* and shirt for weeks on end without having them washed. It seems that whenever new clothes entered the prison, the Count always got to them first. I had seen him wearing everything from the rough canvas uniform of a trusty to sports gear, and once he had come in dressed up like an office PA in a brilliantly white, perfectly starched shirt with a collar and a beige *longyi* wrapped tight around him like a skirt. On that day his hair was slicked down to perfection and he minced more foxily than any office beauty. Tonight, however, he was wrapped up for winter, wearing boots instead of the ubiquitous flip-flops, a great thick jumper and bobble hat and – unbelievably – a pair of jeans. I had never seen jeans in Burma at all, let alone on a prisoner.

He joked with the guards before sidling over to the rear window of my cell. Feeling sociable, I wandered over intent on sounding him out about the midnight celebrations. But before I could begin, he hissed 'prison champagne' at me under his breath and gave a joyfully conspiratorial wink. My face lit up. Aha! So we are not on a different planet after all. He indicated that I should wait till midnight and with that he was gone.

As the last hours of the millennium slowly ebbed away the eight guards around my cell gradually fell asleep. The Buddhist New Year falls in April, so tonight meant little to them. Just before midnight the Count reappeared bearing bowls of rice and vegetables, and two huge fried fish. Without saying a word, he began to pass half of it through to me: a tricky business since he had to squeeze it through the bars without spilling it. I produced my cigar, which we would share, then he pulled out two mugs of 'prison champagne'. It was a clear oily liquid that immediately looked dangerous, the kind of stuff that explodes if you blink at it. But this was a one-in-a-thousand-years occasion and no time to be fussy. We raised our glasses, toasted each other's health and I drank the most wonderful drink I can remember. It burned me from my lips to my stomach and sent all my nerves into an exquisite state of shock. The food was delicious and the cigar a perfect finishing touch.

I looked up to the stars, thinking of the whole world celebrating. Could anyone else have been as satisfied with this night as I was? Then I felt a sorrowful guilt, knowing that people I loved would be sad tonight, thinking of what I was missing out on, and I had no way to tell them just how happy I was.

CHAPTER 24

To be a Christian means to believe in Him, which is to believe in His sacrifice on Golgotha and His teaching that we too must deny ourselves and follow Him. We are meant to be crucified and buried together with Him, not in a physical sense . . . but in fighting to the uttermost against sin, the world and the devil, and never giving up even if you lose many battles.
Richard Wurmbrand

B Y NEW YEAR I was getting sick of the speaker outside my cell. The volume was so loud it seemed surely malicious. At first I used to sing my own songs to drown out the noise of it but this was not very pleasant for the guards. Next I just began shouting in protest whenever it was too loud. They would turn it down for a few minutes but the volume would creep back up again. I detested the way they used supposedly Buddhist teaching to make people's lives miserable. I had put up with it for over 130 days because I did not want to give the regime a chance to say I was attacking Buddhism. I was not. I was protesting against the cruel volume and timing of it. Although I had little patience left, I did not want to get abusive. 'Would the malicious weasel', I shouted as loud as I could, 'who is in control of the volume please turn it down. Listen to what the Lord Buddha says! Learn compassion from him!'

Lieutenant Smo Ki was furious with me for causing disruption, but nevertheless they turned it down and the next day the speaker was removed altogether. Once again I wondered why I had not protested earlier.

Karen had told me that my father would be coming out and sure enough, on the next consular visit he came too. It was great to see him and we had a few laughs together, for the benefit of those watching as well as for our own morale. He told me of the growing campaign back home, which was very encouraging. A Thai businessman had offered 100,000 Baht for the rebuilding of *Pyo Pan Wai*. And another businessman in Britain had offered to donate £20,000 for the same. That was fantastic.

The matter of an appeal was brought up again too. I did not want to appeal. It would be a waste of time and money. But I was the only one who seemed to think so. Vladimir Bukovsky had explained in his autobiography that it is worthwhile to fight even the most corrupt of regimes from a legal angle. I understood that but I wanted to go all out, taking the stand that the SPDC was altogether illegitimate and that the NLD was sovereign. But I was dreaming if I thought the outside world would back that position. Others wanted a softer approach. The FCO especially needed it explicitly demonstrated to them that the charges against me were fraudulent. I hope in the future, in a faster-moving world, that our Foreign Office will show a bit more balls.

So I agreed to appeal. I did not want Burmese lawyers endangered, though, and wrote out some instructions for my father during the meeting. The authorities withheld them for months.

Once again the authorities agreed I should have more exercise time and once again they reneged on it. I decided to take it anyway. Instead of returning to my cell after twenty-five minutes I stayed out for forty-five minutes, including the wash. The guards did not want to create a scene. I got away with it. After a few days this became the established routine and the prison officers agreed to it.

Six days after the consular meeting the authorities were still holding back fruit and blankets that had been brought. Their excuse was that they had to search them. Every other prisoner who received food from outside (twice a week, but only one in five could afford it) was given it within a couple of hours of their meeting. The officers held mine back because I was stroppy. I became more stroppy.

When rice was brought to me in the morning I slipped behind the guards' backs and out of the doors. I went round to the front of the cell and sat down on a rock.

'Hey! What you do?' The guards were worried. 'James, go back inside.'

'Please tell Soe Lin I want to see him.'

Eventually they went to get him. He was dressed in a white vest and a blue *longyi*, the first time I had seen him out of uniform. I wondered briefly what kind of hours he worked, and did he really spend his time off here too. He was tired and angry, but I would not go into my cell.

'Why do you keep back the fruit?'

'We have to search your embassy parcels.'

'Six days to search a bag of fruit?'

'The doctor has to check your food.'

'Does he need six days?'

'The prison superintendent [governor] has to give permission.'

'He does not need to for any other prisoners.'

'Please go into your cell and I will bring the food.'

'You bring me the food and I will go straight in.'

Five minutes later it came, along with a couple of blankets. I went back into my cell. I was still unhappy that they were with-holding books and letters. A week later, after my wash, I refused again to return to the cell. Within half an hour six of the books which my parents had brought were produced. They let me keep two of them.

But I was still not happy with the way things were going. I did not feel that forty-five minutes a day outside the cell was adequate. I had been there for nearly five months. I sat out again. I was wrong to repeat the same tactics. It is best to keep them on their toes by changing your methods but I was getting quite desperate. I demanded to see a doctor. He came and we had a useless chat.

'Do you agree with me', I asked him, 'that solitary confinement

291

is inhumane, that being kept in one room for over twenty-three hours a day is unhealthy?'

But the doctor had no power. He could not even give his opinion for fear of the MI.

'Well, thank you for listening,' I said as he left.

'Ah yes,' he answered quite relieved, 'do you feel better now.' I think he must have seriously overestimated his bedside manner if he thought five minutes of silent listening had cured my woes. I remained outside.

I had been getting on well with the trusties and guards assigned to my cell. Some of them especially I felt a special bond with. They cared for me: there are details I cannot write while the situation is ongoing. But things were turning nasty. They were the executive arm in the prison and I had no illusions about what they would do if they were ordered to give me a hard time. At this point Lieutenant Soe Lin had had enough and he called them over. There was Daddy, an Indian-looking prisoner who weighed well over 200 pounds. The Count, who was slight but ruthless. And there were two prison guards. One was a decrepit old man and the other was a chinless automaton. I might have been able to put up a bit of resistance if it were not for Daddy!

They moved in on me and started hauling me back to the cell. Twice I tried to grab hold of the barbed wire but Daddy would not have it. For want of something better to do I started shouting out that this was a gross violation of my rights, that it was assault and I wanted to see the police. Unfortunately I burst out laughing when I called for the police, which weakened my resistance.

I was still able to put up a good struggle at the door and they could not get me inside. Lieutenant Soe Lin called in a couple more prisoners who had been working on the vegetable patches nearby. They all took a limb and I was dumped with little decorum inside my cell. The door was locked and Soe Lin disappeared.

Immediately Daddy appeared at the window. I smiled at him.

'So sorry,' he said, mildly distressed.

'Hey, never mind,' I answered. Then the Count came too and apologised. There was no point in showing any hard feelings but inside I was deeply worried. I kind of owed my life and sanity to those guards and trusties who looked after me. I could see, though, that we were on a collision course. It was one thing for me to defy the authorities; they could always put a stop to it by sending me home. But it was a completely different matter for the Burmese prisoners to defy the regime. They had learnt that you only ever fight with the junta if you are willing to die or if you are young and idealistic enough to believe that democracy is just around the corner. Otherwise there was no point because for whatever perceived wrong you did the payback would be diabolically out of proportion and you would suffer from it for years.

Until now I had been getting regular visits to my compound and cell from prison officers, usually several times a day. It was a kind of hangover from the novelty of my arrival. But things changed. The atmosphere was turning unpleasant. From now on I would see an officer barely once a week. It was not that I needed their company – in fact, I relished the space. But it was impossible to sort anything out with the low-ranking guards and trusties. If I wanted something to change, I had to slog it out with the higher ranks.

Although prison officers were avoiding my compound, security there was increased. An extra set of steel doors was added to the outside of my cell (quite uselessly) and the number of guards around my cell went up. Five new men were brought in. There were now up to a dozen men assigned to my compound during the day and up to eight through the night. For sleep, three could fit on the sheltered platform. The others had to rough it on the floor. I was angry about that.

These five new men did not look quite so hard as the original five but they did not look friendly either. Not prisoners, then, but prison guards. It was hard to tell just by the uniform. They stood like ramrod sentinels around my compound. As soon as I was let out for exercise I went to each one in turn as I lapped around the cell and spoke with them in an unfriendly way.

'*Mingalaba!*' pretending to be polite, or, 'Democracy, what do you think about it?' or, 'Do you know the NLD, do you know

U Tin Oo, do you know he is good man?' Finally one of them could take it no longer and . . . burst into a big smile. I was rather put out. Only slowly did it dawn on me that they were indeed prisoners too. And again as the days and weeks went by we got to know each other well and the friendships grew. Their warmth and concern were a lifeline to me.

It was not that I had anything against the real guards either. It was just that they could not be trusted at all. They were either broken old men whose fear meant obedience to the junta. Or else they were very young men, uneducated, who sincerely believed that if they tried hard they would do well, or that the junta were just too formidable to fight. And even the senior officers, right up to the generals themselves, were all caught up in a trap. It is greed, ignorance and hate that makes us commit wrong. And therefore the man who commits wrong is to be pitied, not resented. We all commit wrong, so who is going to do the judging anyway.

If I had tried to play power games with the authorities I would have lost. Can I alone beat all of them, with their might and their guns and their bureaucracy? No chance. The effort of trying would kill me. But I was not there to fight against men; I was there to fight against evil. So, much as I disliked Maung Lo, the governor, he was not my enemy. The goodness in him was my friend and the badness in him was my enemy. How do I go about fighting the bad part of him without damaging the good part? Well, it is extremely difficult. In fact, if I want to fight the evil in the world I find that there is only one place where I can be assured of succeeding and that is the evil inside myself. So in prison ninety per cent of my struggle was against myself and it is precisely in striving to overcome the evil in oneself that one consequently has the effect of reducing evil in the world.

When I received a food parcel I had the choice of sharing it with other prisoners or eating it myself. I could be more or less greedy. But if I eat most of it myself, how are the other prisoners supposed to believe me the next time I shout out 'Your cause is my cause' or claim that all human beings are of equal worth? My words will mean nothing if I cannot overcome my greed. I will not be a source of support to other prisoners if I cannot overcome my greed.

As I have a belief in the democratic way and I want the authorities to come to understand that democracy is not their enemy but for the benefit of all, I have to try to convince them. But if I am arrogant they will listen to nothing I say. It does not matter if a man speaks truly or falsely because, if he is doing it offensively, few people are humble enough to listen. So whenever I meet with the authorities I have to try to be humble. If they find the very sight of me obnoxious, I am not going to be able to get across the democratic message. Funnily enough, I have to try to get them even to like me a little. With half the guards this is no problem. But with the high-ranking ones, oh what a struggle for me to rein in my pride! I want to stand up to them, challenge them, confront them. But I have to overcome that anger, that pride. I have to try to be humble. I have to try to see their good points so that I might respect them a little and, noticing that I respect their humanity (if nothing else), they might at least grant an ounce of credibility to what I say about democracy.

It is a paradox. Whoever would change the world must change themselves. Strive to overcome your own pride, greed and anger and this very process will affect the world. It is not something to be done first, to make yourself a goodly person so that you can then deal with the world. To sort oneself out takes more than a lifetime. It is our task from God: to seek perfection, to strive to love our neighbour and our enemy. And by thus striving, by obeying His command, we unknowingly shape the world around us to make it a better place. I should not have spent *ninety* per cent of my effort in prison fighting myself, I should have spent a hundred per cent of it.

To fail to fight this internal fight is to invite disaster. If I was angry with the regime for what they did to me and if I wanted somehow to reverse the situation and hurt them I would fail. Of course I was weaker than they. So anger would turn to frustration and mixed with pride this would become hatred, and I would spend every hour in fury because I wanted to destroy my captors but knew that I could not. If I chose to hate I would not be able to bear prison. I would go mad. If I chose to love I would be free and happy. In practice, I had to struggle all the time.

I managed to make some notes in prison which I kept hidden for over half a year before smuggling them out to England. It is hard for me to remember how I felt when I wrote those words but it must have been intense. '*If I could change the past it would only be the times I have hurt/offended* anyone – *this is how one feels in the face of death.*'

On 9 February Victoria Billing of the British embassy made a visit. I recalled Tiffany, the political secretary she had replaced. What a far away world it was out there. Best not to think about it. Vicky let me know that she had heard me speak at SOAS (School of Oriental and African Studies) while she was studying there the year before. Her manner was immediately supportive. As the meeting got under way I lost my temper far too many times. 'At every meeting', I said to the officials with a raised voice, 'you assure the consular staff that you will pass on the letters they give you for me. But you have not handed over a single letter this year. Why not?' I was not angry because I was deprived of letters; I could expect a hard time in prison for the trouble I was giving them and I knew that far worse things went on in Burma. But it was maddening to look at their shameless faces while they told lie after stupid lie.

The interpreter spoke to his colleagues in Burmese. Their anger was mixed with amusement.

Victoria spoke far better Burmese than I did. 'He is not trans-lating what you say,' she told me. Then I was quite astonished by how robustly she laid into them. She gave the whole rack of them a relentless dressing down. In fact, she got so enthusiastic and aggressive that I was worried she would lose her job, be deported or something. But it was wonderful to watch. At last here was somebody else who believed that the best way to deal with the junta was to stand up to them. It was a massive and much needed boost to my morale. Fantastic that the FCO employed such people. What an indescribable comfort it was. I sorely needed support then and will forever be grateful to Victoria for her courage and spirit. I was so happy to be able to relax a little in the meeting and watch someone else stand up to them.

'Why do you not pass on the books to James?' she asked.

'His books are in Rangoon for censorship.'

'That cannot be true,' I said. 'When I made a protest for books they came within half an hour. They cannot have been brought from Rangoon.' And it was daft anyway to suggest that they went to Rangoon to be censored.

But they would not answer. Or else we would get the eternal response, 'We have to ask with higher authorities.'

In the report back to my parents Victoria mentioned that I appeared stressed. I am sorry my parents had to read that. But she also wrote that '*[a]s James shows little sign of weakening, it appears that the authorities are determined to make life harder for him*'.

Among the messages of love and attempts at humour that I sent back to family and friends, I also wanted to show that I was not going to be put off.

> *A regime which is afraid of schoolchildren cannot be considered strong. If we work hard then within two years this junta could be gone.*

> *Through extreme deprivation of our physical and mental needs they hope to pressure us into becoming moral vegetables. They want us to utterly disregard right and wrong. They want us to turn a blind eye to all injustice whether against ourselves or against others. So you see, they do not want our good behaviour. They want our free will. They cannot have it.*

Regarding the appeal, I was still hoping for a fundamental approach.

> *[Following an appeal], [t]he length of my sentence has little to do with when I will get out. To hope otherwise is a waste of time. However the appeal can be useful as to stand up and speak the truth is the beginning of freedom. I would like to make as the basis of my appeal:*
>
> *1   that the 1990 election was held to determine government (not a constitution drafting assembly) and therefore the NLD/CRPP is sovereign;*
> *2   that, since 1962, this regime has been anti-constitutional and illegitimate. So are its laws and courts etc.*

And most importantly of all:

1 John 5:v:3: For this is the love of God, that we keep His commandments. And His commandments are not burdensome.

Recalling my Christmas request, Victoria had bought a massive cigar for my birthday. It was mammoth, as large as a hippo's leg. I did not want the authorities holding it back for a week, letting it go stale, saying that the doctor had to inspect it. So at the end of the meeting when I was left alone in the office for five seconds (why? basic security!) I popped the cigar down my shirt.

As soon as I was back in my cell with the doors locked I dashed over to the back window and asked a guard for a light. I was laughing so much at the ridiculous size of the cigar that I could not keep it still. He was laughing so much that he could not keep the lighter steady. They were desperate moments; I was expecting Lieutenant Soe Lin to come storming over any second. At last it was lit and I retired to my virtuous couch to enjoy the slow-burning beauty. Blue smoke rose swiftly from the tip in a streamlined column, then burst into rings and swirls of dancing chaos. From my mouth the clouds of smoke billowed out white and soon dispersed. From the butt of the cigar brown smoke trickled out, *downwards*, reminiscent of sewage. You did not need to be a rocket scientist to work out that your mouth was the filter which cleaned the sewage brown smoke to the fluffy white clouds. Terrible habit!

Not until I was halfway through did Lieutenant Soe Lin appear fuming at the window. 'Please give me it,' he said curtly.

'Excuse me?' I replied languidly.

'Please come here!' I walked slowly over to the window. 'Give me it,' demanded the lieutenant again.

'Why?'

'I must search it.'

I held it up to him and turned it from side to side. 'There, you can see it is a good cigar.'

'Give me it. You are stole. Thief.'

'If I give it to you I will not get it back.'

'You stole. You are thief.' As he said it his eyelids were flickering and falling. He could not keep them open.

I turned back to the sleeping platform to carry on smoking. If they really wanted it they could come in and get it. Lieutenant Soe Lin left, unhappy. And I thought about his eyes. He was having the same trouble with them that I had during my mother's visit in November and subsequently. Stress. Enormous stress. In a rather too picturesque analogy my family, myself and the regime were all thrown together in a vice, which was squeezing tighter and tighter. It was going to continue until one party gave way, until one decided they had had enough. I was sad that people like Lieutenant Soe Lin had to start feeling the pressure before the MI did, before the decision-making generals at the top did. I was often tempted to stop fighting altogether and just get along with the regime for the sake of the low-ranking guards. But that would have been a mistake. The junta were brittle, the junta were weak. They would crack before my family or I did.

My birthday was on 14 February. Back in London the Jubilee Campaign, the human rights lobby group, had long since been on my case, largely thanks to Lord Alton. They organised a rally outside the Burmese embassy and my parents went down to present a bamboo cage to the ambassador. The Jubilee Campaign were efficient and committed. My parents were becoming increasingly respected by the media and public. Questions and debates had been raised in the Houses of Lords and Commons. MPs had contacted the FCO regarding my case and had passed a motion deploring my imprisonment. Things were picking up.

CHAPTER 25

The study of Zen is like drilling wood to get fire. The wisest course is to forge straight ahead without stopping. If you pause at the first sign of heat, and then again as the first wisp of smoke arises, even though you go on drilling for years you will never see a spark of fire.

Hakuin, 1686–1769

IN INSEIN I had used the movement of a sunray to tell the time, though it was limited to a few hours in the afternoon. Here in Kengtung I was in a much better position. The roof of my cell was full of holes and thus all day long I had spots of sunlight travelling across the room as well as the rays through the large windows. When the gongs were not working through the day I could nevertheless tell the time with remarkable accuracy – within five or ten minutes. And not just spots of light inside the cell but the shadows outside worked for a very precise timepiece too. But as in Insein, my astronomical ignorance led me down a paranoid path.

I had noticed that afternoon food would come as the shadows of the posts outside my cell all fell into line with the barbed-wire fence itself. I knew it would change a little day by day but became slightly worried when the shadows seemed to take more and more effort to get there. The last few inches would take an interminable time and then the shadows stopped reaching the fence line altogether. I was still being fed on time so this was just academic curiosity.

The only explanation I could come up with was that the whole prison, and the perimeter wall, and the trees whose tops I could glimpse over it, were all on an enormous turntable. The MI had decided to rotate the entire prison by a couple of degrees a day, for no other reason than to disturb the calculations of anyone who was shadow-spotting. Unlikely? Absolutely ridiculous, I know, but what else was happening? So I thought about the sun again and geography lessons from school. How basic the answer was. It was just that the sun's track from east to west was moving progressively southwards in the sky. Everyone knows that, but I had never thought about its implications for shadows before.

I used to think back to my maths lessons too (really there was plenty of time to think!). I wanted paper and pens so I could try to derive all the equations and prove all the proofs that I ever knew, but of course the prison authorities would never fall for that one. So I picked up my water scoop and started drawing on the walls in water. The marks would last a good ten minutes in the cool of the day before evaporating and I was able to get through some wonderful stuff – a kind of pictorial algebra: writing down an algebraic identity and then trying to draw the geometrical picture that it represented, more abstruse than functions. My tiny brain became fouled on ellipses and I gave up.

One of the books I had received from my mother was an encyclopaedia. If prison was supposed to be monotonous, how could it be with a book like that? Imagine having all the time in the world to reflect upon a few of the facts. 'The sun is one million miles in diameter.' 'In World War Two 35 million Chinese civilians were killed.' Who has time to think those through? One fact from God to put you in awesome wonder, and one fact from man that turned the world on its head. Thirty-five million civilians; why had I never heard that before?

Mum also left the complete verse of Kipling. Fantastic: 'Mandalay', 'Gunga Din', 'Cells', 'Tommy', 'The Ballad of East and West', 'The Ballad of Bo Dah Thone' . . . who could be unhappy with these to read?

But I was not allowed to keep these books in my cell. I had to give them back to get a new one and I was annoyed because I could not remember how incredibly long the Zambezi river is, so I wanted the encyclopaedia back. And I knew full well that, 'You may talk of gin and beer/When you're quartered safe out 'ere,/An' you're sent to penny fights an' Aldershot it'. Yet I could not for the life of me remember 'But when it comes to slaughter/You will do your work on water,/An' you'll lick the bloomin' boots of 'im that's got it'. So I wanted Kipling back.

'Can I speak to a prison officer?' I asked one of the guards. Previously prison officers had visited my compound several times every single day. But since the day I had been dragged into my cell they stayed away. For four days I asked to see a prison officer and for four days they refused to come. This is so wrong; no system of accountability at all. Prisoners were not supposed to have complaints. If they had a problem they should endure it in silence. So I had to find a way to make sure they would come.

My father had brought about twenty packets of dried soup when he visited. They were not the sort of things I could easily share with other prisoners as they were so obviously not from Kengtung and could not just be wolfed down on the spot like fruit or bread. With a prisoner's instinct I had not thrown the empty packets away; in prison everything can be useful, keep hold of it, even if you do not know why at the time. I had also saved up several strips of sellotape from packets of the local biscuits, again not sure why. And I had managed to set aside a few small plastic bags. None of this was conspicuous in my cell. The sellotape was hidden and virtually invisible. The soup packets I had scrunched up into little balls and put each one inside the last. These were stuffed into one bag with the other plastic bags and looked no more threatening than a little bag of litter. But they went a long way.

I contrived to make three balls out of them and the result was very satisfactory. Three fairly hard balls, packed tight, wrapped up and taped up, and excellent for juggling. That killed a few hours. Then I stood a flip-flop up at one end of the cell and used it for target practice. Killed a few more hours. I missed one shot wildly and it slammed into the door. Because the doors had been boarded up inside and out they were like drums and there was quite a resounding bang. It gave me an idea.

I threw the balls as hard as I could again and again into the door. The noise was quite dramatic. Very quickly the guards ran to the windows to investigate.

'Hey!' – very excited – 'stop! Be quiet.'

'Get me a prison officer,' I said and continued slamming the balls into the door. For four days the prison officers had been 'too busy' to see me. How remarkable that now two of them came running within four minutes.

'Why you do!?' fumed Lieutenant Soe Lin.

'Soe Lin, I am very bored. I have been in here six months and I am not allowed to keep books. If you will not give me the books then I have to find other things to do. Throwing balls is fun.'

'You cannot have the books.'

'The governor agreed I could have them. The Ministry of Foreign Affairs and MI agreed I could have them.'

'They need to be censored.'

'Soe Lin, I am talking about the books which I have already read. They do not need to be censored twice. Why can I not see these books again?'

'They are in Rangoon.'

'Don't be silly. They do not take each book I have read back to Rangoon.'

'You cannot have the books.'

'Very well, I will continue to play with my balls.'

With that I started slamming them into the door again. For half an hour the officers chose to play music on the loudspeakers at full blast to drown out the sound. It was very pleasant (now that the speaker had been moved away). But they could not disguise the fact that there was a prisoner being defiant.

I gave it a rest to give them a chance to come up with a plan. As midday approached I had to hide the balls, otherwise they would be confiscated while I was on exercise. But how do you hide three balls in an empty room?

Since the ICRC visit I had a toilet roll in my cell. In Asia one generally uses these from the inside out, so there was quite some space in the middle. I slipped one ball in there and crimped the top of it down a bit. I was not sure how long it would last but it was worth a try. The second ball I attached to an elastic band (another piece of booty which I had stashed in my cell against the day it became useful) and wore it round my thigh like a garter. It would be covered by my *longyi* and I doubted they would try a body search. The third ball I kept in my hand. I wanted to give them every chance to be reasonable; it would not do to assume they would confiscate the balls.

At noon the doors were unlocked and a few guards filed into my cell, looking around for the offending items. The Count was first in and immediately he hid around the corner where none of the others could see him and signalled desperately with a winning smile for me to give them to him, but 'shhh!' do not tell the others.

The significance of that gesture dawned on me the following evening. I walked out to Lieutenant Soe Lin, throwing and catching one ball in my right hand. 'Do you have the books?' I asked.

'No.'

'Can I write down the names of the ones I want?'

'Yes.'

I requested Kipling, the encyclopaedia and à Kempis's *Imitation of Christ.*

'Can I keep the balls?'

'Yes.'

'Are you sure?'

'Yes.'

'So if I put this ball down, back in my cell, you will not get them to take it away?'

'No,' Lieutenant Soe Lin assured me, 'you can keep them.'

'Thank you very much,' I said, not believing it for a second. But the game had to go on so I returned to the cell and laid the ball on the sleeping platform. Of course, I had not done one lap round the outside of the cell before it was snatched up by a trusty. *Well,* I thought, *you have shown your hand rather early, but you won't get the other two.*

It was quite amusing to watch what followed. Six men were in my cell searching for the other two balls. They were utterly bemused. Soe Lin was not happy. The toilet roll was on the window ledge and each time I passed by I was delighted to see it unmoved. Then one guard actually picked it up. My heart missed a beat (the trivial games we play! Hide the thimble for democracy!) but even then he did not find the ball. He replaced the loo roll and stared at it in deep thought, but no one checked there again.

I was concerned about the one on my thigh. What would happen in half an hour when I had to wash? I could not avoid giving the game away then because each time I stripped to my pants to wash there would be several pairs of eyes watching me. That was most unpleasant in itself. So while I was round the back of my cell and out of sight I slipped the ball out and buried it under loose clods of earth at the foot of a post. I had to be quick and each time I subsequently walked past it I added a little more soil. It was well hidden. I would leave it there until the next day then contrive to retrieve it.

After my wash when I returned to the cell Lieutenant Soe Lin was visibly annoyed. They had had all that time to search one lousy cell but the only ball they found was the one I had given away. Once I was locked back inside I retrieved the ball from the loo roll and began slamming it into the door again. The rapid-reaction force retaliated in no time at all. One trusty started hurling gravel at me through the window and others brandished catapults. The ammunition for these was large clay pellets, quite hard. They were used for killing rats, which thrived in the prison. One good shot could take a rat's head off. I am quite sure that on a human they could break the smaller bones, blind you or if they hit the right spot on your head they could even kill you.

'Will you give me the books?'

'No.'

So I carried on slamming the ball into the door. Lieutenant Soe Lin ordered them in and they burst through like the Keystone Cops. Knowing I could not win a physical struggle for it, I hurled it through the open door into the main prison beyond. Bit of an after-dinner talking point for the other prisoners. Actually I was terrified that I would miss the narrow gap between the top of the door and the crowd of trusties as they burst in. I would have hated

305

to have caught one of them in the face with it. They now had two balls but the last one was safe. Later on a trusty tipped me off that if I made another disturbance their orders were to give me a thorough stoning.

By the next morning I still had not been given an explanation for the lack of books. I would not mind if they had lost them, or if they were in Rangoon, or if they were just honest enough to tell me that I was not allowed books, or was being punished for being a troublemaker. At least if they were honest we could take the debate forward like civilised adults instead of playing silly ball games. If they said I was not allowed books we could take the matter up with whoever wrote prison regulations. If they said I was being punished I could ask exactly what for. Specify the charges and show me where in your code of regulations the available penalties are stipulated. I had been trying to get the prison code since the first consular visit but the regime would never give it to me freely and the FCO were not really interested in pushing for it. Again it is wickedness for the junta to cut off the path of redress. There is no accountability, no transparency. Punishments are arbitrary and illegal.

But when you begin a protest you must always see it through to the end. I was very afraid. Yesterday they had started throwing stones and wielded catapults. What would happen today? I was going to bang on my door with my fists as hard as I could for the duration of the morning parade. Expecting another stoning, I thought it best if I draped a blanket over my head. My hands were trembling more than ever before. It was so hard to stop shaking.

As the call to attention for parade began I swallowed my heart (which had been trying to pop out of my mouth) and started pounding. I was so enthusiastic about it that the plywood began to splinter. The blanket was over my head and body, and sure enough, within seconds there were angry shouts from outside and stones started flying in. As I slammed the door I was repeating this prayer: 'Dear God, give me the courage to make this action; dear God, give me the strength to persist in this action; dear God, give me the humility not to lose my temper; dear God, give me the wisdom to speak sense afterwards.'

Because the ground outside the windows was so low it was difficult for the guards to get a good angle. The stones came in with reduced vigour and the blanket protected me perfectly. It meant not one cut, not one bruise, not even the slightest sting. It took all my nerve to keep beating the door until the parade singing stopped (about one and a half minutes). It is important as well, when making a protest, that you know beforehand exactly how far you want to go. Make a protest, stop, give the authorities a chance to come up with the goods (and as far as possible try to make sure they have a way of doing it without losing face). If they do not respond favourably, repeat the above steps until they do. But if you do not have an exact target of when to cease each step of the protest you are likely to stop when fear overwhelms you. This will drain your morale. The only thing that gave me courage to beat that door so hard was the knowledge that in one and a half minutes I could stop. And I had to pray that they would not open it before then. It being first thing in the morning, I hoped they were off their guard.

When I stopped beating the door the stones ceased. I walked away slowly with my back to the windows, then carefully removed the blanket. Yes, the stones had stopped. Phew. The blanket could reasonably have protected me from the stones which were thrown, but it was not good enough to shield me from the catapults. But I noticed silently that Anawratha, Chindithe and Moshi had commandeered the catapults. I am sure they used them with great drama, but they had avoided injuring me. That was not an accident. I walked over to the window and outside was a great crowd: twenty-five people, trusties, guards, prison officers, MI, the second-in-command and the governor himself.

I caught the governor's eye. 'It is not right to keep prisoners in solitary confinement,' I began, speaking gently.

The governor dashed out of view. He hated me speaking to him in front of other people.

'I have asked for books,' I continued, 'and you will not even give me an explanation as to why they are refused.'

'*Shut up!*' screamed Lieutenant Sin Po as he leapt on to a block in front of the window, 'don't speaking!'

'You have kept Min Ko Naing in solitary for over ten years . . .' I was nervous so my mouth had fallen into automatic pilot.

Lieutenant Sin Po made as if to punch me. It would have been interesting with the bars in the way but I took a step back all the same. '*Shut up!*' he screamed again.

'. . . it is not right to lock people up and give them no chance to speak . . .'

Sin Po grabbed a catapult from Chindithe and aimed it at my face. Certainly scary, but I remembered a lesson from the torture in Moulmein. Stick to your guns until you cannot. Having a catapult aimed at you is not the same as being shot with a catapult. Put away your fear, do not take heed of imagined pain.

'. . . it is every prisoner's right to make complaints but you deny them this right . . .'

With a final scream Sin Po turned the catapult a few inches to the left and let fly a pellet just past my face. It cracked into the wall behind with startling power.

'. . . I want you to give me a reason why I cannot get the books. I will not protest against hardship; I don't mind hardship. But I will always protest against injustice.' I was trying to speak as politely as I could. I did not want them to have an excuse for violence.

The MI were giving me the most diabolical stares but nobody seemed to know what to do. I fell silent and looked back at them. The tension eased slightly and the crowd milled about. I stayed at the window looking at them until they decided to move out. When I turned back to the cell I could hardly believe it. Virtually the whole floor and sleeping platform were hidden under a layer of stones, gravel and dust. The area by the door especially was blanketed. I brushed down my sleeping mat but that was all. The rest I would leave as a monument to the event.

Outside I noticed the trusties were preparing piles of stones by the windows. Even large sections of brick. Extra catapults were brought in and hung on their sheltered platform. Then one arrived carrying canvas stockings filled with gravel – very nasty truncheons. They were preparing for business.

I was determined to continue but what would I do if they

catapulted me in earnest? I could lose an eye or worse. I thought about wearing a blanket on my head like a turban and draping one over it to protect my neck, and using the rest of it as a cloak for my body. I could stick my spare shirt and *longyi* down my undies to guard my genitals and pick the round wooden lid off the latrine bucket to use as a shield, improvise a full suit of armour. And I could take cover in the latrine corner, which was not in view from the outside. If they tried to stick the catapults through the bars and fire them blind I could duck down and grab the weapons. But where would it end? I could not hide in the corner for ever. They would just have to show their weapons to make me scamper away. And blankets would do me no good if they opened up the doors and came in with their truncheons. If I wanted to persist, I had to be willing to take a beating and, if I was going to get a beating, it would be better to face it bravely rather than trying to escape from something which was not in my control.

So I put aside the idea of my 'suit of armour' (except for the shirt down my pants though; there is bravery and there is fool-hardiness. Risking your testicles comes under the latter). I would give them till after the midday exercise to produce the books. If they did not then I would wash at the beginning of the exercise period and on my laps around the cell I would retrieve the ball I had buried the day before, and once I was back inside I would persist with the protest. Of course I did not need the ball to slam on the door, and I did not even need the door to make a noisy complaint, but I would get a great deal of satisfaction from beating the system by retrieving said ball.

Noon came round once more. I was scared. I was rather hoping noon might be indefinitely postponed. I took my wash first thing and the guards did not make anything out of the changed routine. I began lapping the cell and was pleased to notice the ground was undisturbed at the foot of the post; the ball was still there. My heart was trying to pop out of my mouth again. God had never put me through anything that was not for my own good. Was He about to change His ways? No. But how could a beating be good for me? Not for me to question God, only to trust Him and obey. I do not mean that I had voices in my head telling me to throw soup packets at the door or to demand the complete verse of Kipling. But God has told us very clearly to seek out justice and stand up to the oppressor. Circumstances and our individual disposition will dictate exactly how each one of us chooses to do that.

Then God bestowed His blessing! Lieutenant Soe Lin appeared at the compound gate and handed something to Daddy. Daddy walked over to me. I could hardly believe it. An encyclopaedia, Kipling and *The Imitation of Christ*. Fantastic! I had not just won the books; I had won a battle for the right to complain. I was so happy when Daddy handed them to me that I nearly kissed him. Instead, I grabbed his arm and asked him to follow me round the back of the cell. He looked a bit bemused but came anyway. I dug out the ball and gave it to him. He burst out laughing. I showed him the elastic band and mimed pulling it up round my leg. He was delighted. We went back round the cell and all the boys had a chuckle.

That night there was considerable activity in the compound. Ko Lat, one of the most recently assigned trusties, and a rather too ardent admirer, came in carrying two small chickens by the legs. A knife was produced and he set about killing them and preparing them for the pot. An iron can had a fire built in it and mess tins were used to cook up a delicious chicken stew. Meat was a rare event and more than ten men shared it, including myself.

'Where are the chickens from?' I whispered to Chindithe at a suitable moment.

'Market,' he replied.

'How much?'

'1000 Kyat.' (About two pounds.)

'How come? Why?' I persisted.

'Lieutenant Soe Lin.' Chindithe smiled. 'Give Daddy 1000 Kyat.'

I pondered for a moment. 'Ah!' – as it dawned on me – 'the ball?' and I made a throwing motion at the door. Chindithe winked. So no wonder the Count had wanted me to give the balls to him; they had a bounty on them! There might have been a little enterprise in this for us . . . but if you try to be too clever you will come a cropper. It was interesting, though, to see how things worked.

CHAPTER 26

*It was bad too, to be betrayed by the author of the book you were reading
– if he began to drool over food in the greatest detail. Get away from me,
Gogol! Get away from me, Chekhov, too! They both had too much food
in their books. 'He didn't really feel like eating, but nevertheless he ate a
helping of veal and drank some beer.' The son-of-a-bitch! It was better
to read spiritual things! Yet even in Dostoyevsky you could find the
passage, 'The children went hungry. For several days they had seen
nothing but bread and* **sausage**.'

The Gulag Archipelago, Aleksandr Solzhenitsyn

THE IMMINENT HUNGER strike was very much on my
mind. If the junta had not produced the court record by
the next consular visit I would go ahead with it. When I
had first come to the prison the trusties had taken great risks in
smuggling extra food to me. They won my friendship for life by
that. But as the months went by, and mostly thanks to pressure
from the British embassy staff, I was able to get better prison
rations and better supplies from the market. I also got Val's and
Barry's food parcel at each visit. So the flow of food started going
out of my cell. It was always hard work to find a way to do it
without putting anyone in danger but prisoners are by necessity
cunning creatures and as long as the MI were not watching then
the guards were willing accomplices. Sharing food was not
explicitly outlawed but it was not wise to draw attention to it. I
could get away with it a few times but if it looked like a routine the

311

officers would try to stop it. It was a cat and mouse game. But seeing as I was becoming so well stocked it seemed foolish for the guys to risk bringing food to me. I asked them to stop but still accepted the odd Burmese-style delicacy, which I was unable to get by other means.

Since the stoning most of the guards and trusties had become quite wary of me. It would not help them if they appeared too friendly. From now on any exchanges between us usually took place in the dead of night. The mutual sympathy and support remained but it had to be covert. I accepted this but it hurt to be so cut off. I missed the relaxed camaraderie during the day. But Anawratha, the prisoner, would have none of the nonsense. He realised I was becoming more isolated and he stepped up his efforts to help me. He began bringing me more food than ever and special food as well: whole bags of fish, large chunks of meat, bags of nuts (very nutritious) and new types of fresh fruit. It was perfect timing with the hunger strike coming up, as I wanted to be in the best possible condition when I began. Anawratha of course had no idea that it was on the horizon. His real and symbolic kindness was a great support when others were withdrawing theirs.

Karen Williams came up on 15 March. It was another wonderful blessing. Back in December I had chosen 16 March as the ideal starting date but I knew I would have to change it to whatever day the consular visit fell on because it would not do to give even a few days warning (in order to wait for the 16th). In practice such a delay would only mean more days for my family at home to worry. And it was not as if I could have guessed a 15 March visit. The gap between visits varied, often four weeks, sometimes three weeks, sometimes five. But the dates had worked out perfectly.

As Karen arrived there was a power cut and the meeting room was gloomy. 'Have you been refusing to pay your bills again?' she asked the governor with a grin. Karen's company was very welcome. We were getting on better as the months went by.

The court record had still not arrived. Karen told me that two weeks earlier the ambassador himself had made an official representation to the Burmese deputy foreign minister to produce it. I was heartened that the FCO seemed to be stepping up their interest too. And Paddy Ashdown had visited the Burmese ambassador in London to press for answers. Much time in previous meetings had been spent trying to establish the most basic of conditions: could I keep a toothbrush, could I get out of my cell for exercise, could I receive books? It did not matter that they said yes I could. They invariably reneged on it and it would take weeks and months to make it reality. The only reason they finally agreed to anything was because of consular pressure and because of people like Lord Alton who had been raising the profile back home. But by now we had won enough ground so that we could start turning our attention to the legal battle. I gave Karen a list of the salient points regarding the first day in Tachilek.

Another reason why I had delayed this was because I knew there would have been no point in fighting a legal battle if I did not have the FCO onside and I was not going to get the FCO onside until the media and public were demanding action. The support from individuals in Rangoon and London was marvellous but we had to get the bigger players interested. Baroness Scotland, junior minister at the FCO, had just declined to see my mother to discuss the case. When she heard about the hunger strike she thought again and made herself immediately available. It is democracy at its best: a family has a problem, their friends help them publicise it, the media takes up the case, the public demand action from the government, the government acts. It is the most pragmatic and balanced system available.

I waited until the end of the meeting before I explained to Karen the exact details of the hunger strike. It was necessary for the authorities to hear all about it too. 'Twenty days, one day for each year of Min Ko Naing's sentence, beginning on 16 March to mark the anniversary of Red Bridge. No food or pills at all, just pure water. And I will end it early only if I am allowed to keep an acceptable copy of the court record.'

'You mean the court diary, order and judgement,' Karen corrected me.

'Yes.' She had better legal advice than I did! By an 'acceptable copy' I meant one that reported the truth and one that was in English. I would have been fascinated to see them reporting the truth, just to admit that I was denied a lawyer. But they knew as well as I did that however corruptly and illegally they operated, it would be death to them if they admitted it. It is one thing to commit murder and rape, it is another to do so openly. I wanted to put the regime into an impossible situation. They would not dare to admit the illegality of detaining me and yet it was becoming increasingly hard for them to lie their way out.

After that meeting Karen insisted on seeing my passport. The authorities had kept it hidden since the moment I had been detained. It showed clearly that I had entered Burma legally, a valid visa stamped into my passport. When the court record finally appeared it confirmed that the judge was quoted as saying I was in Tachilek legally. Yet despite this, the junta's media reported I had been given five years of my sentence for illegal entry. Senior officials were writing it in governmental reports. They were doing this even after I was released! And in a move which defies all intelligent scrutiny they had forged a stamp in my passport to say I had *left* Tachilek on the day I came in! What was that supposed to indicate? The border opens at 8.30 a.m. As the police had reported my arrest as occurring at 9 a.m. I would hardly have had time to enter Burma, get my passport stamped then leave Burma before sneaking back in somewhere to reach the market by 9 a.m. and start demonstrating. Even more absurdly, they had neglected to forge a re-entry stamp for Thailand, which meant that once I had allegedly left Burma I must have jumped off the short bridge between the checkpoints, in full view of dozens of Burmese and Thai officials, swum down the Moie river and then perhaps dried myself off in the two seconds I had left before reaching the market at 9 a.m. To the best of my knowledge the FCO never raised the issue of the forged stamp. I only learnt about it when I was back in the UK. But it was exactly this kind of deceit and illegality that I wanted to expose.

Karen reported back to my family that I 'looked extremely fit and well'. I am so glad she made a point of this. It was true and it was important to me that my family heard it. The hunger strike would give them enough to worry about. I also sent back the reference:

Psalm 119:v:71: It is good for me that I was afflicted, that I might learn Thy statutes.

That was true too. Does God want us to suffer? I do not think we are supposed even to pose the question. God wants us to seek His Kingdom, to seek truth. If we encounter suffering in our sincere effort to do that, it will be such suffering as makes us stronger and makes us rejoice. We will be given what strength we need to see it through. But if one seeks suffering for its own sake, some sort of penance, it will be destructive.

When I ate that afternoon I also drank down two tins of condensed milk (a new line on market runs). It was hard work, the syrup being perhaps the sweetest thing on earth outside of a Disney animation. But it was the last sustenance I would get in a while so I forced it down. Then the strike began.

To give the authorities their due, they did not stop bringing food each day at the regular times. Or maybe they knew it would be a trial for me to sit with it uneaten in my cell. In any case I passed it straight back out of the window. This was a rather messy business as the bowls had to be turned vertical to fit through the bars, and after I complained that rats would be attracted if I left it overnight in the cell they agreed to compromise. Each day they brought the food into my cell and laid it on the sleeping platform. Immediately I would pick it up and hand it back to them on their way out. I was sorry, though, that they just left the food to go off in the sun. It would have been so easy to give it to a hungry prisoner.

I did not want to waste an ounce of energy so I spent almost all day either sitting or lying down. When allowed outside my cell for exercise (now an hour a day) I just lay on a bench. The trusties piled plenty of blankets on it so that it was the most comfortable thing I had lain on for months. I had been looking forward to lying in the sun for an hour a day and thus working on my tan (I had become somewhat pasty). But dash it all, within just two minutes of lying before the blazing March sun I was sweating like a pig. That meant a serious loss of salt. Heck! I moved back into the shade. The trusties insisted on carrying the bench for me because they knew I was trying to conserve my strength.

I did not even want to waste energy washing. Although the sun was boiling, the water was freezing. It was hauled out of a well in the prison grounds and unless it had been left to stand in the sun a while it would have given even a penguin a shock. I did not want to lose energy keeping warm. Very perfunctory washes then.

Fortunately it was book season. That is to say my protests over previous weeks had won me the right to reread any books that I had already seen, although it was still impossible to get the half I had not yet seen. I asked again for David Alton's *Signs of Contradiction*. It was an inspiration. Maximilian Kolbe had lasted fourteen days without food *or* water. That was a miracle. At the end of it, with starved corpses all around him, the Nazis ordered that he be given a lethal injection. They wanted the bunker empty for more prisoners to starve in. Kolbe had volunteered for that death to save a man who was afraid to leave his wife and children. How, then, should I consider my own strike a trial when I had water to drink?

I had also asked for German books. When the time came for me to be released, I wanted to be able to speak with Kerstin in her own language. Ever since we had met at my brother's wedding we had been in contact: by e-mail while I was in Thailand and once I was in prison through the consular staff. Almost every month Kerstin sent a letter, sometimes two (although the authorities did not always let them through). And in most of the consular meetings my longest messages out were for her. We had not made any promises to each other, we knew this prison thing was going to happen, but we both also knew that there was chemistry between us which could not be ignored. A perfect reason to learn German then.

Jeremy and Nicole had sent a couple of language books out to me 'for Christmas' and weeks later the authorities agreed that I could keep them in my cell. Karen Williams also spoke with a friend at the German embassy in Rangoon and they very kindly sent up heaps of books. It was another matter to get the authorities to pass them on but the embassy helped. As I studied the language I was falling head over heels in love with the whole country. The course books could not prevent themselves from including humour, philosophy and current affairs. There were also heaps of short stories, literature from the 1800s and 1900s. The writing was so powerful that I really thought I was there, in Bohemia or Bavaria, on a never finalised journey to Gomsk or lost in the bush in Zimbabwe. Some were such sentimental old tales that they nearly broke my heart. Even now, certain German words resonate with me, they take me back to that most intense time, when I was in a backwater Burmese prison but simultaneously away with the fairies in beautiful Prussia.

The only drawback with the German books was . . . '*Kapitel 6 – Essen und Trinken*'. About one week into the hunger strike I came across the chapter on food and drink. The book was full of photographs: Schweinefleisch Schnitzels, Pfeffersteak, Roggenbrot, great steins of Weissbier and Dunkelbier, Frankfurter, Bratwurst, Weisswurst, Leberkäs and, Lord have mercy, even Schwarzwälder Kirschtorte! Blackforest gateau. The bastards!

In fact, I was having increasing problems with my eyes. After just a few minutes of reading they would ache and my vision swim. I had to start rationing the reading, limiting it strictly to the brightest of daylight hours and taking frequent breaks. With the hunger strike continuing, as I could not afford to pace around my cell, I had more time and more reason to pray. The Bible filled much of my allotted reading time and gave me plenty to think about too.

To cope with the twenty days I dedicated each one to a member of my extended family, which happened to be twenty people. I imagined to myself that if I got through that person's day without eating food it would be a blessing to them. I will not claim that it was a blessing to them, but the fear of incurring the opposite by failing kept me going. And, of course, each day was to represent a year in Min Ko Naing's sentence. I pray he will be released today, but if he must do another year in solitary, can I not do another day without food?

I brushed my teeth twice a day even though I was not eating. This was to have the most unpredictable consequences.

The authorities were good enough to send a doctor round each day. But the doctor could not do anything. The first one who came was actually the head doctor at Kengtung general hospital. I told him about my eye trouble but he did not consider it his business. After that I did not bother with making complaints. They would weigh me, take my pulse, take my blood pressure and promptly forget all the results. Despite there being a crowd of a dozen each time (trusties, MI, guards, doctors) none of them bothered taking notes.

One day two giggling nurses came in. They were utterly useless but pleasant company. They did not dare to speak to me with guards in the room but amazingly we were left alone for a few seconds as everyone else left. 'You should eat,' one of them chided me. 'You need to eat for your health.' She had no idea whatsoever. She was not just being friendly; she seemed genuinely to think that I did not know humans needed to eat. She was giving me the benefit of her professional knowledge. After their visit rumours began circulating in the town that I had been moved to a new cell. I think one of those girls had actually thought I usually lived in the wards with the other prisoners and had been moved to this quiet spot for the benefit of my health during the trying period without food.

In the first few days the duty doctor would put a stethoscope to my chest and back. But he was so terrified of the MI that he could not wait to get it all finished, so he moved it about faster than I could breathe in and out. Like everything else the doctors did it was a pointless exercise, only done so that the authorities could claim they gave prisoners medical attention. What a joke.

One of the doctors was different, though. He was a young man, very soft-spoken. He did his job slowly and deliberately.

'You are a good doctor,' I whispered to him on his second visit. 'Why?' he whispered back.

'Because you look, and you listen, and you feel.'

I never saw him again after that. As far as the physical side of things went, after four days you do not feel hunger, at least not in the stomach. Up to day eight I was sorely afraid of what would happen if I did not see it through. But after that I became more peaceful; I knew I would see it through.

On day eleven the authorities asked me to write a note requesting the court transcript. This was a most insidious ploy. In Burmese law one has only thirty, sixty or ninety days (depending on circumstances) after one's trial to lodge an appeal. If that period expires you cannot make an appeal. But the first step is requesting the court record and once this is done, the clock stops until the record is delivered, and then you must lodge the appeal in the remaining days. The British embassy had applied for the court record on 21 September, almost immediately after I asked for it at the first consular visit. Depending what timescale we were on (and how could I find out without a lawyer?) I might have only eight days left to lodge an appeal from when the court transcript arrived. That meant that if I wrote the requested note and they promptly delivered the transcript to me (probably in Burmese) how on earth could I lodge the appeal in time? Stuck in prison, not allowed to write letters out (none of my monthly missives had been allowed out) and denied consular access when the regime felt like it, I would forfeit my right to appeal.

I scrawled out a note to the embassy saying that I would not ask for the transcript but that I hoped they would persist in their efforts to secure it, acting, as per Burmese law, *in loco parentis*, in place of my parents. I was furious with the junta's under-handedness but at least they were getting nervous. Clearly they were considering making the transcript available.

The days dragged on. I hoped my family were not taking it too badly back at home and that I would be able to get word out, as soon as the twenty days were up, that I was fine.

The water we all drank was from the prison well and when I had first arrived they always boiled it before giving it to me. Fortunately they had not yet fallen out of the habit so I had clean drinking water. Some days it would come to me still piping hot. What a discovery! My own regulations for the strike permitted me only to drink water, but I had not specified what temperature it should be at (well, who would?). It turned out that drinking hot water was just like having a meal. It filled me up wonderfully and the warmth was as satisfying as any Sunday roast.

The trusties had been ordered to watch me twenty-four hours a day, sitting right by the window, and to keep a log of what I was doing every fifteen minutes. I think it must have been the most boring tract in the world: 'read, sit, sleep, read, sit, sleep . . .' The trusties hated this invasion of dignity as much as I did.

I began receiving letters of support, which had been written in the main prison and smuggled to my compound. The letters were written on toilet paper, sometimes three sheets long. My goodness how much I would have liked to have kept them . . . but after a couple of quick scans I had to destroy them. One prisoner wrote: 'Thank you so much for everything you have done for us and our country. Be determined, you will make it. Peace be with you.'

Once again it was not just what these other prisoners were giving me that meant so much, but that they were taking such risks to do it. Other letters contained news of political upheavals in Burma, or even contact details for prisoners about to be released. If they had been caught sending these notes to me I have no doubt at all they would have taken a severe beating and found their lives made torment for weeks to follow. They could even have had their term extended.

By day nineteen I was feeling quite relaxed. *Just hang on a little bit more and you are there . . . and thank God you did not go on an open-ended strike.* I was lying on my back with my legs bent and feet flat on the platform when I felt the most odd sensation below my sternum. It was as if there was a cannon ball, compressed to the size of a snooker ball, inside my abdomen and rolling down it. There was an incredible pressure which rolled from my breastbone down to my belly and then dispersed, or broadened. *Odd*, I thought, not unduly concerned, *what could that be?* Edgar Allan Poe was in my head. *'Tis only wind*, thought I, *only wind and nothing more, just some wind moving through my guts and gore, only this and nothing more.* So forgive me if I relaxed a little too much. After all, I had been without food for nineteen days. Thus I was utterly unprepared for what happened next.

Reader, I shat myself. Severely. My astonishment was beyond

320

description. For a few moments I lay paralysed, but the reality of it was unavoidable. With tremendous care, and a look of forlorn betrayal on my slack-jawed face, I made my way to the latrine corner to action some emergency laundry. It took me some time to figure out what had happened. Although I had not been eating, I had nevertheless been brushing my teeth twice a day. When I rinsed out my mouth I must have swallowed a little bit of toothpaste each time. Over the weeks it had built up. It occurred to me that the authorities were not being so fatuous when they said that eating toothpaste could give you diarrhoea. Well, a most unpleasant lesson.

Thankfully the hunger strike finished without further incident. I had a bowl of chickenless chicken soup and shortly afterwards blacked out. I started shaking violently and could not for the life of me think where I was. The UK? Australia? I decided I was on a train but as the floor was bucking and heaving so much I changed that to an aeroplane, one experiencing severe turbulence. Then I fainted. When I came to I only slowly realised I was in Burma, Kengtung, a prison, my old, tiresome, familiar cell.

The British embassy did well; Karen Williams came to see me the day after it ended. Rumours in Kengtung suggested I had started eating again after only seven days. Fortunately these lies spread no further. Karen told me that a lawyer had come forward in the UK offering to take up my case but he wished to remain anonymous until the court transcript arrived. Also the US State Department had called for my release. This was wonderful news and it certainly put a rocket up the FCO. Back in London they began taking the case more seriously.

I had a few requests for my family, most important that they send, '1 packet of freedom, 1 bunch of human rights and 2 bottles of democracy'. Also 'Matthew 11:v:30: *For my yoke is easy, and my burden is light*'. Unfortunately I could not remember the word 'trebuchet'. A trebuchet is the huge siege engine used to catapult great rocks and cauldrons of burning pitch in medieval warfare. But for this elusive word I wanted to request my family send me, 'A wet suit, a crash helmet and a trebuchet' . . . Let the MI figure that one out!

The mood in my compound over the next few days was surreal.
The prison authorities were making it almost impossible for me to
get any food. They only allowed occasional bowls of chickenless
chicken soup. I had to fight harder than I ever had before to get
fruit and bread and rice. But there was quite a breakthrough as
well. In the following weeks, for the first time, I was able to buy
meat from the market: dried fish, pork or tins of beef and chicken.
And the trusties were giving me the best food I had had for
months.

'BBC radio', one of them told me, 'reported you did fourteen-
day hunger strike!'

'What?' I was not chuffed. Maybe fourteen days does not seem
that different from twenty days but I would have liked the editor
responsible to have tried the further six.

There were other bulletins coming in.

'You have', one trusty struggled to tell me in his version of
English, 'freedom of America!'

That was a difficult one to decipher.

CHAPTER 27

For the Lord God helps me; therefore I have not been confounded;
therefore I have set my face like a flint and I know that I shall not be
put to shame; He who vindicates me is near.

Who will contend with me? Let us stand together. Who is my
adversary? Let him come near to me. Behold the Lord God helps me; who
will declare me guilty? Behold all of them will wear out like a garment;
the moth will eat them up.   Isaiah 50:v:7–9

IT WAS APPROACHING 13 April, the Burmese *Thingyan*, New
Year and Water Festival. It is traditional at this time of year
to pour water over your friends. Civilised Burmese ladies will
take a sprig of greenery, dip it in a glass of water and lightly flick
a couple of drops on to your neck. It is very genteel. Those of a
slightly wilder and more youthful disposition tear around town in
a truck with great barrels of water in the back and hurl bucket-
loads over every pedestrian they can find, or else they turn fire
hoses on to the crowd. It goes on for three days, a traditional
celebration of the pending rains. It often degenerates into juvenile
hoodlumity and for that reason it is indescribably good fun.

At *Thingyan*, Anawratha appeared so many times to pour a cup
of water down my neck and offer me the next choice delicacy on
the menu. Then he would turn and let me pour a cup down his
neck. He was the strongest man I have ever seen in my life. Not
the biggest or most muscly but the most solid man who I had no
doubt could crush boulders in his hands. And he had the greatest

323

heart too. His support, and the support from other prisoners, meant the world to me. There would be no point at all in me doing any of this if the Burmese people did not agree with it.

On the main evening of the festival one of the young guards got screaming drunk. The older men were used to alcohol but the youngsters rarely got a chance. This bairn was about twenty-eight years old. He spent four hours that night running around my compound in his underpants with his arms out as an aeroplane. I think he stopped more than a hundred times to salute me and more than a hundred times I smiled and saluted back. He found endless delight in coming to stand on the block in front of my cell window, sticking his arms out and then letting himself fall backwards. Once he was leaning back just a little bit he would stumble and catch himself and burst out laughing. I suppose in his demented mind he thought he was falling near horizontal. I felt like an old man, being so sober.

There were also plenty of drugs in the prison. When I was outside on exercise, the trusties and guards would often sit in my cell, as it was far cooler than sitting in the sun. It was ironic that I spent all day craving the sun outside and they spent all day craving the shade of my cell. While in there they often read my books, or certainly with the encyclopaedia they looked at the pictures. Moshi, sporting yet another tattoo – a bull – surprised me by recognising a photograph of Mussolini. It was great to see six, seven or eight of them crowded around the little 'library', but sad as well that they had nowhere else to satisfy their hunger for education. The magazines allowed in the prison were useless pro-junta rubbish. I was surprised they were even allowed Bibles. Certainly that is not the case in other Burmese prisons. So with this lack of distraction it is no wonder that drugs were rife and especially as Kengtung was the 'Capital of the Golden Triangle'.

I wandered into my cell one day halfway through exercise for a cup of water and there were a couple of trusties in the corner injecting heroin. I had wondered why one had seemed to be guarding the door but they had momentarily slipped up. I got the water and walked out again.

'I see nothing,' I said next time round, and they smiled in

understanding. Some villages in northern Burma have over ninety per cent of the community infected with HIV. An independent group of doctors began tackling the problem, giving away free medicines. The junta forced them to stop, saying they were undermining the stability of the state by trying to show up the government.

In August 1999 the National League for Democracy was giving out free rice in Rangoon to the desperately poor who would otherwise starve. The regime cracked down on them too, raiding the distribution points and forcing the NLD workers on to trucks. They then dumped them miles out of town. Those who returned to persist in giving out food were arrested and gaoled. Again the regime said they were treacherously plotting the overthrow of lawful government by trying to gain popularity.

At Easter Moshi came to my cell with, of all things, a hymn book. The verses were in Burmese but the titles were in English.

'A good one,' I said, pointing to 'What a Friend We Have in Jesus'.

'Shall I sing it for you?' he offered.

'Won't you get into trouble?'

'Never mind.' He sat a few yards from the window and sang. Wonderful Easter. The embassy had arranged for a local priest to see me at Christmas (not allowed until 11 January) and again for Easter. I was so happy to take the Host but after that I asked him not to come again. It was unfair that I was the only Christian in the prison allowed to see a priest.

He was a good and gentle man. 'We must thank the highest authorities for allowing this Mass,' he told me. I interpreted the 'highest authorities' as divine ones and let it pass. No point in beginning a political debate with him. He had chosen his words well. He used to whisper prayers on his way through the prison.

He gave me an Easter lily. I got it back into my cell and wondered what to do with it. I had a tin, which was left over from some fish, and I filled it with water and used a piece of tatty string to stand the lily up in the water by the shuttered windows at the back of my cell. During the day I would move it into the sun. Over the next four days four of its flowers opened and filled my cell with the loveliest delicate scent. I was waiting for the fifth and final flower to open the next day but the prison began another big clean-up. They were expecting a bigwigs' visit. They asked me to pass the flower out.

'I want to keep it alive,' I said.

'Never mind,' answered U Thu, one of the oldest guards, and he mimed to me that he would plant it beside the cell. I gave it to him and he did so. A few minutes later a guard came and tore it out. The bigwigs would no doubt object to me having my own flower.

U Thu was secretly upset. Soon afterwards he planted twenty flowers round the perimeter of my compound and more than half of them burst into colourful life. They survived all subsequent visits.

U Thu was a gentle old creature. He had trouble with his thighs, probably fungus, and used to spend half the day sitting with his pants round his knees trying to get air to his groin. Another sign of poverty – he had only two pairs of undies, wearing each one for days at a time.

One night when I was chatting with some guards I discovered that the old men, like U Thu, with two stripes on their shoulders, were paid £1 per month. Strange, but for the first time in Kengtung something had me cry. How could they avoid corruption when that was their salary? The lieutenants, who worked harder than anyone else, were paid £2 per month. But the lieutenants could take advantage of their position to live well. They extorted money from prisoners and they extorted goods from the system. Even trusties had more power than the ancient guards and lived better. The trusties could afford to give me generous amounts of food. They looked not just healthy but terrifically strong (whereas other prisoners suffered malnutrition). The old guards, on the other hand, could barely afford their own cigarette lighter and, unlike 'rich' trusties who smoked cigarettes, the guards had only cheroots. Very occasionally one of them would give me a banana. It was like the poor widow giving her last ha'penny.

That Easter my sister Emma and brother Jon came to visit too. I do not know how I would have got by if it were not for the family visits. What a blessing to have straightforward and loving company. Most important to speak with people who did not need to be afraid of what they said and whose word you could trust. Once again though, it was impossible to relax while half a dozen goons had their eyes glued to us as if we were the Christmas edition of *EastEnders*.

And for my family it was important to see Burma. They were campaigning hard back home not just for me but for the broader issues. Emma told me that Jared Genser, an American graduate of Harvard, was preparing to submit my case to the United Nations. Jared had first heard about my detention when I was arrested and assumed that somebody somewhere would demonstrate the illegality of it and I would be released. A few months later he noticed in London's *Evening Standard* that I was still inside. He got in touch with my parents and offered to take up the case himself. His success had tremendous consequences.

Emma and Jon were not misguidedly subtle in their conversation. After praising Burma's beauty and the friendliness of the locals, they spoke to me openly and frankly about the dire things they had seen: faces of fear in Kengtung, poverty and disease and starvation in hill villages around. Emma especially made a point of telling me that the international community continued to condemn the junta for their horrendous record and genocidal campaigns. She wanted the authorities to hear it all. It was encouraging for me to be assured this way that we all had the cause close to our hearts.

Karen Williams came the same day. She showed me some newspaper articles about my imprisonment. The media were doing my family and me, as well as Burma, a huge service, by pushing these issues on to the agenda. But I was upset to see one headline, which stated that I had promised to stay out of Burma if I was released. What rubbish. It did not matter what I intended to do, the SPDC had no right to extract any kind of assurances. They were an illegal regime. I sent a message back saying only the National League for Democracy could ban me from Burma.

I was worried about my family, particularly Mum. Could they be as confident as me about when all this would end? For my monthly letters in April and May what I wrote was utterly unobjectionable. The letters basically stated that I was happy and well, that God looked after me and I sent my love to everyone at home. I also thought about Kerstin. She was so strong, so giving, so understanding, so perfect. She gave me all this energy but asked for nothing whatsoever in return. So I wrote half the April letter to her – a tongue-in-cheek fable with themes of humour, gratitude and affection but not the slightest hint of politics. Yet, like all the others, these letters were never passed on. I had written out a couple of lists of Bible references during visits. Despite saying these would be passed on, and despite having them for months, the authorities still have them today. What on earth could be so offensive about Bible references?

Naturally I missed news of the outside world; there was not much time in consular meetings to discuss current affairs. Anawratha, with his deep, brown, thinking eyes, seemed to know this very well. Like everyone he battled to survive in the prison but exceptionally he seemed to win that battle with infinite energy to spare. I could see in his face that he was looking for ways to channel that extra energy, and when I arrived at the prison he decided very quickly that I was a cause worth supporting. He was not just friendly, as others were. He was not just helpful, as others were. He was not just generous, as others were. Anawratha actively searched for ways to make my life easier and so, under-standing that I must be missing the outside world, he decided to treat me to a bulletin of world news. The guards and some trusties, the latter openly flouting prison regulations, had radios to listen to music, or the football, or the regime's propaganda. Anawratha would contrive to get hold of one and sit directly outside the south window of my cell and listen to the BBC World Service. It was done quietly, but always sufficiently loud that I could eavesdrop. I made a vow to myself that however long it took for democracy to come, I would see this man again.

One day on exercise I heard a couple of smacks from the main prison followed by screams. I ran to the bamboo screen around my compound and pressed my eyes to a gap in it. I just missed another smack and then saw a prisoner standing still and crying as Lieutenant Smo Ki stormed away. I shouted out in a fury but what good was it? The prisoner, who was a strong man, just stood there and took it. He then started wailing like a child. If he ever retaliated he would be dead.

A few days later there was another commotion. I peered through the screen again and saw a team of chained men being brought in through the main gates. There was one out in front being roughed along by trusties. His head was being held down, eyes bowed to the ground. I saw them enter the central compound and turn my way. I hurriedly retied my *longyi* from the traditional loose knot to a secure one (you do not want your *longyi* falling down mid-protest) and scrambled up the barbed wire fence round my compound. The group was just approaching. The prisoner who had been singled out looked in a terrible way. His hair was bedraggled and I am not sure there was not blood coming from his face. His whole posture seemed exhausted and terrified. I think he had suffered a terrible beating and was now in for further cruelty. I was livid. 'Take your filthy hands off that man's head!' I cried in anger at the trusty, miming the action to back up the probably incomprehensible English words. He seemed only then to notice me at the top of the fence. His mouth dropped open as wide as his growing eyes but sure enough he took his hand off.

'How can you treat your brother like this?! What do you get for it?' I was still angry. The prisoner, though, did not raise his head and the column moved on. The corporal at the back waved a finger at me to say 'sh' but did nothing else. By now the guards in my compound were trying, gently, to pull me back down. Again I felt helpless. I stormed around the compound wondering what was going to happen to the prisoner.

A few minutes later I was back up the barbed wire and determined to stay there until an officer came. They would not come to my compound if I asked so I had to cause a scene. When Lieutenant Smo Ki came we had a bit of a barney but it got nowhere. I would rant against the abuses in the prison, he would angrily tell me not to cause disturbances, and I could not take it much further. I had no facts and could not find them out: who was beaten, by whom, why, what with, was there any procedure? In any case if an investigator were later to ask the prisoner if he had been beaten he would probably deny it. The only result was that they stopped roughing up prisoners near my cell or when I was on my exercise period, but I could be sure it was continuing at other times.

Once I was walking around my cell and I noticed a prisoner standing on the far side of the bamboo screen. As I came round again he was still there and I could just make out through the gaps that he was facing me. Occasionally the prisoners and I threw food over the fence to each other but only rarely as it was not such a subtle trick. So I stopped by this man and saw his hand reaching up over the wire. Quickly I put my hand up too to accept whatever was given. He took my hand in his and shook it. That was it, then he disappeared. That touched me, made me so happy I could have cried.

Sometimes teams of prisoners were ordered to my compound and told to spend an hour or two scraping the rust off the bars of my windows. Perhaps it happened the first time when a visiting dignitary on a tour of inspection had decided that the bars would look better if they were shiny. This was the limit of their thinking on improving prison conditions. His subordinates, whose brains were equally redundant, decided to keep up the routine for two or three mornings a week over the following months. After the first couple of sessions the bars refused to get any shinier but I was delighted by the prospect that they would be sandpapered so much that they would eventually be worn clean away! But really, the bonus of it was that so many different prisoners came to visit my cell and I could snatch quick conversations or share the vitamin pills or extra food that I had. Many of them were young boys who had deserted from the *Tatmadaw*. Many were Lahu, an ethnic group in Shan State: local boys press-ganged into merciless battles. Many of them were Christians, although I do not know if that is significant. The regime oppresses all.

As one of these young, deprived, uneducated lads whispered lines to me, I realised that he spoke Lahu, Shan, Burmese, Chinese, Thai and English. Six languages. And he did not think that there was anything special about that. What a crime, what a terrible crime, for a regime to deny people reaching their wonderful potential.

Although I had received German language books and had had previously-read books returned to me, there were still many which they were holding back. It might have been understandable if they were considered unsuitable material. You would expect a military dictatorship to be paranoid about the literature people could read. But their discrimination defied understanding.

During my time in prison I read Nelson Mandela's autobiography, *Long Walk to Freedom*. I read Jung Chang's *Wild Swans*, a shocking condemnation of communist China. I read a collection of letters from scores of people who stood up to Nazi Germany and were executed for their defiance. Most of them were Germans, their humility and courage as inspiring as Mandela's. And Brother Andrew's account of defying the USSR, smuggling Bibles behind the iron curtain. I read half a dozen books by Aleksandr Solzhenitsyn – fantastic books: *November 1916, Cancer Ward, The First Circle, One Day in the Life of Ivan Denisovich, The Gulag Archipelago*. All of them ripped totalitarianism apart. I felt that *The Gulag Archipelago* was perhaps the most important book of the century. It destroyed the lies of dictatorship. I even read Airey Neave's *They Have their Exits*, an awesome account of his escape from Colditz! The junta were passing books about defying tyranny and escaping from prison!

But the two books I had to fight longest to receive were . . . *Tess of the D'Urbervilles* and *Huckleberry Finn*. Unbelievable.

After all the fighting there were only five books I was never able to see in prison. Try and make sense of this. They were *Closing Time*, a harmless novel; *Total Consecration*, a religious tract: a Terry Pratchett book and, so help me God, they lied and lied and lied to withhold *Mr Brave* and *Mr Uppity*: two Mr Men books!

Karen Williams offered the only plausible explanation – that the governor had held on to them for his children. More likely for himself, I thought.

It would take me days at a time just to get an officer to come to the compound so that I could get an issue going. And when they came it was rarely of any obvious use. After four days of polite requests Lieutenant Smo Ki finally agreed to come to my compound for a chat. It was midday and I sat down with him in the sun. He heard my request for books and then looked at me out of the side of his eyes. 'James, my friend, let me tell you . . . it is this way here . . . when you try . . . if you do that way . . . we can only use our mind.'

I waited but he seemed to have finished. 'Lieutenant Smo Ki, please, I am only asking, are the books here? Or can't you tell me because of the MI?'

'James, you can tell it if you like . . . we are here . . . how would you know if I did not say . . . it is that way, that you must follow . . . we are the same.'

I nodded slowly. 'Lieutenant Smo Ki, but do you know if the books are here or somewhere else in Kengtung? If you do not want to answer that is fine. I do not want to get you into trouble.'

'Everybody here . . . when the prison . . . to answer your question . . . it must always be. Do you understand?'

'No, I do not.'

'Ah! That is good, thank you.' He smiled, satisfied with my response.

'I did not understand a thing that you just said,' I repeated.

'Yes, good.' He beamed.

'Lieutenant Smo Ki . . .'

This time, he explained it perfectly. 'James. You see my watch.' He put out his wrist and I admired his shiny watch. 'I can see my watch. You can see my watch. So we can talk to each other about what is the time.'

I nodded.

'So if you ask me the time, I can tell you the time, and we both understand.' He waited for me to nod. Well, I was happy that I could understand his words, but I was worried that it was utterly irrelevant. He continued. 'So if somebody has never seen a watch, then how can they?'

'Again please?' I asked.

'For someone who has never seen the watch, they will not understand when we tell them the time.'

Then, in a moment of wonder, I understood what he was

saying. He meant that I did not know the MI, too much was hidden from me, so it was impossible for a Burmese person to talk with me about the MI. Such a subject required its own vocabulary; there was nothing comparable in my experience. And Lieutenant Smo Ki was right. This time I grinned at him. 'Thank you, thank you, Smo Ki, for speaking so clearly. Now I understand what you mean. OK, never mind.' He patted my knee and we rose, both smiling, perhaps chuckling, and he left. But I still wanted to get the books.

Over the preceding fifteen weeks I had received only one of the books that my parents had left. I had to find novel ways of protesting. I picked up the wooden frame from over the latrine bucket and started crashing it into the bars of the window. The frame was already a little bit loose. I hated to cause damage to property but my line was that if they would not give me books, nor a reason why they were being withheld, I needed to have more activity, and outside my cell. If they would not let me out of the cell I would break out.

The bars of the window crashed about a bit, and brick and mortar fell from the surround, but I was quite half-hearted. I was very wary of actually breaking anything because it would be a perfect excuse for the junta to worsen my treatment and the outside world might just say it served me right. A block fell off the foot of the frame. 'Might be useful later,' I thought and hid it under the sleeping platform. By now there were guards and officers threatening me, insisting that I stop. They entered the cell and took away the latrine frame. Never mind, I did not need it. I took the opportunity of their visit to ask for books but again got no answers.

I thought for a while and turned my attention to the strip light. It was kept on all night. Frequently there were blackouts but the guards would then light candles on the window ledges of my cell. I would go and blow the candles out and if it was late enough, the guards would leave it at that. But I hated the strip light. I considered throwing cups of water at it to short-circuit it but was worried that the amateur way in which the guards fixed electricals might mean one of them got electrocuted. I was also worried that cold water on the hot bulb would crack it and asbestos or whatever it is in there would come showering down with shards of glass. I would then be stuck in the dark not daring to move in case I stepped on the glass. But I dearly wanted the books, as well as a symbolic victory.

I retrieved the wooden block and warned the guards that I would break the light if they did not inform the officers that I wanted books. The guards did nothing. I began throwing the block at the light. There was a barbed-wire net across the ceiling which protected it. Most of my shots were not getting through. Again I was relieved because in my heart I did not want to break anything, but I had to look as though I would. My compound soon filled up with the usual entourage plus extras. The prison governor was good enough to come. Just then one shot got through and crashed into the tube fitting. It made quite a racket, sending the light swinging and galvanising the troops. They tumbled into my cell and two of the biggest trusties moved forward to tie me up. I did not resist as they tied my arms behind my back with strips of cloth, but when they wanted to push me back so they could tie my feet too I thought it was a bit much. Fortunately they were two very understanding blokes and they did not persist.

Two minutes after they had all left the cell I managed to slip the bonds and throw them out of the window. There was a small rock used to wedge one of the shutters open and fortunately they had overlooked it when they had taken all other potential missiles out. I started at the light bulb again and very quickly the whole troop was back. This time I was handcuffed. Fortunately the bulb had survived and I had made my point. I was left overnight with the handcuffs on and thought this could only help my cause. Indeed it did. Over the next ten days nine books came through. Emma had sent quotes from Epictetus the Stoic – what a perfect prison companion! And Mum had sent the Meditations of Marcus Aurelius who was an excellent tutor. Mum also sent out George McDonald Fraser's 'McAuslan' books, reading which had me giggling like a schoolboy. But it took many more weeks until I had Tess and Huck to keep me company.

In May I had the chance to dictate to Karen Williams a 'prison appeal letter' for Than Shwe. It was supposed to be a plea for clemency. What rot! I wanted justice not clemency. After I had been persuaded by Karen to tone it down, the final letter read:

Dear Than Shwe,

I was right to come to Burma. I was right to ask the State Peace and Development Council to:

1   *re-open the universities*
2   *release all political prisoners*
3   *hold dialogue with the NLD*

I have broken no law. I will not apologise for doing what is right. As a matter of justice I should be released immediately.

And for Her Majesty's Government:

If there is any intelligence or decency in the SPDC they are far too afraid of each other to show it. Appeals to reason or morality are fruitless. The only way to get results is to force them.

The clock is ticking for certain ethnic groups. If we do not strain ourselves to stop the genocide then their blood will be on our hands too.

The ninth anniversary of the NLD's landslide election victory was on 27 May. I wanted to mark the occasion but was not sure how. I was sick of shouting and causing trouble, even if I felt I had legitimate reason to. As it went, there was yet another blackout the night before and candles were lit. Instead of blowing them out I pinched one and burnt 'NLD' in foot-high letters on the inside of my door. It seemed quite childish and pointless. How was one supposed to express one's feelings here?

In June I discovered that at last the court transcript had been produced. It was supposed to take five or six days. It had taken us over eight months. There was by now sufficient outside interest in my case to make an appeal worthwhile. Not that I would get any justice out of it, but the regime's illegality would be exposed and I was sure that would result in my release. It should not have been necessary to go through a formal (farcical) appeal to do this . . . but that is how the world works at the moment.

Karen Williams came, accompanied by a Burmese lawyer. He was U Kyi Wynn, recommended by the honorary legal adviser to the British embassy and the same lawyer who had offered to defend me in Insein back in May 1998. He had already done plenty of preparation for my case. He was a very special man, willing to put himself in danger to fight for the rule of law. Where foreign lawyers in Rangoon had not dared to tread for fear of losing their posts, U Kyi Wynn had dared to go, despite far more sinister risks.

We discussed the appeal process. U Kyi Wynn explained to me that in Burma the law did not permit detainees to attend any of their own appeal hearings. I learnt later that prisoners are not even supposed to be allowed to read the court transcripts of their own trials! How is that for lack of transparency? But it was clear why. The transcript was a joke, utter deceit.

I was frank with the consular staff about all my protests in the prison (such as burning NLD into the door). It would be no use if the authorities reported their version of events to the embassy and they did not have facts to check them against. I wanted the FCO and my family to be fully informed. I was not going to be able to achieve anything alone and if we did not trust each other implicitly we would not be able to outmanoeuvre the junta.

At the end of June my father visited again. The guards would try to search me before I left my cell but I had long since refused to accept this. 'I am not a prisoner,' I would tell them. There would be a stand-off for a few seconds, then they would wave me through. Dad brought an embarrassingly huge quantity of food with him. Tired of cat and mouse games, I asked the governor straight out if I could share it with other prisoners. He said no. We badgered him and he relented. But that was just for show. It was a real challenge to carry it through. How foul, having to struggle to share your surplus while people all around you are sick with hunger.

Dad lost his temper with the authorities a couple of times, angry at their dumb refusal to answer the simplest of questions. He swore at them. It is always best not to lose one's temper but after months of practice I was still finding it impossible; I could not complain about what Dad did. And it is good, perhaps, for the authorities to glimpse our feelings.

Psalm 4:v:4: Be angry, but sin not.

I was also more than fed up with solitary confinement. Eight months earlier I had requested a transfer to Insein prison. On the one hand it would make family and consular visits a good deal easier; each trip to Kengtung required at least one overnight stay, sometimes more if flights were not available. The consular staff went to a lot of trouble to make the trip each month. And I felt an odd duty to return to Insein, to start fighting there, where conditions were far more murderous than backwater Kengtung. But the authorities did not want to make anything easier for us. Certainly they preferred me in a far-off corner of the country. In the end this worked to my advantage; if I had behaved in Insein as I did in Kengtung there would have been much more of a crackdown.

They were in no mood to end the solitary confinement either. There was no way they would risk putting me in with the other prisoners; we would learn far too much from each other. They would not even move me in with the Indian and Thai prisoners in Rangoon. Nevertheless, I told the authorities that if they did not move me in with the other prisoners, or if they did not give me a short-wave radio, or if they did not come up with a solution to solitary confinement I would break out of my cell.

I explained to my father that I could climb up the back wall, pull aside the barbed wire and haul myself up to the rafters. This would only take a minute and then I could knock out the roof tiles and climb on to the roof. I was a bit stuck about what to do next but it would be a suitable gesture to show that prolonged confinement was inhumane.

When certain people back home heard this they were worried I would be shot in the attempt. That would not have happened. I had seen from the photographs in the governor's office that there was a machine-gun on a tripod in the main watchtower. It was quite chilling to see the photograph. It made it all the clearer why 500 men, most of them battle-hardened soldiers and some of them phenomenally strong, could be subdued by a collection of weak-chinned officers; because those weak-chinned officers were quite prepared to order brainwashed young men to open fire on the prisoners if there was any major sign of disturbance. All other guns were, quite sensibly, kept *outside* the prison.

I would break out on the side blind to the watchtower and besides that I knew the guards who manned the gun there. They did rotating shifts with those in my compound. There was not one single guard in the lower ranks who had the gumption to pass me a toothbrush unless it was authorised from above. There is no way on earth that they would take the initiative with a machine-gun. If I did break out, within a few moments my compound would be full of officials and they would not want anyone firing into that. They would send up a couple of trusties to pull me down. The notion of using guns in this sort of situation comes only from Hollywood.

I was prepared to give them two months to come up with a solution and, if they had not, I would provoke some sort of crisis. I wanted to force them to address the matter of solitary. There were only really three things they could do, as moving me in with other prisoners was not an option. They could give me a radio or let me go. Alternatively they could bury their heads in the sand and hope the problem would go away.

The Count had been somewhat aloof since the stoning, not wanting to appear too friendly with such a troublemaker as myself. But he chilled out over the weeks. Twice more he brought me alcohol. Once it was proper whisky, something that had been refined in a distillery rather than stolen from an oil refinery. But the other time the drink on offer looked like blue-green paint stripper. I was on the midday exercise period and each time I passed him round the back of the cell he offered me another cup. He must have been fairly well oiled himself to be doing it in broad daylight. My tolerance levels were by now naturally very low and the sun was baking hot. After each lap the grin on my face was getting bigger and bigger, my expression more and more inane. Eventually, and with much regret I had to turn the offers down because I could feel myself going away with the fairies. It was very good of the Count. I do not think he wanted anything in return.

CHAPTER 28

Is not my word like a fire, says the Lord, and like a hammer which
breaks the rocks in pieces?   Jeremiah 23:v:29

T HE MANAGING DIRECTOR of Prisons for Shan State came
on an inspection tour at the beginning of July. I hated these
tours, where the whole prison would be spruced up and all
the prisoners locked in the wards for hours or even days as the
authorities were never sure when their chiefs would drop by. This
was not because the visits were supposed to be surprises, it was just
poor organisation. Each time, a couple of bigwigs would stroll
round the prison followed by a crowd of fawning officials. They all
loved to wear peaked caps and sunglasses, and a chestful of medals.
They never spoke with any prisoners; they were not there to
improve conditions. All they were there to do was to improve the
security. Once they decided to cut away sections of the metal grille
on the watchtower so that the machine-gun had a better sweep.
Once they gave orders for the twisted timbers which held up my
compound fence to be replaced by slightly less twisted ones. It was
a joke anyway; in places the lowest strand of barbed wire was a full
foot off the ground. I could have slipped under it any time I liked
while on exercise.

I had found a crack between my cell wall and the door frame,
and could spy on the main prison through it. The guards knew I
did this but were kind enough not to intervene. As soon as I saw
the MD and his fellows enter the central compound I hollered out

my repertoire of slogans. The whole crowd of them winced and cursed but they did nothing more. Just pretend it is not happening, they decided.

Eventually they came to my compound. I was surprised because they had learnt by now not to bring senior officials anywhere near me. I launched into a complaint session. The MD was furious. Two days later he summoned me to the main office for a dressing down. Lieutenant Soe Lin explained that they had eleven charges to be read out against me.

'If you wish to speak to me,' I said to the MD courteously, 'then I ask you to guarantee that I will have the chance to speak to you for three minutes at the end.'

He agreed. The charges got under way. I was rather disappointed that they had found only eleven. I reckoned I had made at least twenty-five serious protests since I had arrived. They were telling me that it was against regulations to do such things as: hunger strike, throwing balls at the door, shouting out words, singing loudly etc. The governor, Maung Lo, was squirming with delight in his seat. As each charge was read out he seemed to feel a rush of pleasure through his body. He detested me and what he thought he saw now was his worshipful superior laying down the law. Perhaps he thought I was as afraid of his superior as he was. I really could not care less what they said.

But they surprised me at the end. 'If you cause another disturbance,' warned the interpreter, 'you will be punished under sections 800 and 808 of the Prison Regulations.'

It was the first time I had ever heard any of them admit that there were codified regulations. How much I would have loved to see them! They were written in the 1800s by the British colonial power. Never mind how old they were, I am sure I could have proved that the junta were breaking all the rules. If I could do that, the whole appeal nonsense would not be necessary.

'The punishments listed are,' continued the interpreter, as the governor felt a spasm of delight, 'number one: that you will have your personal belongings confiscated . . .'

I hardly had any personal belongings.

'Number two: that you will be confined to a punishment cell in solitary confinement for seven to fourteen days.'

I have already been in solitary confinement for ten months, I thought. 'How big is a punishment cell?' I asked quickly.

They conferred. 'About ten feet by eight feet.'

I had already done ninety-nine days' solitary in such a cell in Insein and here they were telling me that the maximum penalty allowed was two weeks. And they were meant for solitary? Such cells in Insein had three, four or more people in them for months on end.

'Number three,' they resumed, 'you will be made to wear rough clothes.'

I could barely keep a straight face. 'Excuse me?'

'You will be given rough clothes. Sacking. The cotton ones you have now will be taken away . . . and number four: you will be given nothing to eat for up to forty-eight hours but glue.'

Inside I was roaring but outwardly I tried not to show too much mirth. This was just a translator's error; he meant *san byo*, rice porridge. Nothing right about laughing at someone's attempt to speak another language and after all, his English was a thousand times better than my Burmese. Was two days of *san byo* supposed to be difficult after twenty days of nothing? There is no doubt that the regime in Burma is stupid in ways that defy belief. But this is a sad fact, not really a funny one.

It was amazing that they thought any of the four stipulated punishments could deter me from continuing. But it was amazing too that they had decided to try to go by the book. To me that seemed like a real breakthrough. I had been demanding due procedure ever since I had arrived. It was a fairly delicate moment and I was not going to spoil it. If they wanted to start trying things by the book, that was fine by me. The MD got up to leave.

I was aghast. 'Hang on!' I said in a panic, 'I have not had my three minutes.' He had spoken for about twenty. He certainly did not think he owed me his word and it was insulting for him to have to listen to a prisoner but I think he was curious about what I had to say. He sat down again and motioned me to speak. I began through the interpreter but it was clear the MD spoke English anyway so I directed it straight to him.

341

I begged him to look at the prisoners on his next inspection tour and to see how sick many of them were. I said nobody deserved this cruelty, especially in a land so fertile and rich in resources as Burma. I protested against the solitary of Min Ko Naing, that he had committed no crime and yet had no avenue of redress. I told him I was not afraid of any man nor any threats they made but that to my last breath I would try to obey God and Buddha.

I had overrun my three minutes, so I stopped. He seemed reluctant to go, hesitating before standing up properly, so I threw in one last bit. 'And can I have a radio? The solitary confinement is doing my nut.'

He promised they would look into it, which they did not. Soe Lin (and team) escorted me back to my cell. Before we got there I had a brainwave, a possible solution to solitary confinement.

'Soe Lin, please, can you ask the MI to arrest a couple of tourists?'

Soe Lin smiled inanely.

'Just for a week or so,' I continued, 'then you can let them go.' Soe Lin smiled on. 'They would be good company for me. After one week you can release them and then arrest another two.' Soe Lin laughed good-naturedly.

'Oh! Cannot!' he told me.

'Oh go on. The MI can arrest anyone. They could start with a German so I can brush up my language.'

For the next two months I made every effort to keep protests to a minimum. If they were even offering the pretence of going by the book then I did not want to give them an excuse to abandon it. Even so, they had a few other punishments up their sleeve.

First they decided I should carry my own latrine bucket out of the cell. I was not allowed out of the compound so I just had to slip it under the wire for Brother Sid to collect. I was pleased as Punch with this development. I hated somebody else having to slop out for me and even if I only got to take it as far as the wire I could at least do it cheerfully to show that carrying sewage is not a low-down job. There are no low-down jobs. And another bonus was it meant I got out of my cell every morning to enjoy a couple of minutes of fresh dawn air. I saw prisoners spaced out alongside the wards sewing up mailbags. Yet another job. I am sure the prisons turned over a profit.

They also started making my rations significantly worse. Smaller quantities, rotten food and eventually adding disinfectant or such incredible amounts of salt to the food that it was inedible.

But the funniest 'punishment' was their decision to stop my laundry. They said I must now do it myself. I answered that I would be delighted to do it so long as they let me have access to the laundry room where all the other prisoners had their clothes cleaned. Of course, they refused this. Instead, they wanted me to clean my clothes without brush, board or bucket, in the muddy swamp behind my cell where the guards used to spit and urinate. They even expected me to do this during my precious exercise period and, I suppose, in the rain. It did not occur to them that I was not so genteel that I needed fresh clothes. I had been a student after all.

For six weeks I swapped between my two shirts and two *longyis*. They became increasingly grubby but I did not give a hoot. The matter was resolved when the British ambassador, with support from the Australian ambassador, raised it in a meeting with the Burmese deputy foreign minister. Unbelievable that it went up to that level. That is what I mean when I say decisions cannot be taken at a low level in Burma. Nobody below the deputy foreign minister had the nous to realise how silly it all looked.

But one thing I was always going to protest for was the right to read the letters which consular staff dropped off on their visits. These letters were an absolute lifeline. In the early months sometimes not a single one would get through. By now though they had learnt it was far less trouble for them just to give the letters to me. I was receiving nearly all of them. When I had read them I asked if I could see the old ones again. After all, they had passed the censors. Everything was hard to arrange in prison and emboldened by the MD's order to stop my laundry, the prison officers thought they could get away with withholding my old letters. I was on the lookout for a new and very effective way of protesting. But what?

On a glorious July day, when the rains were holding off, I was wandering around the outside of my cell during exercise and I noticed the guards had left the keys in the lock of my door. Outrageous opportunity. I tried to hide my excitement and did another couple of laps to make sure all was clear and then, swift as I could, I snatched the keys and buried them behind the cell. I spent the rest of the exercise period walking on air. I was confident that this would work; so long as nobody found the keys I could not lose. The authorities are not strong. Challenge them and they have only bullets and fury. The only method they have of dealing with dissent is violence. As long as they did not use violence on me I could ignore their fury. If they did use violence on me, so long as my behaviour had been innocuous they would find that their actions would damage themselves far more than they damaged me. This is why I felt in control of the whole prison situation. Because if they could not make me afraid they could not possibly win. And the question of whether or not I was afraid was one hundred per cent in my own hands. It was my choice. It is why Vladimir Bukovsky says, 'My freedom is inside of me.'

When the time came for me to return to my cell I refused to go inside and asked to see an officer. Lieutenant Smo Ki turned up with a few heavies. They were expecting trouble.

'Lieutenant Smo Ki,' I began cheerfully, 'I would like to read again the letters I was given earlier this year. Is that possible?'

'OK, Mawdsley,' he answered tensely, 'I will tell the superintendent.'

'Thank you very much,' I responded, and astonished Smo Ki by promptly returning to my cell. He could not hide his sudden pleasure; it had all been so easy.

One minute later he was ranting. 'Where are the keys?' he demanded. The trusties were searching madly.

'Where are the letters?' I replied.

Twenty minutes later they gave me the letters and I told them where to find the keys. I had no more problems at all getting letters after that. Like family and consular visits, and like the trusties around me, the letters were a tremendous source of strength. Thousands of letters had been sent from around the world: to my family, to Western governments, to Asian governments, to the Burmese junta and to myself. Understandably, many people assumed I would not be able to receive letters, or at the very least they would be censored.

It saddened me, though, to get letters from people who were distressed. One day in prison I had taken my sleeping mat out into the sun during exercise and was lying down getting gloriously baked. The prison was quiet, the breeze was cool, the birds were singing. A nearby guard had a radio playing Burmese versions of Gloria Estefan songs. I was melting with happiness. Just the music, the peace and the very same sun which Jon and I used to work under in Australia. I could close my eyes and I was on a beach holiday. I was absolutely absorbed in the present, not that day or that hour (I would be back inside within the hour) but that second. What a lovely time. Then I received the following letter from an elderly lady in Australia:

> Dear David and Family,
>   Am saddened to hear of your dear son and brother, you must all be devastated.
>   I can only suppose that you are doing all you can in England to have James freed from that terrible place.
>   I know Jon is here in Australia and if he is doing anything on behalf of Jon [sic] I would like to help in any way I can.
>   Thinking of you in this very sad time.
>   Yours Truly,
>   Signed

A whole classroom of forty primary schoolchildren in Bournemouth had sent letters too. I received nine of them. One read:

> Dear James,
>   to day father told us all about you . . . you was tough. now I no this is how tough is it to be a christion. Do you miss your family and frinds. is it trrible. in ther. is it hot, dirty, smelly. is there visitors. is it uncomfortable. you been in prison for 17 yours. I think of you every time in bed. I do want to see you. what does it fell like. I know it fells like terrible. I am sorry. I am very very sorry.
>   Hope you are released soon.
>   Sally Wu

345

Sally was just ten years old. It was upsetting to think that elderly people and children back home were suffering pain that I was not suffering. I had been trying so hard to show that I had not lost my spirit, that I was fighting every inch of the way, that I had not lost my sense of humour, that God made this time a blessing not an ordeal. I was so sorry that some people only got to hear about the bleak side of things, rather than the positive aspects. God, it was perfect for me to be in prison: for me personally, for the other prisoners, for the Burma cause.

It must have been so difficult for people to write to a stranger, and one in such apparently grim circumstances. Yet countless people did make the effort and they fairly saved my life. If they did not write news of current affairs or copy out favourite poems, they sent jokes from the Internet or pearls of wisdom from sages, or picture postcards with wonderful landscapes and colours. How many dear, dear people sent letter after letter not knowing if I received any of them? John Thorn, Anthea Hall, Fred Price, Mary Lee. Mary Lee, a grandmother from Buckinghamshire used to send me the most tender letters, telling me of her gardening or her grandchildren or a recent trip to Pembrokeshire. The letters assured me that there remained a beautiful world, where people were honest, gentle and kind, where there was innocence. And what is more this better world is invincibly strong. I began to realise through those letters just how many countless people there are who are doing good things, but doing them quietly. How many kind and gentle hearts there are that you never hear about in a media full of destruction and doom.

I began to appreciate as well how very much the Church does in the world. It had been Jesuits who fed us in Minthamee. It had been Catholics who clothed the children. During my own imprisonment there were Christians of every denomination who were praying, or writing to MPs, or giving talks on Burma in their churches, or out campaigning with my family, or donating money for the Burmese cause. But most of this was done quietly. We cannot easily see the work that the Church does. It was only when I was on the receiving end of the Church's awesome power that I came to recognise it.

So many Christians wrote to me with Bible references, and by their choice of verses they showed their complete understanding of the situation, that there was nothing to fear here, that God has it all in hand.

Most encouraging of all were those wonderful letters from people who were not going to give up their freedom of expression for the sake of appeasing the junta. My great friend from Bristol, Steve Rhodes, penned the following words to me.

. . . you still appear in national newspapers: ALL THIS DRAWS ATTENTION TO THE VIOLATION OF HUMAN RIGHTS IN BURMA; TO THE PLIGHT OF THE KAREN PEOPLE – AND WHEN THE EYES OF THE WORLD TURN TO SEE IT, WE ARE SHOCKED!

We are shocked and upset because we KNOW IT DOESN'T HAVE TO BE LIKE THAT!

. . . I will personally make sure that our Prime Minister, Foreign Secretary and Minister for Far East Asia, Pacific etc. etc. get constantly reminded about

BURMA – THE REGIME – THE 1990 ELECTION
The international responsibility to Burma
You! . . . and other human rights problems

. . . Mate. I've heard that you've been beaten and stuff, which is appalling. What is worse is that I know that what happens to you is the tip of the iceberg, as far as human rights abuses go over there. You're still making the papers and the military junta are getting themselves well-deserved condemnation from the international community. Your case is effectively putting the spotlight on them.

. . . But you will be glad to know that this feeling has not obscured the reason you are there. Sure, we want you out safe and sound, but what we want most of all is to see the military rule at an end; democracy restored; 'Real Freedom' a possibility once more.

All those letters came through. The following one did not:

. . . Anyway I can't help wondering who reads these letters, and how many actually get through. I wonder how many translators' hours are

taken over the word 'pericabobulation' and whether, for that little joke,
my letter has been torn in two! . . .

Many others wrote strong letters too. Letters from Jeremy, my
twin brother, made me feel safe as houses. He was a pillar of
unshakable solid good sense. Nothing would make him flap. It did
not matter if all the world was against me; I knew I would not lose
his support.

The most wonderful thing about those frankly worded letters was
that whether they came through or not they would all be read by a
mixture of prison officers, MI and trusties. When else did they have
the chance to hear what the outside world was thinking? How else
will a pensioner in Ireland give her full and frank opinion of the MI
to them? How else will a politics student in Brisbane give his deep
sympathy and concern to a beleaguered trusty in Kengtung prison?
How else will a despairing prison officer rekindle his hope that the
outside world cares for his country, save that he sees scores of letters
sent to say the very same?

We gain nothing at all by buttoning our lips in the face of
injustice. We put the brakes on progress every time we fall for self-
censorship. And now, today, while we in the West live free, it is
those in other countries who will suffer from our timidity. But
surely when we die, God will reveal to us the pain of His children,
our sisters and brothers, and ask us why did we not speak out
against it. And that pain will fill us up and we will not know for a
second why we ever thought it better or wiser or more beneficial
for us to stand silent while our family cried.

I used to shout out ridiculous slogans time and again into that
prison, not knowing if it was giving prisoners hope or if they
thought I was a loony. And every now and then I would get a
letter or a sign to say 'thank you so much for what you are doing'.
That is how I feel about all those people who wrote to me while I
was in prison, sending letters which they thought read terribly
(how awkward to write to a stranger!) but which were every single
one of them wonderful letters, and writing them with only the
slightest hope that I would ever get to read them. But read them
I did and they kept my heart beating.

It did not matter if the letter was a political one, or a funny one, or a religious one, or a newsy one. The best letter is one that is sincerely written. And that made them all great. Such support was especially appreciated when I lost my best friend in the prison. News reached my cell that Anawratha was being taken to the borders, to do prison labour there. That meant malaria, landmines, possibly death. I saw him chained up, ready to be taken off. When he found an opportunity to say goodbye to me, I retreated to the corner of my cell and cried. It was only the second time in the whole of the first year. In fact, he was not on his way to the border, but being transferred to Mandalay with a dozen others. Our prison was getting overcrowded.

Prison without Anawratha was a fire without any heat. It was hard to carry on; I felt I had lost my ties here. He had been such a wonderful friend: so persistently kind, so fearlessly supportive. His actions were dictated neither by fear nor promise of favour. He was his own man. He is 'the one man in one million' of Ecclesiastes. The only other I had ever met like him was Kublai, the villager who paddled me to Moulmein.

In the July consular visit Karen brought two typed copies of my 'appeal' letter to Than Shwe for me to sign. She handed one copy to the authorities and kept the other herself, intending for U Kyi Wynn, my lawyer, to hand it to a judge when the opportunity arose. When she went to leave she was detained outside. The prison authorities demanded that she hand over her copy of the letter. Karen refused. She knew what would happen if she handed it over.

In May she had given me instructions to write a note appointing Lord Brennan QC as an additional lawyer. I had done this and Karen duly gave it to the authorities for them to 'censor', expecting it would then be returned. Instead they 'lost' the letter. Later the governor said they threw it away because a handwritten letter cannot have been important! My goodness, did they want me to type out a letter requesting a lawyer? As it went, Lord Brennan did not allow the loss of a poxy letter to block his involvement. Instead he brought the most refined and formidable expertise to support my case and the very fact that another member of the Lords, a QC, was giving me his backing went a long way in swinging public opinion back home. It also scared the hell out of the regime.

Karen's flight back to Rangoon was to leave in fifty minutes. The prison authorities would not let her go. They demanded the appeal letter. Karen refused. She had seen that their copy of it had been screwed up and thrown on the floor. Unbelievable. The governor told Karen that he could not process letters which contained political language. I can understand that they hated what I had written but I thought that at least they would pass it on to the MI for their records. (And this is quite regardless of the obscene illegality of their destroying letters by which I was trying to establish an appeal. Criminal obstruction of justice.)

But in Burma officials are so afraid of their superiors that they dare not upset them, even by passing on a message. In my ignorance I thought that the chaps at the top of the MI would want a clear and real picture of my mental health so they could judge how close they were to 'breaking me', when they could extract a full creeping apology and repentance from me. But the guys at the top had no idea. All they would ever hear from their subordinates would be messages of encouragement and that is why they are so prone to blunder down disastrous paths. It is why in 1990 the generals genuinely believed that they would win a general election. They had no idea how much the people hated their rule nor how much the people loved the NLD. They prepared victory banquets on polling day and some broke down in tears when the results came through.

The worst is that the vocabulary of police/MI reports changes as it goes up the ladder. If I admit that I taught refugees on the border, they write down 'operated with insurgent groups'. If I give out pro-democracy literature they call it 'anti-government' (as, unfortunately, do a whole swathe of the Western media). If I ask for the universities to be reopened they write 'an attempt by neo-colonialist foreign imperialist powers to undermine the stability of the Union and usurp political power'. The men at the top have no sources of information other than the garbage fed to them from below. They live in cloud-cuckoo-land.

So it was that nobody in the prison could even think to dare to countenance the consequences if that letter got out. I was unapologetic and still hammering away at my three points. What was worse, I had signed a copy in their very prison and they must have felt that their heads would roll if it ever came to light. Prisoners were not supposed to have legal redress nor stand up to the junta.

Karen still refused to hand over the letter; she had seen enough of their deceit over the past year. She sat in a taxi before the main gate and the authorities refused to open it up. Ten minutes before the flight was due to leave she was still sweltering in the car. Five minutes to go and she was adamant that they had no right to take the letter. The authorities got scared, phoned the airport to hold the plane and finally let Karen go.

That, I think, is going above and beyond the call of duty. What a blessing to have such people around. We are all free to make the right choice. Do academics and philosophers still argue about determinism? Are we determined by our upbringing or by our genes; is our behaviour dictated by our psychological disposition; are we all slaves to the historical process; are we pawns of language; or are we just insignificant cogs in a huge clockwork universe? Freud, Marx, Nietzsche, Derrida, Laplace go jump. You have missed the point. Every single one of us has free will. We can choose to do right and we can choose to do wrong. For sure only God can weigh up the mitigating circumstances. But to deny our choice is to deny our humanity, our very meaning. So much as determinism exists, in whatever form or theory, it is of no importance compared with the part of us that is free. God bless Karen for choosing to hang on to the letter.

My twin brother Jeremy was due to make a visit. Life in the army meant that he only had rare opportunities to do so. The Burmese embassy in London refused for weeks and months to grant him a visa. No explanations were given, enquiries went unanswered. His visit was set for early August. At the last minute they returned his application and granted him the visa, but it was too late by then to book a flight. Jeremy could not make it out there. Meanwhile some of his soldiers were dropping hints that they would like to help 'in any way they could'. It was a kind offer, but I doubt Her Majesty would have approved.

CHAPTER 29

Lucky am I, because, though this befell me, I continue free from sorrow, neither crushed by the present, nor fearing what is to come.

Marcus Aurelius

THERE WAS QUITE a lot of sex going on in my cell, although I hastily add that I was involved in none of it. There were the rats who had become ever bolder since the disappearance of the compound cat. Each evening they would emerge from my sleeping platform and charge around the cell. In the van was a female flying and scrabbling round the room at breakneck speed with a big lusty male in uncontrollable pursuit. They would run round and round in rings and figures of eight, vanishing beneath the sleeping platform for a few moments, then shooting out from the other end.

Every now and then the male would catch the object of his lust and they would tumble in a ball of claws and shrieking teeth. It did not take too long, though, for the drama subtly to change. The female was becoming less and less successful in her attempts to escape and remarkably, the male was becoming less and less desperate to catch her. Eventually they would be lolloping round the cell at an embarrassingly slow place. She even kept stopping and looking back at him, no doubt with quivering eyelashes. He, however, was by now exhausted and pointedly refused to catch her. Whenever she stopped and turned to him, he would stop too and start sheepishly examining his fingernails or looking for a coin he had just dropped. What entertainment. How fortunate that we humans are not at all like the animals.

The spiders had even more extraordinary sexual habits. There was a great big female in the centre of her gorgeous web and a male, about one quarter of her size, gingerly approached the periphery. Before coming any closer he spun himself a huge bow of thread and attached himself to the middle. Then he furtively picked his way across the web towards the grande dame at its centre. Once he was about six inches away he suddenly started pranging on the web strings. His beloved felt the excited vibrations (perhaps the trill of a lover felt different from the crazed throes of a victim insect) and twanged back to him with a quick signal of approval. His amorous overtures accepted, the male would rush in and the two would be lost in a sixteen-legged ball of arachnid copulation. Within seconds, though, the male would flick her away and he would fly off on his bow, catapulted well out of her reach. She would grope around furiously for him, then settle back, fuming at being used like that, with him disappearing before giving her full satisfaction.

This whole process would be repeated about four or five times. Then something different would happen. When the male trilled on the line to his beloved, she did not trill back. Instead, she remained perfectly still, sinisterly still. He trilled again . . . no answer . . . and with that he was off and away. Climbed quickly up the bars of the window and was never seen again. What did all this mean?

I think they must have had one of those relationships where when the female judges that her eggs have been sufficiently serviced, she decides to eat the male. And he knew it. Hence his elaborate 'ejector seat'. How dreadful for those male spiders who went back perhaps once too often, or who, caught up in a frantic orgasmic embrace, found that they did not have the willpower to pull out in time before it was too late.

For me, though, no sex and no matter. For months I had not even thought about it. Celibacy is remarkably easy when all temptation is removed.

When I had first arrived at Kengtung a prisoner had warned

me that the guards with three stripes on their shoulders worked for the MI. They were not prison guard sergeants but MI officers. One of these MI guys was doing his rounds of the prison, stepping through the vegetable patch on the other side of the wire, when on an impulse I called out to him. '*Mingalaba!*' [blessings!] '. . . How are you?'

He pointed to his chest with a startled expression on his face.

'Yes, how do?' I cried across the compound to him. A couple of other guards turned their heads to watch. 'Can I ask, what is your name?'

He looked behind him, to the left and right, then pointed to his chest again. Did I mean him?

'Yes, please, do you mind if I ask you, what is your name?'

Suddenly he looked very pleased. 'My name is Ko Ba Ga.' Actually, he was very friendly.

'Thank you,' I called out, 'and which department do you work for?' He was silent. 'Are you MI? . . . You are Military Intelligence, aren't you . . . What do you do for your job? . . . How do you help Burma? The MI is destroying Burma, you lock up innocent people, Burma's best and bravest, you lock them up and try to destroy them . . .'

Ko Ba Ga had got the message. He stormed off with a sour face and I was surprised at how easy it had been. But I felt sorry as well, because he had answered me so genuinely, so friendlily, and even so proud of himself. He did not seem like a monster at all and I had just been incredibly rude to him.

That incident had occurred back in February and since then I had become increasingly confrontational with the MI characters until I had scared off all seven of them. They avoided my compound wherever possible, only coming if there was a big crowd rushing to investigate a protest.

But a new chap appeared. Ko Gyi Gyi, the fattest and most primitive MI man in Kengtung, waddled into my compound. His presence there changed the whole atmosphere. The guards could no longer lounge around; instead, they sat up attentively or even stood. Ko Gyi Gyi only needed to wave his hand and two or three would come rushing to see what errand they could do for him:

fetch a cheroot, a cup of green tea, go polish his boots. There was no real laughter, except from the Count. And nobody would dream of talking with me while the fat man was there. If I asked for a light they would pass it to me with their head turned away.

I had tried twice before to get rid of Ko Gyi Gyi, by this confrontational method, but he was exceptionally thick-skinned. If I had to take my hour's exercise with him in the compound I would not be able to enjoy it at all. I had taken to sitting on the far side of the cell where we could not see each other, but how many more days could I do that? The very presence of the MI is supposed to be oppressive, and it is. Enough was enough.

As soon as the cell door was opened for my exercise I headed straight to Ko Gyi Gyi, pulled up a stool in front of him and put my face about one foot from his. 'What do you do, what do you MI do that is good for Burma?' He scowled at me, furious, but said nothing. 'This regime is destroying Burma and you support them. They are killing whole families, massacring whole villages in Shan State and you support them. You should be ashamed. You disgust me.' I was speaking with feeling.

Ko Gyi Gyi was holding a tiny plastic cup in front of his face. It was the strangest body language. He was not drinking from it, only holding it close in front of his leathery face, trying to hide his whole huge bulk behind this tiny cup. The other guards were getting uneasy and calling out for me to move on.

'I hate what you are doing to Burma. You know *Tada Phyu*? White Bridge, Red Bridge? Unarmed students protesting against the murder of Phone Maw and Soe Naing and what does your regime do? You shoot at them too! The *Lone Thein* followed fleeing students into Inya lake and clubbed them to death. Drowned and clubbed to death, female students, unarmed, innocent.'

The other guards were around me now, unsure what to do, some trying to pull me away. I did not know how it was going to end either and I was running out of steam.

'*Tada Phyu*, how many killed, and Khin Nyunt dismisses it in his propaganda as a meaningless incident. You know the *Sa Thone Lone*, don't you? Khin Nyunt established these groups of men to kill any villager who has had contact with guerrillas, no matter how little the contact and no matter how many years ago. Do you think that is right? Do you want to work for the same boss? The *Sa Thone Lone* cut villagers' heads off and stick them on poles . . . then they tell the other villagers that they will cut their heads off too if they dare to touch them, to move them . . . what do you think of that? . . . Doesn't it matter to you? . . . You disgust me, I hate what you do. . .'

Mention of Khin Nyunt had galvanised the boys. Brother Sorrow (very strong, very gentle) was standing behind me. 'James, stop!' He put his hands under my arms and picked me up. It seemed like a good moment to leave anyway. I marched off. Brother Sorrow was in for thirty-five years for driving a truckload of amphetamines. He was only nineteen and often I would notice him staring so poignantly over the prison wall. I do not think he dreamt of the world outside. I think his soul was still in shock. And as if I needed another reason to pray for democracy soon, it was so Brother Sorrow could see his parents and three sisters and two brothers again.

Daddy was taking refuge behind my cell and had a huge grin on his face when he saw me. He shook his head and as I walked past he patted me on the shoulder. We did not need to say anything. Each time I came back round to the guards' shelter I threw my meanest Paddington stare at Ko Gyi Gyi but he would not make eye contact. Soon he was laughing again and the guards were making a point of being relaxed. Had it worked? I had to give him a few more minutes, as he would not want to lose face by waddling out immediately. And then sure enough, just a couple of minutes later, he remembered an urgent task and left the compound. What a relief. He did not come back again.

Is it strange that these cruel men are defeated by a show of fearlessness? If I appeared fearless, it was only because we all knew I had the international community watching my back and, if the regime was going to injure me, then they were going to need a pretty good reason to do it. Ko Gyi Gyi left because he did not know how to control the situation and that means death to the regime – if they are seen to have weakness and to be faced with things they cannot control. Had I been Burmese I would have been beaten up immediately. But with this primitive solution always at the ready, the regime has not developed any others. The answer is to talk, to argue the points through. But the regime know they cannot do that because they do not have a leg to stand on. Nobody can excuse genocide. When the regime are made to feel too afraid to use their guns, then they will crumble, because they have nothing else.

When the August consular visit came round I was in for a surprise. The authorities had built a glass room within the governor's office and I was supposed to sit in that for the meeting. I was not at all prepared for it and before it occurred to me to object I stepped inside and the door was locked. I was supposed to communicate with the visitor via an intercom. They gave several ridiculous reasons for this box, then finally admitted it was because Karen had got away with my signed letter (although I did not hear any of that for another month). It must have cost an awful lot to erect; it was permanent and there was a huge air-conditioning unit at the base. It must have been a terrible inconvenience to the governor as it took up almost a third of his office. It was there solely for my once-a-month one-hour visits. This time I was visited again by the ambassador, Dr John Jenkins. It was heartening to see him. The prison staff were intimidated enough by anyone from the embassy; with the ambassador their nervousness was even more apparent.

U Kyi Wynn had submitted my appeal to the district court in July and it had been thrown out. No one was surprised. It was then taken to the high court and Dr Jenkins told me that the previous week it had been thrown out of there too. It was not that the judges had found against me. They had rejected the whole thing, saying there were not even grounds to submit an appeal in the first place. Dr Jenkins asked me if I wanted U Kyi Wynn to take it to the very last stage, applying for special leave to appeal. My answer was that I was in no position to make judgements and would leave it for my family and the FCO to decide. Deep down I wondered when the London side of the FCO were going to admit that there is no judicial system in Burma worthy of the name. Their idea was to exhaust the official procedures first and if there was no joy there they might consider other methods. I had to accept this slower pace of things. I had, after all, put myself in prison. I did not feel I had the right to demand anybody's help.

In any case, I trusted my family's judgement. They had all made quite an impression on the embassy staff over the course of their visits to me and it went a long way in earning support.

'Your sister is very good,' mentioned Dr Jenkins. This was because Emma was so level-headed and clued-up. She was a Cambridge Ph.D. (as well as a Rowing Blue) and could make balanced decisions where others feared to tread. If Mum was my ambassador to the press, Emma was my ambassador to the British government and, with my record, she had her work cut out for her.

We did not bother using the intercom but shouted through the screen instead. Dr Jenkins held up a few letters to the glass for me to read. One was from Kerstin. Once again she had written the most positive and encouraging letter. During some of the very hardest periods in prison it was by thinking of her that I kept myself together. If it were not for Kerstin I might have let myself go. She was my hope. If I wanted to be fit and sane when I came out, it was for her. She is an angel, the best heart in the world.

The ambassador asked again if I would be allowed out of my cell for more time each day, perhaps to work or something. Indeed, my sentence had been 'imprisonment and *hard labour*', yet where was the labour? We had had to fight even for me to sweep out my own cell!

The inevitable reply was: 'We will ask the higher authorities.'

When the meeting was over the ambassador asked three times if the door could be opened so that we could shake hands. Three times the prison governor said no.

I had been in prison for almost a year. The regime appeared completely intransigent. The appeal had been dismissed from the highest court in the land without even a hearing. There was still no indication that I would be moved in with other prisoners or be permitted to keep a radio.

History is full of examples of people rising up to overthrow tyrants. They could succeed because both sides were using similar weapons and the determination of those fighting for greater freedom won the day. But the world has changed since then. Nations have become so much more intertwined. The stage for revolution is nowhere any longer within one nation's boundaries. All oppressive dictatorships in the world today are using funds, weapons and technology from abroad, but the people of these countries do not have the same resources. Therefore the fight is too unequal.

The people of Burma will win their own freedom as only they can. But they will not be able to do it unless the outside world is simultaneously fulfilling its duty. Namely to make sure that the junta in Burma are too afraid to respond to the people with barbaric and disproportionate violence. For democracy to come to Burma there must be a resonance between the forces within the borders and the forces without. For me to get out of prison required the same thing.

There is no way I could get out of prison on my own. It does not bear thinking about. If I were a one-man band, the junta would have slotted me long ago. But neither could I just sit back and wait for the outside world to get me out. If I sat back I would vegetate. For a year the campaign around the world had been gathering momentum and was now almost ripe. I also had had a year in prison to learn as much as I could about how it worked and how the authorities were likely to react to given forms of protest. It was almost time to take the plunge.

CHAPTER 30

But you who are strong and swift, see that you do not limp before the lame, deeming it kindness.   Kahlil Gibran

WHAT HAPPENED WITH me in prison is only one side of the story. I am afraid I cannot do the other side justice. I cannot give a full enough account of what was happening outside. My family had stuck by me all the way. They campaigned relentlessly to bring pressure to bear on the junta.

As soon as news of my arrest was reported, Lord Alton and Baroness Cox contacted my parents to get involved. With my family they began presenting the facts and purpose of my actions to the media and the media had a prize story. The Jubilee Campaign, a Christian human rights lobby group, was also involved straight away. They put together campaign packs to distribute throughout the UK. These concentrated not on my release but on the facts of injustice in Burma.

In October a vigil was held at St Peter and Paul's, the church I had gone to as a child in Mawdesley. A larger one took place at Westminster Cathedral. More followed around the world. Protests were held outside the Burmese embassy in London and my friends from Minthamee demonstrated most fiercely outside the Burmese embassy in Bangkok. Thanks to the efforts of Jubilee, thousands of postcards were sent to our FCO and to the Burmese regime. After a few months the FCO indicated to my family that they had got the message loud and clear, and could the cards now be directed just to the junta!

Thanks to the media and Jubilee's church campaigns, people up and down the UK were writing to their MPs. Hundreds of MPs contacted the FCO on the matter and scores gave their signed backing to questions raised in the Commons. Three times Lord Alton raised questions in the Lords and initiated full debates on the situation in Burma.

My parents began giving talks around the country. At Greenbelt my mother addressed crowds of hundreds and went down a bomb. They loved her. My whole family were giving countless interviews for newspapers, radio and TV. National papers printed articles written by my mum. Local papers kept a steady interest and in the periods when the national press went quiet, the Catholic press never relented. Lord Alton wrote time and again for them on the issue.

By February a businessman had pledged £20,000 to the reconstruction of *Pyo Pan Wai*. Meanwhile, schools in the UK and Australia were taking up my case, most notably Queen Elizabeth High School, where I had spent one year while living in Hexham.

Christian Solidarity Worldwide got things moving in Australia and even more so in America. Congressmen and Senators received countless letters on the matter. When Jared Genser became involved, he wanted not only to take the case to the UN but also to get the American State Department interested. Lord Alton had already visited Washington to draw American interest to my situation. Then Jared and friends of his lobbied so effectively that by May the US was calling for my release. In June five Senators and eighteen Members of Congress sent a letter to the junta urging for my immediate and safe return to the UK. American involvement seemed to spur the UK FCO to greater efforts. On 14 June the Burmese ambassador in London was summoned to the Foreign Office to explain his country's actions.

Andrew Mennear, a councillor in Hampstead and Highgate, had delivered a letter to the Burmese Ambassador's residence calling for my release, then urged the Shadow Foreign Secretary to raise the matter.

Lord Brennan QC agreed to take up my case and, like Jared, completely free of charge. Lord Brennan was Labour, Baroness Cox was Tory, Lord Alton was a crossbencher, previously Liberal. This was not a party matter.

Despite a precedent of a British QC defending a case in Burma, Lord Brennan was not allowed to do so, but in prison I took great heart that although I had faced trial without a lawyer I now had three of the world's best working on my case: a QC at the House of Lords; U Kyi Wynn who I suspect may be Burma's most competent and courageous lawyer still allowed to practise; and Jared. In fact, Jared was not even a lawyer yet! He had got a Master in Public Policy degree from Harvard and was now studying for his law degree in Michigan. In any case he delivered the results.

The embassy staff in Rangoon were working hard too. Over the course of my imprisonment they sent seventy-eight official notes to the authorities in protest over prison conditions. They also made 13 face-to-face representations with senior Burmese officials. That is the reason why I was able to get anywhere with my protests. If the FCO had not said the same thing on the outside, I would just have been beaten up. But the regime were too afraid to beat me up over issues where the FCO gave me backing.

Again and again, meetings were held with Burmese ministers in Rangoon. On 27 July the British Deputy Head of Mission went to see the Burmese Director-General of Consular Affairs. The Director-General responded to criticism of my conditions by saying that I was not in effective solitary confinement because outside the cell were prison guards!

When Dr Jenkins, the British Ambassador, saw the Attorney-General on 9 August he once again asked for the order and judgement lifting the suspension of my 1998 conviction (i.e. why I had to do five more years in prison). The Attorney-General, head of the Burmese legal system, said this was a matter for the Ministry of Foreign Affairs. Dr Jenkins replied that it would be a matter for the judiciary if it was further withheld. The Attorney-general, dodging all his responsibility, suggested a court application should be made to force the Ministry of Foreign Affairs to produce the records. What a nonsense. The very heads of the Ministry of Foreign Affairs were saying 'not our business, see the Home Office' and the Home Office were saying 'not our business, see the Ministry of Foreign Affairs'. And they were not just junior clerks dodging responsibility. The British and Australian embassy staff visited the Deputy Minister for Home Affairs, the Deputy Minister for Foreign Affairs, the Foreign Minister, the Attorney-General and the Director of Prisons. My mother met the Director of Prisons too. He was not willing to make any decisions at all.

My father managed to get an appointment with the Deputy Home Minister. 'Instead of meeting me,' said my dad, 'why don't you meet with James? I'm sure he would love to talk to you.' But no chance.

When my case was dismissed without a hearing from the High Court, US Senator Sam Brownback contacted Lord Brennan with a rather radical idea. He was interested in organising a trip to Thailand and then marching over the Burmese border to raise the matter of my right to legal representation.

On 31 August 2000, the one-year anniversary of my detention, another businessman had paid for a boat to steam up and down the Thames outside Parliament, and a vigil and rally were held on board. TV companies were becoming increasingly interested. On the same day, Francis Maude, Shadow Foreign Secretary, released a statement to the press calling for my release. A week later Robin Cook was in touch with my parents. Tony Blair had already replied to my mother's letters.

There were six key powers involved in this. The power of family, who are your nearest and dearest, who will never abandon you. The power of friends, like And, Tom, Rob, Mike and Ben, who supported my family throughout and Christine Glover, Steve Rhodes, Kerstin Gerlach and Ye Min Aung who went to phenomenal lengths to promote the campaign. The power of the Church, full of individuals who do not count the odds when they join battle because they know it is already won. The power of the media, those journalists and reporters who were not just interested in a sensational story but also in accuracy and truth. The power of those who go above and beyond the call of duty in their job – Mark Rowland, Emily Murray, Lord Alton, Baroness Cox, Victoria Billing, John Jenkins, Senator Sam Brownback, U Kyi Wynn. And the power of people who were perfect strangers but took up the case because of their commitment to justice – Jared Genser, Daniel Brennan QC, Mary Lee.

Letters were coming in from every continent. Thousands of people around the world were becoming increasingly concerned. It was all building up. A month later it would fairly explode.

CHAPTER 31

Good is never accomplished except at the cost of those who do it; truth
never breaks through except through the sacrifice of those who spread it.

Cardinal Newman

A MOST IMPORTANT ASPECT of surviving prison is developing a daily/weekly routine, trying to take control of your time as much as you can. This meant I had very specific times for reading, praying, pacing and, oddly enough, 'free time' (where I could do whatever in the world I liked, be it sit down and think of politics or sit down and think of politics). Even brushing my teeth and the daily wash developed into an exact procedure. A vital part of it all was exercise. One year earlier, on my first morning in Kengtung, I had managed a grand total of sixty exercises. Over the year I built it up: press-ups, sit-ups, using my water bucket as a dumb-bell, enough jumps and step-ups on to the platform to merit a mountain every time. By now I was doing over 2000 in each session, four sessions a week. I usually did these very early in the morning, sometimes starting at 4 a.m. so that I could channel my fury at the inane propaganda to good use, rather than lying on my bench cursing the noise which prohibited sleep. Thus I was probably fitter and stronger than at any other time in my life.

In early September I was gearing myself up to make a major protest against solitary confinement. There had been enough warnings, enough official representations, the regime had had enough time to find a solution. But I knew that whatever I did had to make more impact than everything I had done before. No more symbolic protests, this time I had to win. And I knew that that was going to be an exceedingly painful process. I bottled out.

Soon afterwards Ko Lat, the trusty, whispered to me that my mother was due to visit. What a conundrum. I had already decided that I was going to refuse to go into that glass box for any more visits. It was an unnecessary, cruel and illegal set-up. But I had made an exception. If my mother came I would agree to see her. I thought it might be too hard to refuse. But a line had to be drawn. If you bow to one injustice you will find it harder and harder to fight the next. The more I considered it, the more I had to admit that if I saw my mother through that glass screen I would certainly cry. And if I cried she would cry and then we would weep and then no more would my family be able to believe that I could handle prison. It would be too much of an agony for them to be back home imagining me a broken man in prison.

When I arrived at the main office for the meeting I refused to enter the box. I sat on the chair positioned for my mum. I told the authorities that they had no right to stop me seeing my mother, that no other prisoner in Burma was required to sit in a glass box (although plenty were denied visits altogether) and that it was cruel and unnecessary. 'I will not sit in the box. I want to see my mother,' I told them levelly.

They went out to tell her. Thank God that Mum and I understand each other so well. She had heard about the box from Dr Jenkins who saw it on his last visit. She weighed up the situation in just a few moments and correctly deduced that I was saying we were surely not so weak that we had to accept cravenly the junta's every injustice. She said that she would not see me unless it was outside the box.

The prison governor screamed, a little yelp of panic. They returned to me and told me that my mother did not want to see me. It was a shock for just a split second but then I came to; we were on the same wavelength. I returned to my cell. That was that.

Mum was advised (by some who should have known better) not

to say anything to the press that might antagonise the junta. But she was not going to confuse spinelessness with diplomacy. She immediately got in touch with the Jubilee Campaign and gave the following statement:

> *They are holding James in solitary confinement without fair trial, refusing appeals for a fair trial, lying to the world, and continuing their genocide against the Karen and other ethnic minorities.*

The media pounced on it. My family had also been advised not to involve the UN in my case as this might 'antagonise the authorities'. What absolute rot, as was to be proved.

The isolation had got worse in other ways. In order to ease overcrowding, 200 prisoners were transferred to Taungyi. They included some of my best friends. But it was good that they were gone, and Anawratha had gone, and Chindithe and Moshi too. I would not have liked them to be around for what happened that September.

I had been in prison for over a year and there seemed precious little evidence that my analysis of the regime's weakness had been correct. Should I give up? I could induce my release any time I liked by kissing the junta's ass but frankly I would sooner have died. How, though? Maybe cut my wrists with the barbed wire, or just climb to the rafters and then dive headlong on to the concrete. Nasty thoughts. The very idea of killing myself was a terrible one. It would be a betrayal of everyone who had supported me, an unforgivable pain for my family, a sin against and an insult to God – did I trust Him or not? Feelings are vital but not infallible. They tell us truths which the rational part is incapable of formulating. But feelings can be wrong. I had *felt* back at Bristol that I wanted to commit suicide and had then discovered how wrong those feelings were. So to have them again, now, in prison . . . well the rational side took over. It said, 'These feelings are dangerous. Do not indulge in them. Turn them aside.' I became angry that I had even had the thoughts. I needed to channel that anger into effective action.

The threat of violence against me had been building up. If I was to make a significant protest against the continued injustice of my incarceration I was sooner or later going to get a beating. If I stopped then, after a beating, and gave up, nothing would be achieved. In fact, the regime would have found the way at last to shut me up. If I continued, though, and continued, and kept continuing until there was some kind of breakthrough, some kind of admission on their part that the situation had to change, then it would be worth it. And I knew full well that if I got a beating for making peaceful and legitimate protests the regime would have few places left to run from the outside world.

Back in my cell my eyes were as bad as they had ever been. I could not read more than a few lines before they began to hurt and the vision blurred. It was a torment not being able to read, especially as I had such fantastic books. This was a kind of last straw. If I was degenerating, then it made sense to take my stand sooner rather than later or I would have less resources to do it with.

On 21 September at 9:30 in the morning I removed the loose screw from the shutters. On one wall I scratched in large letters 'prolonged solitary confinement is inhumane' and on another wall 'release all political prisoners'. I replaced the screw and began pacing round the cell in a final effort to collect myself. I was extremely scared.

'OK,' I told myself, 'three more laps and then you begin.' At the end of the third lap I stood before the cell door and beat it and beat it harder than I had ever done before. Always with protests I would give myself specific limits. The heat of the moment is not a good time to decide when to stop and I had told myself this time that I had to belt out the first three verses of 'Lord of the Dance'. A bit of a comic detail but there is nothing like a rousing hymn to keep your courage up and besides, it was sung at Jeremy's and Nicole's wedding so put me in a good mood. It was vitally important, too, that I did not lose my temper. I challenge anybody to lose their temper while singing 'Lord of the Dance'!

It took a good minute and a half. The Keystone Cops were going berserk at the windows and the other side of the door. Because I was rattling it round so much they had great difficulty in slotting the key into the lock and quite often they took to punching the door from their side in fury. This only served to add to the general din.

When I had finished my singing I backed off to the middle of my cell and awaited their entry. Moments later they poured in, the usual crowd, fifteen men including lieutenants, MI and the governor himself. Five had wooden clubs and the Count was at the fore. Before I had a chance to say a word he laid in, swinging the three-foot club with all his power, like a baseball bat, bang! bang! bang! It was a bizarre situation. I literally had not had time to panic and a kind of Zen calm descended on me. So long as he was beating me I was just looking straight into his eyes. How did I know to do that instead of looking at the club? I was speaking to him too, I cannot remember what, but asking him why he was doing it, what good did he think it would achieve.

The blows were crashing into my arms and legs but I could hardly feel them. I was on a kind of autopilot and managing to block each blow from my head, abdomen and groin. All the time I stepped towards him so that he would have less room to swing the club. At the same time he was moving backwards and leaning backwards as well. I think he expected that I would surely punch him in the face. As he sought to keep his face safe, to lean back and to move back, all the while swinging the club into me with all his strength, it was he not I who nearly fell. He was all over the place trying to keep to his feet and the club seemed to be just bouncing off. Nevertheless, it was a savage assault.

After about a minute he stopped. The governor, MI and officers had witnessed it all and did not intervene. They had had permission to do this, I suspect, since the Managing Director's visit in early July. But how stupid of them to come to the cell and witness it. Now they could not deny that they were responsible.

The Count and I got our breath back and I realised the worst was over for the day.

'Look at that,' I said pointing to the writing on the wall. 'I have the right to complain about solitary confinement. Every prisoner has the right to complain about injustice and you must listen to the complaints.'

'No hit on the door!' shouted Lieutenant Soe Lin.

'I will continue until you give me an adequate response.'

One of the trusties was ordered to copy down what I had written. Well, hooray, they were paying attention to it, but would it not have been simpler to give me a pen and paper in the first place?

I was handcuffed and they began filing out, perhaps thinking that was that.

'I will not stop,' I said catching Soe Lin's eye. 'I will not stop.'

My legs were a bit sore and I wondered briefly if my left arm was broken. Later on, the guards returned and replastered over the slogans on the wall. After six hours they took the cuffs off. I would give them the day to find an answer.

The next day was Friday. Throughout the morning wives or sisters of prisoners used to come for their twenty-minute allotted visit. I did not want to cause a disruption then in case the visits were cancelled for the morning. Certainly the authorities would make sure no outsiders were there to hear me banging on the door.

I waited until the afternoon, then removed the old screw and scratched into the wall, '388 days' solitary confinement needs a solution' and 'solutions come from discussion not violence'. Replaced the screw, a few more laps of the cell to calm myself down, then banging on the door again, this time giving it 'Singin' in the Rain' to keep myself in as good a humour as possible.

They were better prepared now and within a minute the door was open. I did not really fancy another beating so instead of retreating to the middle of the cell I just took two steps to the side. It was a tiny detail but it meant that it was that much harder for the first chaps in to swing their clubs and I was hoping that if it did not start straight away I might be able to diffuse the situation. They were, after all, very nervous about what they were doing too.

And sure enough, the first trusties and guards in had to turn round to see me, could not get a quick swing in without hitting their friends and in any case were not sure who should start it off. The Count was at the back this time.

'*Look at that*!' I blurted, more in surprise than anger, and I pointed to what I had written on the wall. It was all silly games but fortunately two of the trusties went to read it, which diverted the room's attention.

'Forget it!' snapped Lieutenant Soe Lin. I had never seen him so angry. He grabbed the front of my shirt and ripped it to shreds. 'You bastard!' he shouted.

One of the ancient guards started brandishing his club at me, two others began threatening to hit me as well, poking me with them but not actually striking. Each time I jerked my arms up to ward off an expected blow, Daddy would growl and pounce forward a step. It was a horrible situation.

I had Lieutenant Soe Lin roughing me up and shouting blue murder. The decrepit old guards thought they should show keen and so were making gestures of violence, and each time I moved to defend myself from one of these blows, Daddy, who was over 200 pounds and could probably pluck a gorilla's head off without effort, would move in to defend the old men. Basically, if those silly old men would stop trying to look tough the situation would diffuse. Fortunately it did.

Lieutenant Soe Lin was exhausting his inventory of abuse on me. I think he managed to call me the penis of every kind of farmyard animal Burma has. He dashed over to the trusty who was copying down what I had written and tore the paper up. 'You don't say this!' he screamed.

Once again, I said as calmly as I could that I had the right to complain and that I wanted a solution to solitary confinement. Once again, they cuffed me and once again I told them that I would not stop.

They took away all my personal belongings – Bible, German books, toothbrush – and once more fixed a loudspeaker outside my cell for the intolerable propaganda. This time the cuffs were left on overnight.

The next morning at half-nine I was ready again. By now the guards had been put under strict orders to keep me under constant observation. This, however, is a job too boring for anyone, no matter how keen they are, so there were, of course, lapses of attention. Instead of using the screw to write on the wall, which after all the regime could fairly object to, I decided to write with water. I took a scoop of water and using my spare shirt as a brush I wrote '*metta*' in huge Burmese letters on one wall and drew a crucifix on another. It would be unmistakable, when the guards walked in, what I was protesting about.

At the window was Pura, a devout Buddhist and one of the trusties who had been very kind to me. He shouted out as he noticed me finishing off the cross.

'Let's go!' I answered him and this time had to stride straight to the door if I was to get any banging done. Within ten seconds the doors were flung open. Again there were about a dozen men but the governor, MI and officers had had the sense to stay away. Five of them had clubs and there was to be no holding back this time.

So long as the blows were on my limbs and body I could stay on my feet, but with five men hitting me I certainly could not do much to block them. I remember seeing the Count's fist, then elbow, smash into my face, then he grabbed a club off one of his colleagues. As hard as he could he swung it into the back of my head. I felt distinctly dizzy and my arms fell down limp. The next thing I saw, though only for a split second, was the Count swinging it again but this time into my face. It was a beautiful strike, catching me almost squarely across the eyes and nose. I fell down on to my knees and somehow managed to guard my head with my hands. The blows kept coming. I was on another planet.

Then Daddy, bless him, put his great arms out and stopped the beating. He had noticed blood pouring from my face and had courage enough to make a decision where nobody else would. 'Enough!' he ordered.

I got back to my feet and, again on autopilot, started asserting my right to complain. My voice was certainly shaky and there was blood gobbing off my lips. I could not see too well either.

Lieutenant Soe Lin and Lieutenant Smo Ki marched in. Soe Lin was triumphant, Smo Ki looked gutted.

Soe Lin was laughing at me. 'So you see what happen when you don't obey the rules!' he cheered. 'You must obey our rules.'

I was cuffed once more, this time for twenty-three hours.

'I have the right to complain', I managed to say in an unsteady voice, 'about injustice and I will not stop.' There was a moment of silence. 'I will not stop.'

The team left. I was just about through. I sat down on the floor of the cell where the guards could not see my face other than from the south window. I dearly wanted privacy now. I wanted to cry but did not dare while they might see it. Blood was pouring from my face down my neck and front. I did not care and made no effort to stop it. I had a broken nose, two extremely black eyes, a cheek swollen out abominably, lumps and welts on my head and back. Because the clubs had been wound round in rubber, there were bruises on my arms and legs which took two weeks to come to the surface. My shirt was still torn to shreds from the day before. I felt so sad. All this confrontation was not with the men I wanted to confront. I was in too much shock to feel pain.

Ten minutes later they all piled back in. I stood up. They had brought a bucket of water and there was a senior trusty I had seen only a few times before. 'Come here,' he ordered. 'The doctor will wash you.'

I had no intention of cleaning myself up and I certainly was not going to let anyone else do it. I wanted the blood to stay, I wanted the governor or the next visitor to see it. But I was being silly. Better that I wash myself than I be washed under force by them. I stripped off the bloody and tatty shirt and used my *longyi* as a sponge to clean myself up. I did it without fuss, not caring for bruises, only going tenderly around my nose and eyes. I was keen for them all to get out. I wanted to be alone.

A 'medic' held out a handful of pills.

'No thanks.' I turned them down. No medicine for months and then a handful all at once! Forget it. I did not even know what they were. The medic seemed upset. He was another gentle man.

I gave them all another brief lecture on the Rights of Man, they milled about a bit, unsure of how to take control, and then piled out.

The Count appeared at my window to say sorry. He had apologised after the first day too. His apology meant 'I wish it had not happened, but I'll do it again if I have to.' 'Sorry,' he said.

'Funny old world, isn't it,' I said very ungraciously. That day I was not allowed out for exercise or a wash. It suited me fine.

I was lying back on my mat, thinking about what would come next. I was finished off. I did not want to fight any more. It was not just the idea of an even more severe beating – broken limbs, maybe a broken skull. It was the pain of fighting with men with whom I had no quarrel. Where were the junta hiding? When were they going to wake up to the challenge? But I had committed myself to carry on until I got a result. I had told the officers that I would not stop and if I had faith in God, faith in what I was doing, then I had to persist. *Dear God*, I thought, *I have nothing left. I cannot face another day like this. God, I will persist if You require it. I pray that something might happen between now and nine-thirty tomorrow, but if not then I will protest again. You have all of me. Thy will be done.*

Early the next morning I told Pura, the trusty, that I wanted the cuffs off.

He went into a kind of rage. 'No, cannot!' he cried hoarsely, and there were tears in his eyes, 'you . . .' and he mimed banging the door. Pura had not laid a finger on me, he had remained in the background throughout the beatings, yet he was more troubled than anyone else. He was a good man. His culpability was minimal, yet he felt the shame of it more than anyone.

The morning wore on. I was going to have to go through it all again. I could not see a way forward, I could not predict what would happen, but I would trust that to God.

Then at half-eight, the cell doors opened. 'Mista James,' crooned Lieutenant Soe Lin, 'what do you want?'

'Excuse me?'

'I am so very sorry,' he went on, 'I am so very sorry about what happen.' He was smiling obscenely. There were new faces with him, three new prisoners acting as guards. He signalled to one of them to take the cuffs off me. 'What can I do for you?' he asked again.

'I want to complain about solitary confinement.'

'OK.'

'I want to write it down.'

'No, never mind, you can tell me.'

'No, I want to write it down.'

We haggled.

'OK, OK.' Soe Lin laughed nervously, then snapped at a trusty to get me paper and pen. I wrote out my complaint, that pro-longed solitary confinement was unjust and I wanted the chance to discuss a solution. 'Tomorrow,' said Soe Lin, 'I will give your complaint. I have meeting, government meeting, many depart-ment. I give them your complaint. And I promise you, Mista James, that this will never happen again. It will not again.' He paused, then continued, 'What would you like? What can I do for you?'

'You can take that speaker down. Get rid if it.' And they did. Straight away.

'Ah, Mr James, I am so very sorry. Are you all right now?' He winced as he looked at my black swollen eyes. 'Is it hurt?' His face was flicking between an obscene grin of appeasement and wounded concern as he mourned over my injuries. Yesterday, he had been gloating over them.

'I want my Bible back.'

'Ah, yes, of course.'

'And all my stuff.'

'Yes.' And they were brought back.

'And I need a long-sleeved shirt.' I had only one *longyi* and one T-shirt.

'Mr James, please. You had an accident . . .'

'Accident?'

'Ah, I am so sorry. Please, Mr James, please, will you . . . can you say you did this . . .' He waved his hands about his face and winced again. 'You say it was an accident?'

'What the devil do you mean? That I fell down the stairs?' I could not believe what I was hearing and I could not believe that Lieutenant Soe Lin was making such a pitiful exhibition of himself in front of so many other prisoners.

'Mr James, I am so sorry for your pain. Will you say it was a mistake, that you made an accident . . .'

'No, I will not. I will say the truth about it.'

375

'James, I will punish those servants who did this to you.'

'Servants?'

'My servants.'

I could not believe the word I was hearing. I asked him to repeat it. Perhaps he had seen the word in a dictionary and read the definition: 'a lowly worker who must do everything his master orders' and figured that was the word for his subordinates.

'Who do you want me to punish?' he asked me frankly.

'Don't punish anyone, man. They were following orders. It is the creatures at the top who need sorting out!' I could not believe what he was saying.

'James, I will give you anything if you say it was an accident. Anything you want.'

'Soe Lin, I want justice. If you can give me that, then wonderful. But I am not going to say this was an accident.'

He persisted and finally left, still grinning, still hoping I would change my mind. Later on I learnt that Maung Lo, the governor, was to be 'transferred to Rangoon'. Someone had to be punished and it turned out that it would be the head of the prison. I felt sorry for him. He too had only been following orders.

Three days later Karen Williams came. The authorities told her that I had inflicted the injuries on myself by bashing my face with my wrists while handcuffed. When Karen saw me she could see for herself the extent of the injuries. I gave a full account of what happened, as well as the usual messages that I was still full of beans and prepared to crack on. I am glad that Karen reported back, *'Despite his [injuries] his spirits are still as bright as ever.'*

She also told me that Mum was still in Rangoon. That surprised me. It had been over three weeks. Mum was not prepared to leave without seeing me first. On 2 October I wrote my monthly prison letter. For a whole year not one of them had got through, but in September I had written just eight words for Kerstin and the authorities relented. If they did not pass it on I could easily have dictated it to consular staff and they would have asked why it was withheld. This meant that the cycle was broken and my next letter got out too. It was delivered to the British embassy with the following note:

No. 4848(1) 2/2000 (1394)

The Ministry of Foreign Affairs of the Union of Myanmar presents its compliments to Her Majesty's Embassy and has the honour to enclose herewith a personal letter entitled 'Dear All' from Mr. James Mawdsley dated 2-10-2000.

The Ministry of Foreign Affairs of the Union of Myanmar avails itself of this opportunity to renew to Her Majesty's Embassy the assurance of its highest consideration.

Yangon, 11 October 2000

Ah the dulcet tones of diplomats! The letter read:

Monday 2 October 2000
Kengtung, Burma

Dear All,

I am, thanks to you, thanks to God, thanks to these balmy mountain evenings, in fine health & spirits. All your efforts to keep me well are working to great effect. God showers me with more blessings than I can count. Again it is wonderfully clear to me what is meant by saying the measure given back to you will not only be a full one, but shaken and tamped down and running over. In the nick one is forced to attend to fine details and so discovers just how rich life is. I have discovered also how much good there is which usually remains hidden, particularly in the kind/gentle/strong letters from strangers. And so I ever remember Romans V:v:3–5, and truly 'rejoice' in this work. I have nothing at all whatsoever in the slightest to fear from man.

Howeverly, I am sorely beset by two things, which I will here tell, though I don't ask you to trouble yourselves searching out solutions – you are doing everything and more already. Instead I look forward to the day when I can solve them myself. Firstly, how on Earth does one pronounce 'Ärtztin', the German word for a female doctor? This has been challenging me for months and I have had to temporarily give up on it for fear of biting my tongue off. Secondly, how do the altimeters on jet aircraft compensate for the speed of the aircraft and variations in air pressure due to climate (particularly turbulence)? This has me grievously perplexed. I assume the altimeters work on air pressure. Perhaps they are ignored during turbulence, perhaps a cunning algorithem (argh! mental block! how to spell algorithum??!) can take the plane's speed into account, BUT what about the vast weather systems of high + low pressure? Well anyway, that is more than enough of my woes.

Such limited opportunity for communication makes this abundantly clear: that love is all that matters, that it endures all things, that it trusts and rejoices in giving. I have so many to tell that I love them, that they have saved my life just by being there to be loved – but a single letter don't hold space for all your names. So I thank God for you in my prayers, and I thank Him several times daily for the exact situation I am in – I am tumbling into Great Love with His Reality, with how things really are ordered. There is wickedness and suffering and hate, but what a joy it is to be a participant in their demise. I know this: that God (or Truth or Love or Good or Justice) has overcome. He is inevitable . . .

I am full of hope, but not some whimsical hope for a particular possibility, a future event which I long for. Rather I hope because all the past is ordered perfectly, and all the present is so very wonderful. I cannot see things being otherwise, I love reality, it's good, in fact it's perfect. Because I love the present, because I am so grateful for all of the past, then I have hope, a belief in good, a certainty that the future is good. By the way, I don't refer to dreamy rapture – that is a rare treat. Most is work. Hard work. Fierce work. Common sense. Calm, reserved, reality. And it's good.

I'll see you tomorrow (or thereabouts)

Jimmy xxxxxx

CHAPTER 32

. . . so shall my word be that goes forth from my mouth;
it shall not return to me empty,
but it shall accomplish that which I purpose,
and prosper in the thing for which I sent it.   Isaiah 55:v:11

ON 24 MARCH Jared Genser had submitted a petition to the United Nations Working Group on Arbitrary Detention detailing the facts of my case. The Burmese regime had been sent a copy and had three months to respond, to present their version of events. Of course they did not respond. They were given a two month extension and still no reply. One month later the UN group would deliver its findings, which would be made public shortly afterwards. Thanks to Jared's excellent work the group upheld every single point of the petition. That is, they found the Burmese regime had violated ten points of international law and that my detention was, from the beginning, arbitrary and illegal. They found:

Mr Mawdsley was doing no more than expressing his opinions . . . Mr Mawdsley has not perpetrated the use of violence. Peaceful expression of opposition to any regime cannot give rise to arbitrary arrest.

There is another aspect which requires consideration in this case. The allegations, unrebutted, demonstrate the violations of all norms of fair play and justice. Mr Mawdsley was not informed of the reasons for his arrest; he was detained incommunicado without legal advice or

379

representation; his trial is a mockery of all legal principles applicable in jurisdictions where the rule of law prevails . . .

The five judges who delivered that verdict came from India, France, Chile, Senegal and the Czech Republic. There could be no accusations of bias. Their verdict was made public on 26 September, the same day that Karen Williams had reported on the assaults. Together these had quite an explosive effect.

For the second time the Burmese ambassador was summoned to the Foreign Office for a dressing down. He gave the line that my injuries were self-inflicted. I am delighted to say that the minister, Baroness Scotland QC, did not hide her fury at his response and announced in the Lords that she rejected 'his tissue of lies'.

The Apostolic Nuncio in London was immediately in touch with the Vatican. The Holy See was already involved. The Holy Father, Pope Jean-Paul II, wrote a letter to the Chinese government urging them to pressure Burma for my release. In the letter the words 'mercy and compassion' were used. It was strange to see where these words next turned up.

Chris Davies, a Liberal MEP for the north-west had put my case forward in Brussels. Nicole Fontaine, President of the European Parliament, agreed to pursue the matter. The pressure bearing on the junta was becoming intense.

When the UN made their decision public the FCO could finally act without restraint. On 10 October the Burmese ambassador was once again summoned to the Foreign Office and Robin Cook published a statement to demand my immediate release and saying 'it is clearer than ever that there is no justification for the detention of James Mawdsley'. The FCO also cabled dozens of its embassies around the world (EU, ASEAN, US, China etc.) instructing them to urge, as far as possible, their host governments to add to the pressure on the Burmese.

If my beating had made all this rather urgent, it was thanks to Jared Genser that the world had the ammunition it needed. Once the UN made its ruling, other less impartial bodies felt they could get behind it.

Just one more straw would break the junta's back and it came from an oil company. In March an FCO minister, John Battle, had asked in the Commons that Premier Oil disinvest from Burma. Pressure was growing on them to get out. Sensing a crisis, Premier suggested to the junta that they should release me as soon as possible. The junta finally woke up to the inevitable. There is reason to believe they also listened to the Chinese government, who had taken notice of the Pope's letter. One of the reasons they finally gave for releasing me was 'to mark the end of the Buddhist "Lent", to show mercy and compassion'. It was not a phrase they had used before.

On 16 October they agreed to release me unconditionally. The news was widely reported in the world press, but nothing happened. Was it another lie?

Back in Kengtung the authorities had built an extension on to the prison. In here they had solitary cells, real solitary cells: small, isolated, surrounded by tall brick walls so that no other part of the prison could be seen. There were no trees to be seen, no plants, only concrete, whitewash and gravel. I was moved in there a couple of hours after Karen's last visit. It would have been a terrible thing to have been here for a year but the timing of it was perfect. I really needed then to be isolated, to get my strength back.

I gave myself a week to recover from the beating and then started gradually increasing my exercise regime again. The prisoners guarding me were new faces: very friendly, very gentle, but very wary.

I was taken to the governor's office for an 'interview with a psychologist'. I did not care what he wanted to talk about, I stuck to human rights. He gave me this defence of the regime: 'You have seen the film *Ben Hur*? Well, in that film the Roman Catholics fed Christians to the lions. And so you see, repression happens.'

What an absolute fruitcake. I talked about the illnesses of other prisoners I had seen and he sniggered. When he did that I stormed out of the room and ordered the guards to take me back to my cell. They did so.

Even in that isolated spot I began to hear rumours that I would be released. It was something I could not afford to get excited about. No point in believing anything until it happens. But it seemed very plausible; I was sure the junta had had enough.

Then one morning Lieutenant Soe Lin came to my cell. 'Your mother is still in Rangoon,' he said.

'Really?' I was surprised. 'Why?'

'She want to rescue you,' he confided.

I could guess that this fitted in with what the other guys had told me, but I tried to pretend I knew nothing of the release. 'What, is she going to ride up and knock down the wall?' I asked.

Soe Lin laughed. He hung around a little, desperate to tell me the good news but he could not think of a way to say it. I was desperate to hear it from him, to confirm the rumours, but I did not want to drop anyone in it by hinting that I already knew. Suddenly he was called away. Argh!

An hour later he was back, marching into my cell with a huge grin. 'Congratulations,' he said happily, 'you are release today.'

Despite all my best efforts to look nonchalant, unfazed and bored I confess that I smiled. But no more than that. Being released was emphatically not an emotional time. I could not afford to let it be so. I had to keep control, see the job through to the end. It was sad that morning, saying goodbye to the guards and trusties. Trying to grab them one by one and tell them in all sincerity that although I was gone from prison I would never forget them, or their country, and that one day we would surely all get roaring drunk together in a Kengtung Karaoke bar. The prisoners were pleased for me. The guards seemed jealous.

Walking through the prison to the main office I felt a bit light but mostly sadness. Every now and then I had imagined what it would be like to be out: lying in an unkempt field on a sunny day, not even bothering to read a book – wonderful! But now, as I approached the prison gates, having for so long pretended that being in prison was no big deal, I had to pretend that being released was no big deal either. And in fact being released was oddly ordinary and, when it eventually happened, somehow too quick.

As I passed my old cell I was sad to see it so changed. Now it was back to its original use as the officers' office. The compound fence had been ripped down, the doors were wide open, there was a wardrobe inside and a badminton racket hanging on the wall. I suppose Smo Ki and Soe Lin were glad to have it back after one year. I hoped they would enjoy discovering the slogans on the walls over the coming days.

I came before the central compound. All the prisoners had been locked in the wards; they always were when I was moved around the prison. I wish I could have gone to every one.

'I ALWAYS NEVER FORGET YOU!' I shouted out to them. It was strange, no one really made an effort to stop me, but I had no heart to continue. And I felt strongly that I *would* indeed see them again.

I met Karen Williams in the main office. Prison officers asked me to sign an inventory to declare my personal belongings had been returned. I refused and Karen signed it instead (the English version, she would not sign the Burmese). Shortly afterwards we flew to Rangoon, accompanied, of course, by several MI. I was not about to let myself go. It was not over yet and I did not want to make a silly error.

At Rangoon airport I met my mum. Grand. She too was keeping all emotions in check while we were still in Burma. Dr Jenkins was also there, as were Vicky Billing, the Australian ambassador and a doctor from the Aussie embassy. I was due to fly out to Bangkok in four hours' time with Mum and Karen Williams.

But the junta had one more surprise. 'Before Mr Mawdsley leaves', they explained, 'he must sign these documents.' They produced a sheet of conditions. I am not even sure what they were as I could not be bothered to read them. There was no way on earth I was going to sign. I shook my head.

'Are you willing to sign?' asked an official.

'No.'

'Are you willing to go back to prison?' he threatened.

'Yes, I'll do another year, c'mon let's go now, back on the plane!' I meant it, I turned back to the plane. For the next two hours the ambassadors did what they are best at doing. Karen and Vicky seemed incredibly busy too.

The doctor took my pulse and blood pressure, and could hardly believe it. The pulse was 55 and my blood pressure was 120 on 80. Perfect. Mum did not suggest that I sign the silly papers and neither did any of the embassy staff. They knew full well that I would not.

The main deprivation in prison was not being able to share with people – not even thoughts. So sitting here in the airport, chatting openly with six others was to me more special than any of them might have imagined. Paul Gorman, the Australian doctor, offered me one of his cigarettes. I accepted, then ambitiously declared that this was to be my last day of smoking and went on to finish the whole pack.

Something occurred to me. A prisoner always knows exactly how many days he has been inside, and if on a fixed term, exactly how many days he has left. I did a quick sum. Recalling Ne Win's superstition about the number nine and that my first imprisonment had been for ninety-nine days, I was disturbed to discover that my total time in Burma for this stretch, from entering Tachilek to finally leaving Burmese airspace, was nine thousand nine hundred and ninety nine hours. The old man is not dead yet.

I saw the sunset for the first time in over a year. Glorious. After two hours the regime realised they were getting nowhere. I was not going to sign the form. They grumbled and postured but they had no wish to carry on fighting. When the plane was ready I got on and left.

There was no sweetness in being released. Where is Kublai? Where is Anawratha?

EPILOGUE

S IX MONTHS AFTER I was released I returned to Burma, to Karen State. At a certain village I met the following three men:

First was Soe Che. He had been a soldier in the Burmese army but had managed to escape. He was only fifteen years old. He had been walking home from his school in Rangoon one day when an army corporal asked him if he wanted to enlist. Soe Che was afraid and said nothing. He continued home. The corporal followed him for a short while, then just grabbed him and dragged him to a truck. That was it; Soe Che was recruited.

Of the 250 people in his training batch, eight were fifteen-year-olds. No one was paid during training. Frequently Soe Che was whipped with a bamboo cane – four strokes, for example, when late for roll-call. One day four of the recruits managed to escape but were recaptured. Then every single one of their 246 colleagues was made to walk past each of them and beat them with the bamboo.

After training, the 250 were sent to the front to fight against the Karen. Soe Che knew nothing about them. His Burmese officers call the Karen '*nga pwey*' (ring worm). Neither did Soe Che know anything about the NLD, but he had heard the name of Daw Aung San Suu Kyi. After one month in the front line, Soe Che was guarding a forty-year-old porter, and the two of them escaped together, and made it into Karen-held territory.

Soe Che has two older sisters. He wants to go home to his family and back to school, but he cannot return to his parents'

385

house or he will be arrested. He could return to a relative in Rangoon but it would be risky. His Burmese army officers warned him that if ever the Karen caught him they would shoot him dead. Instead, the Karen gave him 1000 Kyat, said a prayer for him and are now trying to arrange schooling for him in a refugee camp. Despite their kindness, Soe Che looks racked by homesickness. His family have not heard from him since he was abducted six months before. The only thing Soe Che has to say to me at the end is that he wants to go home.

Then I heard from U Lu Paing, the forty-year-old porter who had escaped with Soe Che. Five years earlier he had run from his house when two gangs of thieves came to rob it. When he returned there was a corpse there. One of the robbers had been shot by his rivals. U Lu Paing immediately went to Ma Taing Police Station to report it. It turned out that the corpse was the nephew of the local head of police. There was no need for an investigation. U Lu Paing was thrown into gaol. Before he was sentenced the police told him that he had 'no quarters here, so your family must send rice to you'. The police are not obliged to feed the people they lock up. U Lu Paing was told to confess to the murder and threatened with beatings. He denied killing anybody. The police put a plastic bag over his head then poured water over it. The result is terrifying suffocation. Still U Lu Paing would not confess. Back on to his head went the bag, once again came the water and soon afterwards U Lu Paing agreed that he was a murderer.

In court he was naturally allowed no lawyer. The prosecutors had two. U Lu Paing pleaded not guilty but that did not matter. He was sentenced to five years' imprisonment in Prome. In prison he shared a cell with forty-five others. One of his duties was to work on the rice fields. He had to drive a tractor to plough the fields. Well, more accurately, he had to get his two sons to do it, because as a prisoner he would not be allowed such a task. But then that is not important. The important point is that U Lu Paing had to pay for the tractor hire and fuel: 60,000 Kyat (£100) for ten days. Over his five-year sentence he had to do this six times. Then his family ran out of money. This meant that they could no longer afford to pay the bribes necessary for prison visits. Well, no more visits for U Lu Paing then.

Three months before his release date the prison authorities told him he would be taken to the border regions to finish his sentence as a porter. He was used as a minesweeper. He had to hold a long bamboo pole with a ball of burning cloth and pitch on the end of it. This he swept from side to side along the track and the heat would detonate any mines. He found three this way. Each one exploded just in front of him. Alternatively he might be given a pole with one spike and two claws on the end of it and he had to use this to prod the ground ahead. Not everyone is allowed even a stick. One and a half months before his release was due U Lu Paing escaped.

Why would a man who had completed over 97.5 per cent of a five-year sentence choose to escape? He told me it is because words like 'freedom' and 'release' are meaningless in Burma because there is *no* rule of law. Like Soe Che, and like the other five porters and the other *Tatmadaw* deserter who escaped with him, U Lu Paing received from the Karen 1000 Kyat, a prayer, and their efforts to find him refuge and work.

The third man I spoke to that day was Thu Po Mu. He was sitting next to a forty-eight-year-old called Po Hla Win. When Po Hla Win told me his neighbour was his grandfather my eyes popped. Not that it was unusual to meet a ninety-seven-year-old out here whose eyes were full of brightness and smiles, but because it meant he obviously would remember World War Two.

It turned out that not only had Thu Po Mu worked with the British from 1930 to 1945 but also that he knew Major Hugh Seagrim. In fact, he had worked with him for many months. In December 1941, Thu Po Mu was the first to be called forward by Seagrim to go out and recruit; they needed men for the day when the Allies would launch their counter-attack against the occupying Japanese. When he later heard about Seagrim's execution, he too had been caught by the Japanese. But Thu Po Mu survived.

'What do you think of the British?' I asked him.

'They are good nation,' Thu Po Mu replied.

'Thank you, but we not come back,' I said, referring to our betrayal of our Karen allies after the war.

Thu Po Mu laughed. '*You* have come back.'

Deep down, I still want to have a face-to-face meeting with the generals of the SPDC. I want to look them in the eye, but most probably that will not answer any questions. Because the answer as to why there is evil in the world is because there is sin in every single one of us and if we would fight evil then let us fight that wrong within our own being.

The freedom which really counts is one which none can take away, just as none can give it. Physical and political freedoms are shadows of a still more vital one – inner freedom, that ability to overcome the obstacles, the fears and temptations, which cloud our choice to do right, to obey God, to love.

APPENDIX

Four open letters prepared in summer 1999.

A   Open letter to the British and Australian Governments

July 1999

cc Tony Blair, John Howard, Robin Cook, Alexander Downer

Dear Sirs,

Re: Our duty in Burma

The military junta in Burma has no legal, moral, popular nor constitutional mandate to govern. They ousted the elected government by force in 1962, and have since maintained their position by extreme violence and terror.

The National League for Democracy is the party of government in Burma, having won 82% of the seats in the 1990 election. The laws, constitution and appointments which they have initiated are the ones I recognise. I sincerely hope the British and Australian governments will have the courage to do the same.

Please never compromise your support for the National League for Democracy to gain short-term trade and investment, or for the sake of playing god with regional balances of power. The people of Australia and Britain do not care for such fleeting reward. It is paid for with Burmese blood.

With the deepest respect I ask that you:

– Formally acknowledge that the CRPP is the only body

389

with legitimacy to appoint Burma's representative at the
UN.
- Formally acknowledge that the SPDC is criminally guilty
of genocide against the Karen, the Shan and the Karenni
peoples of Burma.

I am not asking for gestures; this is as real as politics gets. With
sufficient will, with a dauntless commitment to Truth, these
actions will have a resounding impact in Burma and be of benefit
to all humanity.

'Whoever possesses the world's resources and notices that his
brother is in need and then locks his heart against him, how is the
love of God in him? Dear children, let us not love in word and
tongue, but in deed and truth.' – 1 John 3:v:17–18

Yours sincerely,

James Mawdsley

B   The following is the English version of the letter I wrote to the
people of Burma. The copy which I distributed in Tachilek on 31
August 1999 was in Burmese and *did not include* the paragraphs
italicised below. Clearly there can be no legal objections to the
letter I distributed.

Letter to the People of Burma
cc DVB, BBC, VOA, RFA, ABSDF

Mingalaba. My name is James Mawdsley, I am a British/
Australian citizen and it is my great pleasure and honour to be
involved with the struggle for democracy in Burma. I have spent
many months in your country and I am constantly inspired by the
courage and kindness shown to me by Burmese. I will never
forget the great bravery and commitment to freedom of those I
have met, the Karen, Mon, Burman, Shan, Chin, Kachin,
Arakanese, Karenni, Lahu and others.

I have witnessed the brutal oppression of the SPDC. I have seen
some of their gross violations of human rights. I will not sit idle
while they continue to torture, rape and murder the people of

Burma. *Bogyoke* Aung San founded the army to liberate and protect Burma. Yet now the guns of the *Tatmadaw* have turned on their own people. I have the deepest respect for *Bogyoke* Aung San, and the deepest respect for those who follow him in his love of Burma. And so I join you in your second struggle for independence, and because of the strength and Truth of the movement I have joined I am utterly confident we will succeed.

I have come here to ask for three things.

> That the SPDC release all political hostages.
> (Article 9, UDHR)
> That the SPDC cease its disruption (in fact closure) of the universities.
> (Article 26, UDHR)
> That the SPDC cease its brutal intimidation of Burma's government, the NLD, and holds tripartite dialogue with the NLD and the ethnic groups with the aim of honouring the 1990 election results.
> (Article 21, UDHR)

Do not allow the junta's propaganda to tell you that foreign powers are trying to disrupt your country. That is a despicable lie. You have many many friends abroad who care deeply about your situation. When it comes to human rights, there are no foreigners; we are all the same, human beings, no outsiders. Your cause, is my cause.

There is formidable strength in the democracy movement: the NLD, the ethnic groups fighting against oppression, the countless Burmese both inside and outside Burma who are committed to freedom, those like Min Ko Naing whose fighting spirit is invincible. You are my teachers and I never doubt the justness of your cause. I do not judge the prospects of Burma by the number of guns held by the Tatmadaw. *I am not deceived about the people's desire by the SPDC's wicked lies and propaganda. Instead I am full of hope that democracy will come to Burma because I understand the iron resolve of those who will never give up their fight for freedom.*

But for those others who have not yet joined the movement, it is no use to merely wait for democracy; it will not come as a matter of time. Democracy will only come as a matter of action, from the persistent and courageous efforts

391

of millions. So can I ask all of you who are civil servants, who are police officers, soldiers or other representatives of the junta, if you want democracy then you must work for it. Do not obey orders which you know to be cruel and unjust. Do not agree to serve those generals who are destroying your country. And remember that every single bribe you give or you take is prolonging this intolerable regime. I know it is a hard path to begin on but Burma's freedom depends on you. When sufficient millions withdraw all their co-operation from a corrupt and oppressive system, and instead transfer this support to the honest and lawful groups dedicated to Burma's liberation, then that day you will have won. It is up to you.

I look forward to *mohingha, ye nwey* and your company, in a peaceful, prosperous and free Burma.

'Do not think lightly of good, that not the least consequence will come of it. A whole waterpot will fill up from dripping drops of water' – Lord Buddha, Dhammapada:v:122.

James Mawdsley

C   Open letter to the people of Britain and Australia

July 1999

cc Family, Press Release

Many of you are aware that the military regime in Burma is violently oppressing millions of people. You may have heard of the psychotic violations of human rights, where the sick and elderly are burnt alive in their homes, where villagers are used as human minesweepers, where young girls have broken bottles pushed into their vaginas by soldiers. Like me you find this intolerable and you wish to God you could find a way to stop it.

Many of us write letters of protest or join demonstrations outside Burmese embassies in Canberra and London. We pressurise companies which invest in Burma to pursue ethical policies, or even to withdraw entirely. We might lobby MPs and ask our governments to take a firm line on human rights. Journalists and public speakers can increase awareness, NGOs and charities can give humanitarian assistance and any individual can donate money to fund-raisers. And because of all this effort we now have the UN, the EU and the ILO issuing their strongest condemnation of the junta's brutality. Invaluable, but clearly not enough. Is it not obvious what the next step should be?

As citizens of established democracies we are graced with political freedom. The real beauty of this is not that we are free to clamour for our elected governments to implement our ideas and dreams, but that we can actually work towards them ourselves. We have freedom of movement and association, freedom of assembly and expression, we have economic freedom to earn and save money. These opportunities mean we do not have to rely solely on official channels to carry our hopes. In my case, they mean I am free to take my point of view straight to the Burmese junta.

I am not going simply to protest against injustice, even though it is inside Burma that such protests have the most impact. I am not merely trying to raise awareness of human rights, even though it is in the minds of the junta that such understanding is needed most. And I am not setting out just to challenge, confront and defy the lawless grip of the SPDC, even though I believe this is precisely the key to Burma's freedom. I am going there because it is right: morally, rationally, spiritually, personally. When you sincerely seek to do what is right, and when the answer is burnt across your heart and demands with an irresistible passion that you obey, then it is mortal folly to argue. So I will go, and if that means prison, then so be it.

'Surely Mr Mawdsley is crazy to go back to Burma! Last time he was imprisoned and sentenced to five years. He passed out twice under torture. After four weeks he had a fit and collapsed from lack of nutrition. He caught scabies and the "authorities" refused to hand over the treatment provided by the embassy. He contracted two ear infections and sat for days with half his head on fire as if he'd been smacked in the face with a brick . . .'

Yes it is hell adjusting to Insein, but I will not be languishing. I will be using every ounce of my wit and my strength to bring forward issues of human rights, and I will be in the perfect place to do it. I want to understand the junta, and I want the junta to understand the spirit of freedom.

Very simply, not my will, but His will; not my strength, but His strength: 'Though I walk through the valley of the shadow of death, I will fear no evil . . . for Thou art my Rock . . . my Refuge.' Then there is nothing to fear. But if I were to turn my back on my sisters and brothers as they were tortured and raped and murdered, then I would be ashamed and indeed I would fear. They are not only my family, they are your family too.

If any of you wish to help the people of Burma then this is my very best advice: learn. Learn as much as you can about the situation from the thousands of books and reports available, the hours of video tapes and the Burmese themselves – those here, those on Burma's borders and those inside Burma proper. The more one understands the clearer it becomes what to do.

And finally, if anyone is kind enough to want to help me, then please give all possible support to my family. As long as they are strong, so am I.

'And whatever you ask in prayer, you will receive, if you have faith' – Matthew 21:v:22

James Mawdsley

D   Statement to the Military Junta in Burma

July 1999

cc Khin Nyunt, Than Shwe, Maung Aye, Win Aung

Ladies and Gentlemen of the Junta,
I have come here to ask three things.

That the SPDC release all political hostages.
(Article 9, UDHR)
That the SPDC cease its disruption (in fact closure) of the universities.
(Article 26, UDHR)
That the SPDC cease its brutal intimidation of Burma's government, the NLD, and holds tripartite dialogue with the NLD and the ethnic groups with the aim of honouring the 1990 election results.
(Article 21, UDHR)

There can be no rational, moral or legal objections to these requests. Burma is an original signatory of the Universal Declaration of Human Rights.

You already know that I love Burma, you already know that I want Burma to be strong, to be peaceful and to be prosperous. I have so many dear Burmese friends, those who are bravely and selflessly struggling to bring democracy to their country. I will not sit idle while they are being oppressed.

Please do not embarrass yourselves by trying to turn the truth on its head. I am not your enemy. I fight against brutality, against greed and against deceit – not against people.

You have the chance to help this country. If you co-operate with the democratic forces then Burma will flourish. Trust them, trust the will of Burma, honour the 1990 election result.

Remember, you are not the government of Burma; the National League for Democracy is. You are terrorists. You took power by force and you retain that power through violence and cruelty. You have tortured, raped and murdered thousands of people. You have crippled Burma's economy. You have denied a generation their right to education. And for what you are doing to the Karen, to the Shan, to the Rohingya, for the evil barbarity of your *Sa Thone Lone*, may God have mercy on your souls.

Bogyoke Aung San founded the army to liberate and protect his people. He then left the military to devote himself to politics – he understood that the two must be kept separate. Learn from him.

I hope you will consider my requests. But if you try to ignore them, and if you try to crush my spirit through further torture, deprivation and imprisonment then you should know this: I share the spirit of Min Ko Naing. You may kill me but a thousand like me will rise up to continue our struggle for freedom. We will succeed.

'Do not think lightly of evil, that not the least consequence will come of it. A whole waterpot will fill up from dripping drops of water' – Lord Buddha, Dhammapada:v:121.

Yours most sincerely,

James Mawdsley

E   When I got back to England I received the following letter.

20 October, 2000

Dear Mr Mawdsley,

Welcome home. Thank you so much for your stance against the Burmese junta – you are an extremely brave and courageous man.

The Burmese government has been a constant thorn in my husband's side. They have hindered his career by not letting him take his exams here as they said he could take them in Burma. We had to get married in secret because he should have obtained their permission! He has been in exile in this country for nearly thirty years and could not go back to see his mother when she was dying or even to attend her funeral . . .

When my husband's Burmese passport expired he had to go back there, not knowing if he would be able to get out again, because otherwise the two people who had signed a bond when his passport was issued would have been fined or gaoled, or even both. At the time, we didn't know if we would ever see each other again. Fortunately, after some months he found a way to leave without a passport because of their ineptitude.

They rule by fear, force and blackmail. The expatriates all over the world cannot do much because they all have family and friends in Burma who would suffer if they did. Consequently, I can't put my name and address to this letter.

Once again, very many thanks.

Yours very sincerely,
     A Shan Wife

During my months in prison I became convinced that the best defence against brutally oppressive regimes was widespread education; education is a crucial defence against exploitation and marginalisation.

To this end, in September 2001, the Metta Trust for Children's Education was established. Our mission is to give funding to projects that provide basic education for children in the developing world, and to raise awareness of the need for proper education facilities in all parts of the world.

There have been NO expense or administration costs as the secretary and chairman have agreed to cover all these from their own pocket. MTCE aims for every single penny donated to go directly to the target projects.

For further information, or to make a donation by cheque payable to MTCE, please contact:

MTCE, PO BOX 18833,
LONDON SW7 1WG,
UNITED KINGDOM

BAY OF
BENGAL

ARAKAN STATE

Prome

P E G U

Irrawaddy

IRRAWADDY
STATE

Mouths of the
Irrawaddy

ANDAMAN

ISLANDS

ANDAM

SEA

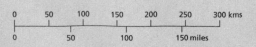